MATT KRAMER

ON WINE

MATT KRAMER
ON WINE

A Matchless Collection *of*

Columns, Essays, *and* Observations

by America's Most Original

and Lucid Wine Writer

STERLING EPICURE

An imprint of Sterling Publishing Co., Inc.

New York / London
www.sterlingpublishing.com

STERLING and the distinctive Sterling logo are registered trademarks of
Sterling Publishing Co., Inc.

Library of Congress Cataloging-in-Publication Data Available

2 4 6 8 10 9 7 5 3 1

Published by Sterling Publishing Co., Inc.
387 Park Avenue South, New York, NY 10016
© 2010 by Matt Kramer
Distributed in Canada by Sterling Publishing
c/o Canadian Manda Group, 165 Dufferin Street
Toronto, Ontario, Canada M6K 3H6
Distributed in the United Kingdom by GMC Distribution Services
Castle Place, 166 High Street, Lewes, East Sussex, England BN7 1XU
Distributed in Australia by Capricorn Link (Australia) Pty. Ltd.
P.O. Box 704, Windsor, NSW 2756, Australia

Manufactured in the United States of America
All rights reserved

Sterling ISBN 978-1-4027-7164-4

For information about custom editions, special sales, premium and
corporate purchases, please contact Sterling Special Sales
Department at 800-805-5489 or specialsales@sterlingpublishing.com.

CONTENTS

PREFACE

The book you are reading is one man's opinion of moonlight.
—Donovan Leitch, *Young Girl Blues*

A JOURNALISTIC RETROSPECTIVE, UNLIKE THAT for art, is a tricky undertaking. After all, journalism is written for the moment and when that moment has passed, well, timing is everything. That said, you could make a case that a retrospective can offer both perspective and insight, illuminating where we once were and how far (or not) we've come.

I like to think that this collection of columns and essays offers such an opportunity. Most of the pieces stand on their own with little need for a comment. They have not been changed from the original, tempting though that sometimes was in the rereading. I have added a comment only when it offers context to what was originally written or completes a picture that has since come into greater perspective or richer detail.

What follows is not merely opinion—which it certainly is—but opinion about something peculiarly ephemeral. After all, when an art critic holds forth about, say, Rembrandt's *Aristotle Contemplating a Bust of Homer*, anyone can trot off to New York's Metropolitan Museum of Art and see whether the critic is full of hooey or not.

The same, however, doesn't work with wine. Not only is it a fast-disappearing item, rendering this year's judgment out of date for next year's vintage, but every taster's experience even of the same wine tasted at the same time is different. This makes it the slipperiest of subjects.

Precisely because of this, I have tried for more than thirty years to write about more than just mere "product evaluation." Wine writing can be more than a string of fruit-and-flower taste descriptors culminating in a slam-bam-thank-you-ma'am score. One hopes so, anyway.

Aiding this ambition was a significant piece of good fortune: I came along at just the right time. I started writing about wine in 1976. That was the year when America began to sense the aesthetic and business possibilities of fine wine, to awaken to life beyond the jug. It was also the year of the now-legendary Paris Tasting of 1976 when American Cabernets and Chardonnays improbably vanquished big-name red Bordeaux and white Burgundies.

Ironically, the Paris Tasting of 1976 was instigated by the British, specifically an

English wine merchant named Steven Spurrier who conceived and organized the event. It turned out to be the opening shot of yet another American revolution. Like his forebears, Spurrier never thought—by his own admission—that the Americans stood a chance. Then again, neither did we at the time.

The last three decades have seen more revolutionary change in wine than in the previous three centuries or longer. This was not just in America, mind you, but everywhere in the world, including such ancient wine cultures as France, Italy, and Spain. They also saw the rise of significant new or dramatically revived wine nations such as Australia, New Zealand, Argentina, Chile, Greece, and South Africa, to name but a few.

Journalistically, what was available to be observed was dazzling in its range: scientific advances, economics, business, real estate, restaurant life, social climbing, and collecting. And, of course, there were thousands of wines to be tasted. But above all, it was a ringside seat in watching an emerging American wine civilization.

Worth noting about this still-evolving American wine culture is how quickly it was exported. European wine producers, especially the younger ones, now freely acknowledge their indebtedness to the liberating influence of America's precocious wine efforts.

This influence began as early as the 1980s and had a demonstrable impact on both the wines and winegrowers everywhere in Europe, especially in Italy and Spain and, to a lesser but still substantial effect, in France.

Of course, influences went both ways. Barnacle-like, we attached ourselves to anything worthwhile from Europe's vast experience: their deep, tacit, traditional knowledge of grape growing and winemaking; their wines; and even their very vines. (Numerous California vineyard owners illegally carried back vine cuttings from famous European vineyards, drolly referring to these cuttings as "suitcase clones.")

For our part, we exported our American openness, scientific verve, and, above all, our naive-to-the-Europeans belief that the future is our friend. While they publicly scoffed, privately they found it irresistible.

To witness all this, earn a living from it, and opine about it, well, what could have been better? It was—and still is—a great privilege. A slice of the results are here for what might be called an aftertaste.

ACKNOWLEDGMENTS

IT ALWAYS SEEMED TO ME that the cliché was incorrect: It's *money* that's the sincerest form of flattery. Imitation is merely a flirtatious wink. This is, of course, the perspective of a freelance writer, a lifelong resident of Grub Street.

So, believe me when I express my appreciation in these "Acknowledgments" for the editors who backed their belief in me with their checkbooks.

Foremost among them is Marvin Shanken, the owner, publisher, and editor of *Wine Spectator* magazine. Among the greatest privileges of my life has been to write for *Wine Spectator*. Whatever misgivings its publisher (and editors) may have had about one or another of my innumerable opinions—and surely they had them— Marvin Shanken has always let me have my say. I am more grateful for his ferocious integrity than I have ever previously expressed to him—which, of course, I should have. Many of the columns in this book originally appeared in *Wine Spectator*. I am grateful for the opportunity to reprint them, and even more grateful for the chance to have originally published in *Wine Spectator*.

I am indebted to Bill Hilliard, the former executive editor of *The Oregonian* in my hometown of Portland, Oregon, who originally hired me as that newspaper's wine critic more than two decades ago. His successor, Sandy Rowe, recently retired, was a supporter as well. I am grateful to them both. Most of all, I am indebted to Karen Brooks, who was for years my direct editor at *The Oregonian*. She is not just a colleague, but also a treasured friend.

The same may also be said of my editors at *Diversion* magazine, which had also published my work for many years. Longtime executive editor (and friend) Tom Passavant and his successor, Cathy Cavender, made a place for me in *Diversion*, even in the hardest of business times. *Diversion*, like so many magazines, ended its run in 2009.

A special mention must be made for my original editor at the *New York Sun* newspaper, Robert Messenger. Although my time with the *Sun* was relatively brief, a mere few years compared with the decades I've enjoyed at other publications, Robert Messenger and his colleagues at the *New York Sun* (which ceased to exist in 2008) offered me the opportunity—and a handsome recompense—to write in a fashion that's now rare in print publications today. A good number of columns in this book originally appeared in the *New York Sun*. I am grateful to the *Sun* for the opportunity to reprint them.

Also due sincere thanks are my many book editors for the seven books I've written. Foremost among them is the editor of my first three books, Maria Guarnaschelli. Without her early encouragement and support, I never would have stretched myself.

More recently, and equally importantly, is Carlo DeVito, who has encouraged and supported me in every sense, through two different publishing houses. This book reflects his convictions as an editor as much as mine as a writer.

One last acknowledgment is in order, for someone who *gets* money from me: my agent, Robert Lescher. This book wouldn't exist without him. And without him, I'd be poorer in far more than money.

THROUGH TWO LENSES—
ONE EYE ON EUROPE
AND ANOTHER ON AMERICA

When I was a boy I had a passion for tropical fish and would spend hours memorizing the Latin names for all sorts of freshwater fish. This made me an almost unbearably pretentious nine-year-old as well as broadened my world considerably.

One of my favorite fish—and fish names—is the wonderfully redundant *Anableps anableps*. A brackish water fish that dwells at the waterline, *Anableps anableps* fascinated me because it can simultaneously see both above and below the waterline, hence its popular name, Four-Eyed Fish. (It actually has just two eyes.)

I mention this bit of esoterica because I sometimes feel, to coin a word, *anableptic* when surveying the landscape of American and European wine cultures. Make no mistake: I am American, born and raised.

However, when I first started writing about wine professionally more than thirty years ago, both the cultural wine vocabulary and, especially, the world of wine writing, were seen almost exclusively from a European perspective. The great majority of wine writers were British and most of the Americans, for their part, were Eurocentric. This made sense, as most of the wines worth writing about back then were European. We Americans had not yet invented a native wine vocabulary or a native wine culture.

Both of these cultures have their own intrinsic worth. Anyone who submits, out of jingoism or chauvinism, that America has nothing to learn from Europe's centuries-old wine culture is a fool. Conversely, anyone who says that America (or Australia or New Zealand or any other "new" wine culture) has nothing significant or worthwhile to contribute is equally ridiculous.

That noted, cultural perspectives do differ. How we Americans go about understanding wine is different from the European approach. I like to think that I understand, and appreciate, both. Over the years, I've commented, er, *anableptically*, on these dual perspectives.

THE TYRANNY OF BEING WELL BROUGHT-UP

IF A DEFINING DISTINCTION CAN be drawn between European and American cultures, it is this: Europeans accept abstract ideas as enormously powerful; Americans find them less persuasive. To Americans, an abstraction is powerful only when proved practical. For example, Einstein became a genius only when his ideas resulted in the atomic bomb.

I mention this cultural difference because, as winemaking has become internationalized, one particular notion is proving hugely powerful—abstract though it is. It is the French notion of *bien élevé*.

A French childhood—not a happy prospect, according to many who survived it—is shaped by the demand of being *bien élevé*. Literally, it means "well bred." But it is more than just a parental admonition. *Bien élevé* is a vision of civilization, a two-word boundary that delineates refinement from savagery. In France, to describe someone or something as *mal élevé*, badly brought-up, is devastating.

Wines, too, are thought to come to no good end without incessant civilizing—a smoothing, refining, buffing. French wine shippers revealingly describe themselves as a *négociant-éleveur*. What's more, it's not enough that something (or someone) be *bien élevé*, it must be *obviously* so. The stamp of civilization must be unmistakable.

This notion of *bien élevé* is powerful and persuasive throughout the wine world. French wines have set the standard by which all others must be judged. So the idea of *bien élevé*—which has shaped all fine French wines—has also covertly shaped the palates of everyone who fancies himself or herself a judge of good wine.

Today, for a wine to be considered fine, it must be noticeably *bien élevé*. The most dramatic effects of this are seen in Italy and California, the two "wine nations" most covetous of rivaling France as sources of the world's finest wines. Producers in both places are frantically signaling, through their winemaking, that their wines are *bien élevé*, never mind indigenous cultures or tastes.

This is most prominent in Italy, which has a wealth of traditions and long-evolved tastes. Italians understand *bien élevé*—theirs is also a mannerly culture—but *bien élevé* lacks the same imperative force. Italians simply don't subscribe to it, at least in their foods and wines.

One of the accusations made against Italian cooking by those trained in, or seduced by, classic French cuisine is that Italian cooking lacks refinement—as the French see refinement. They point, understandably, to the great French repertoire of sauces. To the French culinary mind, a dish is incomplete without an elevating sauce. This has its subtleties, to be sure.

Yet the Italian aesthetic can be even more subtle than the French. The Italian notion of saucing—although they would not choose that word—is, in essence, that a "sauce" should come from *within* the dish itself. If it is external, such as olive oil or balsamic vinegar, the added touch should serve only as something to draw out the "sauce within." Anyone who has had a plate of plain, but perfectly cooked, beans knows that a mere drizzle of superb olive oil unleashes an unsuspected depth of flavor *in the beans themselves*.

This is why Italian winegrowers traditionally never pursued—as did the French—the use of small new oak barrels to infuse their wines with the "saucing" of the vanilla scent that new oak brings. Nor did they seek to impose upon the wine the textural "polish" that these same small oak barrels provide. The sensibility about extracting intrinsic goodness made such refinements alien. It is why the Italian wines made today using small new oak barrels seem so "un-Italian." It's not just the unfamiliar flavors. It's the imposition of a foreign aesthetic premise, namely, *bien élevé*.

Have you had any of the new-style Piedmontese Barberas lately? They are painfully *bien élevé*, never mind the loss of individual expression of site and even grape. Ditto for many of the most obvious worked-on Barolos, Barbarescos, Chiantis, and dozens of other Italian wines that court world opinion.

The most widely praised wines today almost invariably are adjudged "lush," "fine," "well crafted," "gentle," "elegant," "sumptuous," "polished," "stylish," "seductive," "silky," and "velvety." *Bien élevé*, wouldn't you say?

Abstractions *are* powerful. And woe to the winemaker who doesn't recognize it. *(1994)*

DOES AMERICA NEED MASTERS OF WINE?

WE AMERICANS HAVE ALWAYS HAD a fondness for British ways of doing things. Partly, it is the sheer exoticism. Partly, it is the reward of a successful revolution: we can *afford* to love them. We've always been suckers for a title or an accent.

The British way of doing things is fundamentally different than the American. Theirs is an eye-of-the-needle approach, based on ever-finer gradations of exclusion. Great Britain abounds in clubs, fine scholars, and a class system of such nuance as to baffle even the most astute American. We, on the other hand, are all about inclusion. Our system thrives on letting almost anyone have a shot at seemingly almost anything. And then giving them a second chance if at first they don't succeed. It's messy, but it works.

What prompts these musings is watching a friend of mine try, unsuccessfully, to gain entry to the Institute of Masters of Wine. Founded in England in 1953, it has set itself up as a self-appointed arbiter of winedom's elect. It now seeks to extend its reach to these shores. The Institute of Masters of Wine is a peculiarly British institution, which is to say that like so much else in upper-class British life, it exists primarily as a vehicle to distinguish its members from the riffraff. Members award themselves the title of Master of Wine, which they abbreviate to "MW" and brand to their names like prize cows who fear cattle rustlers.

What the Brits do in the privacy of their own island is their business. But why would an American want any part of it? Various wine industry sorts in this country, including the *Wine Spectator*, have lined up in support of extending the reach of the Institute of Masters of Wine to these shores. The usual reason invoked is that, somehow, the acquisition of a credential would make for a better wine trade. If you believe that, you've been watching too much *Masterpiece Theatre*.

One of the compelling attractions of American culture is its very freedom from self-appointed gatekeepers. By promulgating credentials, such gatekeepers feather their nest at the expense of other perfectly well-plumed birds. After all, if they are the masters of wine, so-called, then what are you? Figure it out for yourself.

The Institute, of course, intones about standards, excellence, and whatnot. While credentialing bodies such as the American College of Physicians and Surgeons can make a convincing case for such a need (folks who are about to poke you with a needle or slice you up with a scalpel should be able to present a certificate of some kind), it's a bit much for those who only brandish a corkscrew.

What makes America different—better, even—is its freedom from and nose thumbing at just this sort of exclusionary device. The idea that the American wine trade needs greater professionalism is patently absurd. We have the most vibrant, dynamic wine market in the world. It serves, admirably, the world's greatest collection of connoisseurs, bar none. And this is not because of size. Remember, we don't drink that much wine. As for professionalism, we have a steeplechase of state laws that makes the European Community regulations look like a cakewalk. No wine industry amateur could long survive, let alone thrive, in this environment without soon acquiring a high gloss of professionalism.

As for setting a standard, or raising one, you only need look at the several thousand Americans who import, wholesale, retail, or write about wine. And that doesn't begin to enumerate all of the winemakers and winery representatives across the nation, many of whom know about the world's wines to a fare-thee-well. It's amazing how they all managed to grasp—and improve upon—the subject without so much as a how-de-do from a college of wine cardinals.

So why did my friend, who has had a successful career as a writer and teacher, try so hard to join the club? "To tell you the truth," he replied, "I just wanted to separate myself from everyone else in the field." That pretty much tells you what it's all about, doesn't it? *(1994)*

Wine Spectator *long ago ceased any involvement with the Institute of Masters of Wine.*

———

MUSIC TO NO ONE'S EARS

ONE OF THE MOST TREACHEROUS instruments to play is banging the drum of chauvinism. It takes no talent, yet it attracts attention. The player fancies himself a musician when, in fact, he or she is little more than a noisemaker—a crow among canaries.

These thoughts occurred upon reading, some months ago, a line of self-serving trash by a European writer whom I won't even bother to name. Frankly, it's not important *who* promulgated it. But as the year approaches its close, the words still linger—and they deserve a response. "Ignore the American ignorami," declared the writer. "Read what the knowledgeable Europeans have to say!"

This is poisonous stuff. Heaven knows, Americans have pursued all sorts of mis-guided notions about fine wine. And there's no denying that our influence is out-sized. More than two centuries ago, *The Federalist* papers identified America as a "large commercial republic." This has only become magnified in our time. And as the size of the American purse grows, our interests impinge upon others.

What is worth noting is that, for the most part, Americans themselves are largely innocent of just how potent this influence is. Oh, we hear about it often enough (usually in tones of sputtering outrage). But the average American really doesn't get it. How can we? Only when we live abroad do we discover—and quickly so—to what degree American ideas penetrate other cultures.

This influence is no different with wine. Like it or not, America has become the world's most influential wine country. This is not to say that we are as knowing about wine as the French or Italians. Far from it. Wine has not permeated our cul-ture as it has theirs. No American would even suggest that it has. We know what we don't know.

But we also know what we *do* know. We know that low yields generally mean better wines. So we are pushing winegrowers everywhere—in print and with our pocketbooks—to lower their yields. We know that, generally, unfiltered wines have better texture and flavor than heavily filtered ones. Again, we raise our voices, and we vote with our purses.

Above all, we know—perhaps better than most, if I may say so—that public discussion is absolutely essential to improving wine quality. This discussion can grate on others' ears, in part because—let's face it—American public discourse is not the most genteel. The late A. J. Liebling captured this bare-knuckled quality more than fifty years ago in one of his war correspondent dispatches to *The New Yorker*:

> Americans are the best competitors on earth. A basketball game between
> two high school teams at home will call forth enough hardness of soul
> and flexibility of ethic to win a minor war; the will to win in Americans
> is so strong it is painful, and it is unfettered by any of the polite flummery
> that goes with cricket. This ruthlessness always in stock is one of our great
> national resources.

This is present in wine as well. Witness the velocity of California's rush to wine fame. Sure, chauvinism played a role, but it was the "you always hurt the one you love" kind. Wine writers simultaneously plumped for, and then pummeled, California winegrowers. The push for ever-finer wines has been ferocious—and often unkind.

Nevertheless, what Americans want today in their fine wines has—for the most part—improved wines everywhere. This is not to say that the French or Italians or Spanish would not have pursued ever-better quality on their own. Of course, they would. But the raw, even unpleasant, American push for something ever better surely helped matters along.

Let me be blunt. (I am an American, after all.) A few prominent Burgundians are upset about what they perceive as American incomprehension or mean-spiritedness. Yet the quality of Burgundies has improved because of our vocal involvement in their wines. Witness the celebration of—and the prices so willingly paid for—the likes of Domaine Leroy's extraordinary wines. Or those of Niellon, Sauzet, Lafon, Rousseau, Raveneau, or a few dozen others, some of them unknown only a few vintages ago.

And we are not wrong about these wines. They represent the standards by which others should—indeed, must—be judged. And we do so, vocally, competitively, and yes, sometimes uncomprehendingly. But the discussion is open for all to see and participate in.

So as the year comes to a close, it's worth remembering that the greatest wines come from growers of implacable will and standards. And from an audience that is actively involved with them—never mind their nationality. *(1995)*

The British writer who declared "Ignore the American ignorami" was Clive Coates.

MORE AMERICAN THAN EVER

ONE OF THE CURIOUS FEATURES of being an American abroad is what I call the "talking dog syndrome." You meet a local and they are astonished—stunned, really—that you, as an American, can actually grasp something about their culture. Whoever thought the dog could talk?

This happened yet again during a recent trip to Italy's Piedmont region, which is an old stomping ground for me. I was having dinner with a Piedmontese winegrower, a prominent fellow who travels the world. He knows the American market. But that's not the same as knowing Americans.

"Do you think they'll ever really understand?" he inquired. He meant Americans.

"Well, *I'm* an American," I not so gently pointed out. This was tut-tutted away. "You are different," said my friend. "I mean the others."

I decided to let loose. "We Americans are the easiest people in the world to underestimate," I declared. I believe this with all of my heart, never more so than now.

The next morning, as I walked out of my hotel (a tiny place deep in the countryside) for a stroll, I came across two Japanese wine professionals. Frankly, I was astonished to see them in this tiny, tucked-away hilltop village in foggy Piedmont. But I shouldn't have been. I should have recalled my own words: "We Americans are the easiest people in the world to underestimate."

You see, "we Americans" are really *anybody* new to the culture of wine. And that, by the way, includes a surprising number of newly middle-class French, Spanish, and Italians, too. You'd be amazed—excuse me, I don't want to underestimate you—how many Europeans are as new to fine wine as . . . Americans. Or Japanese.

The learning curve is steep, as we wine-loving Americans well know. But it's surprisingly fast. Pierre-Henry Gagey, the president of the Burgundy shipper Louis Jadot, said to me recently how impressed he is by how quickly the Japanese have turned to wine. "You know, ten years ago they were just like Americans were thirty years ago. They wanted the 'best' and price was no object. But they didn't really know much about Burgundy.

"But today, it's totally different," he added. "Not only are the Japanese important clients, they know what they're doing. They really know Burgundy. Of course, you Americans are in another league now yourselves." This might sound like so much French Shinola except for one thing: it's true.

Right now, there's a new kind of "underestimating" going on in wine today. There's a certain cynicism among fine-wine producers in France, Italy, and yes, California, about what "we Americans" want.

They are convinced that all of us newcomers to wine want big, hulking red wines of implacably dark hue. Indeed, there's a lucrative market for them. In fairness, the best such wines are really good.

But too many are contrived. They are concocted by adding dollops of wine concentrate (California, Piedmont) or by adding to their indigenous varieties of Pinot Noir, Nebbiolo, or Sangiovese such dark, strong "outsiders" as Syrah or Cabernet (Burgundy, Tuscany, Piedmont).

In winemaking, there's the little-reported widespread use of vacuum concentrators, where water from diluted grape juice (from habitually excessive yields) is sluiced off, creating a seemingly denser, darker wine. Bordeaux alone has two thousand such machines, known by the brand name Entropie. According to Entropie, more than half of all of Bordeaux's classed growths own them. They are fast appearing in Burgundy and Italy, too.

At first glance, vacuum concentrators seem innocent enough. You take out some excess water and voilà! you have better wine. Surely in rainy vintages it is a godsend. But we haven't seen many rainy vintages in the last decade. What it's really all about is growing more grapes in the vineyard than is desirable and achieving "concentration" later on in the winery.

Left unsaid is that when water is sluiced off from unfermented grape juice, it's not just water. Also being removed is sugar and the thousands of flavor compounds that create fine wine's complexity.

The sugar can be added back in (chaptalization), as well as acidity (remember, the balance gets changed by this process). Texture and taste can also be affected. But there's no replacing—or creating—flavor that can only be achieved in the vineyard by low yields.

Time will sort it all out. It always does. Bad wines don't last. But good tasters do. And it never pays to underestimate Americans—no matter what country we come from. *(2002)*

Not long after this column appeared, the French company Entropie, which previously proudly proclaimed on its Web site how many classed-growth Bordeaux châteaux purchased their vacuum concentrator, deleted that information. It has never since reappeared.

ROCK, PAPER, SCISSORS—
STYLE CLOBBERS CHARACTER

REMEMBER THE OLD CHILDREN'S GAME Rock, Paper, Scissors? Scissors cut matches. And paper covers seemingly invincible rock—winning every time.

I thought of this game upon reading the results of a blind tasting conducted by the bombastically titled Grand Jury Européen. Although its organizers will vehemently deny it, the Grand Jury Européen is an attempt to redress what Europeans—especially the French—see as the barbaric American domination of wine aesthetics.

Judges had to be European. European palates, you see, are finer, purer, more informed. Even the English were invited. Still, the event was dominated in every way by the French (the judging took place in Bordeaux). This year's examination focused on Chardonnay, with twenty-seven wines from seven countries.

Sounds impressive, right? Not so fast. When you look more closely, you discover that fully 70 percent of the Chardonnays were from Burgundy. California had one— just one—entry, as did Italy, Spain, Germany, and Switzerland. Only one country other than France had multiple entries: Australia had two wines.

What's more, the Europeans judged not just one vintage, but three vintage's worth of every wine, a 1989, '92, and '94. (That all three vintages just so happened to be banner years for Burgundy, we'll leave aside for the moment.)

But wait, it gets better. The French were taking no chances—or so they thought. Their lineup was a regular Hall of Fame of Chardonnay cleanup hitters. Enlisted to the cause were such Burgundian bombers as Meursault Charmes from Domaine Comtes Lafon and Meursault Perrières from Domaine Coche-Dury.

Various hyphenated Montrachets showed up. Two Chevalier-Montrachets rode to the rescue, one from Bouchard Père et Fils, the other from Louis Jadot. A Bienvenue-Bâtard from Olivier Leflaive was enlisted, as were two Corton-Charlemagnes (Louis Latour and Domaine Bonneau du Martray).

As if this were not overkill enough, two Montrachets were present as well, from Marquis de Laguiche/Joseph Drouhin and Domaine Jacques Prieur.

Not impressed, you say? How about Puligny-Montrachet Les Combettes from Domaine Sauzet? Or Puligny-Montrachet Les Pucelles from Domaine Leflaive? Or Chablis *Grand Cru* Valmur from that district's greatest producer, Domaine Raveneau?

Now for the best part: The wine that came in Number One was Robert Mondavi Chardonnay Reserve. The runner-up was Domaine Comtes Lafon's Meursault Charmes. This was not a coincidence—as I'll get to in a moment. Nor was it a coincidence that the wine that finished dead last was Chablis *Grand Cru* Valmur from Domaine Raveneau.

So what do such results tell us? a) European palates are no better at sifting through too many wines at one time than anybody else's. b) There's a lot of good Chardonnay out there all made in an uncomfortably close *style.* c) Wines with a lot of (sweet) oak, extended lees contact, and forward rich fruit (e.g., Mondavi Reserve [#1] and Lafon's Meursault Charmes [#2]) always show best in big blind tastings, while austere, seemingly idiosyncratic, age-needy wines such as Raveneau's Chablis Valmur always show worst.

Chablis *never* does well in big blind tastings. It always comes off as weird rather than characterful. Even Coche-Dury's glorious, stony-tasting Meursault Perrières only came in seventh, which tells us something about how little truth about character—as opposed to style—is extracted in such blind tastings.

In the Rock, Paper, Scissors match of blind tasting, the paper of style always covers the rock of character. European palates are no better at sidestepping this than any others.

The tasting tells us something else: The French had better wise up. If all their indisputably great vineyards can do is deliver a sense of fruitiness magnified by winemaking style, then America, Italy, and Australia (Ca' del Bosco and Montadam came in fifth and sixth, respectively) will mop the floor with them.

How could this happen to fabled Burgundy? Yields. The vast majority of even the greatest white Burgundy vineyards are overcropped, sometimes shamefully so. Their vaunted (and very real) *terroirs* are lost, diluted into insipidity. Mere fruitiness is all that remains, flavored by French barrels, lees stirring, and other winemaking techniques.

Anyone can do that. And everyone is. Just ask the Europeans. *(1997)*

WINE IN THE AMERICAN MAINSTREAM

WHEN WINE EMERGED AFTER ITS post-Prohibition coma twenty-five years ago, the wine industry dream—a fantasy, really—was of a United States that embraced wine in the old European manner. Only when we drank like them, went the thinking, would we have a wine culture. We would know when it happened by looking at the numbers: per capita consumption.

In the meantime, America has declined—and seemingly leveled off—at a modest 1.86 gallons of wine per American adult or about nine bottles a year per person. This is slightly above the average wine consumption during the 1970s (8.5 bottles a year per person) and substantially below that for the 1980s (11.5 bottles a year per person). Despairing at these limp sales figures, the wine industry declared the wine culture dream finished.

As you might expect, the wine industry is wailing like professional keeners at an Irish wake. In the meantime, the corpse is up and about. To see it, you have to look beyond per capita consumption—which was always a myopic measure, anyway. Only now, as we approach the mid-1990s, are we able to see the truly critical feature: wine in America is becoming "normal."

"Normal" cannot be defined simply in terms of per capita consumption. After all, fully half of the adult population of France—whose wine culture is undoubted— *never* drinks wine according to France's National Interprofessional Office of Wine, an industry group. And the French who do drink wine consume half as much wine per capita today as they did fifty years ago. Has their wine culture declined correspondingly? It looks pretty vibrant to me.

The American wine culture dream is coming true. The proof is something frequently overlooked, but enormously significant: wine now is made in forty-three states. When I was a boy growing up in Long Island, New York, the agricultural talk (there still were many farms nearby) was of potatoes. No one I knew grew potatoes, but that was unimportant. They were part of Long Island life. I knew potatoes were there and saw fields on Sunday drives.

Today, Long Island has at least sixteen wineries. They are part of Long Island life, even though I'm sure that only a tiny fraction of Long Island's three million or so residents have ever tried a bottle of their local wine—or even drink wine at all.

Another example is New Mexico. I confess that I never have tasted a New Mexico wine. In fact, I've never even seen a bottle. Professionally, this is an embarrassing admission. After all, New Mexico now has five thousand acres of vines under cultivation. And it has nineteen wineries. With that many acres and wineries, wine in New Mexico has to have become something local and proprietary.

In the Pacific Northwest, Oregon and Washington together have 193 wineries and more than eighteen thousand acres of vines. Some northwesterners may not like that fact, being teetotalers, mossback moralists, or just plain ornery about change. Still, the awareness is there, and most of them have accepted this addition to their vision of northwest life. They are their wines from their place.

This sense of proprietariness now exists—to greater or lesser degrees—in forty-three states. Who's drinking all these wines from the forty-three states? All that Long Island wine? Or New Mexico wine? Or Texas wine? Or Northwest wines, for that matter? Locals and tourists. The great majority of these wines are never seen outside of their areas of origin.

One other element points to the emergence of a wine culture. Increasingly, those Americans who do drink wine are unwilling to pay a high price for it. Wine prices are softening. This is not just because of recessionary times, although that surely plays a role. Something more fundamental—and universal—is at work. It is simply this: wherever wine is viewed as "normal," people are unwilling to pay a high price. Its corollary is that wherever wine is seen as "exceptional," its audience willingly pays a high price.

The new normalcy of wine is making itself felt. Only truly remarkable wines will command a premium, as has long been the case in Europe. This leaves some wine producers uneasy. It's almost, well . . . un-American. *(1994)*

According to Wine Institute, a California-based trade group, in 2006, America's per capita consumption was 2.39 gallons (9 liters) per capita or twelve bottles of wine per person. This figure has been exceeded only twice, in 1985 and 1986, when per capita consumption was 2.43 gallons. Wine is now made in all fifty states; Long Island has fifty-one wineries. Oregon and Washington now have more than 600 wineries and a combined 46,000 acres of vines. I have since tasted New Mexico wines and have enthusiastically and repeatedly recommended the sparkling wines from New Mexico's Gruet winery.

SLIPPERINESS AT THE SMITHSONIAN

IT'S TIME TO TAKE THE gloves off about academics who opine about wine with no more knowledge or insight than what you can glean from reading an old *Time* magazine in the dentist's office. Anyone who is a professor of seemingly anything now feels free to step up and take a swing at wine—or alcohol in general— with impunity.

A choice example of this was on display in May at the Smithsonian Institution, which sponsored a seminar on American wine called "Red, White, and American." Among the speakers was Warren Belasco, who is chairman of the American Studies department at the University of Maryland Baltimore County.

"I'm not sure that I see Americans becoming really significant wine drinkers—or even drinkers of anything alcoholic," says Belasco. "As we hold individuals ever more morally responsible for their own illnesses, I think alcohol may very well go the route of tobacco and red meat."

And what does he base this on? "Seventy-five percent of the wine consumed is drunk just by 5 percent of the adult population," cites Belasco, without attribution. "So, 95 percent of the adults are not drinking much, if at all." Then, out comes that old statistical warhorse: France and Italy consume ten times as much wine per capita as we do.

"Wine," explains the professor, "has a central place in cultures based on very long, leisurely meals and pedestrian transportation. And that's probably not the future in America unless we experience a major economic and environmental collapse."

What a quaint vision of wine and culture. "Significant" wine consumption is the old sot staggering down the country lane. Wine, you see, is one of those rural, horse-drawn reveries like something out of a Merchant-Ivory movie. We Americans, on the other hand, are terminally, internally combustibly busy. Only an economic or environmental collapse could return us to our wine senses.

The professor's remarks remind me of A. J. Liebling's scathing definition of an expert as someone who "writes what he construes to be the meaning of what he hasn't seen."

If we've heard the Europe-vs.-America comparison once, we've heard it a thousand times. The fact is—and it *is* a fact—most Europeans drank surprisingly little wine until quite recently, given their long history of winegrowing.

American wine consumption will never equal Europe's. So what? Modern-day Europe's consumption will never again equal late nineteenth-century Europe's.

Theodore Zeldin in *France 1848–1945, Volume I*, tells us that "The consumption of wine in France increased from 51 liters a head in 1848 to 77 liters in 1872 to 103 liters in 1904 and 136 liters in 1926." This great increase came almost exclusively from the cities, with their higher wages.

Ironically, a disproportionate few now drink wine in France. In a survey of four thousand French adults, 51 percent said they *never* drank wine, according to the National Interprofessional Office of Wine, a French trade group. France drinks less wine today (64.5 liters per capita) than it did 125 years ago.

Does this mean that wine in France is any less vibrant today than it was before? If you look only at the numbers, you'd have no choice but to conclude that not only is wine dying in France, but also all over Western Europe. The numbers are unequivocal: in the last thirty years, wine consumption has declined by nearly half in Italy, France, Spain, and Portugal.

Is wine culture dying in France, Italy, or Spain? Hardly. Yet their wine consumption will continue to decline. Wine is finding a new equilibrium, taking a revised place alongside increased consumption of bottled water, soft drinks, and the like.

If you actually visit France, Italy, or Spain, you will discover that wine—and above all the wine culture—is vibrant and throbbing with vitality. As school kids say, I seen it. This is the *real* measure of wine, a reporter's measure.

What makes for "significant" wine drinking is *culture*, not numbers. I seen it in America, too. Not everywhere, to be sure. But make no mistake: American wine culture is vibrant and growing. You can see it in the explosion of imported and domestic offerings on supermarket and wine-shop shelves: in the eight-hundred-plus wineries in California, to say nothing of the hundreds of other wineries spread (sometimes thinly) across forty-two other states, and in the proliferation of wine newsletters and computer chat lines.

Asking non-wine professionals to publicly ponder the subject is a wonderful thing. But it would also be wise to ask them if they know anything about it. *(1996)*

French wine consumption continues to decline. In 2005 (the latest available data), France consumed 55.85 liters of wine per capita. The United States now has wineries in all fifty states. American per capita consumption of wine has increased 26 percent in the ten years between 1996 and 2006. I never did hear from Mr. Belasco or anyone at the Smithsonian, by the way.

Gen X Nixes Wine? Aw, Quit Worrying

I SUPPOSE IT'S HUMAN NATURE to fret about the future during a gung-ho present. Right now, the wine business is booming everywhere. No matter where you turn, from Chile to Italy, California to Australia, Oregon to Hungary, you can't visit a winery without tripping over a smiling banker and a grinning grower. Prices have never been higher; demand is stronger than ever.

So what's not to like? Ah, then you haven't met the handwringers and doom-sayers. They'll tell you that you're living in a dream world. It's all a bubble, you see, like the once-fabled Japanese economy. Wine's newfound success will also pop and collapse, with comparably disastrous effects.

It's nothing so scenic as wineries being blown up by the aliens in the movie *Independence Day*. Rather, the doomsayers say we're living in a demographic bubble. The famous baby boomers, all 66 million of 'em marching toward the wine aisle, have created a temporary fantasyland. They're the ones drinking fine wine and paying the big bucks.

The doom lies beyond, with the darkly designated Generation X. This group, now in their twenties and early thirties, apparently do not like wine. Focus groups tell us this. Market research by big wineries says that beyond the boomers lies a void, a demographic black hole of wine-spurners. They drink beer. And that, campers, is why you're not safe in your French oak barrel at night. Darkness is falling on wine.

You think I'm joking, right? Not a chance. I heard just this scenario submitted to me in just these melodramatic terms by a winegrower. And he, in turn, heard it at some conference somewhere, presented with even greater certainty by a guy with charts and numbers. So it must be true.

Actually, the numbers *are* pretty incontrovertible. Those pesky Xers really aren't pursuing wine like us insufferable boomers who had the great good luck to be born when houses were affordable and college loans not quite so crushing. We have discretionary income. They have debts.

That's not a small point, by the way. We all know that prices for good wines are almost ludicrously high. Have you tried to buy a house lately? In certain parts of the nation, houses are all but unaffordable for entry-level buyers—which is to say people who are in their twenties and early thirties. And if they do buy, you can be sure that they don't have much dough left over. No wonder beer looks so good.

The fretters and doomsayers are dazzled—stupefied, really—by the numbers. Therein lies the problem: The numbers mean nothing. Every time the wine business starts crunching numbers, they turn out to be wrong.

First, we weren't going to be a true wine nation until our per capita consumption rivaled Europe's. That never happened, of course, and yet, voilà! here we are: a genuine, if fledgling, wine nation.

Then the numbers revealed that our per capita consumption actually was declining. Government warning labels flourished. Anti-drunk driving laws. Sulfite warnings. Fetal alcohol syndrome. All of these, and more, were forecast as crushing blows to wine.

So neo-Prohibitionism became the rallying cry. Haven't heard that in a while, have we? That's because it never existed. What the doomsayers paranoically insisted was neo-Prohibitionism was really just an outgrowth of the much larger issue of health awareness.

All of which tells us of the likely lunacy of the latest bit of doom-and-gloom about Generation Xers. What always is ignored, yet is as powerful as springtime itself, is wine's powerful pull on our senses. Every generation finds its way to wine, if it's allowed to.

So why not believe in wine? Why not recognize that what drew us to fine wine will surely, over time, exert the same attraction on succeeding generations? After all, the same numbers tell us that twenty- and thirty-year-olds are not just drinking any old beer. They want "craft beers." The same quality consciousness they are bringing to beer (not to mention coffee) will lead them inevitably to fine wine.

There's nothing else like wine. No other taste sensation rivals it. No other food offers as much history, culture, variety, and yes, mystery. It's what has made wine so compelling to so many people for so many years. And now, all of a sudden, it's going to stop? Forget the numbers. Wine isn't soda pop. Wine is forever. *(1997)*

Ten years after this column appeared, it turns out that not only was there no cause for worrying about Gen Xers "nixing" wine—they've since embraced it, according to market surveys—but there was cause for even more optimism yet. I had not factored in the succeeding generation designated as Millennials. They are the cohort that reached drinking age (21 years old) around the year 2000, hence the designation.

According to a 2007 "Consumer Tracking Study" from the Wine Market Council, a trade group, "The two youngest segments of the market, Millennials [born starting in 1977] and Generation X [born between 1965 and 1976], are increasing their consumption most rapidly and most decidedly."

What's more, the report notes, Millennials are the more influential for demographic reasons: the Generation X population is about 44 million, while the Millennials number about 70 million. The report further notes that while Generation Xers didn't take to wine until their thirties, Millennials took to wine in their twenties. This is a major reason for the uptick in overall per capita consumption of wine, as Millennials outnumber Baby Boomers as a cohort, although the Baby Boomers (born between 1946 and 1961) are significantly wealthier.

The Consumer Tracking Study calculates America's per capita wine consumption at 3.02 gallons, by the way.

AN OPEN LETTER TO WINING (AND WHINING) GEN XERS

DEAR GEN XERS,

It's a hot topic today, at least in economics circles: The growing gap between income and wealth. Income, as we all know, is what you've got jingling in your pocket right now. Wealth is the result of accumulated income, never mind whether it's in stocks, bonds, real estate, or—here's a thought—a personal wine cellar.

Make no mistake: A wine cellar is a collection of uncashed paychecks. And most of us, especially before we hit our peak earning years, find it tough to set aside even a portion of our paychecks.

I say this from heartfelt personal experience. Although I've got a nice collection of bottles today, it wasn't always so. It was hard won, as many Gen X–generated wine cellars now are.

This brings me to my (slightly uncomfortable) point. I say to those of you who are in your twenties and early thirties, don't give up! You *can* build the cellar—well, a bunch of wines, anyway—of your dreams. But there's a catch: It has to be something crafted from *your* dreams. Not *Wine Spectator*'s. Or mine. Or some other know-all wine pundit.

In other words, don't let us torture you with the sugarplum fantasies that—let's be honest here—are our stock-in-trade. What we taste and write about isn't necessarily what we own. Why? Well, it's the same reason why you don't have these wines either: money.

Now, I'm not going to pretend that I don't have some good bottles in my cellar. I do, although very few of them are blue-chip auction items. I mention this because— brace yourself—I'm tired of hearing the whining about how wines are too expensive today. About how you can't participate in today's wine world.

Get over it. It's not true. Here's a fact: The same wines that are out of reach for you today were out of reach for me twenty years ago. Sure, prices have changed, but not the relative affordability.

Just to confirm this, I rooted around in the cellar and found a dusty box of old wine catalogs. One of them was a Winter 1981 catalog from the (now defunct) San Francisco wine merchant Draper & Esquin. They had good prices, too. And to be fair about this, let me tell you what I was earning back then: $185 a week as a full-time food-and-wine writer.

So what was I tempted by? Well, there was Domaine Leflaive Puligny-Montrachet Les Pucelles 1979, the latest vintage. Price: $31.75. Today, it's $90. It was painful then and now.

I never was tempted by big-name Bordeaux, but just for the record, a '78 Chateau Cheval-Blanc cost $62.50 back in 1981. I was no more able (or willing) to divert one third of my weekly paycheck onto a bottle of wine than you are. By the way, Lafite, Mouton, and Latour were all about the same $60+ price.

My dream wine (yours, too, I'll bet) was Domaine de la Romanée-Conti. Take a guess what the latest release of La Tâche cost in 1981? Time's up. The 1978 La Tâche cost $130 a bottle. It was out of reach then and now.

Some clever economics major can probably figure out the purchasing parity between then and now. But it's pretty clear that the fabled "good old days" really weren't all that dreamy. The fabled wines of the time remained fantasies, just as they do today.

Granted, there are real differences. And I don't want to diminish them. College didn't cost so much two decades ago. Housing was much less expensive. Cars were cheap. All of these have become oppressive.

Also, there are a lot more high-ticket wines today than twenty years ago. Really, there were no expensive California wines, except maybe Hanzell or Heitz. Then again, you can find more really superb California wines today selling at reasonable prices than ever existed two decades ago.

So let me give it to you straight. You're going to have to build your wine collection just the way the rest of us did, by looking for the unknown or under-appreciated regions. Or for new producers who haven't yet got the hype. Or for wine types that are currently out of fashion (remember how cheap Sauternes used to be?).

Most of these won't be trophy wines. They won't be the subjects of magazine cover stories. You won't be the envy of Texas millionaires. But you *will* have a real wine cellar. And if you choose carefully and sift through today's flood of advice—which didn't exist twenty years ago, I might note—you'll have realized your wine cellar dream. And it will be beautiful. *(1997)*

Oh, what a difference a decade makes. Domaine Leflaive Puligny-Montrachet Les Pucelles now fetches $250 a bottle for the latest vintage; Chateau Cheval-Blanc costs $900 to $1,000 a bottle; and the fabled La Tâche asks—and gets—between $1,000 and $5,000 a bottle depending upon the vintage. Nevertheless, there are also more lovely, cellar-worthy wines made today from places such as Spain, Greece, Italy, France, Argentina, Chile, New Zealand, Australia, California, Oregon, Washington, British Columbia, and Ontario than existed even ten years ago. And they sell for very reasonable prices.

SOME TRUTHS OF OUR TIME

WINE HAS AN AGELESS QUALITY about it, what with all of Europe's ancient vineyard areas and lovely old stone buildings. Yet the new structure of wine today is not a simulation of wine's romantic past but a "real time" creation that has transformed our old preconceptions. To understand wine as it really is today—and will be for decades to come—consider the following:

Price has nothing to do with quality. There's absolutely no correlation anymore—if there ever was—between price and quality. None whatsoever. But there's an equally absolute correlation between demand and price. Sure, quality plays a part, but price is mostly a function of scarcity, publicity, and perceived exclusivity. Think of French Champagne, if you're looking for a good example.

Partly the reason for this most-extreme-in-history imbalance between quality and price is technological: Winemakers everywhere now have the same good equipment. And they are equally well equipped with solid scientific educations.

The other reason is globalization. Wine drinkers everywhere—America, Europe, Asia—now drink remarkable wines from a dozen or more countries that sell for modest prices which don't even begin to reflect their intrinsic quality and—this is important—originality.

Most wines will age longer—and better—than we expect. This is a corollary to the uncoupling of price and quality. Precisely because so many of today's wines are so well made—and often from intrinsically fine, yet still low-priced, areas such as Puglia or Argentina—the old intuitive linkage between price and ageability has also been severed.

Mind you, it's not just a matter of a wine's being able to age—that's a matter of mere endurance—but rather, the worth of waiting. A surprising number of today's best wines from just about anywhere will not only make the long march but also will have something interesting to say at the end of it. This applies to just about any wine, from Muscadet and Moscato to Barbera and Blaufränkisch.

Today's most interesting wines get short shrift. Although a number of my winewriting colleagues—and wine retailers, too—have labored mightily to spotlight lesser-known wines and winegrowers, the fact remains that too many deserving wines and whole regions have not had their moment in prime time.

The issue here is not about assigning blame, but about recognizing that, as

Hamlet said, "There are more things in heaven and earth . . . than are dreamt of in your philosophy." Our "wine philosophies"—and I include my own here—are not as creative and inclusionary as they might be.

The great exception to this is restaurant sommeliers. More than any other group, they have vastly enlarged their "wine philosophies," persuasively advocating for the likes of Grüner Veltliner and many of Italy's and Spain's great, but lesser-known, wine regions and producers, to say nothing of the new wines of Greece, Hungary, New Zealand, Oregon, Washington, and, of course, California.

Wines today are either "preinstalled" or "alternative." In the computer business, software makers pay hundreds of millions of dollars to have their products preinstalled on new computers. If you want an "alternative," you have to download it yourself. The same thing is now happening in wine.

In the world of what might be called Big Wine, the past decade has seen a concentration of brand power in relatively few hands. On the production side, you've got three major players: Constellation Brands, Diageo, and E. & J. Gallo.

They, for their part, need comparably big distribution. So you've got Southern Wine & Spirits of America. It distributes 19 percent of all the alcoholic beverages sold in the United States. Southern's new joint venture with Glazer's Distributors, a powerhouse in Texas and the Midwest, will increase that share to an estimated 38 percent nationwide.

What this means is that in retail wine sales, especially in supermarkets, the great majority of the wines on the shelf are preinstalled. You can like it or not, but that's how it is. (Actually, it's been this way for decades. Only the scale has changed.)

The key point is that all other wines—like software you have to actively seek out and download—are "alternative."

More than ever before, wine buyers now fall into two camps: those who are passive and choose from what's put in front of them (by far the larger group) and those who actively seek.

A modern-day Brillat-Savarin might easily declare: "Tell me how you buy, and I will tell what you're drinking." *(2008)*

In 2009, the joint venture between Southern Wine & Spirits of America and Glazer's Distributors was discontinued. Nevertheless, Southern Wine & Spirits remains by far the dominant—and dominating—force in American alcoholic beverage distribution nationwide.

TASTING

Obviously, tasting is central to wine. Yet there's more to tasting than a quick gurgle and a spurt of wine and words. In the same way that listening to, and becoming absorbed by, music expands your world and offers entrée to discoveries that take music beyond its compositional notes, so too is the act of tasting wine a broadening experience. It's nothing to spit at, you might say.

FEAR VS. CONVICTION

RECENTLY, I'VE COME INTO CLOSER-THAN-USUAL contact with California corporate wine types. It's easy to parody corporate wine types. Yes, they often are "suits," as opposed to "wine men and women." Suits move boxes. Indeed, they're proud of it, as that's the coin—in every sense—of their realm.

But what I hadn't understood before was their ever-present fear. Really, they're terrified of you. They won't take a chance on using screw caps, even though they know that 3 to 5 percent of everything they released under cork is tainted. Why not? Because their surveys show that you don't like screw caps.

In fairness, theirs is a profoundly democratic environment. You say you want Chardonnay? You got it. More Syrah? Coming, dear! Whatever you, the customer, wants is what they strive to supply. But precisely because their primary interest is the marketplace, corporate wine types are always playing a nerve-wracking game of catch-up. It's a long lag time from vine to wine to market.

The power of the "suits" has grown along with the vastly increased corporate ownership in today's wine world. And this has given rise to a new way of classifying wines. Never mind grape variety or *terroir*. We now have just two types of wine: wines of fear and wines of conviction.

Look at what happened to Robert Mondavi wines. Robert Mondavi himself was first and foremost a "wine man." Sure, he made a lot of money. But did you ever doubt his ambition to actually *lead* the market? To make wines that helped define, rather than react to, popular taste? He made his reputation making wines of conviction.

During Mondavi's heyday in the 1970s and 1980s, countless critics and wine drinkers expressed surprise at just how good Mondavi's basic Cabernet was, given the large quantity produced. The more expensive Reserve Cabernet was always in the top rank. Mondavi was the one to beat, never mind the big-scale production. But since Mondavi went public in 1993 and the suits took over, that hasn't been the case.

What do wines of fear taste like? In a word, "predictable." Johnny Carson used to do a comedy routine called Karnak the Magnificent in which he would hold a sealed envelope to his forehead and announce the answer to the question inside the envelope.

Today, any moderately experienced taster, upon seeing the label of one of these "wines of fear," can do the same. He or she can accurately tell you what the wine tastes like without opening the bottle.

Wines of fear will be oaky—a little or a lot. They will be intensely fruity, and smooth down the gullet, so much so that you can sometimes think you're drinking grape juice rather than wine. Above all, they will taste interchangeable with any other such wine. This, by the way, crosses national boundaries. You find wines of fear in France, Italy, Australia, California, Spain, Chile, and any other place where suits—rather than individuals—rule.

All of this is thrown into sharp relief (in every sense) when you taste wines of conviction. With a wine of conviction, the element of predictability is absent. The wine tastes original, even provocative.

Do such wines always come from small wineries? Usually they do. But winery size isn't really the defining element. Instead it's winery management. Wines of conviction come from *somebody*. Usually it's a committed owner with the courage of his or her pocketbook, as well as a vision. Occasionally, you can find a manager who behaves like he or she owns the place.

Size complicates conviction, but it doesn't prohibit it. But as every poker player knows, the bigger your pot, the less inclined you are to risk it. This is ironic, of course, because it is precisely the big players who can *afford* to take risks. Yet they almost never do.

Small wineries can psychologically afford the courage of their convictions. Almost all of the innovative wines in California today originally came from small pocket-book producers. It wasn't the Big Boys who first brought to our attention Rhône varieties such as Viognier or Grenache. Neither did they pioneer Pinot Gris, which they're all chasing after now.

So next time you drink a wine, ask yourself one question: Does this taste like a wine of fear? Or a wine of conviction? You'll be surprised how quickly, and readily, the answer will spring to your lips. The difference today is that clear. *(2005)*

CAUGHT IN A BLIND

I HAVE TO TELL YOU right up front: I'm a lousy blind taster. Ethics (and witnesses) force me to make this confession. If you're ever seated next to me at a blind tasting, don't copy from my notes. You're sure to wind up sitting next to me again—at remedial wine-tasting summer school.

With this *mea gulpa*, so to speak, out of the way, I can now proceed to the point of this column. Blind tastings, like sharp instruments, are best handled deftly. Increasingly, I find myself a believer in seeing the label.

Make no mistake—I am a great supporter of blind tastings. *Wine Spectator* rightly employs the practice for nearly all of its tastings. There's no fairer procedure in the land. It leads to a real sort of justice.

But at the same time, there's a "kids-don't-do-this-at-home" element to blind tasting. I can't tell you how often I've found myself at a dinner table where the host says, "I thought you might enjoy comparing a few wines blind tonight with dinner." Boy, the host got that wrong. I most definitely do not enjoy doing that. And others around the table usually aren't shrieking with delight, either.

Blind tasting at table seems to be a specialty of the English, as well as Anglophilic Americans. I cannot ever remember being subjected to it by Italian or—outside of Bordeaux—French hosts. The Bordelais have long had English (and Irish) affiliations.

Just why blind tastings at social occasions are so enjoyed by English wine fanciers is probably best left to them to explain, if they can. My own armchair theory has this love of tableside blind tasting as a bizarre offshoot of their ancient culture of canings in upper-class "public schools." Once you get a taste for that sort of thing . . .

They say that it sharpens one's acuity and appreciation. Right. I'm sure all the great headmasters said the same thing. To the extent that fear of humiliation does heighten the senses, then there may be something to this assertion. Mostly though, it makes those of us on the receiving end miserable.

So this is why I say enough with the blind tasting, already. Leave it to the confines of magazines and newsletters or the structured environment of a wine-tasting class. I've done these sorts of blind tastings (not well, of course), and I'm here to tell you that I've learned more and better by seeing the label.

I've discovered, for example, that within the vast area of Chianti Classico, there's a little nook that cradles three superbly distinctive Chianti Classico estates that all share a strong taste similarity: Castello della Paneretta, Fattoria Monsanto, and Isole e Olena. In a blind tasting, you may like one or another of this trio. But I doubt that even the most acute taster would spot the commonality among them in a large lineup. It's readily seen, though, when you knowingly serve them together.

Allow me to be clear about this: There's no one right way to taste wine. Blind tasting humbles the most pretentious label drinkers. There are no experts in a blind tasting. Also, it can bring to the forefront wines that, ostensibly modest, really are aristocrats. That's why we should never stop blind tasting.

But it also deserves to be said that too much blind tasting leads to a different sort of arrogance. I'll never forget being told by a Napa Valley winemaker that she thought all the distinctions of *terroir* in Burgundy were bunk.

"In our tasting group, we tasted all the different vineyard wines made by Leflaive and Lafon, Niellon, and Sauzet," she said. "And all we could repeatedly do was identify the wines by the producer's style. There is no way you can say which wine is Bâtard-Montrachet and which is Chevalier-Montrachet," she said firmly.

When I suggested that perhaps their problem was that they hadn't first tasted enough of these wines with their labels on, she dismissed that as "prejudiced tasting."

Personally, I prefer the opportunity of deriving insights from knowing where the wine came from. And even who made it. Does that invite prejudice? Sure. So what? Blind tasters are often equally prejudiced by their "we tasted 'em fair and square" approach.

When we listen to music, is our discernment any less acute, or insightful, because we know the composer or the singer? Quite the opposite, I suspect. *(1996)*

— ⁓ —

YET ANOTHER GRAND TASTING

LOS ANGELES—ONE OF THE PECULIARITIES of American wine loving is the grand tasting. Thirty years ago, you considered yourself lucky (and exhausted) to taste fifteen or twenty wines of a certain type at one sitting.

But the rise of American wine collecting, as well as the American wine passion, pumped up this puny approach into extravaganzas involving dozens of wines at a sitting and sometimes hundreds of wines across a "wine weekend."

Just last week, for example, the auction house Acker Merrall & Condit sponsored a blowout Burgundy tasting in New York spanning three days with about 115 wines, including meals at Per Se, Bouley, and Cru. It sold out at $7,999 a person.

Here in Los Angeles, a wine-obsessed physicist named Bipin Desai has for twenty years sponsored similar wine extravaganzas, with meals prepared by Chinois on Main in Santa Monica and Spago in Beverly Hills, both owned by Wolfgang Puck. Floods of Bordeaux and Burgundies have washed through these tastings, which cost thousands of dollars apiece.

This past weekend was unusual, as Mr. Desai acknowledged in his opening remarks, for a first-time-ever featuring of a Riesling wine. "In twenty years, I've never before presented a Riesling," Mr. Desai said. "And I knew that if I ever did, it would have to be Trimbach's Clos Ste. Hune." Mr. Desai admitted that he hadn't tasted many vintages of Clos Ste. Hune, which is widely seen as Alsace's single best Riesling.

This admission likely could have been echoed by many of the evening's forty-three other participants, if only because so little of Clos Ste. Hune is produced—about seven hundred cases a year at most—according to vintner Jean Trimbach, who flew in directly from Alsace for the event.

A single vineyard wine, Clos Ste. Hune occupies a mere handkerchief of a vineyard, just 3.2 acres, with the oldest vines dating to the 1950s. All of the wines at the tasting came directly from Mr. Trimbach's cellar.

Although Clos Ste. Hune was the star attraction, the tasting also included Trimbach's other great Riesling, Cuvée Frédéric Émile, which comes mostly from the *grand cru* Geisberg vineyard, with a small amount drawn from the neighboring Osterberg vineyard. "This is more readily available," Mr. Trimbach said. "We make about 3,500 to 4,000 cases a year of Frédéric Émile."

In all, eighteen vintages of Clos Ste. Hune were offered, from 2000 to 1971, along with sixteen vintages of Cuvée Frédéric Émile, also from 2000 to 1971. With thirty-four Rieslings in an evening—and not just any Rieslings, mind you—this wasn't your average suburban wine and cheese affair. (Actually, no cheese was served at all, which was a pity.)

Apart from the obvious bragging rights, are tastings such as this really worthwhile? The answer is a grandly equivocal yes and no. I've done these sorts of tastings before and have always walked away simultaneously awed and depressed at the extravagance of tasting (and spitting out) so many magnificent wines that each deserve a contemplative, lingering dinner of their own. Instead, they're herded into a beauty contest where their merits are bloodlessly, methodically examined with clinical remove. It's like a conference on lovemaking with a forensic pathologist as the keynote speaker.

That acknowledged, these tastings do offer insights. For example, it was striking to see not just the sublime quality of these two wines over a span of thirty-five years, but also to recognize something exceedingly rare in today's wine world: The style of these wines hasn't changed an iota.

This may not seem at first glance all that significant, yet it's surprisingly rare. Remarkably few wines from Bordeaux, Burgundy, Italy, Spain, California, Australia, or anywhere else—including each nation's most famous and prized estates—have remained stylistically unchanged in the past three decades. Nearly all red Bordeaux have changed, sometimes radically, in this time span. Ditto for red Burgundies and practically all of Italy's best wines.

Yet Trimbach remains true to its exclusive school, nowhere more so than with its two signature Rieslings. What's more, the Trimbach approach is almost a model of what not to do in today's quivering, market-fearful wine business. For example, neither Clos Ste. Hune nor Cuvée Frédéric Émile undergoes malolactic fermentation, where the harsh malic acid is transformed by bacteria into softer lactic acid.

This means that the wines not only retain a zippy acidity but also that it requires years, even decades, for the wines to fully mature—a point brought out dramatically in the tasting at which most of the wines only approached maturity some fifteen years after the harvest date.

Also, neither of these wines spends any time in small vanilla-scented oak barrels. Instead, they are stored in large, flavorless oak casks and even there, not for very long. The wines are put in bottle little more than eighteen months after the harvest, the better to preserve their freshness and fruit. Not least, both wines are almost always exceptionally dry, devoid of the palate-seducing sweetness now commonly found in California Chardonnays, as well as numerous Alsatian wines.

Which wines stood out? There's no question that Clos Ste. Hune is the supreme vehicle for finesse and minerality (the soil is 80 percent pure limestone). It's also the more long-lived of the two. Only today are the 1985 and '83 vintages truly mature, with '79 and '76 showing only slight signs of decline, evidenced by a slight drying out of the fruit. (The '71 was, alas, marred by cork taint.)

Cuvée Frédéric Émile is impressively close to Clos Ste. Hune in quality, displaying superb minerality and a more generous fruitiness, along with a tangerine scent absent in the more austere Clos Ste. Hune. It also matures a bit earlier: The 1990 Cuvée Frédéric Émile was rounding the curve into full maturity while, side by side, the 1990 Clos Ste. Hune was nowhere near as ready. The difference between these two Rieslings is like that between the most refined Swiss cotton and silk.

This is reflected in price as well. Where you can buy the 2000 Cuvée Frédéric Émile for $35 (recently recommended in this column, it showed brilliantly at the tasting as well, confirming my belief that 2000 is one of Trimbach's greatest vintages for this wine), the 2000 Clos Ste. Hune will set you back $160. You get what you pay for in each instance, but there's no doubting that Cuvée Frédéric Émile is the steal. *(2006)*

I've attended several of Bipin Desai's lavish tastings. He is always very cordial to me, even though he surely knows that I do not share his sincere enthusiasm for the worth-whileness of these events. I get invited because the featured wine producer usually has the perquisite of asking a few guests of his or her own choosing. This was the case, I'm sure, with Trimbach. The co-owner of the Trimbach winery, Hubert Trimbach, was the best man at my wedding, which took place in the tiny, ancient church featured on the label of Trimbach's Clos Ste. Hune Riesling.

THE GENIUS OF GREAT WINE

IT WAS A STRAIGHTFORWARD AND not at all naive question: "How do I know when I'm drinking a great wine?" a friend recently asked. I started to reply with the usual blather about layers of flavor, originality of taste, dimensionality, and so forth. Then I stopped myself.

"It's really very easy," I replied. "Great wine makes you feel like a genius."

In all these years of thinking about wine, tasting my unfair share of great wines as well as an equally unfair share of junk, I had never realized just how little work a great wine requires of us. Usually, we're told it's the opposite. That understanding a great wine requires a sense of context; how you really have to know something about wine, etc.

But when you think about your "virginal epiphany," the first time the scales fell away from your palate and you saw the wine light, I'll bet you anything that you barely knew which end of the bottle had the cork.

Far from great wine requiring a reservoir of knowledge, it instead reaches out from the glass, grabs you by both nostrils, and, like some fantastic monster from the deep, pulls you down into its existence and holds you there. Far from suffocating, you're exhilarated. Your senses open; your mind swells. Life seems richer, finer, fuller. You feel like you're in on a great secret. Above all, you feel like you did it.

This is the giveaway to great wine: It does all the work, yet you feel like you're the genius. Everything is laid out so clearly, so comprehendably, it's so unmistakably obvious that you grin shamelessly. "But of course," you say, without a shred of modesty.

This is how I felt when, for example, I first tasted La Tâche, one of Burgundy's ineffably great red wines. I was a wine pup at the time. I was drinking—I swear this is true—Asti Spumante with pepperoni pizza. I thought it was a swell combination. Somehow, I found myself in front of a glass of La Tâche. The rest you know. Every wine lover has such a story.

From there I, like you, tried to explore every wine highway and byway: German Rieslings, red Bordeaux, white Burgundy, Barolo, California Cabernets, and so forth. As I acquired a buildup of vintages, a kind of coral reef of wine experience, I could mentally compare the latest wine in hand with its predecessors. I felt smart. I felt experienced.

Every time I tasted a truly great wine, I thought it was me, that I was the smart one. I was a fool. Great wine has what the Chinese philosopher Lao-Tzu, the founder of Taoism, observed more than twenty-five hundred years ago in the *Tao Te Ching*: "When the best leader is gone, his people will say, 'Amazing, we did it all by ourselves!'"

So why don't we drink great wines all the time? We can't. It's not just the money. Or the rarity. I actually know people who do drink great wines almost exclusively. They're bored and jaded. They're barely aware of what they're experiencing.

The first time I saw this I was shocked. Great wine, by definition, should be a rare experience. Ironically, it's rarer today than ever before. How can this be? It's simple: the quality gap is closing. It wasn't so long ago that your average wine was just that. Great wines stood out like beacons. Think of the huge gap in manners, speech, clothing, and education between peasants and gentlemen. Wine once had the same enormous, obvious distinctions.

When you read the works of once-famous early-twentieth-century British writers such as P. Morton Shand, Maurice Healy, André Simon, or H. Warner Allen, all they ever seemed to taste and talk about was Château Lafite Rothschild, Montrachet, various Champagnes, a few "hocks" (German Rieslings), Port, and the like. Their universe was populated by maybe five dozen wines.

The gap between their habitual great wines and the next level was such that they probably saw it as slumming, like having lunch with the fishmonger. As a character in Disraeli's *Sybil* nicely put it, "I rather like bad wine. One gets so bored with good wine." *(2004)*

— ~ —

How to Be a Wine Guy

MAYBE YOU'VE WONDERED HOW I'VE acquired such vast wine knowledge? Such expertise? Such opportunities to sample old vintages? I'll tell you in one word: *bamboozle.*

It's as simple as that. For example, how is anybody supposed to really know Burgundy? You can taste until your tongue rolls up like a broken window shade and it won't help.

Do you want to know how to differentiate between, say, Savigny-lès-Beaune "Serpentières" and "Narbantons"? Do you want to taste perfectly mature, pristine examples from the grower's cellar at no cost to you? Of course you do.

To acquire true wine expertise, you can taste numerous examples at vast expense over a period of decades. Then maybe, just maybe, you'll get a grip on it. (Actually, you won't. My experience confirms the old saw, "The more you taste, the less you know.")

So here's what you do. You're in some dank cellar somewhere. You're struggling with French or Italian or the jargon of California wine speak ("We sourced this wine from the lower part of the upper bench at just the right pH").

When the time comes for "The Tasting," you project floods of modesty and self-effacement (this is the hardest part for me). You say that, really, if the grower would be so kind, if he wouldn't mind, you would like to taste the wines blind and say where they came from.

Upon hearing that, it's all the grower can do to keep from grabbing his cell phone and calling his neighbors in from the fields to watch you make a fool of yourself—which you surely will.

It helps to understand that most of the world's best winegrowers are farmers. They're close to the land. Theirs is an earthy sense of humor. They like old-time carnival shows where, for a quarter, you can throw a ball at a target and, if you hit it, some hapless victim is plopped into a vat of water.

The idea here is to make yourself that hapless victim. If you're in France, Italy, Spain, or Germany, the winegrower is elaborately courteous, replying with something like, "But of course, monsieur." (Americans are more blunt: "You gotta be kidding," is the usual response.)

Now the fun starts. Six glasses are put in front of you on an upended barrel. The light is dim. The wines are barrel samples with about as much apparent difference between them as yesterday's bank balance from today's.

You swirl. You sniff. And you spit with a certain definitiveness. (Really good spitting is something I've never mastered. This is a pity, because people always credit a good spitter with having a great palate.)

Eventually you hold forth. Here, you let slip your veil of modesty. You verbally stride forth, saying, "I think this first wine is the Serpentières because it has that ethereal delicacy I always associate with this vineyard." This, of course, is nonsense. You haven't a clue. But you persist, going down the line, declaring with professional certitude the distinctions of each wine that unmistakably make it such-and-such vineyard. By now, the winegrower can barely contain himself. He's practically hopping from one foot to the other like a schoolboy with an overfull bladder. He can't wait to gleefully tell you how wrong you are.

And, boy, are you ever wrong. In all the years I've been pulling this stunt, not once have I ever been right.

Finally, the moment arrives. The winegrower, with the sort of false dejection seen at the best funerals, declares that he's so sorry, monsieur, but the first wine is not Serpentières. "No, monsieur, it is the Jarrons vineyard. You see, Jarrons has a rich, meaty quality due to the high clay content, etc."

While the grower is expansive with an eloquence and articulateness you couldn't get from him if you asked a direct question, you are scribbling like mad. Word for word, you download this distilled wisdom of generations of winegrowers.

Then comes the best part. After explaining how you missed all the wines, the grower will then take pity on you. "You know," he says, "it's very hard to see these differences with young wines. Let me show you some mature examples."

With that he goes off to the dark recesses of his cellar, bringing back an armful of filthily lovely old bottles just so you can, someday, get it right.

Can you really ever get it right? Not likely. But you'll get to taste a lot of swell wines—as long as you don't tell 'em Matt sent you. *(2005)*

THE 25-WATT WINE

I'VE ALWAYS TRIED TO PUT whomever I meet—and whatever I drink—in a historical context. (It's the history major in me.) For example, when I visit farmers, I always ask them when their farms first got hooked up to the grid. You'd be amazed at how recent rural electrification was in many areas of the United States. It tells us volumes about how peoples' lives once were lived and how they've changed.

Years ago when I was still a food writer, I visited an onion grower in Vidalia, Georgia. My onion grower was in his early forties at the time. I asked him if he remembered when his farm first got electricity.

"I remember it well," he replied. "I was a boy at the time. This would have been in the 1950s. I remember we had a wire coming down from the ceiling over our kitchen table. At the end of it was a bare light bulb. I tell you, when we flipped that switch for the first time, it was, to this day, the brightest light I've ever seen. It was a 25-watt bulb."

I think of this story whenever I drink a rosé. Because a great rosé—yes, such a thing exists—is not merely pleasant. Instead, a great rosé reminds us that wine wattage isn't everything. A rosé made not as an afterthought, but as what might be called an "intentional wine," proves that even pink can make you think.

Sure, rosés are pleasant. And, granted, no rosé is as symphonic as a full-fledged red wine. But they can be compelling, even original—especially once we get past a color prejudice that dismisses a pale pink wine as inherently insubstantial.

Want proof? Try the Cerasuolo wine from Torre dei Beati, the word *cerasuolo*, or "cherry red," being synonymous with *rosé* in Italy's Montepulciano d'Abruzzo zone. Or the Chiaretto from Provenza in northern Italy's Lake Garda area, *chiaretto* being that zone's local name for *rosé*.

France, of course, is famous for Tavel and nearby Lirac in the southern Rhône Valley, both of which make rosés mostly from Grenache. Tavel has the distinction of being the only appellation in France—the world, most likely—dedicated exclusively to the production of rosé.

These and many other rosés—such as rosados from Spain, most of which are made from Grenache, which is arguably the single best grape for rosé wines—are seductive. And refreshing. And easy to love.

What's more, wine history further proves that rosé is more than a mere slurp. It's worth recalling that in Burgundy the very wines that allowed Burgundians to draw their great vineyard distinctions were, in fact, what we would today unhesitatingly call a rosé.

Red wines as we know them require a prolonged mingling of pigment-rich skins with the juice. (Nearly all grapes have colorless juice.) To do this requires large vats or casks, as the skins are bulky.

When you look at wine harvest scenes in French tapestries from the 1400s, however, you don't see any large fermenting vats. That's because they didn't appear until the 1600s. And even then, the vats were not often used for what the French call *cuvaison*, which is the process of allowing the juice of red grapes to ferment with the skins.

Even as late as 1807, when truly red Burgundies appeared, the French minister of agriculture, Jean-Antoine Chaptal, described Burgundy's still-traditional method of fermentation: "Lighter wines of Burgundy can't take more than six to twelve hours of *cuvaison*. The most famous of these is Volnay. This wine, so fine, so delicate, so agreeable, can't stand a *cuvaison* of more than eighteen hours and doesn't last from one harvest to the next."

Yet by that time, virtually every *premier cru* of Volnay that we revere today—indeed nearly every significant *premier* and *grand cru* vineyard in Burgundy—had already been identified and qualitatively judged.

This tells us that amplification is not substance. Our wine-loving forebears could hear volumes in a mere whisper. They and their sensory world were calibrated differently. As with my onion grower, light was not slight to them.

Our time is different. We need stronger wine statements. But rosés not only still exist, but also the best ones are better than ever, even if we'll never experience the antique insight of, say, a Richebourg rosé.

Rosés at their resonant best are a modern wake-up call, reminding us not merely to kick back, but to throttle back as well. *(2006)*

TASTING AND TALKING

ONE OF THE PHENOMENA OF our time is the wine conference. Now, for those who don't hang on every drip from the bottle, the idea of a wine conference seems, well, a bit silly. After all, what more can you say after "a loaf of bread, a jug of wine, and thou"? The answer is: a lot. Edward Fitzgerald's admirable concision is absent, however. Wine conferences inspire a wealth of wine jabber.

The past two weeks saw me in back-to-back wine conferences, one in the Central Otago area of New Zealand and most recently in the cool-climate Mornington Peninsula of Australia, about an hour's drive south of Melbourne. Both conferences were consecrated—that's the only word for it—to Pinot Noir.

Wine conferences attract particular sorts: winemakers, of course; retailers, wholesalers, and importers; and not least, impassioned consumers. What attracts these die-hard wine drinkers? In a word, passion. And no wine inspires this more than Pinot Noir.

Sure, there are other occasional wine conferences centered on other grape varieties. Chardonnay, Syrah, Cabernet Sauvignon, and even Viognier have had their moment in the spotlight. But no other wine sees such relentless attention, such scrutiny, as Pinot Noir. Oregon has its International Pinot Noir Celebration every year in late July. It's the granddaddy of these Pinot fests, with nearly two decade's worth of annual events to its credit. Inspired by Oregon's example, now New Zealand has its own Pinot Noir Celebration; California has its World of Pinot Noir; and Australia—which is not known for Pinot Noir greatness—has its Mornington Peninsula Pinot Noir Celebration.

Just what goes on in these high-ticket (anywhere from $600 to $1,200 a person depending on the venue) wine romps? Tasting and talking. And then yet more tasting and talking.

Invariably, they are come-ons for the wine region hosting the event. Here in Mornington Peninsula an entire morning was spent tasting the local Pinot Noirs, followed by participants being bussed off to various local wineries that hosted lunch. Every such event I've attended follows this same promotional formula.

But the real attraction is what can only be called geek-speak. You've seen the movie *Sideways*, where the repellent wine geek Miles holds forth on the minutiae of Pinot Noir? That's nothing compared to the pathology of real Pinotphiliacs.

For example, in an afternoon session at the Mornington Peninsula Pinot Noir Celebration, 150 attendees were rapt—*rapt*, I tell you—by a nearly forensic investigation called the "Influence of Clones and Terroir."

One local winery (Stonier Wines) offered a side-by-side comparison of two Pinot Noirs where the winemaker and the clone or strain are the same, but the *terroirs* (vineyard plots) are different, based on soils and exposures. Heavier soils such as clay can create darker, fruitier Pinot Noir than, say, gravel or sandy soil. Exposure—how much sunlight the vines receive based on how early or late they capture the morning sun—can significantly affect ripeness. (One wine was lighter and more floral, while the other was denser and richer, as well as darker.)

Another local winery (Willow Creek) offered a different twist: the same winemaking and *terroir*, but a different clone. This business of clones is always much discussed whenever Pinot Noir is the topic.

Every grape variety has different strains, each creating wines of greater or lesser fruitiness, degrees of color, and, above all, particular taste characteristics. Because

Pinot Noir is more genetically unstable than many other grapes, it creates more mutations. When these mutations are identified, isolated, and asexually reproduced (my grandmother did the same by stealing a leaf stem from a friend's African violet and rooting it in a glass of water), it's called a clone.

Starting in the 1970s, France has methodically cataloged its vast heritage of grape varieties, patiently identifying distinct strains, looking for the grape version of a few good men.

Nowhere was this effort more extensive than with Pinot Noir in Burgundy. Starting in the late 1980s, the French government then commercialized these Pinot Noir clones, offering them to the world's grape growers under the unromantic designations of clone 113, 114, 115, 667, and 777, among others. They became known collectively as the Dijon clones, after the Burgundian town where the research team was based. Today, everybody's got the Dijon clones, in addition to whatever existing clones were already present in their respective nations.

Do these clones make a difference? Boy, do they ever. Even a novice, after just fifteen minutes of training, can tell the difference between, say, Dijon clone 115 (intense red and black raspberry in scent and taste, as well as deep, blackish color) and clone 5, which is more commonly called the Pommard clone (scents of cherry, leather, and gaminess, along with dark color).

Willow Creek winery offered a comparison of clone 115 with a local Australian clone called MV6 (which stands for Mother Vine), a strain that has no American equivalent. The difference was dramatic, with 115 offering strikingly dark color and rich, intense, pure berry flavors while MV6 was lighter in every sense, but with lovely floral notes. The winemaker said he would blend the two for the finished wine.

California winemaker Merry Edwards of Merry Edwards Wines (she was recently named winemaker of the year by the *San Francisco Chronicle*) schlepped two samples offering different *terroir* and winemaking, but using the same clone (115).

As if this wasn't headache-making enough, winemaker Tony Rynders of Oregon's Domaine Serene proffered clone 777 made identically, but on two distinct soil types. And, yes, they were discernibly different.

Not satiated yet? You could attend tastings comparing Pinot Noirs from different countries or Pinot Noirs made in different fashions, e.g., short macerations, higher or lower fermentation temperatures, filtered vs. unfiltered and so forth. And did I mention oak barrels? Never mind. That's serious geek-speak indeed.

Why pay all this money and lavish all this attention on what is, after all, just a pleasing drink? Fair question. The answer is surprisingly simple: Fine wine is a compelling beauty. As with paintings, you can move along, gazing briefly and enjoying its effect without probing further. Or you can delve deeper, losing yourself in brush-strokes and scholarship. Fine wine admits just such investigation, no wine more so than Pinot Noir.

Don't laugh. Someday you may find yourself at one of these convocations of the impassioned. And you may find yourself nodding in agreement when someone insists that clone 115 is just too potent for real Pinot Noir subtlety. That's when you know you're far gone indeed—but oh so happily. *(2005)*

BUDDY, CAN YOU SPARE A PARADIGM?

ONE OF THE MOST INFLUENTIAL books of the last fifty years was Thomas S. Kuhn's *The Structure of Scientific Revolutions* (1962). Kuhn submitted that "progress" in science was achieved not by a step-by-step accretive process but rather by radical new ways of looking at things, what he called *paradigms*. It was Kuhn's book that popularized the terms *paradigm* and *paradigm shift*.

I thought of Kuhn, of all people, in the middle of a blind tasting when someone asked the group, "Do you think this wine is Old World or New World?" When I heard that, I couldn't help but think of how outdated this perspective has become. It's an inappropriate, even lazy, way to taste and talk about wine today.

Are you still defining wines along the Old World/New World paradigm? At one time, maybe twenty-five years ago, it was a plausible lens that offered focus or insight. But now it's more than merely a dead end. It's a fallacy.

Conventionally, Old World is thought to reflect a sensibility of delicate, refined fruit expression often reflecting a site specificity while New World is seen as driven by powerful, vibrant fruitiness and a preference for multi-site blending.

The fact is—and it *is* a fact—that it's increasingly hard to delineate wines today using the Old World/New World platform. Does the Old World paradigm really tell us anything about, say, Spanish reds? Or wines from southwest France? Or many red and white Bordeaux, for that matter? How about Syrah and Merlot from just about anywhere in Italy? Or the so-called Super Tuscans? All of these wines, and many others, cannot be identified in a tasting by thinking of Old World vs. New World.

Differentiating wines this way is also, consciously or not, political. Europeans who feel threatened by competition like to invoke the Old World designation as a protectionist means of stigmatizing anything not their own. Ironically, the very same effort is used by boosters of so-called New World wines, particularly in places like Australia and New Zealand.

I can hear you saying: "But surely there's a difference between the really great Old World wines and upstarts from the New World?" Well, actually not.

How many more blind tastings do we need before we accept that even the best, most astute, most informed tasters can no longer distinguish between, say, the best Syrahs from California and from the Rhône? How many more showdowns between Napa Valley Cabernets and red Bordeaux are required before everyone acknowledges that not only are the best wines from each place qualitatively equal but often stylistically indistinguishable?

So if Old World/New World is a dusty, dead-end paradigm, what should we use instead? One possibility is to talk of "site-deferential" wines. Call it *terroir* if you must, but it's really more than that. It's a kind of humility, a reverence for the sanctity of place over the glory of self-expression.

"Site-deference" is a mentality rather than a locality. This is the key point. We know, of course, that great vineyard sites are hardly confined only to Europe. So the informing difference today is not so much *where* they're from but rather, *how* they're from.

This is why, by the way, philosophical paradigms such as biodynamic agriculture are gaining ground. The jury is still out on whether this extreme form of organic cultivation and winemaking makes a scientifically verifiable difference. But the mentality *does* make a difference—at least to the winegrowers. It enables them to see "wine life" through a different lens. And that, in turn, affects their wines.

Recently, I tasted what struck me as one of the most site-magnified American Pinot Noirs I've yet experienced. The not-yet-released Rhys Vineyards Swan Terrace Pinot Noir 2006 is almost monastically about sanctity of place. You can barely find the winemaking in the wine. The fact that the grapes came from a high-elevation vineyard in the Santa Cruz Mountains is a mere detail. (That they're also grown along biodynamic lines is another detail.)

Had you tasted this Pinot Noir and insisted on using the Old World/New World paradigm, you would have been forced to declare it as Old World. And how wrong you would have been—about a lot more than just merely where the wine came from.

To see wine through the Old World/New World paradigm is to blind yourself to today's borderless wine reality. Thomas Kuhn put it best: "You do not perceive something until you have the right metaphor to receive it." *(2008)*

STOP ME BEFORE I JUDGE AGAIN

THERE ARE THREE WAYS YOU can approach wine: You can taste it. Or you can judge it. Or you can drink it with a meal. What you conclude about the wine will depend upon whether you are tasting, judging, or drinking. And I can guarantee that your conclusions about the wine will differ—wildly so.

Since this is the silly season of wine competitions, state fair judging, and the like, it's worth noting just what "judging" is all about. Occasionally I let myself get roped into judging, which I do only because I like the locale where it's being held. For example, I'll judge in Venice anytime, which I once had the opportunity to do. The *Dallas Morning News* holds an annual wine judging to which I go when invited because I like Texas, in general, and Dallas, in particular.

Maybe my Dallas experience has flavored my imagination, but wherever I've judged, it always reminds me of a cattle roundup. Judges are herded together, before being cut into smaller, more manageable groups. Then they are corralled into wine-tasting feed lots, where invariably there's a lot of noise about the quality of the wine "feed."

Under such circumstances, not only aren't you drinking—which would be physically impossible given the number of wines—but you really aren't even tasting. Oh, at the time, you think you are. You go through the wine-tasting version of cud chewing and ruminating. You sniff and swirl and spit. You take notes. Finally you ruminate and then hold forth, bellowing your opinion in one mighty moo.

But really, you're not tasting so much as you are judging. All wines that pass before you are in approved competition with all other wines in the category. What began as something aesthetic, like ballet, becomes competitive. We have become so used to the idea that anything can be compared and quantified—witness those Olympic figure-skating judges who adjudicate grace itself down to a tenth of a point—that doing the same thing for wine seems more than plausible.

To a degree, it *is* sensible. After all, some wines are better than others. And one way to tell is to line them up, fair and square, and see which wines emerge victorious. The problem is that, almost without exception, idiosyncratic wines lose. It is inevitable. They stand out as being somehow too extreme: too tart, too flavorful, too different.

Once, tasting through a bunch of Chardonnays, I came across one that was unusual in the extreme. Actually, it was reminiscent of an older white Burgundy, which means a Chardonnay of a very particular taste. But we all knew that such a wine couldn't possibly be in the tasting. So it got marked down into oblivion.

But what would we have thought if we believed otherwise? What if a real French Chablis—which is perhaps the most idiosyncratic Chardonnay on the planet—was inserted into a competition where everyone assumed that only American Chardonnays were entered? My guess is that such a wine, and its producer, would quickly become extinct thanks to a fatal lack of attraction.

This is not an academic issue, especially for New World winegrowers. Anyone making a wine that doesn't "judge well"—too austere, too different—dances with doom. Chablis producers, with centuries of acclaim and tradition behind them, do not face such ready oblivion. But I'll bet you anything that someone making just such a wine in California—or Australia, Chile, or New Zealand—would struggle mightily merely to survive.

How much acclaim have you heard for Renaissance Cabernet (grown on ungrafted vines in decomposed granite soil at 2,000 feet in the foothills of the Sierra Nevadas)? Or for Soda Canyon Vineyards Chardonnay and Mayacamas Vineyards Chardonnay— both in publicity-drenched Napa Valley—which never see malolactic fermentations? Or many huzzahs, either. These wines are too austere to "judge well," especially against a lineup of sluttish Chardonnays and Cabernets offering immediate gratification.

All of which is to say that judging isn't tasting, which isn't drinking. It's drinking that counts. Only then can you know how convincing—as opposed to conquering—a wine can be. This is not to say that wine competitions do not reveal some genuinely fine wines. They do. But wines, like photographs, have to be taken one at a time. *(1995)*

JUDGMENT DAY

IT'S A QUESTION THAT SEEMINGLY won't go away: How can anyone taste fifty or one hundred wines in one sitting and actually do a good job at it?

I've lost count of the number of winery owners and winemakers who have insisted that it cannot be done. (Rarely are they producers who have received high scores, however.) These critics point to the undeniable fact that palate fatigue and/or habituation sets in quite soon. The cutoff point varies with whatever study is cited (if any), but the usual number is around a dozen wines.

I am not a taster who, as part of my daily work, regularly sifts through one hundred or so wines in a single tasting. I've done it—on more than a few occasions, in fact. But it's not my beat, as it were. So I don't feel the least bit defensive in discussing the matter.

Let me be straightforward: tasting one hundred wines in a day can be done. And done well. Granted, it depends on the wine. Tasting one hundred Mosel Rieslings is tough on the gums (all that acidity), but it's actually pretty easy compared with, say, tasting one hundred Barolos. I've tasted that many Barolos in one go and I'm here to testify that it's brutal.

But what's so often missing in this sometimes volatile issue is the critical element of judgment. You see, what the naysayers forget is that such studies are designed to test the consistency of a taster's acuity, not his or her capacity for evaluation.

Palate fatigue is really a red herring. Yes, it exists. And every good taster knows it. Sometimes you step aside and refresh yourself, as you would on a long day's drive. Sometimes you power past it, attempting to compensate for your limitations.

Also, there are many ways to judge a wine. The simplest is the Coliseum approach—thumbs up or thumbs down. Believe me, you can rip through fifty or one hundred wines that way in short order.

But if your professional requirement is jotting down detailed tasting notes on each wine, no matter how banal, things slow considerably. Ironically, it's these very tasting notes that give a misleading impression about the essentialness of palate acuity.

Today's tasting notes emphasize an "I Spy" approach: I spy apples, I spy toasted oak, I spy coconut, and so on. So a reader can be forgiven for thinking that the ability to nail these elements is the most important aspect of wine tasting. It's not.

Journalists write tasting notes plumped with flavor descriptors because they need to convey to readers what the wines taste like. But it's the taster's *conclusions* that matter. (This is why scores are so powerful, by the way. Scores are an instantly and intuitively grasped summation of a taster's conclusions.)

Consistency in tasting is not about an unerring ability to identify flavors, like a retriever fetching a stick, producing the exact same results every time. Real consistency is about the values you bring to the wine. It's not the answers you get from the wine, courtesy of your acuity, but rather, the questions you ask of it.

Good tasters know what to ask, and they're not easily diverted. This is the difference between mere competence and insight. A competent taster knows the basics, e.g., that this wine is a good Cabernet or Chardonnay.

Insightful tasting occurs when you know enough to ask different, more demanding questions. An insightful taster asks a Stags Leap District Cabernet to be dense, rich, and velvety and offer whiffs of dark chocolate and black currant. A different question would be asked of a Howell Mountain Cabernet. It should have harder tannins, a dusty note, and a texture that allows the wine to go down almost like water.

Insightful tasting takes a lot of study. Lazy tasters ask the same questions of all wines, expecting, say, a Barolo to somehow comply with the same inquiry appropriate to a Bordeaux.

Also, there's an element of emotional affinity. Insightful tasting is more than technical ability. It requires an identification with the grape or region under investigation. An expert on Renaissance art only rarely teases out insights from a work of, say, abstract expressionism. This is why someone may be a great Cabernet taster but a lousy judge of Pinot Noir. So whenever you read someone's wine notes, set aside whether he or she tasted one wine or a hundred. The real issue is whether we think they're asking the right questions. And whether they ask those questions consistently.

It's a matter of a sustained sensibility. Because what matters is the final dish you get, not the sharpness of the chef's knife. *(2005)*

TREE HUGGING

IT ALL BEGAN WHEN I went down to the cellar and hauled up a bottle of Chablis Fourchaume Premier Cru 1995 from the *négociant* Verget. I own a case of this wine, which I bought fairly cheaply on futures because it received glowing reviews from several critics, both French and American.

Now, I have to say that I have never liked this wine. I didn't like it when it first arrived. But I figured, "Well, it's a Chablis. It needs more time." But I knew in my heart—and on my palate—that time wasn't the issue. Oak was the issue.

A couple of years later, I tried the wine again, this time in a blind tasting with several other Chablis from top-rank producers. There were ten of us doing the tasting. Once again, it surfaced like a bad penny. "A pleasant wine," said one taster. "But what the hell is it?"

So the other night I decided to open yet another bottle. Same story. There was more Weyerhauser in the wine than Chablis. It smelled of "toasty oak."

My reaction was visceral: I've had it with toasty oak. And I don't mind suggesting that everybody else should, too. Yes, I know that's small-minded, dictatorial, and downright non-democratic. But let me at least try to convince you that toasty oak is one of the most dangerous phrases in wine today (followed closely by "limited availability").

Time was when relatively few wines saw any oak flavor at all, let alone the pronounced, slightly charred/bread toast/caramel/vanilla whiff of toasty oak. Whole categories of wines—Barolo, Chianti, Sauvignon Blanc, even many red and white Burgundies—were devoid of any evident intrusion of wood flavors into wine purity.

Chablis, of course, is a particularly famous example. More than elsewhere in Burgundy, producers in Chablis recognized that the singularity of their particular Chardonnay—its intense stony/minerally scent and taste—required winemaking transparency. In other words, no makeup.

Then came toasty oak. This phrase isn't just about oak. It also typically involves extended lees contact and stirring while the wine is in barrel, the better to impart the flavor of the dead, autolyzing yeast cells. Above all, the aesthetic of toasty oak means intervention, a winemaking declaration that "Kilroy was here."

Far from objecting, a lot of folks thought it was swell. They *liked* seeing the hand of the winemaker. They could recognize the toasty oak signature, which was gratifying to be able to spot. After all, it's a helluva lot easier to find toasty oak than it is to understand the authentic, intrinsic taste of an unsullied Chablis.

Today, toasty oak rules. You can find it everywhere. I had a Valpolicella the other day that reeked of toasty oak. I mean, do we really need toasty oak in Valpolicella? Does it really add anything to the pleasure of that supremely fruity wine?

Toasty oak is the hidden sugar of wine processing. It provides flavor where, like canned peas, there's not much else there.

Sometimes the toasty-oak regimen is used to make an otherwise uncommercial wine palatable. Barbera is a choice example. Although Barbera producers are (understandably) loath to tell you this, the signature smell of Barbera is rubber. Now, most folks really don't like the smell of rubber in their wines. Also, Barbera is acidic and, when tasted without food, this too isn't exactly a come-hither quality.

So when Piedmontese wine producers discovered that a good dollop of toasty oak not only obscured Barbera's intrinsic rubber smell, but also sensorially softened its acidic hit, it was a no-brainer. What's more, the toasty oak made a largely unfamiliar wine taste very familiar, like Bordeaux or Burgundy.

This was brought home to me several years ago when I visited a well-known Barolo producer in the company of two very famous wine writers, one French and the other English.

Anyway, we tasted the producer's Barolos, none of which saw any new oak. And then we tasted his Barbera, as well as his Nebbiolo d'Alba, both of which spent time in new French oak. To my astonishment, my tasting companions pronounced both wines superior to any of the Barolos! They liked best what they knew best: toasty oak.

It's tempting to say, "Look, it's all just a matter of taste." True enough. But the taste of *what* exactly? The less that comes between us and the actual taste of wine, the better. Otherwise, all wines really will start to taste alike—of guess what? *(2002)*

RIGHT DOWN THE MIDDLE

NEXT TIME YOU DRIVE BY a tree that's fallen in a storm, snapped off at trunk-level, look inside. You'll find that it's hollow at the core, rotted from the inside out.

Now, look at some of your wines. You may find the same thing. Wines, like trees, die from the inside out—sometimes sooner than you might imagine.

Nothing about wine is simple. Wines, again like trees, die for all sorts of reasons. Foremost among them is temperature. If your wines are stored at a year-round temperature of much above 65 degrees Fahrenheit (18 degrees Celsius), kiss them good-bye before they kiss you off forever.

But even this varies. Pinot Noir will give you the big smooch long before Cabernet Sauvignon will. And I don't think anything, short of swinging it against the prow of a ship, can hurt a bottle of Port. As for dry white wines, they are indeed as delicate as they look. Yet well-balanced sweet white wines can be impressively tough.

But let's look past the sins of cellaring. Better to look at what's in the bottle upon arrival. How can one know that today's sapling won't turn out to be tomorrow's hollow tree? There's no certainty, but I'll tell you what I look for, anyway, when I buy the latest vintage. You can taste a few of your own wines and see if your experience confirms what I'm about to suggest.

But first, as the philosophers say, a few *a priori* premises: First, most of today's wines are technically well made. Second, many of today's most expensive wines come from grapevines with excessive yields. Third (and most important), there are no shortcuts. Flashy intellectualisms such as "extended cold maceration," "differential extraction," or "200 percent new oak" can never substitute for the gritty integrity of low yields and honest, discreet winemaking.

So what does one look for? With just-released wines, the first place my palate proceeds is to the "middle taste." Actually, it's not so much to the middle taste as the middle *texture*. This is where the wine will hollow-out first. And it's where, almost invariably, you can separate the hucksters from the honorable.

These days, it's pretty easy to create a wine that, on first sip, seems promising. The color is deep, bright, and fresh—as it should be. The scent is (too often) redolent of oak, with its wafting, come-hither scent of vanilla. And make no mistake: vanilla is catnip for humans. So we are seduced. Upon tasting the wine, there's usually a good immediate impact. The tannins don't grab; there's a sense of roundness and suppleness, like stroking a freshly shaved face.

So far, so good—so predictable, even. It's astonishing how many wines today, both red and white, fit the preceding description: Barolo, Barbaresco, Bordeaux, Cabernets from everywhere, Chianti, and red and white Burgundies, among many others.

But when you get to the middle taste and, above all, texture, the truth telling begins. You see, no amount of extended cold maceration (for Pinot Noir) or differential extraction (for Cabernet) or new oak barrels can put the stuffing into the sofa. Oh, these devices can make a wine *seem* well upholstered.

But when you concentrate on the core of the wine—its middle taste and texture—there's no concealing a wine's essential shallowness. What one wants is density. You can feel it; it's practically a whole-body experience. And that comes, above all, from low yields.

When you taste some of the world's greatest red wines—the ones with real density and honest, unmanipulated texture—and you ask the winemaker how he or she achieved it, the answer is always breathtaking in its simplicity. They really don't do much—except labor in their vineyards nursing old, low-yielding vines and praying for fine weather. In the winery, the winemaking is surprisingly straightforward.

Ask Aldo Conterno how he makes his Barolo, Dominique Lafon about his Volnay Santenots-du-Milieu, or Randy Dunn about almost any of his Howell Mountain Cabernets.

Even for white wines—which lend themselves to cosmetic treatments—ask Jeffrey Patterson how he makes his Mount Eden Estate Chardonnay, or Bernard Trimbach about his Clos Ste. Hune Riesling, or Francois Jobard about his magnificent Meursaults.

All of these producers, and many others, will tell you the same thing: "Old vines. Low yields. Careful, clean, deferential winemaking." They have no tricks, they take no shortcuts. They—and their wines—go right down the middle. *(1996)*

WINE VIAGRA

"SO YOU SEE, DOC, I'VE got this problem," I confessed. "I'm a wine writer. A pro, you understand. I'm supposed to be able to get, er, excited, every time I meet a nice wine. But lately I just don't seem to respond. I can't be the only one who's had this problem. Surely there are others, right?"

"Of course there are," he said soothingly. "Why, I myself have had the same problem from time to time. It happens to everybody."

"Yeah, that's what my wife says," I said bitterly. "She suggested that I buy some new Riedel glasses. 'That always gets you going,' she said. But it didn't work. And I bought those big ones, too. I'm really running out of options here, Doc."

"Well," he said brightly, "what you need is wine Viagra."

This was news to me. "Does such a thing exist?" I asked, excited (at last!) at the prospect.

"Not in the way you think. Don't look so downcast," he added. "A pill is just a pill, after all. Wine is what pills would like to be. What was it that Brillat-Savarin said when somebody offered him grapes for dessert? 'I am not in the habit of taking my wine in pills.'"

Great, I thought to myself, of all the doctors in the world, I get one who was a French major.

"Really, what you need is a change of wine scenery," he continued. "In my experience this is usually the cause of the—what shall we call it?—ennui. You're a Burgundy sort, if I remember correctly."

I told him that was so. Burgundy always worked for me. *Grands crus*, *premiers crus*, even shy little *village* wines would always do the trick. But not anymore.

"I dunno, Doc. I tried with Burgundy, believe me. Why, just the other night I opened a Chambolle-Musigny that used to make me weak in the knees. Now, nothing."

"Yes, yes, *terroir* and all that," he sighed. "But this *terroir* obsession can get a little hothouse, you know. What was it that Proust said? 'The real voyage of discovery consists not in seeking new landscapes, but in having new eyes.'"

"Enough with French literature," I cried. "What about my problem? Believe me, Proust ain't gonna help."

"Quite so," he said contritely. "All right, first, you start with white wines. But no white Burgundies," he said sternly. "Didn't you once say that you loved Muscadet? Start there. The 2003s are now available. It was an exceptional vintage: very warm, creating unusually rich, full, intense Muscadets. Granted, Muscadet may not be the wine Viagra you're imagining, but as my Chinese acupuncturist colleagues like to say, one must first cool the hot wind.

"Then after you've had a few 2003 Muscadets—try Domaine de la Pépière, Domaine de l'Ecu, Château de Chasseloir, Domaine les Hautes Noëlles—you should move on to a slightly more substantial white wine, say, Sauvignon Blanc. Really, it will be good for you to savor all those lovely Sauvignon Blancs the world has to offer today: Loire, Bordeaux, South Africa, California, northern Italy, Washington, New Zealand. That's the kind of stimulation you need."

"But when do I return to red wines?" I pleaded. "Real men drink red wine."

"Pish," he said dismissively. "It was red wine that got you into this problem. Get some flexibility. Tune yourself. Too many men think red wine is the answer. Women know better. Ask your wife, she'll tell you."

"Yeah, well, my wife likes rosés."

"Excellent!" he exclaimed. "I should have thought of that myself. Anything made with Grenache is always a good choice. It's really the best grape for *rosé* because it's so fruity. I had a wonderful rosé just the other night from the Lake Garda area in northern Italy called Chiaretto from a producer called Provenza. Oh, it was lovely, with a whiff of strawberries. And the grapes are Groppello, Marzemino, Sangiovese, and Barbera. How's that for distinction, eh?"

"Sounds wonderful, Doc. But will this get me excited about wine again?"

"Guaranteed," he replied confidently. "You see, the problem is all mental. Put out of your mind those big buck, I'm-saving-this-for-a-special-occasion wines—for a while, anyway. They're not the real wine Viagra. Rather, it's the small beauties, the daily delights.

"Iris Murdoch put it best: 'One of the secrets of a happy life is continuous small treats.' And she wasn't even French, you know." *(2004)*

THE CRITICAL HALF-INCH

"WELL, DOC, I'M BACK AGAIN," I said forlornly.

"It's been awhile," he said rather tersely. "Let's see, according to my notes you were here about four years ago. You were having a problem about getting, um, excited again. By the way, how's that going?"

"Oh, fine, just fine," I replied. "Your prescription of—what did you call it?—a 'change of wine scenery' did the trick. I followed your advice and chased after Muscadets and Sauvignon Blancs. And you were right about smelling the *rosés*, too. Very invigorating."

"Excellent, excellent," he said, practically rubbing his hands together. "So what seems to be the problem?"

"This is gonna be a little difficult to explain," I said. "I'm afraid that I'm becoming a geek."

"You're joking," he said. "Why, you've been a geek—or something very near like one—ever since you started coming here. You had tendencies even when you had hair. And you know how long ago that was."

"Well, I never thought so," I said defensively. "Sure, I knew how it looked to outsiders. Although I have to say that you weren't so quick to diagnose geekiness when I tipped you off about that incredible Spanish white from the Basque country, a Txakolina if I recall correctly."

"Quite so, quite so," he said contritely. "So why now, all of a sudden, do you yourself think you might be afflicted with geekiness?"

"Actually, it didn't begin with wine at all," I explained. "I was reading *Stereophile* magazine."

"Stop right there," said the doc. "If you hang around with audiophiles, you know what you're likely to pick up—and I'm not talking about dust on the record needle."

"They're not so bad," I said weakly. "Anyway, I was reading some guy's column and he wrote . . . wait, I tore it out. Let me get it for you. He said, 'I don't have enough fingers on my two hands to count the number of times I've read about the importance of proper speaker placement, and the difference a half-inch can make.' And I found myself nodding in agreement!"

"Not good," grumbled the doc. "Not good at all."

"Wait, there's more," I said hurriedly. "Then I picked up the latest issue of a food magazine I rather like. Let me show you," I said, pulling a tightly folded piece of paper out of my wallet. "Take a look at this," I offered, handing him the page about making an acceptable cup of coffee.

"Coffee? What's the big deal about coffee?" asked the doc. "You get some good beans, maybe a nice little espresso maker, and you're good to go."

Then he began to read. "I don't believe this," he exclaimed. "According to this guy, the water must be between 200 to 202 degrees Fahrenheit. That doesn't leave a lot of margin. What does he think he's doing, building a stealth bomber? He's kidding, right?"

"No he's not," I said. "I myself have been thinking a lot about just the right wine temperature.

"And lately I've been wondering about the right glasses for various *cru* Beaujolais. You know, Morgon *is* different from Fleurie. Also, have you ever thought about the best wine to serve with *vitello tonnato*? Veal with a tuna sauce is an odd combination. Maybe an Arneis. What do you think?"

"I think it's a good thing you came in when you did," said the doc sternly. "This has got to stop. Now. Are you listening to me? Let me give you a little professional advice. This isn't connoisseurship. Or appreciation. This is nuttiness.

"Here's my prescription: Enjoy life. Enjoy your wine and your coffee and your stereo stuff. Buy more and better, if that's what turns you on. But *enjoy* the stuff. A half-inch here or one degree Fahrenheit there isn't going to make your music or your coffee one bit better. All it's going to do is make you . . . well, you know what it'll make you.

"So go home. Open up a nice bottle. Pour it into whatever glass you like—you hear me?—slice up some salami, put some music on the system, maybe a little Bill Evans, kick off your shoes and enjoy the world as it comes to you.

"Because you know," he said, looking me straight in the eye, "losing your hair was one thing. But someday, you're going to lose something a helluva lot more important. And at that moment you're not likely to say, 'If only I moved the speaker a half-inch to the left.'" *(2008)*

❧

WHAT MAKES A WINE A LANDMARK

> "We've got to struggle to get above taste . . . Landmarking is not to
> select what's pretty, it's to select what's significant."
> —Robert A. M. Stern (architect), *New York Times*, April 7, 1996

WHEN I READ ROBERT A. M. STERN'S forthright declaration, I sat bolt upright. Stern was talking about the challenge of giving valuable landmark designation to certain modernist buildings in midtown Manhattan that—brace yourself—some people don't like.

For wine drinkers, the idea of "getting above taste" seems absurd. Isn't taste what fine wine is all about? Nope. You'd think it would be, but it's not so. Let me push this further: the purpose of fine wine is not to give pleasure, but to give insight.

When I said this in a wine-tasting class not long ago, I was very nearly lynched. "What do you mean the purpose of wine isn't to give pleasure?" demanded one participant. "Isn't pleasure the idea here?" It's a fair question. And the fair answer is: Pleasure is a measure only for ordinary wines. Once you reach the realm of really fine wines, we must ask more.

That's what struck me about Robert A. M. Stern's insight. He's right. For "landmark wines," we've all got to struggle to get above taste—whether we like it or not. For wines that are put forward as great (by price or the producer's declared intent), what matters is how much insight it offers us.

Enough abstraction. Let's talk specifics. Collectively, the extended cold maceration red Burgundies championed by the consulting enologist Guy Accad (who has since left Burgundy) have proved to be failures. None of Accad's former clients—such domaines as Grivot, Chicotot, Confuron-Cotétidot, Pernin-Rossin, Senard, Château de la Tour—is in Burgundy's top rank. This, despite their owning choice *grands* and *premiers crus* vineyards.

Once everyone got above "taste" and demanded insight from these wines, disaffection set in. The wines simply have little to say. They could come from many possible places, which of course is not what great Burgundy is all about.

More specifics: Eventually tasters will tire of the repetitious taste of the extended "lees contact" used by many Chardonnay producers around the world. This will take longer to "get above," if only because the practice does make for white wines that are tasty and texturally rich when young.

Nevertheless, time will show that many—although by no means all—of these Chardonnays will wind up tasting more alike than not. Granted, at first taste, they are impressive, which is the idea. It's not a coincidence that many of the most prominent practitioners of extensive lees contact and stirring are either consulting enologists or *négociants* who must purchase grapes that might not stand on their own.

Witness the white Burgundies from the shippers Olivier Leflaive Frères and Verget, both of whose wines are lauded as rich, unctuous, and striking. Yet it's amazing how similar, in their respective lineups, one wine is to another, never mind where the grapes are grown. Indeed, Verget's owner, Jean-Marie Guffens, is known to use the lees of, say, Corton-Charlemagne, to enhance the flavor of a lesser wine such as Saint-Aubin. Does that give us insight? Hardly. It merely offers taste.

This is by no means confined to Burgundy, by the way. Numerous California wine-makers—especially those with extensive consulting practices—make similarly swoopy white wines. They taste good out of the (new) barrel. Their clients are happy, critics' attention is snared—especially in big, blind tastings—and buyers are impressed.

Nevertheless, for those on the prowl for truly great wine, the idea is "not to select what's pretty, it's to select what's significant." For fine wine, significance is site. The more we can taste that, the more significant the wine. Winemaking techniques that magnify this sense of somewhereness are welcome indeed. Those who substitute "some other overriding originality" (as the poet W. S. Merwin put it) are suspect—or should be.

The greatest wines literally mark the land for us. They tell us something about the earth that we could not otherwise know. This is their pleasure, an insight so intrinsic that it endures and repeats itself over generations. Everything else is just, well, taste. *(1996)*

SCHLEPPING OLD WINE BAGGAGE

WHAT IS IT ABOUT WINE lore that, like dust balls under the bed, all sorts of musty, outmoded notions accumulate? Take the old prescription that cheese is best with red wine. We've all heard it. And, yes, certain cheeses, such as Parmigiano-Reggiano, really do taste best with red wines.

But the old dictum about red wine with cheese was unbending. The famous Paris cheese merchant Pierre Androuët in his book *Guide du Fromage* (1973) states flatly, "Cheese is eaten with red wine, pure and simple." He was echoing generations of French gourmands.

Yet nothing could be more outdated. Experience reveals that white wines, with their flavor transparency, mineraliness, and crisp acidity, better accompany many more cheeses than do most reds.

So how did this old prescription get started? Until recently, most Europeans disdained white wine. I recall an Italian wine producer dismissing white wine as "good for nothing except getting out red wine stains." Wine was red. It was as simple as that.

Indeed, many districts now famous for white wines once grew only red grapes. Take Sancerre, for example. Prior to World War I, if you asked for Sancerre, you got a red. It was Pinot Noir. Today, of course, Sancerre means white, made from Sauvignon Blanc. A red Sancerre is now a rarity.

Also, white wines were once much less stable than reds. They lacked red wine's protective tannins and could not easily resist poor winemaking or storage. Whites oxidized quickly and didn't ship well.

Here's where we part company with the past: The red wines cheese lovers once enjoyed aren't the red wines we drink today. Not only are today's reds richer and bolder, but we drink them far younger than anything cheese fanciers would once have paired with their cheese plate.

Back when the "red wine with cheese" dictum was universally accepted, wine lovers wouldn't dream of drinking a red wine that didn't have at least twenty years of age on it. Many red Bordeaux didn't even appear on the market until a decade after the vintage. And good merchants would often cellar them for yet another ten years.

Such aged red wines are more delicately fruity and consequently more deferential to cheese. So when they said "red wine with cheese," they were really thinking of a very different red wine than we drink today.

This same divergence from past tastes can be seen with, say, the choice of wine for oysters. A century ago, in France, *the* wine for oysters was Sauternes. Today, of course, it's something light, crisp, and very dry such as Muscadet or Alsatian Riesling.

I've tried Sauternes with oysters in America, and at least to my palate, it doesn't work. Why not? Because our oysters are different. American oysters are nowhere near as metallic-tasting as France's fabled Belons. The taste set-up between oyster and wine is different.

Above all, it's a matter of the taste of your time. In the Victorian and Edwardian eras, richness of all sorts was expected. I suspect that they particularly liked the plushness of Sauternes with the famously (and to some, objectionably) pillowy texture of oysters.

In this, we've lost something—namely, a greater awareness of texture. Think of all those mainstay sauces of yesteryear's table: hollandaise, béarnaise, and that all-time winner, *sauce mousseline*, which was a hollandaise that had lightly whipped cream incorporated into it. Now, *that's* texture. Can you imagine drinking a thin-bodied wine with that?

This is why so many of the white wines (and even some reds) preferred in that era were, by today's standards, relatively sweet. Really, these wines are better described as "rich" rather than sweet. Besides, many of them were drunk after ten or twenty years of age, when their sweetness mellowed. Wines we think of today as conventionally dry—Vouvray, Savennières, Champagne, and even the odd white Burgundy or white Rhône—were a little or a lot sweet. (I recently tasted an 1889 Montrachet that was most definitely sweet, a result of a stuck fermentation, I'm sure.)

Did those old wine lovers know something we don't know today? Absolutely. But we, too, know something. We know what works best for our food in our time—just as they did for theirs. *(2002)*

THE LOW-CUT DRESS SYNDROME

ONE ELEMENT OF TODAY'S MEGA-TASTINGS cannot be seen (or even known) by the average wine buyer. It is a structural limitation inherent to large-scale tasting that has absolutely nothing to do with the abilities of the taster. Every taster, no matter how acute or self-aware, falls prey to it. I call it the "Low-Cut Dress Syndrome." Allow me to explain.

A man walks into an elegant party. The room is filled with beautiful women wearing lovely evening clothes. Now, all women know that men are hardwired for visual stimulation. It's in the species. Male arousal is strongly, irresistibly visual.

So our archetypal (heterosexual) man scans the room, looking at all the women. No matter how cultured a fellow he is, how tasteful, how refined and delicate his sensibilities, the fact remains that he will first be involuntarily drawn to the woman wearing the lowest-cut dress that's filled out the best.

Perhaps, by the end of the evening, our (male) critic will conclude that the woman wearing the finely detailed, high-neck, austere Armani is truly the most beautiful, but his eyes will not lock on to her in that initial survey of the room. For that, Versace beats Armani every time.

However frivolous (or worse) you may think this analogy, the fact remains that the

Low-Cut Dress Syndrome affects all mega-validators. You're tasting, say, two dozen or more red wines at one sitting. It really doesn't matter if the labels are unseen, what's called a blind tasting, although that does further exaggerate the Low-Cut Dress Syndrome.

No matter how conscious you are of trying to give each wine its due—no matter how aware you are of the low-cut dress syndrome—you will be drawn to the wine with the deepest color and the most open, accessible, attractive "nose" or scent. These come-hither wines invite closer investigation, which you willingly give them.

Now comes the critical juncture. The mega-validators are very good tasters. They're not going to affirm a lesser quality wine, no matter how dark the color or accessible the taste, if the wine lacks real quality. If upon further investigation the wine is found wanting, it's marked down accordingly, and you move on to other wines. However, if the wine is very good, you begin—quite unconsciously—to calibrate all the other wines in the lineup from this benchmark, a kind of tasting telemetry.

This is the Low-Cut Dress Syndrome. The darkest, biggest, richest, *good* wines with the greatest accessibility always score highest. *Always.* They are the low-cut dress wines.

I can say quite frankly that this phenomenon happens to me repeatedly when I engage in large-scale tastings. No matter how aware I am of the Low-Cut Dress Syndrome, the fact is that when faced with a large array of wines at one sitting, you cannot help but seek to impose some order, some hierarchy, upon the chaos of competing tastes.

You may not choose to accept the inevitability of the Low-Cut Dress Syndrome. You might well (and justifiably) say, "Surely there are better, more disciplined, more experienced tasters than you." Certainly there are.

But the proof is in the scores. If you have the chance, over time, to taste the wines scored most highly by the mega-validators across a wide array of grape varieties and vintages, you will discover that nearly all of the highest-scoring wines are large-scale, intense, deeply colored (if red), rich wines that almost always are noticeably oaky (which always makes a wine more accessible, as well as familiar tasting).

It's important to note that all of these high-scoring wines are almost always the finest versions within their style. Mega-validator tasters are really good at what they do. They don't land on bad wines. But their choices are *structurally* affected by the Low-Cut Dress Syndrome.

This structural problem is the most significant challenge in the modern attempt to honorably taste hundreds of wines in a relatively short time.

From Making Sense of Wine—Second Edition *(Running Press, 2004). Reprinted by permission of the publisher.*

ALL NOIR, ALL THE TIME

FOR A WHILE THERE—OH, FROM the early 1970s to the late 1980s—it looked like Cabernet Sauvignon ruled. It invaded every emerging wine nation. Every winemaker, no matter how newly minted, could handle it easily. What's more, Cabernet performs at what, for other grapes, are scandalously high yields. It always tastes good, ships without spoilage, and makes scads of money for everyone.

Yet something happened. While it decisively won commercially, it lost intellectually. No wine today wants to grow up and be Cabernet. And few winemakers hold dear the old Cabernet model in their hearts and minds. Instead everybody's making Pinot Noir, never mind whether it's from Cabernet, Syrah, Zinfandel, or Malbec.

You might call this the "Pinot Paradigm." It turns out that what we all wanted— including Cabernet lovers—was red wine with Pinot Noir's characteristics. While Cabernet won the shelves, it lost the "hearts and minds." Pinot Noir, it turns out, inspired the populace.

Winemakers—and wine drinkers—everywhere seek red wines with Pinot Noir-ish traits: suppleness, silkiness, and delicacy. Above all, there must be a fresh-tasting, berryish scent and taste. In short, Pinot Noir.

This came home to me bigtime while visiting Aldo Conterno. At sixty-eight, he is, in my opinion, Barolo's greatest winemaker. But he's no pushover. Although modern minded, Aldo is deliberate. He looks mighty hard before he takes a step, never mind leaping.

Yet when Aldo offered me his not-yet-released 1995 Barolos, one taste told a revolutionary tale. I offered the wine critic's version of "Quick, Watson! Something's afoot."

"It's those new roto-fermenters, isn't it?" I demanded. Aldo agreed.

I knew that Aldo's three sons, Franco, Stefano, and Giacomo, had been pushing Dad toward this not-so-new-fangled device. Imagine a front-loading washing machine and you've pretty much got a roto-fermenter. It looks like a conventional wine press. But where regular presses just sit around and squeeze, a roto-fermenter does the hokeypokey. It rotates, sloshing around the grape skins and juice like laundry in a front-loader.

The idea has been around for decades. Forward-thinking winemakers tried it and found it wanting. Roto-fermenters extracted deep color very quickly, but also too many harsh tannins. Wines emerged over-extracted, with no subtlety or delicacy.

Not anymore. Thanks to computerized controls, a deft winemaker can precisely control how much the laundry, er, the grape skins and juice are tossed around. You can rotate for five minutes in one direction. Then let it rest for a predetermined time and rotate in the opposite direction for two minutes more. You can do this day and night, designing as many variations as you like. The computer never sleeps. Of course, you've got to know what you're doing.

Now, you'd think that Nebbiolo, famous for its high tannin content, would be absolutely the last grape variety you'd want to subject to this device. But Aldo was convinced otherwise. He's not the first winemaker in the Langhe to use the machine. But he's the proof of the power of the Pinot Paradigm. Because what Aldo wants from Nebbiolo is what winegrowers in the Langhe have secretly suspected for generations: Inside their native Nebbiolo is a Pinot Noir screaming to get out.

"I've always known there was a connection between Nebbiolo and Pinot Noir," says Aldo. "But I've never been able to fully capture it until now. In my opinion what I'm making now is the *real* Nebbiolo, filled with perfume and berries. Not the old dried-out wines that were nothing but tar and tannins."

What's important—and what makes Aldo Conterno's 1995 Barolos so significant—is that someone at the very height of his game is changing it. Lalou Bize-Leroy did the same thing with Pinot Noir itself with her revolutionary wines from Domaine Leroy. Neither of these sixty-somethings had any reason to change. The world declared them and their wines as supreme. Yet the Pinot Paradigm pushed them on.

It's doing the same to winemakers everywhere. Look at today's best Cabernets, whether from Bordeaux, California, or Italy. Look at today's best Zinfandels. Or the best Chiantis, Australian Shiraz, Loire reds such as Chinon and Bourgueil, various Rhône reds, Barbera, and so on. They're all pursuing the Pinot Paradigm. It's turned out to be the taste of our time—never mind what's on the label. *(1999)*

THE MYTH OF THE ALL-PURPOSE PALATE

IT MAY BE WINE'S MOST universal experience: You walk into a wine shop, as I recently did, and you ask the sales person for a recommendation. "Not too much money," you say. (At least, that's what I always say.) A wine is heartily commended: "It's one of our favorites right now."

So you take it home, taste it and . . . *bleh*. You wonder how in heaven's name could anyone recommend *this*?

I'll tell you how. It's because there's no such thing as an all-purpose palate. How you live with wine can decidedly affect how you taste and what you conclude. For example:

THE RETAILER PALATE

THE GOOD: Merchants taste more wines from more places than anyone else. Wholesale distributors bring by or drop off dozens of samples every day. If you want an intensive, worldwide exposure to wine, work in a wine shop.

THE BAD: Once you start selling wine to consumers, you can't help but start thinking—quite reasonably—about what they'll buy. That, in turn, starts skewing your palate. Many wine shop sales people start as connoisseurs, but commerce starts insinuating itself.

THE UGLY: When a merchant concludes that what sells is, by definition, what's good.

THE WINE CRITIC PALATE

THE GOOD: Wine critics, at their best, are wine's version of museum curators. Wine writing really is (or should be) art for art's sake. The opportunity to engage in extensive research, thanks to access to wineries and winemakers, is unequaled. Ditto for the chance to taste massive numbers of wines.

THE BAD: Critics are susceptible to an "itch" for something different and dramatic in wine. After all, when you taste a lot of wines, it's inevitable that most of them occupy a middle ground. You begin to crave standouts. Often these standout wines are indeed better (lower yields; new vineyard areas; superior winemaking), but not always.

THE UGLY: Bigger, more dramatic wines (more oak, deeper color, higher alcohol) get the nod over more delicate wines.

THE WINEMAKER PALATE

THE GOOD: No one knows better how wines are *really* put together. No taster is better at telling you *why* a wine tastes a certain way. Winemakers look at the grain, the joints, the finish, and the craftsmanship of wine "furniture."

THE BAD: Most winemakers are not connoisseurs. They don't "pull back" from the wine and see it in a larger context. It's the difference between looking at an armoire with an experienced collector and looking at the same object with a carpenter. Also, many winemakers rarely taste regularly much beyond their own and their neighbors' wines.

THE UGLY: The temptation to see winemaking as the source of a wine's intrinsic goodness.

THE SOMMELIER PALATE

THE GOOD: Sommeliers see more wines from more places than any other category except wine merchants. Similarly, the best sommeliers are wine's best students.

THE BAD: Multiple personality syndrome. Sommeliers usually start as wine-loving consumers, evolve into wine sales on the restaurant floor, and moonlight as genuine wine critics. Like art gallery owners, sommeliers can talk like critics but their real job is to sell. Sometimes, *à la Sybil*, you never know which sommelier personality you'll meet.

THE UGLY: "Three times cost really is reasonable."

THE CONSUMER PALATE

THE GOOD: No one tastes wines with greater joy, even love, than wine consumers. The range of knowledge is vast, from beginners to genuine experts. The consumer palate is the most receptive to the pleasure of wine. And the most curiosity-driven, too. No palate enjoys wine more.

THE BAD: A certain easygoingness. Precisely because most (although far from all) consumers do not have the chance to taste competing versions of numerous wines side by side, it's hard to grasp how a wine falls short.

THE UGLY: "If I like it, it's good."

Even if all of these generalizations are true, are they also inevitable? Of course not. The best tasters can try—and often succeed in—changing roles. But it's not as easy as you might think.

The nineteenth-century French writer Brillat-Savarin famously said, "Tell me what you eat and I'll tell you who you are."

But with wine it's: "Tell me what you do and I'll tell you how you taste." *(2003)*

THE RULE OF GOOD BONES

IN NEARLY EVERY WINE TASTING class I've taught—even the so-called "advanced" ones—I always had to remind the group not to pay so much attention to the *taste*. This, on the face of it, seems absurd. I mean, it's a wine *tasting* class, right? Wrong.

What I was running—whether anyone knew it or not—was a wine *judging* class. Taste is one thing, while judgment is something else again. Let me give you an example.

We've all seen glossy home-decorating magazines that have those "before and after" photos. You know the drill. First, there's a photo of some dump of a room that looks like one of your old college dorms. Then there's the "after" photo that shows what Good Taste can do. (Money, of course, is never mentioned.)

Most folks are wowed because, well, it's an eyeful. The room is filled to the rafters with stuff; the walls are glazed with umpteen (expensive) coats of fancy paint; and there's always a just-so piece the decorator found in the Paris flea market (cost: $6,500) that the accompanying text always calls the "focal point" of the room.

The pros, however, are not fooled. You know why? Because they never really look at the decorating. They're never actually "tasting." Instead, they immediately go past the nonstop stuff and get to what's important, namely, what kind of "bones" does the room have? Does it have high ceilings? (That's good.) Big windows? (Very good). Above all, what are the proportions?

As a decorator friend once said to me, "The better the bones, the less you need to do. *Anybody* can make a room with a stunning fireplace, twelve-foot ceilings, and wonderful windows looking out onto, say, Central Park look beautiful."

It's the same with wine. *Of course* you're going to like a good vintage of La Tâche. Talk about a (wine) room with a view! The flavor just pours out of the glass. But, believe it or not, flavor is not what makes La Tâche a great red Burgundy. You know the reason: it's dem bones.

It's not taste alone that you should be judging. Instead, you've got to look past it, at least in the judging phase, to determine whether what you're getting is something really built-in or just "decoration," such as new oak.

This is not as much fun as just rolling around in the catnip, which is why so many tasters don't do it. But if you really want to understand wine, it's essential.

What's more, it's the only way to beat the system. Too many of today's priciest wines are "decorated" with lavish amounts of new oak and a glitzy fruitiness. And it works, too. Buyers are lining up for such wines, wowed by sheer lavishness. Sound familiar?

But they never think about the "bones." Does the wine have an invigorating acidity? (Usually not.) Is the fruit really distinctive, even idiosyncratic, or is it just palate-popping intense? (Guess which.) Above all, does it have the structure that allows a wine to evolve?

When you start asking these questions, you'll find yourself choosing wines that are far more magnificent than their prices or their labels. Recently, for example, I hauled out a ten-year-old Sauvignon Blanc from California's Renaissance Vineyard and Winery. It had great bones from the start, and ten years later, the wine was superb. I forget the original cost, maybe six bucks. Today the latest release is ten bucks, tops—and it's even better.

The "rule of good bones" is true for all wines everywhere. It's what separates great wines—never mind the price—from merely showy ones. It's why some wines from low yields and less celebrated vineyard sites can be superior to big-name bottles.

Wines with great bones are all around us. They're in Chianti and Sicily, Mosel-Saar-Ruwer and Languedoc. Burgundy has unheralded villages such as Auxey-Duresses and Saint-Aubin that have bones (and flesh) that a movie star would envy.

California has a long roll call, usually involving grapes grown in places more famous for "easier" wines like Chardonnay. A wine like Limerick Lane Zinfandel in Sonoma's Russian River Valley comes to mind in this category.

In short, if you really want to be a wine judge—and a deal-spotter—ignore the taste of tinsel and go bone deep. *(1999)*

FIT FOR A PRINCE

IT MAY NOT SEEM LIKE much of an accomplishment, but one of the rarest pleasures of the table is finding interesting wines through the entire course of a dinner. Too often, in their attempt to achieve this, hosts spend too much money serving blockbusters.

Now, there's nothing wrong with such wines. One feels flattered. But it's a rare blockbuster-serving host who can restrain himself (it does seem to be a guy thing) to just one solitaire jewel of a wine. Usually it's an embarrassment of riches, in every sense.

One of the great literary examples of this is found in an unjustly forgotten 1924 book called *La Vie et la Passion de Dodin-Bouffant, Gourmet*, which became *The Passionate Epicure* when it was translated into English in 1961. The author, Marcel Rouff, was the sidekick of the famous French gastronome, Curnonsky.

Its fictional hero, Dodin-Bouffant, lived for his not-inconsiderable stomach and was renowned as an epicure of true refinement. Indeed, the depiction of Dodin-Bouffant—once past the parody on the real-life Brillat-Savarin on whom he is modeled—is a portrait of thoughtful restraint.

One of the more memorable chapters has the Prince of Eurasia, who fancies himself a great connoisseur, taking the waters near Dodin-Bouffant's town in the Jura region bordering Switzerland. (Marcel Rouff was Swiss born.) Dodin-Bouffant's fame was such that the prince sought him out as a guest for a dinner in his honor.

Dodin-Bouffant assented, only to be appalled at the unthinking excess and lavishness of the prince's over-the-top banquet, which he had been told was carefully chosen by the prince himself, who fancied himself Dodin-Bouffant's equal in matters of the table.

Dodin-Bouffant subsequently invited the prince to his home for dinner and served him, as the centerpiece dish, the homely *pot-au-feu*—boiled beef! Of course, it was a *pot-au-feu* such as no one had ever eaten, accompanied by wines throughout the meal that were, as the French might say, *comme il faut*. (The *pot-au-feu* was served with a Chambolle-Musigny, a Burgundian Pinot Noir notable for its delicacy and exceptional perfume.)

The prince, shown the error of his meretricious ways, was both suitably abashed and uplifted. "Dodin, perfectly happy, gave a little smile. He triumphed. To the vain sumptuosities of the prince, he had responded with a meal that was simple, short, home-spun but done with an artistry so profound it had persuaded even the dispenser of those superfluous luxuries of his own superficiality."

An overripe depiction, to be sure. But no less true for that. For a summertime dinner, you want wines that are unimposing yet invigorating, but still replete with refinement and even intrigue. *(2006)*

BEYOND "I LIKE IT" AND "I DON'T"

WINE PROSELYTIZERS SEEM PERENNIALLY TORN about how best to evangelize the stuff. One school advocates the "you have to study it" approach. The other is more defiantly populist. Its rallying cry is "Pull the cork, pour, and glug."

The wine formalists believe the complications of wine are such that mere drinking isn't enough and that study is essential. The "pull, pour, and glug" adherents find this approach overly prescriptive and pretentious. They believe that if you leave wine drinkers to their own learning devices, they'll come to a profound appreciation in their own good fashion.

Indeed, no less a wine connoisseur than the late Alexis Lichine, a famed wine writer, once declared, "There is no substitute for pulling corks."

My experience in teaching wine classes during several decades leads me to conclude that pulling random corks, no matter how well selected, is like visiting a museum where you gaze at everything and understand nothing. What's missing is focus—and the insight that comes from it.

What I learned at school, admittedly in the teacher's seat rather than in the student's, is that when left to their own devices, most wine drinkers—including many well beyond the novice level—assess wines from an "I like it/I don't like it" platform.

Refreshing as the "pull, pour, and glug" approach is, all of us need guidance or even a gentle push along our wine way, teaching us to distinguish between the fundamentally important elements of wine and those that are insignificant or just transitory (such as tannins or the latest winemaking style).

Hard as it may be to accept, pleasure is not the measure of fine wine. Rather, the best measure judges complexity, finesse, cohesion of flavors, and an indefinable but unmistakable sense of originality.

True, these attributes usually result in pleasure. But it's a pleasure more substantive than, say, the seduction of residual sugar.

When my students would begin their discourse with, "Well, I like this wine . . . ," I had to gently remind them that I didn't care whether they liked it or not. "Tell me what you think of it," I asked the students. "What you like is, for the moment, immaterial." Tough wine love, you might say.

Obviously, there's nothing wrong with a hedonistic approach. Hedonism doesn't lead to insight, though, but only to reactive pleasure or distaste. It's awareness that enables even absolute beginners to swim from the shallows of mere preference—"I like it" or "I don't like it"—to the deeper waters of insight.

Most wine drinkers, especially beginners, are put off by tannins and, to a lesser degree, acidity. The astringency of tannin, like learning verb conjugations in a foreign language, can be formidable. There's a strong inclination to reject wines with even a smidgen of tannin or a poke of acidity as unpleasant and therefore "not good." What a mistake that is.

The most important thing I learned at school—the thing that has made teaching wine such a joy—is how quickly, even easily, interested wine lovers can learn about what's really important in wine. I'm not referring to the grammar of the label (which is why many people take a wine class), but the knowing of wine itself.

I've seen many times how, in just one evening focusing on just six (progressively more complex) wines, absolute beginners could grasp why some wines are intrinsically better than others. You can't get that from merely pulling corks. *(2007)*

TELLING THE DIFFERENCE

ONE OF THE MOST FREQUENTLY repeated refrains I've heard about wine is "Oh, I couldn't tell the difference." The assumption, of course, is that the differences that make fine wine distinct from ordinary wine is somehow beyond an "average" person's grasp.

I've never heard this about food, by the way. Everyone fancies himself or herself an expert—or at least a competent—judge when it comes to food. But something about wine loving suggests a secret knowledge, a discernment beyond that of the everyday.

Mind you, this is not confined to wine. I've come across it frequently with stereo equipment, which is yet another sphere of the seemingly occult, with a vocabulary so obscure that it borders on the shamanistic.

I've gotten the same "Oh, I couldn't hear the difference" with stereo stuff, most forcefully by friends of mine who suffer from partial hearing loss, enough so that they wear hearing aids. You can't blame them for thinking that the mysteries are unavailable to them.

Yet I was able to demonstrate, much to their astonishment, that they can hear the difference. That's the crucial phrase: the difference. Can my hearing-impaired friends hear all of the frequencies? No, they can't. But the key is that they do get *all* of what does come in, as it were.

Put another way, even if you don't fully understand the contextual greatness of, say, Mount Eden Vineyards Estate Chardonnay from the Santa Cruz Mountains, you'll still be able to say, "Wow, this isn't like any other Chardonnay I've ever had."

When we taste a wine, we're really evaluating not the wine itself but rather the difference it conveys. We automatically compare it, consciously or not, with other wines we've had. Our sense of its goodness comes from our sense of its "difference."

This is why "Oh, I couldn't tell the difference" is so mistaken. *Everyone* can tell—or at least sense—the difference. Novices usually can't find the words to describe the differences they discover, which is a frustration.

It's also why it's so instructive to taste wine with other people—and with other wines, too—and to talk about it. Invariably, someone spots something in a wine that you missed. I've seen this with the greatest, most informed palates I know, as well as with novice drinkers. Once a wine achieves a certain level of complexity, none of us can grasp it in its entirety.

What's more, in a lineup of several such finely distinguished wines tasted together, their differences soon blur. The difference between, say, a Chambolle-Musigny and a Morey-St.-Denis (both Burgundian Pinot Noirs) is a close call. The smaller and finer the differences, the less likely the general discernment of them.

This is one reason, by the way, why such differences are almost never discovered in big tastings, even by acute palates. Anybody who has watched *Law & Order* knows that one perp quickly begins to look like another in the lineup, because "telling the difference," especially at this level, requires not just examination but, interestingly, a lack of pressure to produce results.

In 1981, psychologists Roy Malpass and Patricia Devine published the results of a landmark experiment on eyewitness accuracy. In the experiment, a male "vandal" entered a lecture hall, exchanged words with the instructor, and knocked over a rack of machines. The audience was then asked to view a lineup to identify the perpetrator.

The accuracy of the witness identifications, the experiment revealed, depended on the instructions the witnesses were given. One group received instructions that implied they had to choose among the suspects in the lineup. The other group got instructions implying there was no pressure to choose.

When witnesses thought they had to choose, they more frequently chose the wrong suspect. (This happens to me in blind tastings all the time.) Yet when witnesses thought they didn't have to choose—when they were more relaxed and not in a forced-judgment mode—they rarely made false identifications.

Europe's greatest wine districts achieved such exquisite—and real—vineyard distinctions because not only did their caretakers have the generation-spanning time, which is essential, but they were free from a demand for results. Consequently, their "eyewitness" accuracy was uncanny.

Can you tell the difference? Sure you can. Just relax—and take your time. *(2007)*

10,000 HOURS

OCCASIONALLY I HAVE BEEN INTERVIEWED or asked for a quote by a magazine or newspaper. Invariably, I have been described as an "expert," a designation that makes me cringe.

Compared with the general run of the population, I suppose I am an expert. By that measure, it's a good bet you are, too. But is either of us the real thing? And, more to the point, are we always so expert about every wine we taste?

Some intriguing insights about this are found in a recent book, *This Is Your Brain on Music* (Dutton), by Daniel Levitin, who is, well, an expert on cognitive psychology. He runs the Laboratory for Musical Perception, Cognition, and Expertise at McGill University in Montreal.

Deep inside this fascinating book, Levitin declares: "Ten thousand hours of practice is required to achieve the level of mastery associated with being a world-class expert—in anything.

"In study after study of composers, basketball players, fiction writers, ice skaters, concert pianists, chess players, master criminals, and what have you, this number comes up again and again. Ten thousand hours is equivalent to roughly three hours a day, or twenty hours a week, of practice over ten years.

"No one," he says, "has yet found a case in which true world-class expertise was accomplished in less time."

There's nothing wishy-washy about it: Ten thousand hours is the great divide between wannabe and mastery. So, right there you can ask yourself the age-old question: Have I put in the time?

"The ten-thousand-hours theory is consistent with what we know about how the brain learns," says Levitin. "Learning requires the assimilation and consolidation of information in neural tissue. The more experiences we have with something, the stronger the memory/learning trace for the experience becomes."

I thought of this when reading one of Rajat Parr's blog entries on the *Wine Spectator* Web site. The sommelier of Michael Mina restaurant in San Francisco, Parr is an extremely talented taster in a city full of real tasting pros. In his blog, Parr mentions that he and several other sommeliers get together regularly to engage in cutthroat blind tastings.

"We typically get together late at night and try to stump each other with difficult wines, the one constant being that the wines are classic examples," he reports. He describes (quite concisely and well) how to be good at this game. But he adds that "there's a deeper way of tasting and feeling the wine that is impossible to put into words. That's something that you just learn by doing it over and over again."

Levitin agrees: "Increased practice leads to a greater number of neural traces which can combine to create a stronger memory representation."

Still, it's not enough to just suck down wine three hours a day over ten years. If that were true, every barfly in America would be an expert on beer or Bourbon. You've got to care about what you're doing.

"We tend to code as important things that carry with them a lot of emotion, either positive or negative," says Levitin. "Caring may, in part, account for some of the early differences we see in how quickly people acquire new skills."

He reports that we have neurochemical tags in our brains that effectively prioritize memory access based on their emotional importance to us.

Those sure-shot blind tasters care intensely about learning the taste markers within various wines. It's very likely why, apart from the essential study-for-the-test repetition, they're so good at this specialized skill.

All of this brings us to the nub of things: Have you achieved ten-thousand-hour mastery? I can say in all honesty that, when it comes to wines such as Champagne or red Bordeaux, I have not. Not only haven't I clocked in the requisite ten thousand hours of real attention and repetition, but I also don't deeply care about these wines. They don't move me.

I mention this because I'm prepared to go one step further: I've yet to meet a taster who is a universal wine expert. When you think about what Levitin describes, it's not possible. Not only is there the ten-thousand-hour hurdle, but you can't ignore the matter of emotional affinity—a passion for what you're drinking.

Really great tasters not only put in the time, they put in their hearts. Even among the most ardent of wine Casanovas, there's only so much of the real thing to go around. The rest is just . . . technique. *(2007)*

VOTING (WINE) CONSERVATIVE

IN THIS MOST POLITICAL OF moments, everything—even wine—gets politicized. Just look at the hardball politics of direct shipping to consumers still throbbing in several state legislatures. But politics plays no role in my table life. I've served equally good wines to both right-wing nut cases and Lexus liberals alike.

But lately, I've come to realize that I'm not politically wine neutral. While I may be welcoming in *who* I serve, I've found that I'm a card-carrying conservative in *what* I serve.

Oddly, I never knew until recently that I was so (wine) conservative. I knew that I had tendencies. After all, my first great—and still ardent—wine love was the late Jacques d'Angerville's various Volnays. They're a strict constructionist's red wine: no apparent oak; no overt "hand of the winemaker"; not even any vigorous pumping-over sufficient to penetrate the cap of grape skins or any punching-down to extract a deeper color from the skins during fermentation.

Compare that with, say, the once-ballyhooed practice of extended cold maceration, where Pinot Noir grape juice was dosed with abundant sulfur to prevent fermentation from wild yeasts, then refrigerated to barely above freezing and kept in contact with color-rich skins for as long as three weeks. Finally, fermentation was allowed to proceed by warming the juice and inoculating it with cultured yeasts.

Back in the late 1980s that practice was billed as Burgundy's Great Leap Forward. It proved nothing of the sort. Today, almost no one uses this extreme technique.

In California, we're now seeing yet another sort of extremism. And as before, we're told that it's a Good Thing. This time, it's a matter of leaving grapes on the vine until they are so ripe that, if fermented conventionally, the resulting wine would reach 17 percent alcohol. That's about the limit of what a yeast can ferment before it dies from alcohol toxicity.

What happens next is that the winemaker "waters back" the juice. This is jargon for taking a garden hose and pumping water into the vat. This dilutes the juice and effectively lowers the final alcohol percentage to, say, a mere 15.5 percent.

This is why you can't—and shouldn't—believe the alcohol percentage declared on the label, even when winemakers insist that they are indeed citing a wine's exact alcohol content. An equally spurious exactitude is just as easily achieved by lowering alcohol from ultra-ripe grapes by such high-tech means as spinning cones or reverse osmosis.

The issue, as always, is a matter of extremes. (Chaptalization or adding sugar to fermenting grape juice is another case in point. A little is fine, even admirable, while a lot creates a wine grotesque.) At what point does a wine, *à la* Michael Jackson, become so distorted that it no longer reflects anything except what's been done to it?

The wine conservative in me recoils. To push a grape to an extreme of dehydrated ripeness only to revive it later with a splash of water may seem harmlessly mechanistic. If that were so, then a freeze-dried dehydrated soup should taste the same as the original version, once "revived." Yet it never does.

I once was much more willing to believe what I was told by "forward-thinking" winegrowers. Over the years I've been told how better trellising systems could create high-yielding vines that would deliver the same quality as low-yielding vines.

I've been told how oak chips and sawdust are just as good as traditional barrels. I've been told that using only certain clones selected in scientific trials for better color, flavor, and disease resistance creates the best wines.

I've been told about the desirability of regularly using centrifuges, filters, enzymes, fertilizers, anti-rot sprays, mechanical harvesters, and vacuum concentrators.

So now I'm telling you: Most of what I've been told has been wrong. Not totally, utterly wrong. But most of these "advances" have been followed by retreats.

One of the great ironies of our time is that many of the "improvements" in today's best wines are achieved by returning to practices once derided as outdated: the precepts of organic or biodynamic cultivation; gravity-flow winery design; cultivation of "weeds" between rows; and employing numerous strains of a variety in one vineyard rather than a few selected clones.

If experience is anything to go by—and it's worth something, I think—wines that are revolutionary are almost never revelatory. It's as simple, and as conservative, as that. *(2008)*

My Wine, My Self

ARGUABLY, FOR THE FIRST TIME ever in its millennia-old history, wine now serves as a vehicle for what might be called the public proclamation of self.

This became apparent to me during a recent trip to South Korea where I was giving a series of talks. I had already heard about how, in Japan, a wine-loving, self-educating comic book character called Shizuku in a weekly manga series called *The Drops of the Gods* has become hugely influential.

After being translated, it became wildly popular in South Korea, too. Today, one of South Korea's most-watched television shows is a wine-drenched soap opera called *Terroir*. This, in a country where imported alcohol—which means wine—was banned until 1987. My kind of people.

Anyway, after one of my talks, a young woman came up to me and said, "I've been trying to learn about wine. A lot of what I read is complicated and seems to talk about what happened yesterday. What I'm trying to say is: What do I need to know *now*?"

I was a little taken aback by this, not because I thought she was being rude or accusatory (she wasn't). Rather, it was because she had put her finger on something that guys like me standing in the front of the room too often forget, namely, that wine today is *really* different from what it was as recently as ten years ago.

For newbies to wine, whether Asian or American or European, twenty-first-century wine life is vastly different from what it was just two decades ago. It's become a norm—and a form—of self-definition. For example:

In today's twenty-first-century wine world, you will define your "wine self," consciously or not, by identifying between what might be called a Land Mentality or a Brand Mentality.

The Land Mentality emphasizes site specificity; single-variety wines over blends; an almost obsessive celebration of differences; and so-called naturalistic winemaking and grape-growing practices. Although available to all wines, this mentality is ascendant with Cabernet Franc, cool-climate Syrah, Nebbiolo, Riesling, and, of course, Pinot Noir.

The Brand Mentality, for its part, is more open minded in its pragmatism. It sees the winemaker, rather than the vineyard, as critical. An interventionist approach in winemaking is endorsed, even celebrated. Blending is seen as an opportunity to improve a wine.

An emphasis on brand rather than land is seen as an opportunity to offer exceptional value and higher quality at lower price points, as demonstrated by wines from Australia and Chile. Although available to all wines, this mentality is ascendant with Sangiovese, many—although not all—Chardonnays, Semillon, warm-climate Syrah, Merlot, and, of course, Cabernet Sauvignon.

In today's twenty-first-century wine world, you will define your "wine self" by ignoring the world's most famous wines.

Most newcomers to wine today have almost no exposure to the old benchmarks represented by the great wines of Bordeaux or Burgundy or the most celebrated wines of Napa Valley. They're all simply too expensive. Effectively, they're not even real anymore for the vast majority of wine drinkers. One savors them as a "virtual wine experience" through tasting notes and chat boards.

Today's twenty-first-century wine drinkers increasingly define their wine selves and their idea of wine goodness by other, newer, benchmarks.

For example, many fans of California Pinot Noirs—most, I would submit— have only a glancing interest in Pinot Noirs from Burgundy. And often, when they taste many red Burgundies, they find them unrewarding. Instead, their measure of Pinot Noir goodness, which was once exclusively Burgundy's prerogative, is now the California item.

Don't be shocked. Precisely the same pattern emerged among American new-comers to wine twenty years ago between Bordeaux and California Cabernets. Today, Bordeaux is now only a distinct frequency along the spectrum of modern Cabernet appreciation rather than the entire wavelength.

In today's twenty-first-century wine world, you will define your "wine self" increasingly through "social media" such as Yelp, Twitter, Facebook, and YouTube, along with blogs and chat boards.

This is not good news for professional critics of any kind, never mind wine scribes such as myself. Am I ambivalent about this? Sure I am. Professional critics labor—or should, anyway—under standards that exceed "Do I like it?"

The mass of opinions—informed or otherwise—expressed through these social media will increasingly be how newcomers to twenty-first-century wine will amplify and fine-tune their wine selves.

One thing, however, remains constant: the pull and beauty of wine. Whatever happens will only be new wrinkles in a very old fabric. *(2009)*

BURROWING DEEP INTO
WINE LISTS AND WINE CELLARS

Dining in America has never been as sophisticated, expensive, varied, and qualitatively better as it is today. Where once fine dining was confined to a few coastal cities where untraveled or insecure Americans were cowed by French restaurants into a submissive cringe, the dining landscape has been utterly transformed.

The force came—and continues to derive—from America's exhilarating democratization of both food and wine. Not only was American food itself celebrated, starting in the 1980s, but so too was domestic wine. (So successful has American wine become that even the phrase *domestic wine*, suggesting as it does a contrast to the European item, now seems antiquated.)

Of course, Americans traveled in vast numbers, fanning out across the world and bringing home not just experiences with authentic native versions of all sorts of cuisines, but also returning with a newfound and justifiable self-confidence about their hard-earned knowledge about fine dining. Restaurateurs, for their part, recognized this—indeed, they were among the participants themselves—and all sorts of restaurants emerged.

Wine, however, became a bit of a battlefield. High restaurant wine prices have always been a flash point and still remain so. The fact is that many restaurants make the bulk of their profits from sales of alcoholic beverages (booze is far more lucrative than wine, by the way).

With the mushrooming of brand-new restaurants, few wine lists could boast older vintages. So diner and restaurateur found themselves effectively buying the same wines—with ever-savvier diners knowing full well what that bottle actually cost. The typical restaurant markup of three times cost (a bottle selling wholesale for $20 is sold for $60 in the restaurant) seemed extortionate for a wine that was probably fresher than the fish on the plate. Consequently, the relationship—if that's the word—between diners and restaurateurs has never seen so much friction.

That noted, a parallel trend has mitigated at least some of this ongoing friction: better-quality wine glasses and the emergence of a cadre of young sommeliers who take their jobs (and their customers) seriously but not snootily.

This business of wine glasses became both real and symbolic in the 1990s, fueled by the spectacular success of the Austrian glass company called Riedel. Its namesake owner, Georg Riedel, persuaded American wine lovers that the size and shape of a wine glass affected the scent, taste, and, above all, the sheer sensual pleasure of wine at the table. Georg Riedel reports that America is, by far, his largest market.

Restaurateurs, for their part, were initially reluctant to switch from their traditional thick-rimmed, too-small glasses. Not only were Riedel glasses expensive (even the "seconds" that Riedel made available to restaurants were costly), but also the breakage was even more prohibitive. Still both critics and diners clamored for better glasses. While the demand for better pricing went unheeded, the campaign for better wine glasses proved an unqualified success. Good wine glasses are today the norm rather than the exception—at least in wine-oriented restaurants, anyway.

Most good restaurants now use lovely glasses, nearly all of them made by various competitors that have knocked off Riedel's distinctive designs. (The German company Spiegelau was so successful at knocking off Riedel glasses that in 2004 Riedel simply bought Spiegelau's much-larger parent company, F. X. Nachtmann. But they've kept the Spiegelau brand. So now Riedel is, effectively, knocking off Riedel.)

The columns to follow give at least a hint of the push-pull tug that helped birth this ubiquity of good wine glasses and sophisticated wine lists. The subjects discussed were—and still are—hot-button issues with readers.

THE MENTALIST OF THE MENU

WE LIVE IN A CONFESSIONAL era. And so, in the spirit of the age, I should tell you that I once loved pepperoni pizza with Asti Spumante. Granted, this was in my formative wine years, which, like my hair, are now long gone. But I thought you should know.

The reason I mention this is because I am frequently importuned for advice—and sometimes magazine articles—about matching food and wine.

Now, you're probably thinking—quite reasonably—that a fellow who once thought that the frothy sweetness of Asti Spumante was splendid with pepperoni pizza is hardly an ideal arbiter in matters of food and wine. So you might well choose to dismiss what I'm about to say: I don't believe in spending much time or energy pondering the pairing of food and wine. I say this as a former food writer who's banged out one cookbook (about Piedmontese cuisine) and six books about wine.

As best as I know, I am alone among my wine-writing colleagues in my belief that this business about "marrying"—which is the preferred term—the just-so wine with the just-right dish is just so much eyewash.

So why do my colleagues persist in what is either an intimidating exercise in culinary pretension or a pursuit of wine geek persnicketyness—or both? For starters, there's money in it.

Just last week, I received a call from a man who took a wine-tasting class I taught more than twenty years ago. I had not heard from him since. Yet he was so stricken with wine doubt that he felt compelled to call, reintroduce himself, and ask—I swear this is true—what he should serve with the Loire Chenin Blanc called Clos de la Coulée de Serrant.

Now, I already knew the answer. But our supplicant was in distress. After a suitable pause pretending to consider the illimitable possibilities, I declared, "You should serve smoked trout with a horseradish mayonnaise." He blubbered his thanks, so gratifyingly exact was my prescription. He vowed to take more wine classes.

In the magic business, especially in the field of mentalism or mind-reading, this is known as "working strong." The air of authority is everything.

For instance, if you said to me, "I'm serving Vietnamese spring rolls tonight. What's the best wine for this dish?" you'd be disappointed—dismayed even—if I told you to serve a Chardonnay. After all, you already know about Chardonnay. Anybody could choose that.

So instead, I rummage around for something that you've probably never heard of or tasted. So I suggest—nay, insist—that Grüner Veltliner is the ideal dry white wine for Vietnamese spring rolls. Does the pairing work? Sure it does. So too does dry Riesling, Arneis, Pinot Grigio, and about two dozen other dry white wines.

But you're impressed. Who knew from Grüner Veltliner? You look at me with respect. I'm a mentalist of the menu, a priest of the palate, a shaman of the senses. You feel the need to return for my services. In short, I'm golden.

This, I submit, is the calculation behind the mysterious synergy of food and wine. It's the stock in trade of sommeliers in high-end restaurants. You're presented with some wacko dish—halibut topped with cappuccino foam on a bed of huckleberry *jus*—and you're baffled. What wine goes with this?

The sommelier-shaman is, of course, at the religious ready to confirm that, yes, this is a serious business. After a contemplative frown, as if calling upon the gods for divine inspiration, the sommelier concludes that a Hautes Côtes de Nuits Blanc would be ideal, adding, with a swirl of intellectual incense, that you want the 2003 vintage because its richness—"It was an unusually warm year"—will balance "the torrefaction of the cappuccino foam."

So what do I really believe? It's simple if unremunerative: Good wines can take care of themselves. They can work wonderfully with any food that is remotely plausible for the wine.

There are limits, of course. You don't want to serve a so-called "steakhouse red"—one of those monster California Cabs practically *mit schlag* with creamy oak—with your grilled sole. But you already knew that.

Lousy wine, however, needs all the help it can get—good food and a seductive ambience—to distract you from its inadequacy. (This is why, by the way, that charming little wine you had in that country French bistro or trattoria in the golden hills of Tuscany tastes so awful when you finally track it down here at home.)

Marrying food and wine is the mother of all misgivings. My advice? Elope with the first good wine you find. You'll live happily ever after. *(2006)*

An Open Letter to America's Restaurateurs

DEAR RESTAURATEURS,

If someone gave you $30 or $50 or as much as $100 for a single plate of food, wouldn't you pay plenty of attention to the plate that food was served on? You know you would. Yet when it comes to wine—at just those prices—this same care is nowhere to be found.

Let's look at three facts:

> Fact 1: At least 50 percent of your profits come from bar
> sales, of which wine is a major part.

> Fact 2: The typical restaurant marks up a wine three times
> its cost; e.g., a wine bought wholesale for $10 will appear
> on a list for $30. Cheaper wines see even higher margins,
> upward of four or five times cost.

> Fact 3: Facts 1 and 2 are not going to change. This is a
> critical point.

Most of you—a few saints excepted—are *never* going to price your wines modestly. So there's no sense in continuing to beat the dead horse of high restaurant wine prices.

That critter is beyond resurrection. And there's also no sense in pretending that the premium we pay is for service. Today's wine service, so-called, typically involves no more expertise than is required for pouring water. (I take that back: Pouring water is harder. Wine doesn't have ice cubes that can embarrassingly plop out of the glass.)

All of which brings me to the point of this letter: Can't we at least get a decent wine glass? The typical high-end American restaurant serves its high-priced wines in glasses no better than what we used to get free out of detergent boxes. Oh, I know, I know. We don't understand about how much breakage you have (truly, an astonishing amount). That your employees are thieves (some really are). That patrons can be inexcusable deadbeats (I recently saw a table of fifteen fail to show on a Saturday night at a packed Denver restaurant). Still, enough with the complaints.

What's a "decent glass"? Well, for starters, if your glasses come from a restaurant supply house, the odds are overwhelming that they are junk, no more suitable for enjoying that fifty-buck wine than a Fred Flintstone jam jar.

A "decent glass" is something like Riedel's Vinum series. I can hear you already: "Oh my God! Does this *yold* know what he's asking? Those glasses cost a fortune. Don't you know about our breakage? And then there's the help. Don't get me started on the busboys." Sorry, no complaining allowed. If you're willing to put us on the rack and twist the profit wheel three excruciating turns, don't blame us for screaming.

But you may be surprised to learn that I am not entirely unsympathetic. This probably is what psychologists call the "hostage syndrome," where the hostage identifies with the plight of his custodians. So I have a proposal sympathetic to your plight and yet designed to free our own captivity from junk wine glasses.

Continue to put your regular Fred Flintstone–type glasses on the table. But offer us the option of paying, say, $5 per person to have all of our wines served in appropriately shaped, high-quality wine glasses of the Riedel Vinum sort. Just note the option on the wine list. Surely a $5 per person surcharge would quickly cover the costs of your new inventory, new glass-washing racks, breakage, and thievery.

Some restaurant patrons reading this might well howl, "But we're already paying them a premium! Why should we have to pay yet again?" Good point. But let's be realistic: They are not going to invest in good glasses without an incentive, no matter how valid our claim that we've already paid for this service. If we have to pay for it—which we will—so be it.

I, for one, would like the *option* of good wine glasses without having to make an issue out of it in front of my guests. Or having to plead for what might be the restaurant's secret stash of good glasses for privileged clients.

So, America's restaurateurs, what's wrong with this idea? It seems sensible to me. You get your costs covered. We get what we should have gotten all along—wine glasses that allow us to enjoy our wines. Right now, we don't even have the option. How about it? *(1994)*

This column was received with no little derision from some (probably all) readers when it first appeared, largely because of my proposed willingness to fork over five bucks to get a decent glass.

WAS MY LAST OPEN LETTER TOO SUBTLE?

DEAR RESTAURATEURS,

When I last wrote to you, I mentioned the matter of poor-quality wine glasses used in better-quality American restaurants. Several of you were kind enough to write back suggesting—not to put too fine a point on it—that my concerns were unjust and misplaced.

For their part, readers wrote to decry (and cry about) their unpleasant experiences trying to enjoy their wines in your restaurants. Some were upset about pricing.

But all agreed that, whatever the price, a good wine glass is a necessity. I meekly suggested paying a surcharge in exchange for a decent glass. This—like so many of my ideas—was classed as lunatic. Readers declared that paying two or three times your cost for a wine is remuneration enough, never mind having to pay extra for a decent glass.

Now, you'd think that with this sort of obvious discontent, you restaurateurs would get the message. After all, I am hardly the only writer who's mentioned the matter. And surely you're not insensible to your customers' discomforts. But then again, maybe you are.

I'll give you a specific example. Not long ago I went with some friends to Rubicon, which is one of San Francisco's hotsy-totsiest restaurants. It has received great reviews and is packing them in like sardines. I went to Rubicon because it's where you can find Larry Stone, who is Rubicon's wine steward.

I've watched Larry Stone at work for years, first at Seattle's Four Seasons Olympic Hotel and later at Charlie Trotter's, the great Chicago restaurant. He was enticed to Rubicon (one of whose owners is movie director and winegrower Francis Ford Coppola) because Stone is not just one of America's best wine stewards, but also one of the *world's* best wine stewards. Stone was the first (and only) American to win the international French Wine Sommelier competition, as well as secure a Master Sommelier credential from both the British and French accreditation bodies.

Now, here you have a restaurant that went out of its way—and, no doubt, deep into its pocket—to hire the likes of Larry Stone. As you might expect, Stone created a discriminating wine list for Rubicon, not one of those engorged, king-of-the-wine-jungle lists, but a real jewel, where each selection sparkles with insight.

So everything is in place: a superb sommelier, a masterly wine list . . . and junk wine glasses. I was dumbfounded. Why have such a bijou wine list, polished and presented with lapidary care by such a star as Larry Stone, only to have him pour wine into glasses only slightly more useful than a goatskin bota?

As you might expect, I raised this point—none too delicately—with Stone. He replied that Rubicon had originally started with Riedel glasses (which were sold to them at a good price, he noted), but that the breakage was insupportable, about $10,000 worth before Rubicon called it quits. A surcharge was out, he said, because customers resented that. Fair enough.

Finally, I said, "Look, Larry, just slap on an extra buck per bottle for every wine you sell. Surely that will cover your breakage until the employees get the hang of handling better-quality wine glasses?" Then came the kicker. "Oh no, we couldn't do that," he said. "Our customers are very price sensitive. They know exactly how much certain wines sell for in every good restaurant in San Francisco."

I've heard lame excuses in my time, but this was champion. Rubicon's dining room was truffled with *soigné* patrons who can barely recognize the one-dollar denomination, let alone notice its keeping company with a fifty-dollar Cabernet.

Frankly, I didn't get the sense that Stone was all that enthusiastic about having to serve his wines in Rubicon's con-the-customer wine glasses. But he was too professional to let on. I do recall that at Charlie Trotter's—whose eponymous owner-chef is fanatical about quality—even the water came in fine glasses.

So, America's restaurateurs, why do you bother? I mean, why do you pretend to care about fine food and wine when—for something as elemental as wine glasses—you so obviously don't care? Why do you bother hiring and encouraging people like Larry Stone, only to hamstring their professionalism? For that matter, why do you thwart your customers' pleasure? Why not just open a diner, with a big, flashing neon sign that says "Eat"? Think of how much you can save on breakage. *(1995)*

Rubicon did eventually return to using excellent wine glasses. In 2006, Larry Stone left the sommelier trade to become general manager of Rubicon Estate, which is Francis Ford Coppola's Napa Valley winery. Rubicon (the restaurant) closed in August 2008.

HERE'S THE WINE LIST, HEH, HEH, HEH

JUDGING FROM THE LETTERS THAT steadily stream into this publication, seemingly nothing irritates *Wine Spectator* readers quite so much as high restaurant wine prices. No sooner, however, does a hapless wine columnist let loose a puny little salvo, than a volley is loosed from the restaurant armada.

"There are . . . but a few restaurateurs who unreasonably stamp their wines up three, four, or five times," insists Kirk R. Bergsma, the general manager of the Waterfront Inn in Traverse City, Michigan. Michael Ballon of Castle Street Cafe in Great Barrington, Massachusetts, in that same issue, takes up the cudgel, "Any restaurant that marks up its wine three times its cost is doing a gross disservice to both itself and its customers."

This is the "Say it ain't so, Joe" school of denial. Well, folks, it is so. Not only did Shoeless Joe do the dirty deed, but American restaurants are chronic pickpockets of wine-loving patrons. I've said it before and I'll happily say it again: There *are* saints out there. The landscape is dotted with restaurants that offer fine wines at good prices. Even the miracle of well-selected wines at reasonable prices served in good glasses has been sighted. It's even shaping up into—dare I say it?—a trend.

Nevertheless, the fact remains that the majority of restaurants typically mark up wines at three times their cost; e.g., a $10 bottle wholesale sells for $30. Cheaper wines see even higher margins, upward of four or five times cost. Want proof?

Not long ago, in my capacity as wine critic of *The Oregonian* newspaper, I favorably reviewed a wine labeled Nathanson Creek Cabernet Sauvignon. It was a deal: $4.95 a bottle retail. No such winery as Nathanson Creek exists. It is one of several labels created by Sebastiani Vineyards.

Sebastiani seeks to limit sales of Nathanson Creek to restaurants (known in the trade as on-premise sales) and exclude it from retail shops (called off-premise sales). Such restriction is illegal in Oregon, as well as in other states. I surmised that they sought to do this to prevent Nathanson Creek from encroaching on yet another Sebastiani label, called Vendange, which is intended for retail sales.

Subsequently, I received a letter from Louis Willsea, a brand manager for Sebastiani, who wrote to offer both clarification and justification. Willsea provides an unusually frank—and accurate—depiction of the reality of the wine business, especially as it concerns the grotesque markups applied to wines by most restaurants.

Confirming that Nathanson Creek is a brand created for restaurant or on-premise sales, brand manager Willsea observes, "To maintain typical wine list margins, most restaurateurs avoid wines that are visibly promoted off-premise. This is not a comment on wine list pricing, simply a statement of reality that faces every winery which wishes to build off- and on-premise sales simultaneously."

Put plainly, restaurants do not want their patrons to know just how much they are gouging them on wine prices. They particularly do not want to present low-cost/high-profit wines that their patrons might stumble across at the supermarket. But how do they know you won't see such wines at Safeway or Costco?

"Most important to the restaurateur is the lack of a UPC bar code," reveals

Willsea. So *that's* how restaurant wine lists are created: Never mind what's on the front label, look for a bar code on the back. "This means it is effectively unsalable in a scanned-sales supermarket context." No zebra-stripe bar code, no supermarket sales. Nathanson Creek has no bar code; Vendange does.

Pity the poor restaurateur. It's tough to convince some poor dupe to pay fifteen bucks for a bottle of Nathanson Creek Cabernet when that same dupe just bought it at the supermarket for $4.95. Of course, for this whacking premium one does get the wine served in schlock glasses designed to meet or exceed the federal bumper safety standards.

Sebastiani Vineyards—which simply does what dozens of other wineries do—is whipsawing between the differing demands of restaurants and supermarkets. "There is no subterfuge or ulterior motive in our marketing strategy for the two brands," says Willsea. "We are simply attempting to provide two distinct products that will satisfy two equally distinct retail needs."

Have you hugged your restaurateur today? *(1994)*

In 2001, Sebastiani Vineyards sold the Nathanson Creek and Vendange brands, along with several others, to a division of Constellation Brands, Inc., a conglomerate wine company that has gobbled dozens of wineries and labels. The sale slimmed Sebastiani from a seven-million-case wine business to one selling fewer than two-hundred-thousand cases. Today, both Nathanson Creek and Vendange have UPCs (Universal Product Codes), often called bar codes.

UPCs are today commonplace. While some big wineries continue to offer what the wholesale distribution trade calls "restaurant packs," which lack the UPC codes, the presence of a bar code on a label has pretty much ceased to be a distinguishing feature if only because many high-end wines are now sold in supermarkets.

━━━◆━━━

"ACCOMMODATE THEM," HE SAID.

DEAR RESTAURATEURS,

When I last wrote to you last year at this time, the subject was wine glasses. I so enjoyed our little chat that I thought I'd drop you a line to let you know how things are going.

At the risk of being labeled a meddler (or worse), I have one more suggestion for you. In fact, my advice comes from one of your own. And it doesn't even involve wine, at least not directly.

About twice weekly, my wife and I have coffee at a restaurant called Il Fornaio. One rainy, chill Sunday morning we stopped by for some coffee. While I ordered, my wife, Karen, went to the hostess and asked if we could sit near the grill, which had a dancing fire.

Mind you that it was Karen who made this inquiry, not me. She is notoriously nice. I insist that she only *seems* that way because she's married to the Dark Side, but friends say otherwise.

Anyway, she nicely asks if we could sit at a booth near the fire. The hostess gets flustered and says, "I don't think so. You have to sit in the other section."

"Why don't you ask?" suggests my wife sweetly.

The hostess goes to the chef in charge, who was working nearby. After hearing her inquiry, he looks at her with astonishment and says, with asperity, "Accommodate them."

That's it in a two-word nutshell, restaurateurs.

The problem is pervasive. I recently was at a restaurant where I ordered a wine and politely (I thought) asked the waiter if they had any better wine glasses. "Yes," he replied, "but not for the wine you ordered."

Or there was the time I showed up for lunch at the three-star Paris restaurant Taillevent during one of the hottest days of the year. Trust me on this: I was very well dressed. But I wasn't wearing a jacket and tie because of the heat. The restaurant insisted I wear one. When I protested, pointing out that I was hardly going to be an eyesore in their dining room, their reply was the classic: "It's the rule."

I would have left on the spot, but I was with some guests who desperately wanted to eat there, so I submitted. Owner Jean-Claude Vrinat came over to our table, having heard that he had (the rare) unhappy client. "It's the rule," he explained. "Who owns this restaurant?" I inquired, already knowing the answer. "I do," he said.

The message was clear: We exist for him. He doesn't exist for us. When I pointed this out, noting that, after all, *we're* paying the bill, Vrinat murmured, "You are very French, monsieur." I took it as a compliment, but maybe I missed something.

Not all three-star French restaurants are so snooty, by the way. Years ago, during a long cycling trip, my wife and I bicycled from Sauternes to Eugénie-les-Bains, which is where Michel Guérard's three-star restaurant is found. We had a reservation for dinner, but had not booked a room. We were young and poor. But we also were hot and sweaty, so we decided that if they had a room, we'd take it.

Upon arriving at the reception desk, we were told that there was no room at the inn. "But you are cycling, no?" she asked. "Ah, then you have a *petite tente*." We most certainly did. "Voilà!" she exclaimed. "There is a little campground near the post office just a few blocks away. Why don't you put up your tent there? And then come back here and use our pool. You are most welcome here."

Or there's the restaurant l'Antica Posta in the town of San Casciano in Val di Pesa, ten miles south of Florence. While traveling with a colleague, I touted it as the source of the best Chianina beef I'd ever eaten.

Upon arriving at the restaurant we discovered that l'Antica Posta did not (at that time) take credit cards. We had cash, but maybe not enough, we explained to the owner. "No problem," he said. "If it's not enough, you will send me the difference."

So, restaurateurs, why do you turn dining into a high school experience of dress codes, seating assignments, and rigidity? Why does dining out so often become adversarial? And it's not just me, you know. Even my wife agrees. *(1996)*

Some readers came to the defense of Mr. Vrinat, who died from lung cancer at age seventy-one in January 2008. He was a gentlemanly fellow who devoted his life to his restaurant and his vast and beloved wine cellar.

I did subsequently interview Mr. Vrinat for Wine Spectator. *Prior to the interview, his secretary called to invite me and my wife to come to Taillevent as Mr. Vrinat's guests. I declined with elaborate (French) courtesy. Baffled, she switched to English, fearing that my French, which is indeed limited, lacked sufficient comprehension. Who, after all, turns down a free meal at Taillevent? I said, courteously, that I was most grateful but that it was simply not possible.*

When I interviewed Mr. Vrinat, he, too, expressed puzzlement. I reminded him of his position—and mine. He smiled and said, "Oh yes, I remember now." Mr. Vrinat eventually did change his dress policy, about a decade after the sartorial dust-up (which took place in 1985) described in this article.

IS IT REAL? OR IS IT PRETENTIOUS?

FRANK J. PRIAL, LONGTIME WINE columnist for the *New York Times*, was on the beat again. "I'd heard about this newest restaurant routine and, highly skeptical, had gone . . . to see if it was true: Were they really rinsing out wine glasses with the wine about to be served in them?"

Prial was shocked, shocked! to discover that this was going on "right in the dining room." Apparently this was too much. "To me," pronounced Prial, "the wine rinse is show business, another dramatic but unnecessary touch meant to impress the customers."

The funny thing is, I used to feel the same way. But I don't anymore.

The first time I saw the "glass rinsing" procedure that so disturbed my colleague was more than a decade ago in Italy. Now, the Italians are famous for their love of *bella figura*, the "beautiful gesture" that so often is utterly meaningless. I figured this was a choice example, like a chilled salad fork. I was wrong.

The Italians call it "seasoning" the glass. The waiter splashes a tiny amount of your wine—a half-ounce at most—into a wine glass and swirls the wine to fully coat the interior of the glass. He or she then pours the wine from the first glass into another glass, performs the same swirling trick, and so on until all the glasses on the table are "seasoned." The seasoning wine (which also allows the sommelier to judge the soundness of the wine) is discarded, and the bottle is then poured in the conventional fashion.

The usual explanation of why this gets done—the same as that proffered by Prial—is "soapy residue" in the glass. That's possible, to be sure. It happens, although not that often.

The problem, I learned from experience, involves the amplification of smells that comes from big Riedel-type glasses. When I lived in Italy, we used to store our glasses in an old armoire, just like many Italian restaurants do. It was then that I discovered why "seasoning the glasses" is more than an empty ritual to wow the rubes.

No matter how fastidiously we cleaned that old armoire, the wine glasses quickly picked up a musty smell. Really, it could happen literally overnight. There was only one way to insure that you didn't present a musty-smelling glass to your guests: "season" it with the wine to be served.

What at first seemed unbearably pretentious soon became normal practice.

Over time, I discovered that I *liked* seasoning the glass. It seems to bring the scent of the wine alive, especially in glasses with big bowls, like those intended for Pinot Noir.

So, for once, I leap to the defense of sommeliers everywhere trying to give their customers a first-class wine experience.

Of course, a few prerequisites are in order. The wine glass has to *deserve* this treatment. Doing it in some stupid little glass really *is* pretentious—or at least unnecessary—if only because a small glass won't amplify any smell very much.

Second, some care is required in pouring out the minimum amount of wine necessary for the "seasoning." This is a touchy point, especially considering the sky-high cost of restaurant wine prices. Every ounce counts—or so it feels, unfortunately. Still, a half-ounce or so is no big deal and savvy customers recognize that.

The problem with wine service is that it's so much a matter of tasteful presentation. And it so easily mutates into bad theater, like the old at-the-table Caesar salad preparation or the making of flaming cherries jubilee.

Decanting is a good example. More people see decanting a wine as more pretentious than any other activity short of smelling the cork. (The latter isn't so much pretentious as unnecessary.)

What is it about decanting a wine that makes it seem so snooty? Is it the candle? (I use a flashlight myself.) Is it the "drum roll effect"? Or does it just seem too fussy?

I've yet to have a wine that was the worse for decanting—and a good many that were the better for the quick aeration decanting offers. But decanting so easily lends itself to "show time."

Pity the poor wine server. He or she is damned if they do and denounced if they don't. Maybe it really would be better if they just opened the bottle, put it on the table, and walked away. *(2001)*

YOU HAVE THE RIGHT TO . . .

RECENTLY, THE U.S. SUPREME COURT, in a lopsided 7–2 ruling, reaffirmed the landmark Miranda decision. It's the one that requires the recital: "You have the right . . ."

Imagine if there were some sort of wine service Miranda, a recital of your wine rights in restaurants. Such as:

You have the right to a wine list with a genuine range of prices. How many times have you scanned a wine list, only to discover that nearly all the wines on the list *start* at $40 or $50 a bottle? Then there are the lists—rarer, I admit—on which most of the wines hit triple digits. (Did you ever notice how these same lists never put an actual dollar sign next to the price? I guess they don't want to remind us that the spare, elegant "125" is actually *dollars*.)

Restaurateurs insist that their customers only want high-priced bottles. Maybe that's so, but frankly, it sounds a little too self-serving to me. We have a right to an honest range of prices—and not just a couple of industrial, "who'd-want-to-drink-that?" bottles as a sop to the frugal.

You have the right to a good wine glass. Well, of course. And I'll say this much: It is happening. But it's far from universal. *Maybe* you'll get a good glass—if you order an expensive enough wine. Or if you're a regular. Or if you make a stink. We shouldn't have to do or be any of these. We have a *right* to a good wine glass.

You have the right to have a wine at a proper temperature. This is a biggie. I can't tell you the number of times I've been served white wines at near-cryogenic coldness and reds served warmer than my seared tuna.

Now, I understand that serving wines at appropriate temperatures is a tricky task. Restaurants frequently have limited storage space for wine and, worse, it's rarely temperature controlled.

I also recognize that "appropriate temperature" is up to the palate of the beholder. My ideal red wine temperature (pretty cool) may be too chilly for you. So a restaurant can't hit everybody's mark.

Still, it's got to be said: Restaurants have a responsibility to at least *care* about appropriate temperatures. There's simply no excuse not to. If facilities are lacking for cooling wines, then by all means use an ice bucket.

It's not exactly higher math to figure out how long a wine at restaurant room temperature needs to stay in an ice bucket to cool down to, say, 60 degrees Fahrenheit. The formula is pretty straightforward: Figure on roughly one degree Fahrenheit per minute. If the wine is 70 degrees Fahrenheit, it will take 10 minutes to reach 60 degrees Fahrenheit. (A refrigerator, in comparison, takes seven to eight minutes to achieve a one-degree drop.)

You have the right to an appropriate pour. I'll bet you that everyone reading this has had the experience of having a wine poured nearly to the top of the glass. Mostly, it's ignorance. No one trained the server otherwise. That's easily corrected.

But some waiters (and restaurant managers) are sly. They know that if they top up the glass, they can then remove the empty bottle. This creates a feeling that, really, we ought to order another bottle. And that, in turn, adds to the bill and thus to the tip. It happens because it works. You have a right to have a good wine glass filled only a third of the way up, at most.

You have a right to an effortless wine experience. Wine lists that are endlessly long, overlarge in format, or haphazard in such basic details such as vintage and producer all send the same message: it's the World Wine Wrestling Federation.

You have the right to a list that's up to date. How often have you ordered a wine only to discover that it's no longer available? Sure, it can happen, but it occurs a bit too often to believe that "Oh, we just ran out of that wine." In an era of laser printers, there's no excuse for an outdated wine list.

You have the right to consult about a wine's soundness. This is phrased carefully for a reason. The key is *consult*. It's the restaurant's job to know whether a wine is unsound, which usually means that fruit-suppressing, wet cardboard scent commonly called "corkiness." If you're not sure—and in many cases it's damnably hard—you have the right to call for a non-challenging consult. If you're sure, fine. But "consulting" is more graceful, as well as effective.

Above all, you have the right *not* to remain silent. *(2000)*

⌒‿⌒

WHY TODAY'S WINE LISTS FAIL

THE DIRTY LITTLE SECRET OF many—most, I'd say—restaurant wine lists is that they're worthless to the majority of their audience.

Sommeliers go to expensive lengths to construct ever longer, more elaborate lists. Yet I'm sure most of their clients look at these lists and say (if only to themselves), "What am I supposed to do with this?" Even those of us who can speak "wine" don't have *time* to reasonably peruse such lists.

Recently, my wife and I had lunch with another couple where the hubby, like myself, is wine-crazed. The two women convulsed in laughter over how they would have to sit numbly across the table from their respective husbands while we, like Talmud students, tried to absorb these gonzo wine lists.

"In the meantime, I'm *starving*!" declared our friend. "The least the restaurant could do is serve me something—say, the first five courses—while my husband sits there sorting out the entire wine genome."

That said, wine lists fail today not because of length. Instead, it's how they are put together. Today's wine lists no longer make any sense. I spend as much time trying to remember (if I know it at all) the characteristics of the wines as in actually scanning the list.

Today's wine lists are—with a few admirable exceptions—based on a model that's more than a century old. Back in the late 1800s, restaurants served only a few wines from a few places. You had Bordeaux, above all. You saw Burgundy, Champagne, and German wines. And that was about it, give or take the odd Tokaji, Rhône, or Chianti.

Above all, there was no differentiation about how wines were made—and no need to. You didn't look at a wine and wonder whether it was a new-style Barolo or a traditional version. Or whether a wine had oak or no oak; malolactic fermentation or no malo; was filtered or unfiltered, etc. Today, of course, there's really no way to know what you're getting.

Let's say you want a Chianti. Now, short of actually knowing the specific wine on the list, what can you divine about it? Today's Chianti could be new-wave oaky or made in large old vats. It could be 100 percent Sangiovese or plumped with Cabernet. Indeed, it may not even be "Chianti" but instead some goofy *fantasia* bottling or a Super Tuscan. In short, you're lost.

Does the wine list itself help you? It does not. Because all the list does, as it did one hundred years ago, is categorize the wine under *Chianti* or *Tuscany* or even just *Italian*. This is worthless.

It's time instead for wine list creators—whether they style themselves as sommeliers or not—to restructure modern restaurant wine lists to insightfully reveal the true underlying linkages of today's wines.

Grape variety or even districts are fast becoming unrevealing of what's in the bottle. Elio Altare's oaky, suave, almost tannin-free Nebbiolo "Vigna Arborina" stylistically has more in common with many Merlot-based garagiste Bordeaux bottlings than it does with what you would traditionally think of as Nebbiolo. But how would you know that?

It's time for wine lists to show us what might be called "new commonalities." Think of it as wine hyperlinks, as in: "If you like this, then you'll also like. . . ."

I'll give you an example. An insightful wine list today could have a category called "High-Elevation Artisanal." It could note: "These are producers making fewer than five thousand cases a year whose grapes are grown at relatively high elevations, which typically result in lower yields, more intense flavors, and refreshing acidity."

All of a sudden, all sorts of wines, both red and white, that previously were confined to unrevealing, straightjacket designations such as *Napa Valley* or *Piedmont* are reunited with their true family members.

Or you could have a category called "Extremely Low Yields." Mayacamas Vineyards's stunning ton-to-the-acre Sauvignon Blanc has more in common with Domaine Leroy's ultra-low-yield Burgundies than either producer has with their ostensible "relations" of mere Napa Valley or Burgundy.

The dots need to be connected differently today. And the only people who can do it are the ones who are paid to do it: the best sommeliers. If their lists simply plow the same old furrows laid down long ago, then they're no help to us.

It's time to create twenty-first-century wine lists. *(2002)*

OLD WINES, COLLECTING, AND OTHER WINE MADNESS

You would think, what with writing about wine for so long, that I would have a trove of stories about tasting old wines. After all, I have tasted a good number of old—sometimes very old—wines. And in most cases I've had the same reaction: they're boring. Many of these old wines are relics in every sense. Sure, one is struck by their venerability ("Lindbergh landed in Paris the year this wine was born") but once past the awe of that, too often I haven't found much else.

Also, unlike some of my colleagues, I find both writing and reading about old wines off-putting. Not only are old wines now phenomenally expensive, but their very rarity—assuming they're not counterfeit—means that you are one of a select few who will ever have such an experience. Intended or not, an element of paraded privilege clings to these tales of old wines. "And then the Baron brought out his prized 1947 . . ."

When I mentioned this to one of my colleagues, he gently reproved me. "But readers dote on this stuff," he said. That's true. So much of wine involves fantasy, nowhere more so than in tales of something ancient that's still alive, like in *Jurassic Park*.

OK, So It Was the Vintage of the Century

ALL MY WINE LIFE—AND STILL TODAY—I have had a ferocious affection for what might be called "real world" wines. More than most folks, I've been privileged to taste what others can only dream about. And I'm grateful, believe me. But my heart lies elsewhere.

For example, an extraordinarily generous wine lover invited me to a tasting of Burgundies from the fabled 1945 vintage. There were just ten of us tasting the likes of 1945 Krug Champagne (a little something to calibrate the palate), Leroy Corton-Bressandes, Domaine de la Romanée-Conti Richebourg, a 1945 Musigny from G. Roumier and another from Comte Georges de Vogüé, and DRC Romanée-Conti, among others. These 1945s were capped by a 1919 Romanée-Conti alongside a 1919 de Vogüé Musigny.

Were they swell? You bet they were. But none of these made my "wines of the year" list. *(2005)*

—~·~—

Finally, the Truth about Old Wines

YOU'D THINK I WOULD HAVE figured it out by now. I've been among the fortunate few at various rare wine opportunities. I'm not ungrateful. But will somebody please explain to me the appeal of old wines?

Now "old" is a relative term. I still recall the time, years ago when I was a wine puppy, being invited to a small private lunch in Napa Valley honoring a famous English wine critic. I was flattered to be invited.

The lunch was one of those long, drunken ones. It was just a few of us eating outdoors in that fragrant eucalyptus-scented California air. The food was great, the wines were lovely, and I was feeling content.

The hosts had a collection of old wines that they wanted to show to the English wine critic. So they staggered off, leaving me alone with the critic's (very English) wife. She had seen enough old, dusty bottles in dank cellars for one lifetime. I was to keep her company.

I did try—really, I did. But I was young. And American. And I think she was annoyed that I was at this lunch at all. Anyway, I tried to make small talk. Somehow, the subject of Sauternes came up. I was enthusiastic about them (she was not). But I persevered and, wagging my puppy tail, confessed, "You know, I've never had an old one."

"What do you mean by 'old'?" she drawled. I hadn't realized until then that *old* could have three or four syllables.

"Well, you know," I replied, my tail wagging more energetically than ever. "Like a '21."

"18 or 19?" she inquired disdainfully.

OK, so *old* is a relative thing. Still, there is such a thing as an old wine. My rule of thumb for old wine is this: If you can't tell what the hell it is, it's too old.

Talk about label drinking. If most of the swooned-over old wines didn't have their labels, I'll bet you anything these same swooners would taste the wine and say, "It's shot." But knowing its pedigree somehow makes an old wine fascinating, like a boring dinner guest who's very rich.

The amount of time required for a wine to age into anonymity varies enormously. Sweet wines with high acidity—Sauternes, German Rieslings, Quarts de Chaume, Bonnezeaux, Vouvray *moelleux*—are barely mature after twenty years, let alone old. On the other hand, most Pinot Noirs top out at twenty years, if they haven't already toppled over.

I once was a guest at a large luncheon hosted by André Gagey, then the director of the Burgundy shipper Louis Jadot. Gagey is a wonderful guy and a genial host. Since I really like Jadot wines, I thought it was a swell lunch. Toward the end, he brought out an old bottle of a single-vineyard Beaune, something like a 1919. Everyone oohed and aahed.

But as bad luck would have it, Gagey turned to me and said, "So what do you think of this, Matt?" I sighed and said, "Well, André, it's pleasant enough, but if it didn't have a label I doubt that even you would know what it was. And since Burgundy, more than any other wine, is all about place, I'd have to say that when you can't possibly tell where it's from, then it's too old." Some years later, Jadot had a huge tasting of their oldest wines. I was not invited.

I don't get old wines. Recently, I was moderating a panel at the KCBX Central Coast Wine Classic where everyone was tasting multiple vintages of Ridge Monte Bello Cabernet, presented by Ridge's longtime winemaker, Paul Draper. The oldest bottle was a 1974.

Now Ridge Monte Bello Cabernet can go the distance better than most Cabernets. The 1970 is still a stunner. But I thought the 1974 was fading. When I said so, everyone looked at me incredulously. It was the old story: Like babies, they're all beautiful, never mind what they really look like.

Afterward, some guy came up to me and told me the truth about old wines. "You don't get it, do you?" he asked. "Look at me," he said. "I'm fifty-five years old. I had a heart attack recently. Sense of mortality and all that. When that happens, you see old wines differently. You start rooting for them. You start shouting at Beaujolais *nouveau*, 'Hang in there! Hang in there!' As long as they live, you live."

That's it. *As long as they live, you live.* I finally understand. *(1997)*

The memorable lunch in Napa Valley all those years ago was given by the late Joe Heitz, who was a generous host and a lover of old wines. The honored guests were Michael Broadbent and his wife, Daphne.

WHEN GOOD WINES SAY GOOD-BYE

LET ME BREAK THIS TO you as gently as I can: You've got a problem. Not all of you, to be sure. But a lot of you. What is it? You can't let go. You just can't believe that—sob!—your wine has departed. That it's kaput. Not merely over the hill, but six feet under it.

Not *my* wines, you say, my wines still retain ethereal qualities, wafting fragrances, delightful wafts of winsome whatever. Nonsense. It's dead. Get over it.

All right, this is a bit, ahem, hyperbolic. But still, there's a point here. Too many wine lovers really can't let go. They just can't bring themselves to believe that a wine, no matter how decrepit, doesn't retain *some* virtue. I'll give you an example.

Recently, I was moderating (hah!) a panel where the winemaker presented a 1986 Pinot Noir from Santa Barbara County. Now, the 1986 vintage wasn't especially good for them and besides, it was early days in Santa Barbara County winemaking. The wine was almost brown in color. Strong gusts of degradation emerged from the glass. It was doggo. And I said so.

I asked the audience who else thought the wine was dead? Not a single hand was raised. The crowd actually hissed! I was Bruno the Bad at the Friday night wrestling match. (It was wonderful.)

Of course, I could have been wrong. But, officer, what about this corpse? That's not a corpse, my boy. That's an elegantly declining body filled with rapturous fragrances.

Apparently, I was the only one who saw (or smelled) a corpse. Was the wine dead? Sure it was. But nobody wanted to believe it. Tender-hearted souls that we Americans are, nobody wanted to say so in front of the winemaker. That's my theory anyway, and I'm sticking to it.

Obviously, exactly when a wine no longer has a pulse is not definitive. Okay, so maybe it wasn't dead. But that Pinot Noir sure was down for the count. This brings us to the serious question: How do you known when a wine is too old?

My answer to this is straightforward: A wine is too old when you have to imagine it. When you have to bring to a wine a lot more than it's bringing to you, time's up. The wine is no more.

This is not the same, by the way, as appreciating a fading—but still present—loveliness. Only a couple of days after happily tangling with necrophiliac Pinot Noir lovers, I was generously (foolishly?) served a magnum of 1966 Montrachet bottled by the *négociant* Leroy. It was at a private dinner where, according to my wife, I was supposed to be on my best behavior. ("For God's sake, don't tell them their wines are dead.")

Anyway, out came this thirty-three-year-old Montrachet, and I'm here to testify that it was lovely. It was older, no doubt about it. And, yes, I would have preferred drinking it a decade ago when its fruit was surely fresher. But I didn't have to use my imagination to see its compelling beauty. It was all there to be savored, in a mature fashion.

A wine has got to do its part. As Woody Allen memorably said, "Eighty percent of success is showing up." That's a good measure of successful old wine. Most of what was there originally, namely fruit, should still be there.

This is why cold (52 degrees Fahrenheit) wine cellars are ideal. They preserve a wine's fruit. It's why so many otherwise implausibly old wines taste so young and fresh when hauled out of old stone cellars in Burgundy or those vast carved-from-chalk wine vaults in Champagne or from tufa caves in the Loire Valley.

As it happens, this same (generous) host hauled out a magnum of 1978 Volnay Clos des Ducs, Marquis d'Angerville, that same evening. It was spectacular. From the beginning, this 1978 Volnay was packed with fruit and now, two decades later, it has retained seemingly everything it had in its youth. Not only didn't you need to use your imagination, but also your senses could barely keep up with it. It out-raced my senses like a Russian wolfhound on a frisky walk with its owner. There was no keeping up with it.

So clearly there are old wines that are nothing of the sort. But, regrettably, too often most old wines are just that. They're simply shadows of what they once were. Wines die. And it's best to bury them and move on.

By the way, this only applies to what *you* bought. If its mine, it's an "exquisite reminiscence," an artifact of history, a wonder to behold. Your miserable bottle, on the other hand, is dead. *(1999)*

COUNTERFEIT CONFIDENTIAL

LAST WEEK AT A SMALL private dinner, the host, a wine importer, brought forth a bottle of 1928 Château Desmirail, a third-growth red Bordeaux from the Margaux district. Normally, at such a "tah-dah" moment, the wine is presented with academic reverence about its historicity or fetishistic fussing about the condition of its cork.

But the first thing the host said upon presenting the wine was, "I bought this years ago, before there was any likelihood that anyone would fake a wine like this."

Until very recently, anyone who bought an old wine, typically at auction, took it at its label's word, as it were. If it said Château Lafite Rothschild 1961, then it was so. If the wine proved disappointing, you assumed that it was either your inexperience as a taster or it was a bad bottle. After all, that can happen, especially with decades-old wines potentially subject to overly warm cellaring or an imperfect cork.

Today, however, more than a mere worm of doubt has insinuated itself. Instead, it's a serpent in an Eden of wine innocence. The root of the problem is what the proverb has always told us: It's money. Old wines from famous estates (nearly all European) now sell for extraordinary sums. For example, at a Zachys wine auction earlier this month, six bottles of 1945 Château Latour—a great vintage—sold for $78,210, or $13,035 a bottle.

That is a relatively paltry sum these days. Last month Sotheby's sold a jeroboam—six bottles in one—of 1945 Château Mouton Rothschild that came directly from Baroness Philippine de Rothschild's personal cellar for $310,700, or the equivalent of $51,783 a bottle. I could fill the page with lists of wines that effortlessly fetch thousands of dollars a bottle, including some from California, Italy, and the Rhône, that originally sold for mere hundreds of dollars just a few years ago. The key point is clear: The incentive to counterfeit wines has exploded along with the prices.

It's pretty easy to convincingly counterfeit an old wine bottle. Also, until recently, nobody was scrutinizing those bottles very closely, auction house protestations notwithstanding about their wine experts' careful scrutiny of labels and concerns about provenance. The auction house wine buyers, many of whom are knowledgeable, do catch the obvious ones, to be sure, but as in the art world, the really good forgeries slip through unnoticed—especially if buyers aren't complaining.

What about the wine in the bottle, you ask? Who among us knows so much about old wines—or young ones either, for that matter—that we can declare with absolute certainty that the purported 1961 Château Pétrus is definitively as declared? A savvy counterfeiter can concoct a Pétrus-like red wine convincing enough to allow even a so-called expert to concede that it might possibly be the real thing, never mind a twenty-something Wall Street whiz.

Wine has always been subject to counterfeiting. This is why we're presented the cork when served a wine in a restaurant and why that bottle is opened in front of us. Until the late 1800s, it was commonplace for wine in restaurants to be opened away from the guests and served in a decanter. It's easy enough to see how an empty bottle of Château Lafite Rothschild could be filled with something much cheaper and passed off as the real thing.

It's also why some wineries would wrap each bottle in a wire mesh, a practice you still see today with some traditional Spanish wines. This made it that much more difficult for a restaurateur to switch labels.

How was that 1928 Château Desmirail, you ask? It was amazingly fresh in color, more resembling a twenty-year-old red wine rather than something closer to an octogenarian. The 1928s were famously long-lived, and the Desmirail was consistent with the reputation of the vintage.

The greatest assurance of its authenticity, however, was less a matter of connoisseurship and more a matter of the improbability of a con. As the host said, he bought it long enough ago that it was unlikely that anyone would have bothered to fake it. So we took it for the real thing. *(2007)*

Collecting wine is a phenomenon unique to our time. It is different than simply accumulating a bunch of wine bottles, what's commonly known as building a wine cellar. Wine lovers everywhere have been doing that for centuries. "Collecting" is a different matter, as psychologists have long noted. It can have a faint (or sometimes strong) whiff of neuroticism, to say nothing of obsession.

However, collecting is good for business. So it's not surprising that auction houses and magazines actively promote collecting as an admirable, even wholesome, pursuit. Wineries profit, too, which is why they almost always accommodate requests by big collectors for a winery representative (and some hard-to-find vintages) when these collectors put on multi-day extravaganzas featuring a winery's high-priced, fabled wine.

Originally, this business of wine collecting—and especially collectors putting on vast "vertical" tastings (numerous vintages of one wine)—was exclusively an American phenomenon. It has since become worldwide. Today, the leading practitioners are rich, show-off wine drinkers in Europe and Asia.

Wine collecting continues to grow, fueled by economics and publicity. Magazines and wine newsletters regularly trumpet the emergence of a new "cult wine," making it an instant collectible. Auction houses then clean up, like street sweepers after the elephant parade.

REAL COLLECTING VS. PHONY COLLECTING

IT'S PRESUMPTUOUS TO SAY SO (but then, what else are columnists?) but a lot of wine collecting is bunk. I've met a number of these so-called "collectors," and I'll bet you have, too. What's more, I'll also bet that we both walked away with the same mixture of envy and annoyance: So many lovely wines and so little real appreciation.

I thought of this upon reading about the "Ganz collection." They were the opposite of so many of today's collectors. Victor and Sally Ganz were lifelong art lovers. He ran a costume jewelry business; she devoted her time to philanthropy. They weren't rich by today's tycoonish standards. Sure, they had money. But what they really had was passion, devotion, and above all, insight into modern art.

Their fifty-years-in-the-making art collection was auctioned this past November. Newspapers everywhere couldn't resist pointing out that over fifty years the Ganzes spent about $2 million. Their collection brought $206.5 million at auction. We all know the lesson here, don't we?

Everyone, it would seem, but Victor and Sally Ganz. By all accounts, they were devoted to art, not profit. Although there's no denying the hypnotic effect of seeing a $2 million investment reap a 10,000 percent return, the real lesson is that money has little to do with love.

The proof was in what—and how—they bought. Sure, they had the largest private collection of Picassos in the country. But they didn't buy the so-called "easy" Picassos. Instead, they bought the Picassos that made others—at the time—uncomfortable.

An appraisal of the Ganzes in the *New York Times* put it succinctly: "Unlike most collectors of their generation, they did not try to form an encyclopedic collection. In fact, their taste did not follow the conventional. Instead of gravitating toward pretty, commercial paintings, they bought challenging ones. . . ."

What's more, when the price of Picassos rose beyond their means, the Ganzes shifted their highly focused interest—and insights—elsewhere. Almost unerringly, it seems, whatever they bought proved over time to be enduring and enlightening. "They had sure eyes," said the *Times*. "And an uncanny talent for choosing just the right work."

What was evident about the Ganzes was that they loved art for art's sake. For example, in the late 1960s, Victor Ganz spotted the work of a then-unknown sculptor named Hesse. He saw her stuff after visiting a big-name gallery where the big-ticket work of a famous painter was being shown. According to the *Times* account, Ganz described the scene as "Filled with wealthy collectors chatting away like a giant cocktail party." Sound familiar?

Anyway, Ganz goes around the corner to a much less acclaimed gallery and spies the first-ever showing of Hesse's pretty weird sculptures. After intense absorption, he bought three. His son, Tony Ganz, observed, "My father was not a young man when he discovered Hesse, yet even though it was tough stuff, he didn't flinch. Everyone thought he'd lost his mind, even curators. They didn't get it."

The analogy to much of today's wine collecting is pretty obvious, I would think. Look at the prices of the blue-chip auction items. Does anybody who really knows and loves wine believe that today's first-growth Bordeaux, each of which is 30,000+

cases upon release, are worth, as *wine*, even a fraction of what they command today? Would a wine-loving Victor Ganz buy them? I think not. He knew too much.

There are so many wines today that are so beautiful. Yet you'd never know it from the stampede to just a handful of ever more expensive, ever more hyped wines. Are these wines admirable? Some of them are, yes. Do they represent today's expanding universe of beautiful wines? Hardly.

The lesson here for all of us is that real collecting, whether wine or art, is all about knowledge. It's not contrarianism or bargain-hunting. Real collectors, by definition, are loving investigators—connoisseurs, if you will. Their palate is sure not because they can infallibly name a wine blind, but because the beauty they're looking for is not on the label. Above all, as the Ganzes so admirably demonstrated, money is the least of it. *(1998)*

WINE AND WOMEN
(AND MEN, TOO)

Few subjects are more fraught with tension and possibilities for misunderstanding than journalistic generalizations about men and women. It's the third rail of journalism. (Allow me to rephrase that: Few subjects are more fraught with tension and possibilities for misunderstanding than men generalizing about women.)

The wine passion is overwhelmingly male. And white. And upper-middle class. Wine collecting makes even the most restrictive country clubs look like models of affirmative action. Of course, nothing and nobody prevents women or minorities from participating, but largely they don't. It's a (white) guy thing.

I won't pretend to have any impeccable explanations for this phenomenon. History provides some reasons; e.g., women were in the kitchen, and men once were home wine handymen, bottling wines bought by the barrel into their home cellars. This was common in Europe until the early twentieth century. Also, men typically got drunk more than women. And rich men developed refined wine appreciation in their male-only private clubs.

Still, none of that now-ancient history explains today's male passion for wine. Plenty of women—most, it appears—love wine.

But the panting pursuit of it, and the willingness to spend eye-opening sums of money, is apparently not part of it. Then again, men don't spend absurd amounts on handbags or shoes. So it all evens out, I suppose.

THIS BUD'S FOR THEM:
WOMEN ARE BETTER TASTERS

ARE WOMEN BETTER WINE TASTERS than men? My experience in teaching wine classes leads me to reply: "Emphatically, yes." Since Mother's Day is soon to arrive, this is a good moment to note the superior ability of women as wine tasters. I cannot say that mothers, as a group, show any particular gift at wine tasting. But women as a group certainly do. I know this from twenty years of teaching wine.

But for those who prefer not to rely upon wine writers—an admirable instinct—science is marshalling evidence of women's superior tasting abilities. For example, the Clinical Smell and Taste Research Center of the University of Pennsylvania conducted a smell identification experiment involving 1,955 people ranging in age from five to ninety-nine. Among other things, the study revealed that women outperformed men as more acute in all age groups.

What's more, it has been discovered that not all of us are born with equal tasting abilities—at least as far as taste buds take us. Linda Bartoshuk, a professor at the Yale University School of Medicine, asserts that people can be divided into three groups: nontasters, regular tasters, and supertasters.

Supertasters, she says, have more taste buds than others—as much as one hundred times as many taste buds per square centimeter compared to a nontaster. It is strictly an inherited advantage. Roughly one-quarter of the population are so endowed. Another one-quarter are nontasters, and the remaining half of the population are regular sorts. Bartoshuk reports that women generally have more taste buds than men. Then comes the clincher: Two-thirds of all the supertasters are women.

But everybody knows that wine tasting involves more than just taste buds, in the same way that music appreciation is more than just having a pair of what audio sorts call "golden ears." I submit that what makes women better wine tasters than men is an early (and lifelong) training in matters of nuance. After all, fine wine is really just a collection of nuances. Many men have a hard time even grasping the *notion* of nuance, let alone finding it in a glass of wine.

Take clothes, for example. The most profound aesthetic decision a man makes in the course of a day is choosing the tie to go with his shirt. And most men, once having decided upon a particular tie with a particular shirt, subsequently never vary from what quickly becomes a routine decision. Women, on the other hand, engage in a mind-boggling array of aesthetic decisions about look, fit, feel, and smell just simply to get dressed and out of the house each morning. It's a daily training exercise in nuance.

Men tend to keep things simple to the point of mental oblivion. As a (male) fashion writer pointed out not long ago, boys learn from their fathers only one way to knot a tie and one way to part their hair. They subsequently never learn a different tie knot and continue to part their hair the same way for the rest of their lives, never mind whether there's any hair left. Can you expect such creatures to become astute wine tasters?

My ideal wine tasting class would be women lawyers. Why? Because as women, they are already advantaged; and as lawyers, they are trained to think analytically and also to express themselves with some precision. My nightmare class, in comparison, would be nothing but men engineers. They seem almost incapable of accepting the idea of the existence of something that cannot be pinned down to the satisfaction and verification of all observers. Nuance drives them nuts.

Actually, I do know an impressive number of men who are good wine tasters. But I've met only a few who haven't had to work surprisingly hard at it. Granted, everyone—male or female—has to apply himself or herself if they're going to be knowledgeable about wine. Like basketball, sewing, or auto repair, it takes exposure, opportunity, practice, and keen interest. But men appear to have a tougher time at grasping the nuances of fine wine than do women, at least at first. Eventually, the two groups become equal in ability. But the early advantage belongs to women. *(1995)*

THE HEADY MIX OF MEN AND WINE

WHEN MOTHER'S DAY ROLLED AROUND this year, it seemed an opportune moment to acknowledge—indeed, to celebrate—the superior tasting ability of women. I asserted, with certitude, that women are better wine tasters than men. I also noted that I could find nothing about mothers that differentiated them from other women wine tasters.

Now, I am faced with the Father's Day dilemma. What to say? I can say this much: As with mothers, I cannot discern any difference in wine tasting ability between fathers and nonfathers. All men are pretty much equally bad at wine tasting compared to all women.

I'm sorry about this, if for no other than personal reasons. Having said it, I feel that I must rise in defense of mankind (literally). Whatever men lack in innate ability, they make up for in passion. This might strike some people, men and women alike, as a little odd. After all, passion usually is thought to be women's province.

Rarely have I seen a woman swoon over wine. I have seen them enjoy wine immensely. Taste wine acutely. Talk wine articulately. But when it comes to the wine passion, women are no match for men. For some, this masculine swoon over fine wine is, well, unseemly. Embarrassing. Affected. Frequently, it can turn rancid with snobbery.

I have known men like this—too many, in fact. They start out innocently enough. After all, it's not easy being a man when it comes to wine. Think of all the fictional accounts of sophisticated men who command a wine list, like a powerful sports car, with bravura, sureness, and flourish.

Somehow, wine and masculinity became entangled. The twisted connection between drunkenness and masculinity was bad enough. But *knowing* about wine, that was brutal. After all, until recently, knowing about fine wine meant knowing French—or at least pretending to. And you had to know about vintages. And know which wine was supposed to go with which dishes. Who, apart from James Bond, actually knew these things?

What resulted was predictable: Pretension substituted for knowledge. Still does. But the urge to acquire the knowledge still lingered. Here's the odd part: Somewhere along the greased path of wine pretension, a surprising number of men discovered real, honest-to-gosh beauty in wine. No longer did they pursue wine for sheer sport. They became ensnared in the real beauty of fine wine.

Sad to say, some of these guys just get worse. More snobbish. More insufferable. They become wine beasts with voracious appetites for trivia, condescension, and tediousness. They are beyond hope or redemption.

But a goodly number of men—a majority, even—are transformed. They begin to love wine for wine's sake. They want to share the beauty. They become generous souls, rather than hoarders or wine jocks hoisting a quick *grand cru* at the local wine bar. True, they do shop with avidity, poring over the numerous wine shop catalogs. And yes, they do read wine columns (usually for the delicious pleasure of disagreeing). But they always come home, shining with hope over some newly acquired glory that they can't wait to share with—guess who?

This passion can make shy guys who previously would barely squeak at a social function, suddenly become engaged and entertaining. It can make reserved men who normally frown from habit smile warmly when the subject turns to wine.

Perhaps most impressive of all, I've seen cheapskates, real money creeps, who suddenly turn generous and openhanded when faced with the chance to buy a fine wine. It changes men more than it does women. Fine wine melts something in men.

So this Father's Day, those of you who are bystanders to the wine passion—especially women—take hope. True, for some men wine leads to nothing admirable. There are still too many men who take up wine as a competitive sport after their knees give out. But for every jerk who fits that description, five times as many men are transformed by wine.

Fine wine may not be the answer to the world's problems. But surely, it's a skip farther down the road to civilization than a passion for, say . . . boxing? *(1995)*

Your Cheatin' Wine Locker

ALL RIGHT, GUYS, YOU KNOW you're doing it. And—heh, heh, heh—your wives don't know, do they? But remember our boy Bill. Look what happened to him. Maybe it's best to fess up—before your wife reads this column.

You know what I'm talking about: the wine locker you're keeping on the side.

That cool-space honey that's costing you as much as a mistress. Hell, it *is* a mistress of sorts: It costs the same; you think about it as much; you lavish as much attention on it as you would on the more conventional sort. And the bills, well, they ain't cheap. And they're never, ever, sent to your home address.

One of the best-kept secrets of fine wine in America is how many men keep a wine locker on the side. "Oh, there's definitely a lot of it," confirms Peter Morrell of Morrell & Co., a major New York retailer. "There's a substantial number of men—it's always men—who have a wine hobby on the side. You're right, it's a little secret affair."

On the opposite coast, in Emeryville, California, John Fox, co-owner of Premier Cru, a major Bay Area retailer, agrees that it's a widespread practice. "Certainly, a lot of customers we deal with, we can't send an invoice or wines to their homes," says Fox.

What about women who keep a secret locker on the side? "Absolutely not," says Fox. "No women. I've never seen it."

The truth is that an awful lot of married, wine-loving men with cellars at home have a secret wine locker somewhere else. Why? It's simple: They don't want their wives to know how much money they spend on wine. "Their wives don't see the point of spending $50 or $100 for a bottle. Wines should be $8 or $10, they think," says Fox.

What's interesting is that this wine passion is no secret. Quite the opposite. I'm sure that a goodly percentage of the deceived wives have no problem with hubby's wine love. Yet the men keep sneaking around.

I have a friend who is probably the Everyman of wine philandering. He makes a sizable chunk of money. And he has a huge cellar right at home. His wife knows all about it. Yet he keeps a secret locker on the side. When I ask him why, he says, "Well, she thinks I'm spending too much money on wine. She's probably right," he concedes.

So why does he do it? Because he can't stop himself. "I see a new offering that I know won't last long, or I taste a wine that's really fantastic, and I've got to have it. And why not? I can afford it," he adds defensively.

His wife, I happen to know, doesn't dispute their ability to absorb the cost. But she does wonder what *else* they might do with their money if not quite so much of it was diverted to fine wine. Good point.

Bob Liner of Liner & Elsen Ltd. in Portland, Oregon—a retailer with private wine lockers on the premises—says, "The real secret is not that the guy has a wine locker, but rather what's in it. Their wives have no clue about the number of cases or the dollar amount. *That's* the secret." He adds, "A lot of lockers are used as a way for guys to buy wine in quantity and then trickle it into the house. That way their wives don't know how much they've really bought."

All across America, men are squirreling away expensive wines. With these guys, for every bottle that makes it home-sweet-home, there's probably a case put up across town in pricey digs.

And for every wife who thinks she generously tolerates—indeed, encourages—her husband's wine indulgence, there's another who will be shocked to learn that she literally only knows the half of it.

Of course, it all comes out in the divorce proceedings. And when the wife learns just how many cases of 1982 classed-growth Bordeaux hubby owns—and how they've zoomed in value—that probably does take the sting out of it.

This is, by the way, one of the great ironies of wine philandering: Most of these wines are trophies. After all, these guys aren't afraid of bringing home Beaujolais. It's the high-ticket bottles that have them doing the old soft-shoe.

In the meantime, the perennial *Ladies' Home Journal* question must be asked: Can these marriages be saved?

Only by a corkscrew. *(1998)*

THIS JUST IN! WOMEN COLLECT WINE

LET'S SEE, WHERE WERE WE? Ah yes, women wine collectors. As you may recall, I opined previously that we never seem to hear—or rather, read—about women wine collectors. All I ever recall is one or another article about Mr. Big Cork and his ever-expanding vertical of double-magnums of Chateau Bombast. But I cannot, for the professional life of me, remember reading about any women who engage in such activity.

As you might have gathered, I look askance at these Frank Bigbuck, bring-'em-back-in-case-lots collectors. Can women be subject to this, too? I always thought there was a difference between merely buying wine and collecting the stuff. Whoever thought that women wanted verticals, too? So I sought professional help, turning to Dr. Irvin Wolkoff, MD, FRCP, a practicing psychiatrist in Toronto and wine writer there for *The Medical Post*. He really exists, by the way.

I told him about the letter I received from Cynthia M. York of Ann Arbor, Michigan. "I chuckled when I read that you had never heard about a woman wine collector," she wrote. "I don't know how you define 'wine collector,' but a 'woman' I am."

She then went on to describe her very considerable cellar, chockablock with wines from every nation except maybe Mauritius. "Do I qualify?" she asks, rather unnecessarily I thought. "I know of no other woman like myself," adds York. "I have many wine-collecting friends—all male—and we can talk for hours about wine."

"So how about that?" I asked Dr. Wolkoff. "Talking for hours about wine! Isn't that a sign of collector psychopathology?" The look of scorn was withering. "Psychopathology? You talk for hours yourself, about nothing at all. Talking about wine seems pretty healthy to me," he pontificated.

So then I told him about another letter writer who, because she sounded pretty nice (if a little nuts to me), I shall call Suzanne. An American woman who has been living in France for twenty years, Suzanne wrote to describe herself as a "bona fide woman wine collector." She writes: "I developed an all-consuming desire to know about and taste wines from all over France. This passion has become a costly pastime. My husband is basically supportive. Of course, he should be since I do all the wine buying in the household."

"So what's not to like?" asked Dr. Wolkoff. "Wait!" I cried. "However," continued Suzanne, "there were times when my husband became annoyed when he came home from work to find five to eight cases of wine stacked in the vestibule. 'It's no wonder you say you don't have any money,' he would snap. I then learned to schedule the arrivals so I could sneak the wine down into the cellar without him knowing."

Closing in for the psychopathological kill, I then told him that Suzanne reported that she had between eight thousand and ten thousand bottles in her cellar. "Did you say she was married?" Dr. Wolkoff wistfully inquired. "Yes," I replied, "and hubby sounds like a level-headed sort to me. Come on, you've got to admit that when you start sneaking wines into the cellar, you've got a problem, right?"

I happen to know quite a few fellows who sneak (wine) around their wives. They do this by renting lockers at wine shops. I called the owner of one such shop who admitted that, in all his years of locker-renting to wine-sneaking husbands, he had never once had a wine-sneaking *wife* rent a locker from him. "She sounds exciting," he said.

I pressed Dr. Wolkoff. "Is this or is this not strange behavior?" "Hers, no," he replied. "About you, I'm not so sure. Look," he added, "is she drinking her wine?" I replied that it sounded like she did. "Well then, healthy collecting is based on hedonic pleasure," explained Dr. Wolkoff.

"Unhealthy collecting," he continued, "is when you don't drink it. It's when you keep buying wines only to generate a feeling of control and security. Or there's a narcissistic quality, where you have no self-esteem unless it's connected to an artificially-constructed grandiosity. And what could be better than, say, a collection of big bottles of Chateau Petrus or Chateau Lafite—which you never quite get around to drinking?"

But Suzanne's got eight thousand to ten thousand bottles of wine!" I sputtered. "Do you know how much wine that is? She'll never get around to drinking that much." "So what?" he coolly replied. "There's nothing wrong with that. But," he added reproachfully, "there is something wrong with envy, don't you think?" *(1995)*

OBSERVATIONS

F INE WINES TASTE LIKE THEY come from somewhere. Mediocre wines taste like they could come from anywhere. They are interchangeable. However unscientific this "sensation of somewhereness" may be, you can trust it all the same.

•

PROPONENTS OF BLIND TASTING—where you can't see the label or the price tag—are great believers in human weakness. According to them, a mere glimpse of a label, like that of an ankle in another era, is an irresistible temptation that renders tasters involuntarily bereft of judgment, willpower, and resolution. Seeing the label can allow you to evaluate a wine for what you know it's supposed to be, rather than for what you're guessing it might be.

•

TO DRINK HIS DOM PERIGNON OENOTHÈQUE, Georg [Riedel] served it in Riedel's enormous Sommelier series Burgundy glass. If filled to the brim, it holds 37 ounces. (A standard wine bottle holds 25.3 ounces.) This is a glass so big you could auction its air rights.

But for Champagne? What about the bubbles?

"To hell with the bubbles," Georg replied. "Taste the wine."

He was right. Georg was interested in the profoundly Pinot-Noirish quality, and the big glass emphasized that. This was wine, not just fizz. It was a revelation.

•

ALTHOUGH IT'S NOT OFTEN NOTED, there's an odd confluence between wine lovers and audiophiles. (Somehow, I find the term oenophile unbearably pretentious yet audiophile sounds all right.) Put another way, a lot of wine geeks are also stereo geeks.

What's the common denominator? Probably it's an appetite for what Henry James called "the wear and tear of discrimination." Both wine lovers and audiophiles are into differences.

For more normal sorts, the trick is to have wine lovers and audiophiles as friends. That cuts down considerably on the Jamesian wear and tear, but with no lack of benefits. You can get a steady stream of wine advice without having to be a nutter yourself. There is one downside: Crazies never recommend anything even vaguely familiar. The rule of thumb—this is especially true for stereo equipment and estate-bottled Burgundies—is that if you've heard of it, it isn't any good.

•

BELLA FIGURA, OR THE BEAUTIFUL FORM, gesture, style, is the phrase that sweeps into a neat pile all those small, elegant, and—to Italian eyes—oh-so-meaningful details that make, as the poet Jack Gilbert puts it, "the grand Italy of meanwhile."

Bella figura vitalizes Italian daily life and helps justify the new—or at least the different—in a culture that, for all its seeming effervescence, wrestles almost daily with the weight of centuries, like a ship with a hull so barnacle encrusted that it struggles to make headway. An overtly public change requires an excuse, however flimsy. *La bella figura* serves, in its seemingly superficial fashion, to restore life to the living.

•

THE CHALLENGE OF MAKING WINE TODAY can be summed up in a single word: *originality*. In the same way the digital age has made duplication easy, modern wine technology allows a similar capacity. A winemaker can now easily copy at least the style, if not the substance, of the world's greatest wines.

Although this looks dark on the face of it, the reality is not all bad. The overall quality of ordinary, everyday wines is the better for this "duplication." Everyday wines are now fresher tasting, better defined, and better made than before. In looking to, and copying, their betters, as it were, they have acquired the wine version of social graces.

More expensive wines have suffered, however. Too many ambitiously priced wines now confuse style with substance, reminding one of the 1946 movie *Great Expectations*, where Pip says, "I realized that in becoming a gentleman, I had only succeeded in becoming a snob."

•

IN MY INCREASINGLY DISTANT YOUTH, humanity was divided into two categories: those who rooted for the Mets and those who backed the Yankees. This was in the days, mind you, when the Mets proffered the likes of Ed Kranepool and Marv Throneberry. It was hardly *grand cru* baseball.

The Yankees, of course, represented Success. I was always suspicious of Yankee fans, much in the same way that I wondered about young Republicans. As the conductor Sir John Barbirolli said about the impetuous young cellist Jacqueline du Pré, "If you have no excesses in the full bloom of youth, what will there be to pare away on the long road to maturity?"

I'm still suspicious of the wine equivalent of rooting for the gold-plated Yankees, where my colleagues tell you about yet another $100 Napa Valley Cabernet or extol a first-growth Bordeaux. Are such wines good, even extraordinary? Sure they are. Big deal. Where's the challenge? Where's the heart? It's like rooting for General Electric.

•

AMONG THE MANY TRAUMAS I seem to inflict upon my friends and relations, two are noted more than others. One is "I'd be terrified to cook for you." For the record, I'm easygoing as a guest. But I was a food writer for many years and that, like an unflattering school nickname, dogs you forever.

The other involves wine, of course, for pretty much the same reason. "I can't imagine what I could buy you" is the refrain I always hear.

It has to be noted that there's a practical, rather self-serving side to these laments. By blaming the victim, as it were, they're off the hook. Not only do prospective gift givers save themselves money, but also they feel smugly better about themselves in the process. "Everyone knows that *I'm* easy to buy for, so it's his own fault that he's so impossible."

•

ALTHOUGH I'M ALL FOR THE cheer and generosity of the holiday season, I feel compelled to point out the obvious: Your friends will happily, even gleefully, drink your expensive wines with nary a qualm, let alone a pause. In fact, they consider it a public service, like pushing a stick through a clogged street grate. "Let the wine flow!" they exclaim.

People will pillage your cellar if you let them. There's the famous story of the English wine writer who, while visiting one of the great Bordeaux châteaux, was asked which wine he might like to try during lunch. "Well, I haven't had the 1899," he suggested. The host, who'd met his sort before, said simply, "It's not a luncheon wine, dear boy."

All of which is to suggest that you not get too carried away by holiday expansiveness. You don't want to later suffer wine lover's remorse, which is seeing your lovingly and carefully cellared bottles of special wines, sequestered like prize witnesses in an important trial, slurped down like so much grog.

•

CHAMPAGNE IS NO MORE A "real wine" than President Clinton is a real saxophone player. Both noodle at the game, but their real ambitions profitably lie elsewhere. With Champagne, it's all about big bucks—yours especially. The glossy super-luxury Champagnes selling for between $200 and $600 are meant for those who believe that air pumped into your tires by a liveried footman gives your car a better ride.

•

SAY WHAT YOU LIKE ABOUT wine banter—and yes, too much of it is piffle—one of the pleasures of wine is talking about it. A good wine drunk without comment is like a prayer without an "amen."

•

FORMER SPEAKER OF THE HOUSE Thomas P. "Tip" O'Neill famously (if ungrammatically) said, "All politics is local." Had he squandered his talents on wine writing, O'Neill would surely have observed, "All fine wines are local."

You might call this the "subway truth" of fine wine: Only the local will get you there. The express is a fast ticket to wine nowhere.

Now, a lot of marketing forces seek to convince you otherwise. The idea—the Big Lie, really—is that you can have it all: the quality that comes from artisanal craftsmanship available in unlimited quantity with you-can't-miss-it distribution. Such wines, with their ultra-heavy bottles, lavish amounts of oak and Teflon-smooth textures, trade on the trappings of the real thing, like suburban plywood paneling aping authentic boiserie.

•

WHEN I FIRST BEGAN WRITING about wine several decades ago, no one warned me about a certain professional pitfall: you won't fall in love with a wine quite as easily as you once did.

At the beginning of one's wine journey—and I include all devoted wine drinkers in this, not just pro scribblers—you are subject to what can only be called puppy love. You never forget your first La Tâche. Or your first great German Riesling. Or a revelatory red Bordeaux or California Cabernet. Like Ira Gershwin, you hug yourself with amazed pleasure, wondering how long has this been going on? The answer, of course, is: a helluva lot longer than you.

So, like book or music lovers on similar journeys of delicious discovery, you (literally) drink deeply of civilization. You become ardent about Riesling or Pinot Noir or Cabernet Sauvignon. You declare your undying devotion to a wine or a region, only to promiscuously fawn over yet another site or producer.

Inevitably, your ardor cools. This takes years, decades even. Been there, loved that. It's not so much that you've become a hard (wine) case or even a victim of ennui. Rather, it's the price of experience. This is an occupational hazard, maybe even a life hazard. After all, you can't just keep falling in love—even with wine—at every turn. It takes too much out of you.

•

WINE WRITING THRIVES ON INSECURITY. Take wine scores for example. They're like a bad Borscht Belt act. What's the difference between an eighty-nine and a ninety? So, what's your point? (Rim shot.)

What *is* the difference between an eighty-nine-point wine and a ninety? Obviously nothing. It's like distinguishing between tonight's full moon and last night's fingernail-shaving difference. Is one really less luminous than the other? Nevertheless, the difference between eighty-nine points and ninety points is real in the marketplace. Ninety points is an endorsement, while eighty-nine points feels like equivocation.

•

ALL MY PROFESSIONAL LIFE, I'VE been conflicted—a little ashamed, even—about the obsessive tug of wine loving. Let's be honest: Wine loving lends itself to what might be called single-mindedness.

Something about wine excites not only the usual sins of greed, covetousness, and avarice, but also an elaborate fantasy life about idealized beauty. Wine, like stereo equipment, lends itself to a kind of perfectionism. If this Pinot Noir tastes good from vines yielding two tons to the acre, how much better would it be if a grower pruned the vines for a yield half that size?

So it goes, spiraling merrily into a delightful madness. You become transfixed by the possibilities and, Ahab-like, press on to pursue one or another winegrower's new take on wine perfection.

I must confess that I, too, feel the tidal pull of wine obsession. However, because of my professional camouflage, when I practically fondle the latest wine newsletter or merchant offering, it's research. But when your average wine-fantasizing doctor or stockbroker does it, it's borderline obsessive.

•

BIODYNAMICS IS THE "NEW KOSHER." Unlike actual kosher wines, of which no one suggests taste superiority by virtue of the process, biodynamic wines have attracted an ardent cohort of wine lovers who submit that both the process and the resulting expression are superior. British wine writer Jancis Robinson, for one, says biodynamic wines "seem wilder and more intense."

There's even a rabbinate, of sorts. An organization called Demeter—the American branch of which is based in Philomath, Oregon—promulgates an orthodoxy of biodynamic rules and acts as a private certifying agency.

For this observer, biodynamic processes are a form of discipline, some of which may well actually work, while other practices may be more emotionally and psychologically sustaining to the practitioner than practical to the plant or wine.

What matters is that biodynamic cultivation signals a willingness to pay extreme attention to vines and wines. Like driving a race car, if you take your eyes off the road—or in this case, a highly vulnerable vineyard—an irremediable disaster can result. Ask any farmer: Attentiveness is always a good thing.

Are biodynamic wines actually superior? Here again, causality is hardly clear. What is clear is that biodynamic practitioners, by virtue of their practices, are much more likely to have lower yields in the vineyards (good), more deferential winemaking practices in the winery (good), and will be interested in wines that are anything but conventionally commercial (ditto).

Bottom line: If I see a wine that's proclaimed as biodynamic, my ears (and palate) perk up. If nothing else, I know I'm dealing with a winegrower committed to something that often results in characterful, interesting, and occasionally even profound wines.

•

TODAY'S WINE NEWBIE IS LEFT to believe that there are no great wines, only great producers and vintages. A certain wonderment has been lost, a recognition that however important the winemaker and the vintage, greatness really derives from the land itself.

Vineyards need tending, of course, but in places like Burgundy or the Mosel-Saar-Ruwer, where the same varieties have been cultivated in the same spots without interruption for as long as a millennium, these vineyards are really life-forms, like coral reefs.

Modern rationality and consumerism discourages the kind of awe that these ancient vineyard "creatures" should instill in us. Of course the producer matters. Wines from great vineyards don't create themselves. Yet the reverse, however illogical, is equally true: Winemakers don't really create the wines either. They tease them from the earth and tickle them into life.

Today's wine newbies need something now in short supply: a sense of the marvel of fine wine. If there is no magic of place, tell me: where, then, do great wines come from?

To marvel about fine wine is not to romanticize it, but to grasp its real meaning. Fine wine, like birdsong, is fundamentally wild.

IN LOVE WITH FRANCE—WITH A
COOL EYE ON BORDEAUX

Like so many other wine lovers everywhere in the world, I found myself enthralled by wine, thanks to France. In my case, however, it wasn't just wine. I first saw France by bicycle and was captivated by the beauty of the landscape and the courteous, formal warmth of the French themselves. My wife and I have cycled almost everywhere in France, as well as walked a good portion of its extensive system of trails. We've lived, briefly, in Paris. And we were married in France.

Yes, the French can be overly rigid. And self-glorifying. They can be exasperating. But beneath the brittle shellac of their chauvinism, they are in possession of great truths—none more so than about wine. My affection for, and devotion to, France comes from a deeper need within me than mere wine loving. The closest I have come, so far, to writing about this is revealed in one of the columns to follow, "Forever Francoholic."

In retrospect, the odd thing about my writings about France is that they're usually critical. Conveniently, I blame the French themselves. After all, they taught me. French discourse is almost always captious. France is a nation where the highest form of praise is the grudging (but subtly affectionate) *pas mal*—not bad.

In Defense of France

EVERY WEEK, *WINE SPECTATOR'S* WEB site submits a poll to its readers. Recently it offered this provocative topic: "Does France Matter?"

No stranger to provocation, this one nevertheless rocked me. If it had appeared in the journal *Foreign Affairs*, I could understand. But how could a publication called *Wine Spectator* ask such a question? How could France *not* matter?

When asked the question "Does France have an image problem?" 53 percent of the respondents said yes. Various zingers were duly applied ("arrogance," "declining market share," etc.), but the giveaway was revealed by the follow-up question: "What's the biggest problem with French wine?"

A whacking 51 percent of the respondents pointed to "Price—the good stuff costs a fortune." No other category—such as availability (9 percent), labeling (8 percent), or even quality (15 percent)—came close.

I don't get it. Once you strip away the glossy veneer of France's most famous wines—Bordeaux's classified growths, Burgundy's *grands crus*, Champagne's luxury cuvées—French wines are amazingly well priced.

Today, you can pick up all kinds of swell wines from Languedoc, Rhône, Loire, Alsace, even Burgundy for less than $20 or even $10 a bottle.

If high price is your issue, take the battering ram to California. There's probably no place on the planet today where you get less for your wine buck than you do with California. France is laden with wine bargains compared with California.

Here's the nub: What does it mean to *matter*? The notion centers only on the blockbuster mentality that if you don't have a best-seller or a *Star Wars* generating vast numbers, you're nothing.

But is that true for wine? Let's be blunt: If you're Australian, it's true. The Aussies know how to create wine brands better than anyone else. Blending is the Australian mantra. You want more fruit? No worries, mate. More oak? Ditto. You need it by the tanker load? No problem. Roughly three-quarters of all of Australia's vineyards are controlled by five companies.

No wine country anywhere is *less* concerned about sanctity of place than Australia. Bordeaux alone, in comparison, has some twenty thousand producers.

I mention the Aussies because, at the moment, their wine-marketing model is currently seen as *the* model. Everyone has by now heard of Australia's impressive success in snatching the British market from French suppliers, to say nothing of the American.

But France has something that none of these global gobblers offer: It still sets the standard. No wine country anywhere is *more* concerned about sanctity of place than France. That's what makes French wines great. It's why France matters. To borrow a line from those smirky bumper stickers, "French winemakers do it more originally."

What's more, France *can* beat even the Australian über-blenders at their own game, if they choose.

Take Côtes de Ventoux for example. This one Rhône appellation alone has some 17,500 acres of vines. And its wines can be terrific, especially when some Syrah is mixed in.

Then there's the vast Languedoc region. Quick, take a guess about the vineyard acreage of Languedoc. Try 736,000 acres. That's roughly twice either California's or Australia's wine-grape acreage.

Clearly, France can take on all comers. It's still the unbeaten champ at the high end. No one makes better Pinot Noir, Sauvignon Blanc, Chardonnay, Cabernet Franc, Pinot Blanc, dry Riesling, and yes, Cabernet Sauvignon and Syrah. No country, not even Italy, has more expression of place than France.

So what's keeping France from creating low-priced blockbusters as well as it does high-priced ones? The problem—*quelle surprise*—is complacency. It's nothing new. Jane Kramer (no relation), writing fourteen years ago about the French in her "Letter From Europe" in *The New Yorker*, put it as well as anybody ever has:

> "People here have been so confident for so long, so accustomed to the idea of being sharper, smarter, deeper, more elegant, more eloquent, more discerning, and certainly more civilized than anybody else, that it has made them provincial, listening mainly to each other and in the end whistling in the dark against failure."

Does France matter? You bet it does. But does France know *how* to matter in today's markets? Ah, that's a different question. *(2002)*

BURGUNDY AND ITS ENEMIES

"*NOUS AVONS RENCONTRÉ L'ENNEMI ET IL EST NOUS.*"

That's what the comic strip character Pogo famously said (if he spoke French, anyway): "We have met the enemy and he is us." It's what the Burgundians should be saying right now.

The news from Burgundy is not good. Recently, my colleague Per-Henrik Mansson reported on the annual meeting of the Burgundian trade organization, the Bureau Interprofessionnel des Vins de Bourgogne, which met on July 4. Numerous growers, especially in the southern Burgundy districts of Côte Chalonnaise, Mâconnais, and Beaujolais are facing bankruptcy. The cause is simple to identify: far too much mediocre wine. Yields are too high and quality is correspondingly low.

According to Mansson's report, "angry growers heckled BIVB executives." What did these luminaries say to deserve such treatment? They told their constituency the half-truth.

"Competition is hurting us," said BIVB president Hubert Camus. "We use practices that lack any base in reality and are uselessly heavy. We have fantastic *terroirs*, but have not always worked them properly. Our Californian and Australian competitors came to Burgundy twenty years ago to study our values and standards. They couldn't take our *terroirs*, but they also left behind everything that weighs us down."

Just what it is that weighs down Burgundy's growers is a matter of perspective. But a good start is old-fashioned greed.

Everyone knows that less is more when it comes to Chardonnay and, especially, Pinot Noir. Lower yields translate to higher quality.

But does that elemental truth translate to action? It does not. Burgundy's growers are *encouraged* to stretch their yields until their vines are practically screaming. (In the 1999 vintage, growers in the Côte d'Or were allowed to increase their yields by up to 40 percent over that vintage's already generous annual maximum yield. They knew the fix was in, as it is every year.)

In Beaujolais, over-planting, along with excess yields for their Gamay vines, has been disastrous. This summer, Beaujolais growers had to destroy, distill, or make into vinegar more than 13 million bottles worth of Beaujolais, about 7 percent of their annual production.

But is it their fault? Apparently not, at least according to Maurice Large, president of the Union Interprofessionnelle des Vins du Beaujolais. "More and more, consumers 'zap' from one appellation to another. There's no longer any loyalty. This evolution does not favor quality over quantity."

I get it now. It's not that Beaujolais makes crummy wine in vast quantity. Rather, it's that "Many new wine drinkers are attracted to Australian or Argentine labels because they know no better than to treat wine like Coca-Cola or beer," according to Monsieur Large.

It takes a lot of crust—even by French standards—for the folks who invented and relentlessly marketed Beaujolais Nouveau to blame *us* for treating wine like Coca-Cola.

In fairness, the BIVB has a five-year program in place, calling for lower yields (which call is hardly new and always toothless) and a multi-million dollar advertising campaign involving a new Burgundy logo and simplified labels.

It reminds me of what President Gerald Ford did back in 1974 when inflation was 12 percent a year. He went before the American people and asked them to wear a button emblazoned with "WIN" (Whip Inflation Now).

I'll bet you a bottle of (mediocre) Bourgogne that Burgundy's latest anti-inflation campaign will be just as hapless as Gerald Ford's.

Could it be that, at long last, the moment has arrived when Burgundians will look at themselves and see, à la Pogo, their true enemy? The French government is not their friend. It's their enabler.

Burgundy has no business making vast quantities of wines. Instead, it has a very *good* business making very small quantities of uniquely outstanding wines.

Elitist, you say? Well, who does elitism better or more unashamedly than France? Even at $200 or more a bottle, Burgundy's best wines are bargains, as no one else anywhere can equal them.

Instead, their most expensive wines are the junk with high-priced names that the growers think they're smart to make and that their government (and trade representatives) condone and even encourage.

Don't blame us, *mes chers amis*. We're voting with our feet—and our palates. We buy the best and leave the rest. *(2002)*

MY DEAREST FRANCE . . .

IT'S BEEN A LONG TIME since I've written to you. And I know that you're not happy that I ran off to Italy for all those months. But believe me, I've never stopped thinking about you. Of course, you've been in the news lately, and it's not been pretty—what with all your hand wringing about how the New World is eating your *déjeuner*.

You should know that you have always been my great love. Was my 528-page book on Burgundy anything other than one of the world's longer love letters? And please don't forget all those many cycling and walking trips, sometimes for months at a time. There's almost no part of your lovely octagonal self that I have not traversed.

So why did I run off to Italy? I'll tell you why. You're getting cranky. The world is changing, and far from leading the charge—and the change—you're insisting that everyone else is at fault.

Remember your headline-making tantrum in 2001 via the French Ministry of Agriculture? "Until recent years, wine was with us," you said. "We were the center, the unavoidable reference point. Today, the barbarians are at our gates: Australia, New Zealand, the United States, Chile, Argentina, South Africa."

Sure, the barbarian bit was meant to be ironic. But you don't have to be Sigmund Freud to know that beneath the irony is a seething resentment. It's an old story: *Others* are doing this to you.

Well, it's not so. You've done it to yourself. Take controlled appellations, for example. Back in April, René Renou, president of the Institut National des Appellations d'Origine wine division, announced a plan to overhaul your controlled appellation system for the first time since its creation in the mid-1930s.

Controlled appellations have proliferated like aphids on a rose. The original idea was conservative. Famous names, such as Chambertin and Champagne, were being usurped by fraudulent wines with fake labels. Producers of the originals were going bankrupt, swamped by counterfeits.

But no sooner did your few acknowledged great wine zones get such protection—at a price of heavy regulation and bureaucratization—than every other wine-growing area, no matter how insignificant, clamored for similar status.

So now, most of your winegrowers are constrained, Gulliver-like, by chafing regulations they—and we—hardly need. Does it matter whether a red Burgundy can legally contain Cabernet Sauvignon when its ancient tradition was exclusively Pinot Noir? You bet it does. But do we care about the sanctity of Côteaux du Languedoc? Hardly.

How did you propose to fix this mess? Fewer regulations and more freedom, right? Wrong. Instead, you proposed yet another layer of regulation called an Appellation d'Origine Contrôlée d'Excellence, or AOCE, a kind of parental, "This time we really mean it."

The Italians did this, by the way, with their much-ballyhooed designation of DOCG—*garantita*—to differentiate its holders from the hoi polloi of plain old DOC. It's been worthless. (When was the last time a buyer asked, "Excuse me, but is this bottle of Italian wine a DOCG?")

Then there's your *crise de pocketbook* in Bordeaux. In just three years, prices of everyday Bordeaux wine have plummeted by half.

In late June, the Bordeaux wine authorities announced that, for the 2004 vintage, winegrowers can sell only fifty hectoliters per hectare. This will reduce overall sales by one-third. Mind you, actual production—or rather, over-production—is not being limited, just the sales.

My dearest France, you're an aging beauty, unwilling to look in the mirror. Do you still have what it takes? Of course you do. There's nobody like you.

But the time has come—hell, it's long past due—for you to wake up from a reverie of past glories and recognize that what you really have to sell is quality. Not just proclaimed quality—"This is a *French* wine, monsieur"—but the real thing. The kind not proclaimed by regulation, but earned by sweat. And courage.

Remember, you used to be the world's greatest wine marketer. You invented Beaujolais Nouveau and made it an event. You invented Champagne and made it the wine of celebration. You invented grand châteaus and the concept of *terroir*. You made wine glamorous, exciting, provocative. *You, and you alone, made wine culturally essential.* And you sold all this to the world, not just to yourself.

My dearest France, I love you. You're perfect. Now change. *(2004)*

FOREVER FRANCOHOLIC

HI. MY NAME IS MATT and I'm a Francoholic.

I'm at this meeting because I felt myself slipping again. It began when the *Michelin Guide San Francisco Bay Area & Wine Country 2007* recently appeared. I knew this might cause problems for me, and, well, that's why I'm here.

I think I was born this way. No one else in my family suffers from Francoholism. They are all from Brooklyn; my father was a printer for the *New York Times*. If they suffer from anything, it is terminal New Yorkism. But I was different. I knew this for certain when I first saw the movie *Sabrina*.

Do you remember that movie? Audrey Hepburn played a chauffeur's daughter who lived on a grand Gold Coast estate on Long Island. She mooned over the playboy scion of the family for whom her father worked.

She had been sent away to Paris to a Cordon Bleu–type cooking school. But, of course, she learned more than just how to make a soufflé. She left Long Island a working girl and returned, unrecognizably radiant, attired in the height of Parisian couture chic. I identified with Audrey Hepburn. (What this says about early age gender confusion, I'll leave to those more qualified.)

It was then that I realized I was a Francoholic. France was redemptive. It could transform a chauffeur's daughter (or a printer's son) into something *raffiné*.

Anyway, when I first went to France I'd never felt so at peace. Partly it was the sheer beauty of the French landscape. But mostly it was the appeal of "the form." France is a culture where everything is—or should be—"just so," *soigné, à point.* "The form" is essential, as it is the means to the beauty of perfection.

"The form" involves the right way of doing things. (You may recall in *Sabrina* that she was instructed about the right way to crack an egg.) When something isn't done in the prescribed way, then the result is inevitably lesser—*c'est évident*, as the French would (and do) say: "It's obvious."

As with so much of French beauty, it's all terrifically well thought out and abundantly articulated. This is what makes one a Francoholic. You get addicted to the inarguable logic and the sheer certainty of it all. The French don't just have their particular tastes, but they have reasons for those tastes. Things are "correct," or they're not.

It is this very word *correct*, often used in France, that has made French culture so unreceptive to modernity—especially, but not exclusively, American modernity, which too often conflicts with correct. Much that is modern can seem overly relaxed and insufficiently rigorous. And indeed sometimes, that's so.

Where correct presupposes a right way (and often a single way) of doing things, modern suggests a more easygoing, open-minded—dare I say it?—diverse way of doing things. Which brings me back to those red guidebooks. Michelin, for all its protestations to open-mindedness, is the cop on the "correct" beat.

So when Michelin released its ratings of San Francisco restaurants, I knew they'd get it wrong, just as they do in Italy, where Michelin also completely misses the glorious Italian point. In Italy, correct simply doesn't exist—and few Italians would want it anyway.

Reflective of its originating culture, Michelin is obsessed with "the form." A three-star restaurant in Italy must resemble a three-star in California, which must, in turn, resemble a three-star in France. Equivalency is paramount. There is only one true *c'est évident* way to be, especially, a two- or three-star restaurant. Even the one-star category, which allows a certain laxity in "the form," is still remarkably restrictive.

This is why Michelin missed it so badly in San Francisco. A restaurant guide that cannot see and celebrate the compelling food beauty of, say, a restaurant such as A-16—which takes exquisite, even obsessive, care with the cuisine of Italy's Campania—is blinded by "the form." (Want more proof? In New York, does anyone—other than Michelin—believe that Gramercy Tavern merits only one star?)

What's missing is a certain understanding, a recognition of another legitimacy, with its own needs and expressions, but Michelin is like a man admiring a woman's fashions only when they resemble his own tailoring.

All that's left is the all-important form. And if you conform, you are rewarded. If not, you are dismissed. *C'est évident. (2006)*

⸻

THE FOLLY THAT IS FRANCE

IN THIS MOST POLITICAL OF seasons, it's comforting to know that the politics of other nations can be even nuttier than our own. Proof comes from France, where two recent court decisions out of Paris this month have demonstrated the zealousness of France's insistence on curtailing the promotion of alcohol, which inevitably means wine in this most wine-centric of countries.

In one case, the magnificently named Tribunal de Grande Instance (the French equivalent of a small claims court) ruled that an utterly conventional newspaper article, one that recommended various French Champagnes, could be construed as advertising, and that the newspaper *Le Parisien*, therefore, was in violation of the strictures of the so-called Évin law.

Back in 1991, an increasingly health-obsessed French government passed a law named after its legislative proponent, Claude Évin, banning alcohol advertising on television and at sporting events and severely limiting advertising in print (it also regulated tobacco advertising).

Under the Évin law, wine producers were forbidden to make any claims about quality. Indeed, they couldn't mention anything relating to smell, taste, or color. Just the name, manufacturer, alcohol content, and appellation of origin were allowed. Only in 2005, over the objection of France's then-minister of social affairs, was the law modestly amended to allow "references to the qualitative characteristics of the product." (President Sarkozy says he is in favor of softening the severity of the Évin law, but so far has taken no legislative action.)

This is why, and how, the Paris court on January 9 could declare that a newspaper article recommending wines could be seen, in the words of the court, as "intended to promote sales of alcoholic beverages in exercising a psychological effect on the reader that incited him or her to buy alcohol."

The case was brought to court by the National Association for the Prevention of Alcoholism and Addiction, which actively litigates on behalf of the Évin law. The court awarded damages of 5,000 euros to be paid to the association.

A week later, on January 16, in yet another case initiated by the association, the local court for the Paris region found against the Champagne producer Moët et Chandon and the restaurant group Brasseries Flo (which owns fifteen restaurants, including such famous Parisian establishments as Bofinger, Balzar, La Coupole, and Vaudeville) for their joint promotional campaign for a rosé Champagne using the slogan *"La nuit est rose"* ("The night is pink"), accompanied by a photograph of a bottle of Moët rosé Champagne surrounded by rose petals.

The use of this phrase, the court said, "creates an association of ideas between the consumption of rosé Champagne and seeing 'la vie en rose,' which in everyday usage signifies having a euphoric approach to life."

Demonstrating that it wasn't taken in by subversive subliminal imagery, the court showed its contextual chops by noting that Moët's promotional photo "accentuated by the pink color against a black background that symbolizes the night refers to a party, the effervescent rose petals reinforcing the idea of euphoria."

"It was precisely this sort of symbolic imagery," the court declared, "that the legislature wanted to limit in the interests of public health, allowing instead only the most objective references possible."

In an era of political correctness—usually seen by Europeans as an American affliction—the French have gratifyingly made us seem a model of sensibility. Fueled by a law only a Jacobin could love, two different French courts have managed, in the space of little more than a week, to both trample on freedom of the press and proclaim that in France, of all places, *la vie en rose* is not worth living.

One can only wonder what Edith Piaf would be singing today—and where? *(2008)*

ABOUT THAT COOL EYE . . .

MOST WINE WRITERS ARE ENTHRALLED by Bordeaux. I seem not to have inherited that gene. While there's no disputing that Bordeaux makes some lovely wines, mostly it seems that Bordeaux is really all about money and status. This is because red Bordeaux is overwhelmingly the wine of choice of Big Money Guys on Wall Street—or their equivalents in Europe, Russia, and Asia.

The reasons are simple: By fine-wine standards, the supply is substantial (Burgundy production is minuscule in comparison). Everybody's heard of the most famous Bordeaux châteaux, so you get guaranteed recognition. Also, Bordeaux's top properties are ranked first growth through fifth growth, so you know precisely where you stand. Not least, Bordeaux's best wines are traded worldwide, so there's liquidity and the real possibility of turning a profit.

BORDEAUX MEGA-DOUGH

There's only one wine in the world that really matters: Bordeaux. I can't put it straighter than that. Because it's the truth.

The latest Bordeaux à go-go, the vintage 2000 follies, proves it. They are selling for the highest opening prices in history. First growths, such as Château

Lafite Rothschild, will appear on the retail shelves for nearly $400 a bottle when released.

"I don't believe it," you say. "A Burgundy boy like you saying that Bordeaux is the only wine that really matters? What about *terroir*? What about the sanctity of site?"

Yeah, well, what about it? I'm not going to tell you that Bordeaux has much in the way of *terroir*—and even less of sanctity of site—because I don't believe it does, at least not in the needlepoint fashion of Burgundy, Piedmont, or Germany's Mosel-Saar-Ruwer.

But Bordeaux does something like no other wine: Bordeaux establishes *value*. This is why it is the only wine in the world that really matters.

Bordeaux, you see, is the world's vision and definition of a luxury wine. It demonstrates the power of aristocracy—or at least the aristocratic vision.

Never mind that the overwhelming majority of Bordeaux's vast regional production is perfectly ordinary. Never mind that Bordeaux has real quality competitors elsewhere, such as in California. Unique quality has little to do with it. Except for Sauternes, Bordeaux is no longer uniquely fine. But its image is.

This, by the way, is not lost on Bordeaux's main rival, Napa Valley. Everyone in Napa Valley knows the secret to the fine-wine economics of California Cabernet: Its pricing is pegged to Bordeaux. Even buyers with exclusive fidelity to California Cabernet still assess "value" based upon what Bordeaux costs.

Want proof? Consider this: What happens to Bordeaux if Napa Valley Cabernets plunge in price? Nothing. But what happens to California's Cabernet prices if Bordeaux plunges? You got it.

What's more, this value-setting power is not confined to Cabernet Sauvignon. Rather, it affects almost all luxury wines everywhere. Bordeaux is the wine equivalent of the American dollar in currency markets. There's a potency of image, as well as the genuine strength of world distribution.

This is because Bordeaux is *everyone's* notion of what a luxury wine costs. Sure, one wine fancier or another may prize—and willingly pay more for—a wine such as Romanée-Conti. Or a cult California Cabernet. Or even one of the new cult Bordeaux bottlings from the Right Bank.

But none of these wines set value. Nothing is benchmarked against them. But when Château Lafite Rothschild, or any of its fellow first growths (Latour, Mouton, Margaux, Haut-Brion) command $400 a bottle, the whole wine world recalibrates accordingly. That's because *all* of their customers know about Bordeaux.

This recalibration is all about perceived value. Take Chris Ringland, owner-wine-maker of Australia's cult Shiraz called Three Rivers, for example. He recently upped his world retail price to $300 a bottle after seeing his (previously under-priced) wine skyrocket at wine auctions. Some buyers are now aghast at this new price. But now Ringland can say, "Hey, it's still 100 bucks less than Lafite."

Ditto for every California Cabernet producer. Ditto for every newly high-priced Barolo producer. And for Brunello di Montalcino. And Hermitage. And for newly spendy Spanish wines such as those from the Priorat and Ribera del Duero districts.

What's more, the auction markets will recalibrate, too. Prices for older great Bordeaux vintages will be seen in a new light, too. After all, if the 2000 vintage first growths sell for $400 a bottle, then what happens to the prices of other equally good (or even better) vintages such as 1989, 1990, or 1996 first growths, all of which are currently selling at auction for less? You know the answer: They'll go up in order to keep up.

Former U.S. senator Jacob Javits once defined power as "making them jump." No other wine can make 'em jump the way Bordeaux can. That's power. And the prices for the 2000 vintage demonstrates that however you might keep time on your own private "fine-wine watch"—Pinot Noir time, Shiraz time, Napa Valley time—the market mainspring is still Bordeaux. It's what keeps things ticking.

So next time you hear French bleat about "American hegemony," think again. Because in fine wine, it's really Bordeaux mega-money. *(2001)*

To prove that what seems insupportably expensive today becomes tomorrow's bargain, you need only look at the asking prices of the 2005 Bordeaux when the first offerings appeared, as reported in the following column.

To Splurge or Not to Splurge

A FRIEND CALLED THE OTHER day, practically hyperventilating. "So, whaddya think?" he said. "Should I buy 2005 Bordeaux?"

In case you missed this particular tumult, 2005 vintage red Bordeaux have been universally declared by the big barrel-tasting mandarins as not to be missed. Even by florid and hyperbolic wine writing standards, the gush has been extraordinary—and doubtless sincere.

"I can't remember tasting such fabulously aromatic young Bordeaux before," James Suckling wrote in *Wine Spectator*. Robert M. Parker Jr. in his newsletter, the *Wine Advocate*, headlined his own glowing tasting report "Is 2005 the Perfect Vintage?"

You won't be surprised to learn that Bordeaux fanciers around the world—rich ones, anyway—are snapping up 2005 red Bordeaux futures like ravenous trout at the first hatch. (The 2005s will not actually be released until 2007, at the earliest.)

The most expensive wines, first growths such as Château Lafite Rothschild and Château Margaux, will sell as futures in America for—brace yourself—as much as $700 a bottle. This, mind you, for wineries each producing about 20,000 cases.

If you want to do the envy-inducing math, the opening offer from Châteaux Latour and Margaux to the Bordeaux wine trade last week was 350 euros ($438) a bottle. That's just what's called the first *tranche*, or slice, a kind of test-the-waters approach. Buyers quickly flipped these futures to yet other intermediaries for more than 400 euros ($500). Knowing this, you can be sure that the second tranche will be offered by the château at a higher price.

Now for the math: If a first-growth château sells, let's say, 15,000 cases at $500 a bottle, that's $90 million. *Pas mal*, as the French might say, especially considering that the cost to produce and bottle a first-growth red Bordeaux wine is about $10 a bottle. Who says the French don't believe in the free market?

So what did I say to my futures-hungry friend? The answer is obvious: If you've got the dough, go. This kind of Bordeaux-buying hysteria occurs quite regularly, by the way. It always acquires an intensity of desire that cannot be slaked except in the time-tested, classic way.

Yet everyone wins. The wine producers win, of course. Also the merchants win, as their customers pay them the full price two years in advance of delivery. And the buyers, for their part, get to savor an exquisitely prolonged anticipation between—as T. S. Eliot so memorably put it—"the desire and the spasm." *(2006)*

AN OPEN LETTER TO BORDEAUX LOVERS

DEAR BORDEAUX LOVERS,

Are you folks nuts? (Ahem. Let me start over.) My dear brothers and sisters in wine buying. (That's better.) You're really wacko, aren't you? I can't help it. Try as I might to be a kinder, gentler columnist, it won't work. And today's Bordeaux market proves it.

Have you Bordeaux lovers lost your minds? I walked into a wine shop the other day—this is the truth, the convenient truth—and saw a bottle of Château Calon-Ségur 1995 selling for $90. Ninety dollars! For a ho-hum third growth? Who in his or her right mind pays that kind of money for Calon-Ségur?

Now, don't tell me that I'm not in sync with today's wine prices. I know what it's like to be whipsawed (to say nothing of flayed alive) by Burgundy's *grand cru* pricing and spiraling Barolo prices, among other precious gems.

Yet today's Bordeaux—its wines, its most prestigious growers, and its prices—are more bloated than at any time in living memory.

You don't believe me? Try this on for size. When the Champagne house Louis Roederer recently invited thirty wine producers that Roederer's director, Jean-Claude Rouzaud, personally deemed the greatest in the world, all five first-growth owners were invited to the gala dinner at Tour d'Argent in Paris. A free meal and kiss-kiss acclamation was all right with them

But when the time came for a group photograph, these same first-growth owners who so graciously assented to be fed and smooched balked at being photographed with the others. The others, you see, were commoners. For their Majesties, it was inconceivable that they would be publicly seen in the same place, at the same time, with lesser sorts from Burgundy, Italy, California, Germany, and Australia. Why, people might think that everyone present were *equals*.

A group photograph finally was taken. But their Tumescences absolutely refused to allow their wines to be served at the same dinner with everyone else's wines. "The photo was a social question, so that was easier," said Roederer marketing director François-Xavier d'Halluin. "But getting the Bordelais to have their wines served with the others', that was out of the question."

Can you believe that? Who do they think they are? I'll tell you: They think they're geniuses. Why? Because they've bamboozled wine buyers like no one else in history. Never has Bordeaux seen such a run of lucrative luck. And the ones with the bluest chips rake in the biggest pot.

Think about the numbers for a moment. Each of the five first growths—Châteaux Lafite, Latour, Mouton, Margaux, and Haut-Brion—pocketed about $100 a bottle in the 1995 vintage. (The first tranche, or slice, opened in May 1996 at $56 a bottle. It's typically a toe-in-the-water 10 percent of a château's production. By November they were asking $120 a bottle.)

That's *their* price. Now look at how much wine each of them produces on average: Château Lafite Rothschild (240,000 bottles); Château Latour (408,000 bottles); Château Mouton Rothschild (390,000 bottles); Château Margaux (396,000 bottles); and Château Haut-Brion (192,000 bottles).

Now, let's put fresh batteries in the calculator. At 100 bucks a bottle times, say, 300,000 bottles . . . why, that's $30 million! Now that's not chump change. Well, *they're* not the chumps anyway.

Keep in mind that Bordeaux pricing is almost always lockstep. First growths typically get twice as much as second growths. And they, in turn, get twice as much or more as fifth growths. But everything starts at the top.

Now you can't blame these producers for asking such prices. It's a free market. That's why I addressed this open letter to you Bordeaux lovers and buyers. What's the matter with you? Have you lost your minds? Do you really think that in buying classed-growth Bordeaux you're getting something *exclusive*? There's not a lot of exclusivity to a winery cranking out several hundred thousand bottles a year.

So, to paraphrase Aretha Franklin, who's zoomin' whom? Do you really think that plunking down ridiculous sums of money for classed-growth Bordeaux makes you a wine lover? That it makes you knowledgeable? That it shows the world how *smart* you are?

I'll let you in on a little secret: The folks who really know about wine think you're something, all right. But smart ain't it. *(1998)*

WHAT IT MEANS TO BE BULLISH ON BORDEAUX

MANY YEARS AGO I DISCOVERED something about wine lovers that surprised me. They're sensitive souls.

Long ago, I once described Bordeaux lovers as "wacko." Now, I happen to know some Bordeaux lovers. I don't hang with them, if you know what I mean, but they're all right. Like wine lovers everywhere, Bordeaux lovers are open-handed, generous souls who look for like-minded sorts with whom to crack open their precious bottles. (I'm not their first choice, I know, but they graciously don't mention that.)

Anyway, I once wrote about the lunacies of today's Bordeaux market, what with prices reaching nosebleed levels (as much as $400 a bottle for first growths that annually gush 20,000 cases a year or more). I asked, "You're really wacko, aren't you?"

I was prepared to take on those who are bullish about Bordeaux. I figured they'd fight for Bordeaux's sacred honor, its fine traditions, its venerability, and its worthy track record over centuries. Not a bit of it.

What brought 'em out of the woodwork, I discovered, was characterizing them as "wackos." Bordeaux lovers see themselves as the deepest channel of the mainstream. Whatever they do, by definition, is the essence of common sense.

The reason I was so surprised is that if you call a Burgundy lover "wacko," he or she would grin and say, "Yeah, sure." Ditto for Zinfandel lovers and fanciers of Italian wines. We know we're loony. Is there any other way? (Full disclosure: I wrote a book on Burgundy that was so nutty that it promptly went out of print and now sells for as much as $150 on Amazon.com.)

I met a self-declared Bordeaux lover who insisted—quite strenuously—that the attraction of Burgundy is in direct proportion to its unavailability; i.e., the harder a Burgundy is to locate, the more we lust after it.

"Well, of course," I replied. "Everyone knows that's the real appeal of Burgundy. We love the hunt as much as the critter itself."

"Hah!" he crowed. "I always knew that was the real reason you guys are so nuts."

This seemed self-evident to me, but he took it as a tremendous admission. I didn't bother pointing out that it's really no different with the best California or Italian wines, both of which require the tracking skills and perseverance of a Sioux warrior.

Steeped in this culture, I've always assumed that Bordeaux lovers, too, must know they're wacko in their own way. What else can explain their devotion? They must know that for all the Bordelais's talk about *terroir*, the classed-growth designations (first through fifth) go with the château brand, not with the land, as elsewhere in France.

A word about this business of *crus classés*, or classed growths. The short version is that in 1855, Napoleon III hosted a big Paris Exposition. The Bordeaux Chamber of Commerce was asked for a ranking of their best wines. They bungled the job. Their list, based on historical prices, was deemed fusty by the Paris organizers. The job fell to local Bordeaux wine brokers. They, too, looked at historical prices, but they did a tasting as well.

The Bordeaux *syndicat* of wine brokers came up with sixty estates in Bordeaux's best red wine zone, the Médoc. (They also ranked Sauternes, but separately.) These properties were given orders of merit from first growth through fifth growth, with just four properties at the pinnacle (Châteaux Lafite, Latour, Margaux, and Haut-Brion). Then trailed fourteen second growths, fourteen third growths, ten fourth growths, and eighteen fifth growths.

Somehow, this ranking—which was really only one of many over the centuries—has become Holy Writ. It has not changed, with the singular exception of the elevation of Château Mouton Rothschild in 1973 from its original second-growth status to first growth.

Here's the interesting part: If a classed-growth property wants to expand—and most of them have—it's no problem. Classed growths can purchase any vineyard they want in the same district or commune, regardless of vineyard quality, and voilà. The acquired land automatically becomes a first growth, second growth, whatever.

This "Cinderella effect" doesn't work in reverse, though. If a non-classed-growth estate buys vineyard land from a classed growth, the land reverts to the lowly status of its new owner.

Burgundy, on the other hand, is all about the sanctity of the land, not the brand. A *grand cru* vineyard is *grand cru* no matter who owns it—and no matter how badly made the wine.

Then there are yields. Everyone who loves Pinot Noir knows that low yields are essential. If you get too much over two tons of grapes to the acre (thirty hectoliters per hectare in European terms), you're asking for mediocrity. Some of Burgundy's greatest growers, such as Domaine Leroy, strive for half of that level. (And, yes, the wines are greater for it.)

But try raising the subject of yields with the Bordelais. The great American expert on Bordeaux, Robert Parker Jr. asked in his book *Bordeaux*, "Is it really possible to make great wines today from yields that are six times what they were in 1961 or 1959?" No prizes for guessing the Bordelais response.

Knowing this, I figured that Bordeaux lovers must be as wacko as the rest of us. I was wrong. They see themselves as the soul of sanity. If they pay $250 or $400 a bottle for the latest release of a winery selling 25,000 cases, well, that's mainstream, fella. *(2005)*

WHAT IT REALLY COSTS

ONE OF THE PERNICIOUS ELEMENTS of modern-day wine life is the persistent impression that a cheap wine can't be good. The reason this is so pervasive is that wine producers, like parents of teenagers, are forever harping on how expensive it is to raise good wines. We have no idea, they say, of the costs, cares, perils, and woes they endure. Sound familiar?

Actually, we *do* have an idea of what it costs to grow grapes and make wine. And you'd be surprised how little it is.

François Mauss, a French wine lover who, as president of the Grand Jury Européen, organizes extravagant tastings, knows quite a lot about Bordeaux. On an Internet wine chat board, Mr. Mauss flatly states, "The annual cost of a bottle of top Bordeaux reaches a maximum of 8 euros (about $10)," adding that this "includes the food of the dog of the concierge."

"I have seen the balance sheets of the great châteaux," he further notes. "Employee cost is included in my statement. . . . Annual barrels are included in my statement. Dinner, travel expenses for promotion, hotel expenses are included in my statement. . . . I do not count investment or land value. I just count what cash is needed to pay all direct expenses linked to the production."

Mr. Mauss's opinion sounds about right. My own research on the cost of production for California wines comes out about the same on a bottle basis. And $10 a bottle, mind you, is for creating very great wine such as a first-growth red Bordeaux or a top California Cabernet. Yields for these wines are (or should be) lower than for more modest bottlings. Most wines cost far less to produce, especially when grown in areas where land values are low or yields are high.

All of which is to say that the price of a wine on the shelf, like so many other things we buy, is less about actual production cost and more about marketing, supply and demand, and perceived value.

Winegrowers everywhere know the truth of what Paul Newman said to the prim Joanne Woodward in *The Long, Hot Summer*: "Life's very long and full of salesmanship, Miss Clara. You might buy something yet." *(2006)*

RUNNING AWAY TO ITALY

Although France was my first—and, therefore, most indel-ible—love, in recent years, I've spent more time in Italy. Like so many other Americans, I've found myself captivated by Italy's highly localized food, its enormous and original-tasting array of wines, its dynamism, and, above all, of course, by the Italians themselves. They famously need no introduction.

Happily, I've lived in Italy for extended periods, once for a year in the Piedmont region to research my book on Piedmontese cuisine. Another time was eight months in Venice, which was indeed as magical and privileged a sojourn as you might imagine.

I do have to say that I am glad that my first love was France, because it was the French who taught me, a somewhat oblivious American, how to penetrate a "closed" culture. I mention this because, despite Italy's genuinely accommodating and easygoing demeanor, theirs is a more secretive, even furtive, culture than it appears on the surface.

Although the French would recoil upon hearing this, Italy's is a more subtle culture than France's. French rules (which abound) are right on the surface—and if you misread them, you are immediately corrected and instructed. Italian rules are numerous as well, but they're sub rosa—and you have to figure them out on your own. The Italians never say anything. But they do notice everything.

BEING AN "*ESPERTO*"

I HAVE POINTED MEMORIES OF Rouchet, a rare red Piedmontese wine that's a specialty of the town of Castagnole Monferrato, about forty-five miles east of Turin, if only because of a dinner with friends in a famous Turin restaurant called San Giors, which is located near Turin's vast and fabulous food market. San Giors (Piedmontese dialect for Saint George) is an ancient establishment, with hotel rooms upstairs, that looks like my imaginings of an early 1800s Italian brothel.

No sooner had we sat down than one of our Piedmontese gang announced, in a voice the envy of any Swiss yodeler, that they had with them a true wine *esperto*. And not only that, he went on to say, this fellow was an American *esperto* of, particularly, Piedmontese wines. The waiter goggled at me as if I was an albino rhinoceros. I smiled weakly.

As it happens, I had quickly looked around the restaurant when we had entered, looking for their cache of wines. The only way that you can discover which wines are available in an Italian restaurant is to peruse the shelf where the wines are stored. Sometimes it is an easily seen, obvious location. Sometimes, it is near the chef's ankle next to the oven. Here, it was helpfully in full view.

The restaurant's limited selection of wines happened to include a Rouchet, which, fortunately, I spied. So when the time came to pronounce—an *esperto* does not merely order wine in Italy—I played the Rouchet card. If Mister Ed, the talking horse, had done the ordering, the waiter could not have been more astonished. He immediately commenced upon a discussion of the many fine points of Rouchet. As an *esperto*, I had no choice but to hold up my side, undeterred by the fact that, until then, I previously had tasted only one other Rouchet in my life.

You will be relieved to know that I held up the American side with honor. There really isn't much about Rouchet that distinguishes it from several hundred other red Italian wines. I have a pretty extensive vocabulary of wine-tasting terms, even in Italian, so I was able to hold forth on this with, if not eloquence, then at least the usual obscure wine babble.

It worked. And I was feeling pretty good. I had been publicly exposed as an *esperto*, yet managed to find a wine that none of the natives at the table had ever heard of. I had managed to talk convincingly, if not necessarily grammatically, and at length, with a waiter who, understandably, no more believed in the existence of an American *esperto* of Piedmontese wines than in the tooth fairy.

But no sooner had two bottles of the Rouchet arrived and been tasted, than somebody at the other end of the long table pronounced it unsuitable. As an *esperto*, let alone a foreign one, I was not in a position to call the man a *cretino*, which he was. Granted, I had only tasted one other Rouchet in my life. But we *esperti* know a good Rouchet when we taste one. This one was fine, which is to say that it was clean tasting, well made, and, I thought, appropriately young. (Italians can't drink a wine young enough.) After all, it was from the 1990 vintage. Not only should that have been young enough, but 1990 also was a great year.

But it wasn't young enough. The fellow summoned the waiter and asked—I swear this is true—if the restaurant didn't have something younger. I was boggled. This Rouchet was something of a palate scraper as it was. The waiter assured him that not only did the restaurant have such a wine, but in fact, Signore, it just so happened to be a Barbera of their own making.

Naturally, I was urged to inquire more about the wine. So I asked the waiter if it came from a single vineyard, as opposed to being sluiced from one of Piedmont's many god-awful winegrowers' cooperatives. He beamed and declared that it was. I then inquired where the vineyard was located and was told of a site equivalent to growing grapes in a landfill. What's more, he said proudly, the wine was a 1992. With this, I felt genuine fear.

I was present for the 1992 vintage and can tell you that 1992 was a great vintage for frogs, tadpoles, and anything aquatic. The autumn rains just before and during the harvest were nearly biblical in their vengeance. Piedmont experienced flash floods and power outages. The vineyards looked like rice paddies, at least those on flat ground. The roads were clogged with soil runoff from the hillsides. The average 1992 wine is fairly described as "watery."

So out comes this restaurant's homemade 1992 Barbera. It was mean enough to have been the house wine of Italy's terrorist Red Brigade. Whether out of solidarity, or simple fear, the folks at my end of the table pronounced themselves much more satisfied with the 1990 Rouchet and rather ostentatiously called for another bottle.

However, the fellow at the other end of the table tasted the wine, loudly smacked his lips, and declared that this was more like it. The Piedmontese at his end of the table assented quietly, but without the usual Italian fanfare that accompanies even the flimsiest proclamation. I noticed that several of them, almost in unison, asked for more bottled mineral water.

From A Passion for Piedmont: Italy's Most Glorious Regional Table, *1997.*

<hr>

AGED IN AN ATTIC, ENJOYED AT THE TABLE

ONE OF THE FRUSTRATIONS OF wine writing is the inability to reach out beyond the page and put a glass of wine in the reader's hand. Now, this would be nice for an awful lot of wines. But it's utterly essential—and yet so sorrowfully impossible—for the antique magnificence of the Italian wine called vin santo.

The problem here is one of familiarity—or rather, the lack of it. If I praise a Pinot Noir or a Chardonnay, the usual flavor descriptors suffice to give you at least a notion of the wine, aided by your own mental referencing to Pinot Noirs or Chardonnays you've already had. It's like saying, "I saw the best-looking cocker spaniel the other day." You nod knowingly. We're on the same (doggy) wavelength.

But with some wines, such as vin santo, this is all but impossible. Sure, some wine fanciers are deeply knowing about vin santo (saint wine, or holy wine). But more casual wine drinkers likely never even have heard of it, let alone tasted a glass.

Worse, if they have indeed had one, chances are good that the vin santo they tried was an insipid soulless vin santo cranked out in industrial quantity. The vin santo recommended is the real thing. But before getting to it, allow me to explain just what it is about vin santo—the authentic ones, anyway—that's so compelling.

A specialty of Tuscany—although not exclusively so—vin santo at first glance is not that different from what Italians call a *passito* wine, made from the juice of carefully selected bunches of dried grapes. (France had a similar winemaking tradition called *vin de paille*, or straw wine, as did Germany for their *strohwein*.)

To make vin santo, the grower picks ripe and undamaged grape clusters and places them on straw or plastic mats. The grapes are allowed to dry for several months, shriveling into near-raisins. Because there is so little juice when the near-raisins get pressed, the containers used for vin santo are commensurately small, just 50 liters, or 13 gallons. (The conventional small oak barrel or barrique used by wineries everywhere holds 60 gallons.)

Here's the twist: Vin santo is aged not in a cool cellar like most wines but in the attic of a winery or the grower's house, subjected to the (oxidizing) heat of the summer as well as the cold of winter. And it remains there, untouched in tightly sealed barrels for years, sometimes even decades.

Finally, like opening a time capsule—which, in a way, it is—the bung is prized from the barrel and the winemaker finally gets to taste the vin santo. This is an apprehensive moment, as there's no guarantee that the wine will be good. A bacterial infection could have occurred, making the wine undrinkable. Or the fermentation may never have completed. (It's pretty slow anyway, taking the better part of three years due to the sluggishness of the yeasts in such sugar-rich juice.)

In an age in which near-absolute control extends to every part of the winemaking process, such literally hands-off winemaking is a true act of faith. To do so calls for a sincere reverence for the wisdom of one's forebears, along with an extravagance of time uncommon today.

If all went well, what emerges is an amber-hued wine with an oxidized, i.e., sherry-like, scent. But vin santo is very different from sherry. A good vin santo will deliver scents of nuts, apples, raisins, caramel or toffee, honey, and salty-mineral notes. It can be completely dry or retain an edge of sweetness. The texture can be like table wine or it can be almost viscous. In short, there's no one, definitive vin santo.

But what is easy to establish, effortlessly, is a bad vin santo. It will be thin, fruitless, and somehow lifeless. You won't have a peacock's tail of flavor shadings. It will be dull and you'll wonder (rightly) why anybody bothered. *(2006)*

A FORTUITOUS MISTAKE

"I MADE A MISTAKE," ALDO CONTERNO growled. After a lifetime of winemaking, Mr. Conterno, seventy-five, is not used to making mistakes. Indeed, he has made very few, which explains why he is recognized as one of Barolo's greatest winemakers. His Barolos routinely fetch triple-digit prices and are collected with the same obsessive attention lavished on Bordeaux and Burgundy.

Barolo—made 100 percent from the Nebbiolo grape variety—is universally recognized as Italy's greatest red wine. But it's not an easy grape to make into wine, unlike, say, Cabernet Sauvignon. Nebbiolo is both tannic and acidic, neither of which features is considered desirable in today's drink-now world.

To wrestle with Nebbiolo is a winemaking task like no other. Creating Barolos with the elegance and finesse achieved by Mr. Conterno is as improbable as a smooth ride on a motocross circuit. Yet this is precisely what Mr. Conterno routinely accomplishes. His five different Barolos brim with character, all the while delivering their respective messages as elegantly as a professional courtier.

This helps explain why it was so shocking, during a recent visit to the winery, to hear Mr. Conterno submit that he made a mistake. "It was the 2003 vintage," he explained. "As you know, it was very hot. It was a very difficult vintage."

In the tricky 2003 vintage, where the grapes were often scorched by the excessive heat of the hot summer, Mr. Conterno made a fateful decision.

"I didn't like it after one month," he said. "I thought it didn't have the balance. I was wrong. But we had to declare to the authorities whether we were making Barolo or declassifying it into basic Nebbiolo. My sons said, 'Dad, give the wine some time. You'll see. It's really good.'

"I'm ashamed to say that not only did I disagree with them, but I even suggested that they didn't know what they were doing." Mr. Conterno looked remorseful as he recalled his harsh paternal words.

"Anyway, about a month after we had decided not to make any wine labeled Barolo in 2003 and instead eventually sell all the wine under our Nebbiolo label called Il Favot, one of my sons came to me with a glass of wine in hand. 'Try this,' he said. He didn't tell me what it was. So I tasted it and I said, 'This is very great wine.' And my son said, 'Well, Dad, it's the 2003 Il Favot.'"

As the preceding story explains, the 2003 Il Favot (a Piedmontese dialect word pronounced fah-vuht) is both unique and unprecedented. It contains all of the grapes normally used for the five Barolo bottlings, each of which sells for between $125 and $200 a bottle.

"After I tasted that glass of wine, I realized my mistake," Mr. Conterno said. "Normally, we put the Nebbiolo for Il Favot into small oak barrels. But I refuse to put my Barolo wines into small oak barrels because I personally don't like the taste of oak. So I said to my boys, 'Let's get this wine out of the small barrels and into the big casks like we use for Barolo. Because this wine is really Barolo.'"

So the 2003 Il Favot has no oak influence, which is unusual for that label and most welcome. An exceptionally rich, dense, magnificently structured Nebbiolo, the 2003 Il Favot has a deep blackish garnet color and offers an intense, penetrating perfuminess and a remarkable textural density on the palate.

Although technically a "Langhe Nebbiolo," the 2003 Il Favot is really a very great Barolo. And it will age, as great Barolos do, for upward of twenty years. Poderi Aldo Conterno winery has never made an Il Favot quite like this and very likely never will again.

If this same wine had been labeled Barolo—as it could have been—it would sell for $125 bottle. But because it appears under the Il Favot name, the price is $50. That's hardly cheap, to be sure, but for a "Barolo" of this extraordinary quality with this kind of pedigree, it's a flat-out steal. Any Barolo fan will tell you that you can't get an Aldo Conterno Barolo today for fifty bucks. Except, this once, you can. *(2006)*

A TUSCAN VINEYARD KEEPS IT DECEPTIVELY SIMPLE

MASSA MARITTIMA, ITALY—AN UNWRITTEN CONVENTION among wine scribes is that you write about wines your readers can obtain. This makes sense, of course. There's nothing more frustrating than to read about some wonderful bottle but—oh, by the way—you can't get it. Well, thanks, pal.

Still, occasionally you come across a producer so distinctive, so fundamentally worthy, that this prerequisite of availability is ignored in exchange for the greater good of knowledge for its own sake. Such is the case with the tiny Tuscan producer called Massa Vecchia.

Now, you can get Massa Vecchia wines. They're imported in minuscule quantity. But the reality is that finding Massa Vecchia requires the perseverance and tracking skills of a Sioux warrior.

Finding the Massa Vecchia winery itself is no easier. After winding my way up to the Tuscan hill town of Massa Marittima, only to fail to see any winery direction signs, I spiraled down the other side to the main road and pulled into an old Esso gas station. Neither the cashier nor the station's young barista knew of Massa Vecchia.

But just then a beautiful young blonde woman arrived to pay her bill. Hearing my inquiry, she turned to the cashier, whom she clearly knew, and said, "But of course you know it. It's the winery of Fabrizio Niccolaini and Patrizia Bartolini."

With that, there were smiles all round. But, of course. Fabrizio and Patrizia! "It's right nearby," the cashier said.

Mr. Niccolaini, thirty-eight, happened to be standing outside when I arrived. Massa Vecchia is a Tinkerbelle of a winery, something you feel you can hold in the palm of your hand. The cellar contains an assortment of barrels and small casks, some made of oak and others, called *tini*, crafted from chestnut, which was once Tuscany's preferred wood for casks before the now-universal use of oak, which has a tighter grain and admits less oxygen through its denser wood staves.

Mr. Niccolaini's wine vision is, if not unique, then original and of another era. His vineyard, which he inherited from his father and grandfather, is just 8.6 acres. And within that tiny plot are such white grapes as Vermentino, Ansonica, Sauvignon Blanc, Trebbiano, and Malvasia di Candia, and red varieties such as Merlot, Cabernet Sauvignon, Aleatico, Sangiovese, Alicante, and Malvasia Nera. All are at least thirty-five years old, including the Cabernet and Merlot, which is unusual as these two varieties are generally only newly planted in Tuscany. He has also recently planted another vineyard with only Sangiovese.

Mr. Niccolaini subscribes to the deceptively simple sustainable agriculture theories of the Japanese farmer-philosopher Masanobu Fukuoka, detailed in his 1975 book, *The One-Straw Revolution*. "We use no chemicals, no herbicides, really not even much in the way of machines," Mr. Niccolaini said.

What little plowing is done, usually to "rip" the soil between the vine rows to turn over the crop cover, is performed by one of two white, longhorn oxen kept by Mr. Niccolaini for this purpose. "We'll be selling them soon," he said with regret. "They're getting too old. We need to get younger oxen to replace them."

The wines are as original and uncompromising as everything else about this exercise in puristic winegrowing. For example, Mr. Niccolaini's dry white wine, now simply called Bianco (it was previously called Arriento), is 60 percent vermentino with a balance of roughly 10 percent each of Sauvignon Blanc, Malvasia di Candia, Ansonica, and Trebbiano. He ferments this white wine with the skins, which is conventional for red wines but almost unknown for whites.

"The grapes are pressed by foot twice a day for five days," he explained. "Then the wine spends three weeks on the skins, with a daily punch down." Aged in small chestnut casks, the resulting dry white wine is nothing short of thrilling, with a surprisingly bright gold color and a powerful scent of wild herbs and just the slightest astringency (from the skins) in the finish. It's like no other white wine from anywhere.

And so it goes, wine after wine. Not least is a vin santo with the texture and color of the world's most luscious motor oil, so dense and unctuous is this sweet, honey-hued dessert wine. Made entirely from Sangiovese, Massa Vecchia's vin santo rivals Tuscany's universally acknowledged greatest vin santo, the one made by Avignonesi.

For Mr. Niccolaini, simplicity and deference is everything. "Wine is not something separate from the earth, from the planet, or from us. When you cultivate vineyards with care and you make wine in a way that allows everything to come through, then it's enough, don't you think?" *(2006)*

THE WORLD'S BEST LAGREIN. NOW, WHAT EXACTLY IS LAGREIN?

TRAMIN, ITALY—A SMALL, PICTURESQUE TYROLEAN village just south of the city of Bolzano, the village of Tramin is not counted among the world's great wine destinations. Yet if you're on the hunt for great Lagrein, then eventually you'll find your way to Tramin, specifically to the winery of J. Hofstätter. Because this winery, now run by Martin Foradori Hofstätter, thirty-six, makes what is arguably the world's finest Lagrein.

Even Mr. Hofstätter laughs amiably at the phrase "world's finest Lagrein." "I mean, how much Lagrein is there?" he asked. "And how many people have heard of it?" The answers are: not much and almost no one.

Lagrein is a red grape variety indigenous to Italy's Alto Adige/Südtirol region, which borders the Austrian Alps and has been the scene of considerable political and cultural conflict. German is the native and much-preferred language in the zone, even though everyone now also speaks Italian, which is a school requirement starting in the first grade.

Everything, including the official name of the region, is Solomonically divided into two languages. This was partly the price, and consequence, of a carefully crafted peace between the Italian state and the decidedly Austro-centric South Tyroleans.

The area was a geopolitical football, originally part of the Austro-Hungarian Empire, which was ceded to Italy after World War I. Subsequently seized by Germany during World War II, it was returned to Italy at the end of the war. The ensuing cultural and political friction was so intense, involving decades of separatist violence, that Italy, in what might be called subversive accommodation, granted the region extensive political autonomy, as well as offered massive economic aid as an incentive to peaceful acceptance. It worked. A recent newspaper poll showed that 54 percent of the population would not wish the zone to return to Austria even if it were possible.

Lagrein, for its part, is not a matter of local dispute. The only question is whether and how to plant more. One of Mr. Hofstätter's colleagues, Christian Werth, forty-five, oversees what might be called the epicenter of the Lagrein culture, the Benedictine monastery called Klosterkellerei Muri-Gries.

Within the walls of this venerable monastery now surrounded by the urban bustle of Bolzano, Mr. Werth has identified dozens of clones or strains of Lagrein in the monastery's vineyard. The grape, for all its heritage in the area, is still in surprisingly small supply. He said that in 1990 there were 618 acres of Lagrein, while today there are no more than 840 acres.

This is surprising because Lagrein is one of the world's most inviting red wines. A deep, almost opaque blackish garnet, Lagrein is a rich red that delivers intense, inviting scents of blackberries and blueberries along with hints of nutmeg, anise, and violets. Often there's a distinct minerality thanks to the limestone soils commonly found in Alto Adige/Südtirol.

What's more, despite its formidable appearance, Lagrein is almost shockingly smooth down the gullet as the variety is not especially tannic. Also, it has a bright acidity that allows it to pair beautifully with meats of all kinds, as well as game.

Mr. Hofstätter, for his part, is doing all he can to bring Lagrein to world attention. He does this by making an extraordinarily rich single-vineyard Lagrein from his Steinraffler vineyard ($45), as well as a fine Lagrein without a vineyard designation ($25).

But it's the Steinraffler vineyard bottling, with its basso profundo opulence, that can seduce palates to the beauty of Lagrein. Aged in small French oak barrels, the vanilla scent of new oak marries nicely with Lagrein's blackberry scent. Think of a fruit cobbler with a pastry crust endowed with the tiny seeds of a vanilla bean and you won't be far off.

A tasting of multiple vintages of this exceptionally rich, dense, dimensional red makes one wonder why Mr. Hofstätter, and others, don't produce yet more of such beauty. "It's because it's insanely expensive to buy land here in Alto Adige," he said with unconcealed exasperation.

As we looked out over the narrow valley from a high-elevation vineyard perch, Mr. Hofstätter pointed to several large processing plants scattered about the valley floor. "You see those big buildings there? They're apple processing cooperatives. The co-ops control everything here in this region. They get huge subsidies, which means that the apple and grape growers are living in a kind of economic fairy tale that has no real connection to the real marketplace."

With this, Mr. Hofstätter hopped on what was clearly a favorite hobbyhorse about the economic inequities of subsidized agriculture. "I bought a one-hectare [2½ acres] vineyard last year. You know what it cost me?" he asked, his voice rising. "350,000 euros." That works out to about $176,000 an acre, which is about what a choice parcel in Napa Valley might ask. "Yet the wine from that vineyard sells for less than $10 a bottle from the cooperative. It makes no sense," he said, almost shouting in frustration.

Still, Mr. Hofstätter perseveres. "I love Lagrein. I think it's a fabulous red wine. And I'd like to make even more of it, if I can find the right vineyards."

This is an opinion echoed by others in the area, such as Mr. Werth of Klosterkellerei Muri-Gries, whose own "Abtei Muri Vineyard" (abbey walls) Lagrein is one of the benchmarks of the zone.

According to Mr. Werth, Lagrein is still embryonic. "We need more Lagrein vineyards," he said. "And we need yet more investigation about the right clones. It's amazing that, for such an old variety, how very new Lagrein really is around here." *(2006)*

ON THE WATERFRONT, FRESH FISH
AND GREAT WINE

VENICE, ITALY—AT FIFTY-FOUR, CESARE BENELLI is a handsome, solidly built man with a full head of white curling hair who exudes an animated warmth. A chef by trade and a former amateur boxer, Mr. Benelli is a martyr to a cause that other, more cynical sorts in this most touristed of cities likely consider a folly.

As the chef-owner of a forty-seat restaurant called Al Covo (the lair), Mr. Benelli has a cause that is hairshirt-simple: serving the freshest fish imaginable with deference to Venetian tradition, accompanied by some of Italy's (and France's) greatest wines chosen with no deference at all to conventional taste.

Elsewhere—which is to say on terra firma, as the Venetians refer to the mainland—Mr. Benelli's efforts would be easier and certainly less expensive. Everything in Venice seems doled out a tablespoon at a time, from the hotel laundry bags tossed one by one onto waiting boats to cases of wine wheeled on hand trucks through the side streets, like bread crumbs carried off by ants.

Tourists consequently pay some of Europe's highest hotel prices and withstand some pretty steep restaurant tabs, especially given the you-won't-be-back insouciance about quality. Venetians themselves pay significantly less, as the locals typically get a *sconto*, or discount, in restaurants that can be as much as a third to half off.

Mr. Benelli is a man in perpetual high gear. "It's getting so much harder to find really fresh fish," he said, somewhat unconvincingly, as his guest mentions Venice's famous fish market near the Rialto bridge. "Oh sure, we have plenty of fish here in Venice," he said affably. "But where does it come from? Norway. Spain. Fish farms. Those fish come from anywhere and everywhere but here."

Since fish is the soul of both Venice's and Mr. Benelli's cooking, the primacy and freshness of the raw material—which is served raw or crudo at Al Covo in the case of scampi and scallops—are his obsession. "People don't believe what it costs to get the kind of quality I look for," he said. "So now what I do is post my invoices from my suppliers right here in the restaurant. You can see what I pay and, more importantly, where the fish comes from."

With that, he hustled over to the invoice shrine, which indeed prominently holds a sheaf of bills to show a visitor the price—or rather, prices—of his integrity.

"Look at this," he said. "See where it says *Pescato* in parentheses? That means it was caught by a fisherman in the wild. That it's not *Allevamento*, or farmed."

With that out of the way, the talk turned to wine. Mr. Benelli loves wine and, like his fish, he chooses it with curatorial care. "I learned about wines in America, not Italy. I worked as a food-and-beverage manager at a Hyatt hotel in Austin, Texas, from 1979 to 1985. So I got to taste all sorts of wines. Really, it was a terrific education."

It was there Mr. Benelli met his Texas-born wife, Diane, who makes the desserts at Al Covo and greets guests in Texas-accented English and rapid-fire Italian. ("She even has a Venetian accent," one local admiringly commented upon hearing Ms. Benelli's Italian.)

"After I started Al Covo in 1987, I took a sommelier course here in Italy, eventually getting a certificate after passing the professional-level course. Whether that's really worth anything . . ." He shrugged, leaving the matter hanging in the air. "It was during that time that I developed my own point of view."

Mr. Benelli's "own point of view" on wine is consonant with his feelings about fish. "I try to choose wines that represent their *terroirs* in the most profound way possible. I don't care about whether producers use oak or not. But I do care about whether they use indigenous wild yeasts rather than cultured yeasts. I do care about whether they add enzymes during the fermentation, use concentrators, or reverse osmosis, or any other form of artificial concentration."

According to Mr. Benelli, at least 80 percent of all the wines in Italy use some kind of technique to concentrate wine. "Wines are getting too heavy, too rich," he said. "You drink a glass, but you don't want any more than that. There's too much alcohol, too much extract in many of today's wines."

Mr. Benelli's wine list, which changes weekly, has 192 wines, a number of which are annotated with a heart symbol signaling "wines that, in our judgment, we appreciate for their uniqueness."

"Those are the wines I really love," Mr. Benelli explained. "They're really unusual wines, which, I have to say, may not be to the conventional taste."

Among them are Jacque Selosse Brut Initial Champagne ("Not everybody's idea of French Champagne, but extraordinary"); Josko Gravner Ribolla Gialla and his blend called Breg ("Gravner is a genius. The wines can be shocking even, but I love them."); and Recioto di Gambellara from La Bianacara, a sweet dessert wine made from dried Garganega grapes grown in the Soave district.

Almost everything on the list, it should be noted, is exceptionally well priced and, by Venetian standards, downright cheap.

"I choose wines that are not 'perfect,'" he said. "Often, they're not very well known, which is great because that way the prices are lower, as we're not paying for marketing. And I like to offer indigenous wines that my customers won't usually see. Americans really like that," he added. "You guys are great students of wine. Not like my Italian customers," he said with a grin, rolling his eyes. "They don't know anything." *(2006)*

Cesare Benelli and his wife, Diane, are still pursuing their implacably purist dream in Venice, where Al Covo remains one of that city's—and the world's, for that matter—finest restaurants.

RARE TREAT

WHEN WINE DRINKERS GATHER 'ROUND the campfire to tell tales of their greatest wine triumphs, they talk about the rare and the precious. Sagas abound about 1947 Cheval-Blanc. Or you get stories about double magnums of Château Lafite Rothschild bought directly from the estate. And there's always a raconteur holding forth about Romanée-Conti.

But when my turn comes, I tell them that the rarest wine I ever drank was filtered through a sock.

Since it's summer, and since the wine in question is the single greatest summer wine I know, it seems a good time to tell the tale again. So gather 'round the, er, air conditioner and let me tell you the true story of the rarest wine I ever drank.

Now, it's true that in my line of work, I've guzzled a fair share of the world's most precious wines. Why, only a few months ago, I was at a tasting of a dozen or so 1945 red Burgundies, including, yes, a 1945 Romanée-Conti. (It was all right, but not as great as you might imagine. Such old wines rarely live up to one's fantasies.)

Still, the rarest wine I ever drank remains the one filtered through a sock. It was a Moscato d'Asti.

Nobody thinks about Moscato d'Asti as a rare wine, for good reason. It isn't. Made entirely from the Moscato Bianco grape grown on the very steep, chalky-clay hillsides in northwest Italy's Piedmont region, Moscato d'Asti has a delicacy, an ethereal quality, that almost no other wine can rival. Not least, it's extraordinarily low in alcohol, with less than 6 percent alcohol. (A Chardonnay, in comparison, typically clocks in at 14 percent.)

When I was living in the Piedmont region researching a book, I felt duty-bound to become expert in Moscato d'Asti. (It's the sort of rugged challenge we wine writers take on.)

I knew, of course, about its big-name brother, the world-famous Asti Spumante, which is produced in industrial quantities by big wineries. It, too, is 100 percent Moscato Bianco, but even the best Asti Spumante gives only a hint of what the far more artisanal Moscato d'Asti can achieve.

What's the difference? Essentially, it's that between a workhorse and a racehorse. Moscato d'Asti is the thoroughbred, thanks to the way it's made and its vineyard lineage. It's what the growers make for themselves. Production is small. The wine is what the Italians call *frizzante*, which means, "lightly bubbling." A grower could make such a wine in his home cellar. A fully foaming (*spumante*) Moscato, however, requires expensive, special vats that only big wineries can afford.

Because it was so artisanal and localized, Moscato d'Asti was only rarely commercialized. A grower made it for himself, his family and friends, and a few private customers. It was—and is—the ideal conclusion to one of Piedmont's heroic dinners, with their six successive plates of antipasti, two pasta courses, and then a meat course. By the end of such a siege, you had no room left for anything but a refreshing glass of light Moscato accompanied by the delightful cornmeal cookies called *krumiri*.

So there I was, trying to become expert in Moscato d'Asti. I sniffed, I tasted, I swirled—but I never spit. What the hell, it's only 6 percent alcohol. I was getting a pretty good notion of who the best producers are. More about them in a moment.

I was feeling pretty good about my efforts until I mentioned them to Barolo producer Aldo Conterno. He likes Moscato, too, but he doesn't make any himself. Aldo sees it as his life's work to instruct me on any number of important matters, such as why "America is the greatest country in the world" (he served in the U.S. Army), among other issues.

"Moscato?" said Aldo contemptuously. "Why you've never tasted the real Moscato. You have to taste Signora Gemma Chionetti's homemade Moscato. That's the real thing. She puts it through a sock."

When I heard that, I was quivering like a springer spaniel on the scent. I had read about how traditional Moscato was made by filtering the wine through a sock. But I never thought that even in Piedmont, a pretty hidebound place, anybody was still doing it.

You see, the way Moscato is made *frizzante*, or lightly bubbling, is by bottling the very young wine while it's still fermenting. But you don't want all the yeasts in the bottle, as it will then explode from the pressure of too much carbon dioxide. (When yeasts feed on the sugar in the grape juice, they create alcohol and carbon dioxide. Put this process in an airtight bottle or tank and, voilà! you've got sparkling wine.)

So the old-timers used to filter the still fermenting wine through a series of hemp tubes or socks. This would remove any dead yeast cells, as well as most of the living, still-engaged-in-fermenting ones. A rough filtration, it was performed multiple times until the wine emerged reasonably clear. Then it was bottled.

To say that this was an inexact science hardly captures the rough and ready quality of the procedure. As a result, part—sometimes all—of a year's production would explode in the cellar. Too many live yeasts made it through the sock and continued fermenting inside the corked bottle, creating more pressure than the bottle could withstand.

A month or two later, you'd hear a shockingly loud explosion in the cellar and find a fragrant mess with glass shards everywhere. And heaven help you if you're in the cellar when a bottle explodes. You can be seriously injured. (In the old days, cellar workers in big wineries making sparkling wines wore stiff leather chest protectors and fencing masks.)

But things weren't always so predictable. Cellars would be so cold in the winter that yeasts went dormant. But once summer arrived, cellars warmed up and the dormant yeasts would resume feeding and multiplying inside the bottle. And then, boom! (Today, filtration is exact. You can remove every yeast cell.)

Now you know why I was so surprised—and excited—to hear that Signora Gemma Chionetti made a Moscato the old way. (Her husband, Quinto Chionetti, is famous for his red Dolcetto wine.) I pleaded with Aldo Conterno to ask Signora Chionetti to let me taste her filtered-through-a-sock Moscato. She assented.

"Oh, I make maybe 120 bottles a year for ourselves and our friends," she said when I visited her. By the time I got there, it was summer and she was down to her last dozen bottles. "At least I think that's how many I've got," she laughed. "I haven't been down to the cellar to see if anything has broken."

She returned with three bottles carefully held upright so as not to disturb the heavy sediment from the dead yeasts that had made the wine bubbly in the bottle. "You don't want to shake it too much," she said. She was not smiling when she said that.

She pulled the cork, and the wine that emerged was glorious. It was similar to today's best Moscato d'Asti bottlings in its freshness, vibrancy, and incisive, delineated flavors.

But there was one big difference: texture. Her Moscato was thick on the tongue, denser than any other I'd tasted before or since. It was the most dramatic demonstration of the effects of filtering—or rather, non-filtering—that I've experienced. The glycerine richness of that texture is absent in today's necessarily more finely filtered renditions.

She offered me two bottles to take home that evening. "How far away do you live?" she inquired. "Not far," I replied, "maybe thirty minutes away." "Then it's okay," she said. "The bottles should make it there safely. Because once they warm up, well, you never know. Anyway, you'd better drink them fast."

I made it home in record time and gingerly cradled the two bottles to the refrigerator as if they were gelignite. They didn't explode in the night. Figuring that such luck wouldn't hold forever, my wife and I greedily polished off both bottles the next day. To this day, it is the rarest wine I've ever drunk. *(2005)*

CALIFORNIA DREAMING

No one involved with wine today anywhere in the world can escape the gravitational pull of California—its wines, its culture, its freely spent wealth, and, above all, its remarkably innocent joyousness.

It was California, remember, that inspired a (younger) generation of European winegrowers to share their professional lives with each other. Their fathers, in contrast, largely kept to themselves, afraid that their neighbor would somehow "steal" their hard-won winemaking knowledge. California showed a younger generation of European winegrowers the professional advantages and personal pleasures of openness. They returned home saying, "Why not us?"

For wine writers, this same openness offered generous inclusion in not just endless tastings, but also in having the curtain pulled back on the winemaking process itself. Such a behind-the-scenes experience was unavailable in Europe, where a class divide, if nothing else, kept you tied to the estate owner or general manager (or sales director) rather than to the actual hands-on winemaker or vineyard manager. It's different today—thanks to California.

For someone who's spent more than three decades professionally observing California's wine transformation, the changes in wine fashions (remember "food wines"?), aesthetics, technology, and, not least, California's very wine vocabulary, have been nothing less than tumultuous. It's still ongoing, but now more at a simmer than at the rolling boil it once was.

ENGAGEMENT WITH THE FUTURE

"I was talking about music with a friend of my teenage daughter. I asked, 'Can you play the piano?' She replied, 'I don't know. I've never tried.' It was then that I realized what it meant to be an American."
—Michel Salgues, Founding Winemaker, Roederer Estate

TO THOSE FAMILIAR WITH CALIFORNIA today, it seems inevitable that California would be a winegrowing state. After all, it is so Mediterranean: its coastal hills are so contoured, sunlit, so amenable to cultivation of all kinds. Yet wine was not inevitable, at least not fine wine.

It is important to underscore this distinction between mere "wine" and "fine wine." They are kin, but not twins. Virtually any temperate zone can create some sort of wine. It needn't even be from grapes. But the leap to "fine wine" is something else again. At that moment, the ambition becomes more than agrarian. It becomes more than just preserving and reducing a bulky fruit. Not least, it becomes more than a vehicle for intoxication.

Fine wine is a different ambition. It is a refinement, an amalgam of urban and rural. Fine wine is to fruit what the refined English country house is to rural living: a hybridization of studied pleasure with raw nature. As in the English countryside, this does not come about casually. It is the result of economic, cultural, and social forces.

Although it rarely is discussed, one of the underlying elements in the creation of fine wine is an engagement with the future. This phrase, "engagement with the future," refers to several ingredients. Foremost among them is money. Fine wine is capital-intensive. Grapevines require four years before they bear fruit. Tanks, barrels, filters, presses, and bottling lines all chew up capital. Many wines require at least two years of aging in tank, barrel, or bottle before being released. Then there are labor costs. Vineyards are labor-intensive: planting, pruning, spraying, and harvesting. In the cellar, there's the actual winemaking; the transfer of wines from vat to barrel to bottle. Clearly, an "engagement with the future" requires a belief that there will be a return on one's investment. With fine wine comes a magnification: you need more and better.

But this engagement is more than monetary. The political and cultural climates must be conducive. There must be a sense of political stability. And there must be a cultural sensibility that fine wine is a socially endorsed pursuit. This is not just a matter of wine being fashionable, but actually important. Fine wine must be seen as being an expression of civilization. It has to be a vehicle of local pride.

When these elements of finance, politics, and culture coalesce, you will discover a blossoming of fine wines. When just one of these same ingredients is absent, fine wine is suffocated. The examples are numerous. From the Middle Ages to the present, France has issued an unrivaled array of fine wines. It also has been a nation of considerable and continuing wealth that has functioned, for the most part, with a sense of stability since at least the 1400s. Not least, it shares a common cultural vision of the importance of fine wine as a national cultural aesthetic.

The importance of stability can be seen in the ancient fine wine tradition of Germany. Until about 1870, Germany was in a state of almost constant political flux. Politically, it could not be described as stable. But it was for wine. The reason was the presence of the powerful and rich Benedictine and Cistercian orders in the Mosel-Saar-Ruwer and the Rheingau. Their enduring presence meant that an engagement with the future could be made. The monastic example also spurred the ambitions of the local nobility for their own vineyards, thereby furthering the social and cultural prestige of fine wine.

In comparison, Italy has seen the quality—and the public estimation—of its wines vary dramatically over the same period. As a nation, it lacked the widespread wealth of France; cultural unification; monastic presence; or even a national government until the Risorgimento in the 1860s. Even then, Italy remained a collection of isolated regions with little sense of national pride until the mid-twentieth century. What sort of engagement in the future could evolve out of such a circumstance? Who would risk capital on such instability?

California's first such engagement with the future appeared in the 1870s. Not only had a wine industry become widespread, but an ambition for fine wine was revealed. Witness the creation of the Vina Ranch by railroad baron, California governor, and United States senator, Leland Stanford. After traveling to France in 1880, Stanford returned to California fired with the fine-wine ambition. The following year, he began buying land along the Sacramento River between the towns of Red Bluff and Chico, an area in central northern California that once had a minor wine-growing history. Today, it is confined to crops such as rice and olives.

Stanford announced that he would create wines that would rival the best of France; planted more than 1,000 irrigated acres in one year; imported French vineyard workers; built a brandy distillery; and by 1885, had amassed a whopping 55,000 acres of pasture and farmland. By 1887, Stanford's Vina Ranch had 3,575 acres of vines and a wine cellar with a two million gallon capacity. As if this were not enough, in 1888, Stanford built yet another winery to handle the grapes grown farther south on his ranch in Palo Alto, the site of which is today Stanford University. (I am indebted to Thomas Pinney's superb book *A History of Wine in America From the Beginnings to Prohibition* for these details.)

Yet where is the Vina Ranch and the residue of Stanford's ambition today? Gone. It dwindled upon his death in 1893 and then was swallowed utterly with the advent of Prohibition. Vina Ranch became part of the endowment of Stanford University, along with the Palo Alto vineyard. (Ironically, Stanford University's first president was an ardent prohibitionist.) Its final harvest was in 1915, after which the vines were uprooted. By that date, already two-thirds of the forty-eight states were "dry." Four years later national Prohibition would be enacted by amending the Constitution of the United States. The political stability, upon which this nation has long prided itself, actually was absent for wine.

Nor was Stanford's undertaking unique. Instead, it was emblematic. Apart from knowing that they existed, what do we retain of such ambitions as the two-thousand-acre Fountain Grove winery near Santa Rosa? Or the two-thousand-acre St. George Vineyard in Fresno? Or the sixteen-hundred-acre Natoma Vineyard near Sacramento? The list of smaller, but still significant, wineries that disappeared numbers in the hundreds. Although a few winery names from this first "civilization" remain, such as Schramsberg, Gundlach-Bundschu, and Inglenook, they scarcely represent a continuity. Nearly all are either revivals of something previously defunct (such as Schramsberg) or are wineries that soldiered on by selling the grapes or bulk wines demanded by the market.

Stanford's Vina Ranch is worth noting because the very obscurity today of so high flown an ambition reveals the degree of loss of California's original fine wine culture. The loss represents more than just a passing amnesia. It does not figure in our collective cultural memory today because we have no authentic linkage to the original ambition, except for a few shards of documentary evidence. When the fine wine ambition was revived in the late 1960s and early 1970s, it had no memory of prior efforts. There were only scraps of evidence of the ambition, as the few wine-growers who survived Prohibition of necessity were devoted or resigned to making bulk wines. The exceptions that existed by way of wines or men were too few to reconstitute a real memory, let alone a tradition. After all, the fine wine ambition had only just been forming before the prohibitionist campaign gained momentum in the early 1900s.

Nevertheless, starting in the late 1960s (1968 marks the first year when table wine production exceeded dessert wines) and continuing to this day, all of the ingredients coalesced in California for an "engagement with the future." The state's economy boomed, creating widespread wealth. The local population increased dramatically, making California virtually a nation unto itself. Politically, the memory of Prohibition faded. An individual California culture emerged, which valued and celebrated fine wine as a statement of civilization and refinement. All of the ingredients were present: capital, politics, and culture. California erupted with wineries: In 1966, California had 227 wineries, mostly concentrating on bulk wines. By 1989, California counted 771 wineries, most of which pursue fine wines.

California wine historians have labored mightily to establish a record of wine-growing in California. But their work is closer to archeology than history. The telling point is the absence of tradition. The *effect* of California's original fine wine ambition is as lost to us today as the Etruscans are to modern-day Tuscans. We, like them, have various remains from which we can extrapolate—and identify with—but as in post-Etruscan Tuscany, the modern culture has been built entirely from scratch. We know that others passed this way before, but the path—if discernible at all—leads nowhere.

But this lack of tradition extends beyond the trauma of Prohibition. An absence of another sort of tradition also preceded it. Unlike the fine-wine regions of Europe, California never experienced what might be called true primitivism. This phrase is deliberately chosen. With respect to wine, *true primitivism* means "a fixity on the land, an anchoring to place." Nearly all of the great wine districts of Europe came into being as a result of generations of vine-tenders being anchored to their spot, unable to relocate due to economic, political, or social reasons. However unpromising their spot of earth, they had to make it work. There was no choice. If, as in southern Italy, only grapes could grow in dry, sun-drenched, and otherwise barren spots, then grapes would be planted. If the wine was good, all the better. If not, what was the alternative?

It is this true primitivism, this adhesion to a place, however unpromising, that accounts for the creation of wines such as Côte-Rôtie in France's Rhône Valley and Bernkastel in Germany's Mosel Valley. There, the hillsides are so steep that no farmer who had any choice in the matter would consider cultivating such sites. As it happens, they turned out to be supreme on the planet for their wine types. But that was just happenstance. It was all the local farmers had to work with, so they tried to make it work.

Yet California winegrowing never was as primitive as European. This was not necessarily for the better. If a piece of land looked the least bit unpromising for grape growing, the California winegrower either moved on or moved in grapes grown somewhere else. The scale of the land, and the ability to move at will, meant that almost no one chose difficult vineyard locations. And when such sites were chosen, almost invariably you could find a madman or a visionary behind the search. Anyone who has visited Chalone Vineyard perched two thousand feet in the Gavilan Range just under the Pinnacles National Monument cannot help but be awed that this dry, impossibly remote hermitage of a vineyard was first founded in the late 1800s. Its unnamed discoverer was known to be a Frenchman, probably a Burgundian. (For that matter, he was probably a reincarnated Cistercian monk, so austere is the site.)

That said, it must also be pointed out that easily cultivated sites are not necessarily the lesser for being so. But ease of cultivation extends beyond the application of the plow. With fine wine it extends to the very applicability of the area for winegrowing at all. The European example has great wines emerging from "marginal" locales—marginal, that is, for the grape variety in question. Pinot Noir planted in the Bordeaux region of southwest France undoubtedly would thrive—as a plant. But the resulting wine just as undoubtedly would lack the character achieved farther north in the Côte d'Or. There, the reach of the grape matches perfectly the grasp of the wine. When Pinot Noir reaches farther north—such as in Champagne—the grasp is weakened. The wine is too thin, too light, too acid for greatness. In California, ease of cultivation means more than choosing between fertile valley floors and rocky hillside slopes. The absence of a true primitivism meant that implausible places would be explored episodically, if at all, because there was no reason to do so.

Ironically, it is only now that such a primitivism is emerging. The driving force is economics. As land prices increased dramatically in California since the mid-1970s, aspiring grape growers and winery owners began to look beyond the borders of the most established areas. The pattern was largely centrifugal, spinning off from the center point of Napa Valley. It was in Napa Valley, after all, that the fine wine ambition was born anew in the late 1960s and early 1970s. Anyone newly interested in pursuing an ambition to make fine wine looked there first—and then settled. There was no need to look farther.

For example, in 1973, the French Champagne house of Moet-Hennessy decided to establish an outpost in Napa Valley. It purchased 900 acres of unplanted vineyard land in the Carneros district for $1,500 an acre. Subsequently, it bought an additional 800 acres, paying $4,000 an acre. But when, in 1986, Joseph E. Seagram & Sons purchased Rene di Rosa's already-planted Carneros vineyard called Winery Lake, it paid ten times as much: a reported $42,500 per acre of vineyard. In the decade between Moet's bold stroke and Seagram's belated one, only players with pockets as deep as Seagram's could afford to locate there.

Also in that intervening decade, vineyard prices elsewhere in Napa Valley saw similar increases. Many aspiring winegrowers who originally looked at Napa found themselves examining other neighborhoods, namely nearby Sonoma County. And then the same escalation in land values occurred there. So the circle of investigation became wider.

At the same time, the fine wine ambition was emerging elsewhere in the state. The ambition took hold of well-heeled professionals never previously involved with winegrowing: doctors, lawyers, aerospace engineers. They began to plant vines on land they happened to own—whether it was suitable for fine wine grapes or not. It happened in Mendocino County in the north; the Santa Cruz mountains south of San Francisco; and into Santa Barbara. What's more, corporate executives exercised similar options, using corporate money, often with no greater knowledge than the wine hobbyists. The vast—and often ill-advised—plantings in Monterey County are the most dramatic example of that.

Some of these ambitions grew. Home winemakers became professionals. Sometimes they stayed put; often they left for more promising or at least recognized vineyard locations. Land still was cheap enough and sufficiently plentiful for such fluidity. But by the mid-1980s, the opportunities for movement were severely reduced. Housing costs skyrocketed. Vineyard land became both expensive and scarce. Development costs increased dramatically, as the simple-to-cultivate sites in sought-after districts were all snapped up or were affordable only by the likes of Seagram.

For the first time since the revival of the fine wine ambition, Californians found themselves stuck in whatever chair they were sitting in when the music stopped. The California and the national wine market stagnated or contracted in the 1980s. Yet the number of wineries increased, spawned in part by the inability of grape growers to find an outlet for their grapes. In desperation, they entered the processing business and hung out a winery shingle.

Some were happy; others felt thwarted. Economics fixed them to their place—and continues to do so. For the first time ever, true primitivism appeared in California winegrowing. And it is typically Californian in its creation. Where in Europe the forced adhesion to place occurred because of a deficit—of money, social and political freedom, or just knowledge—in California it occurred because of a surfeit: too much money, too many people, even too much ambition.

The result is a forced rethinking of what works best for one's spot. This would have occurred anyway, but the new immobility—like a hanging—clears the mind. There's nowhere to look except inward: perhaps only to a local audience; perhaps to a greater degree of specialization; perhaps to a renewed determination to find one's opportunities within one's new limits.

It cannot be said now what the outcome will be. But the likelihood is strong that the economic motivation of this new "primitivism" will lead to more specialized wineries and wine districts. It will likely lead to redefined ambitions. Not every fine wine producer will strive to make ever more expensive wines. Or even try to outdo some other producer's ballyhooed Cabernet or Chardonnay. Producers will be content to find reliable, lucrative niche markets. This, of course, is what long ago happened in Europe.

To the outside observer, it seems a promising development. The investigation of this book—to view California wine from the perspective of the land—makes evident that many relatively young districts already have found, or are on the verge of finding, true vocations of place. It now is apparent that certain grape varieties do perform particularly well in certain places. The new limitations can act to magnify this. The greater focus will lead to social and economic rewards that come from shared identity. It is far easier to sell your previously unwanted Cabernet Franc or Gewurztraminer if your place on the map gains recognition as being *the* place for that wine. This already is happening: sparkling wine and Pinot Noir in Carneros; Cabernet Sauvignon in the Stags Leap District; and Chardonnay in Santa Maria Valley, to name but a few.

Only now is California wine approaching a sensibility of place. The fine wine ambition has taken root. So, too, have the vines. The combination means a new steadiness of accomplishment. The poet Jack Gilbert captures it: "The marriage, not the month's rapture. Not the exception. The beauty of many days. Steady and clear. It is the normal excellence of long accomplishment." *(2004)*

BOTTLED POETRY

MOST NEW YORKERS OF MY acquaintance are unfamiliar with the normal lapse rate, which involves temperature and altitude. Granted, my circle may be confined to dunderheads—as I've long suspected—but I don't think the normal lapse rate is the stuff of cocktail conversation even among a better class. Likely this is because—you don't want to hear this, I know—New York City is height challenged. For example, Manhattan's highest point, once stripped to its structural skivvies, is just 265 feet at Bennett Park on 184th Street and Fort Washington Boulevard.

New York City's pinnacle is Todt Hill on Staten Island. However, its 410-foot elevation wouldn't give even a Habsburg hemophiliac a nosebleed. Still, it lays surprising claim to being the highest point on the Eastern Seaboard south of Maine.

What's all this got to do with wine? Everything. Here's where the normal lapse rate returns to the picture: The general rule of shivering thumb is that temperature drops 3.5 degrees Fahrenheit for every 1,000 feet in elevation. The higher you go, the cooler it gets.

This is why Californians have a fascination with what they call "mountain wines." In California winegrowing, elevations of 1,500 to 2,300 feet—which is getting up there for achieving full ripeness in a grapevine—are far from rare, although they're not common either.

Most grape growers shy from high elevation sites: Ripeness is hard won; yields are significantly lower; soils are sparse and rocky; and cultivation on hillsides is often complicated by steep slopes. The higher you go, the tougher it gets.

Why bother? Because some of the greatest wines made in California today— not necessarily the most famous or expensive ones, mind you—are grown at high elevations.

Why aren't they more famous? Partly it's a function of limited supply. Mountain wines generally come from small estates, and yields are low. And partly it's because these wines are highly individual. They don't have the sort of universal, one-size-fits-all appeal guaranteed to secure high scores from all tasters.

If wine is, as Robert Louis Stevenson wrote, "bottled poetry," then mountain wines are poems closer to what E. E. Cummings had in mind when he prefaced one of his collections with the unapologetically elitist declaration: "The poems to come are for you and for me and are not for mostpeople."

When I tasted Mayacamas Vineyards "Mt. Veeder-Napa Valley" Chardonnay 2003, I had, after a single sip, an instant, involuntary reaction: "Gosh, this is good." It got more operatic, if not necessarily any more eloquent, by the time the bottle was finished.

One of Napa Valley's oldest vineyards, dating to 1880, Mayacamas Vineyards is probably what E. E. Cummings was drinking when he typed the line "not for mostpeople." I can tell you now that you won't see high scores or effusive praise from "mostpeople" wine writers.

Why not? Because owner-winemaker Robert Travers agrees with physicist Richard Feynman who wrote, "The job of a scientist is to listen carefully to nature, not to tell nature how to behave." Mr. Travers studied geology at Stanford University and knows a thing or two about respectful science. His vineyards, which he's tended since 1968, are at some of the highest elevations in California. He's not about to tell nature—or the wine that comes from it—how to behave.

Mayacamas Vineyards "Mt. Veeder-Napa Valley" Chardonnay 2003 comes from Chardonnay vines grown between 2,200 feet and 2,400 feet elevation. What's more, they're old by any measure, boasting an average age of between thirty-five and forty, with a "sizable chunk," according to Mr. Travers, of fifty-five-year-old vines. Yields never top two tons to the acre. (On the Napa Valley floor, growers get twice that yield or even more.)

This is California Chardonnay of the old school. Mr. Travers uses just 10 percent new oak barrels in his winemaking. So you're not getting the vanilla and coconut scent that new oak barrels impart and that "mostpeople" so like.

Also, Mr. Travers does not put his Chardonnay through a malolactic fermentation, in which the harder malic acid is changed by a secondary bacterial fermentation into softer lactic acid. He wants the invigoration of malic acidity and the long life it helps infuse into a wine.

Mayacamas Chardonnays can and do age for decades. To this day, the 1976 Chardonnay, which had similar vintage characteristics of exceptional warmth of the 2003, drinks superbly and has an almost eerie freshness.

This is original, dramatically fine Chardonnay like almost no other in California—or anywhere else for that matter. (*Grand cru* Chablis is the Chardonnay it most resembles.) Lemon yellow with a hint of green, it's a rich yet restrained pure-play Chardonnay with a scent of minerals, lemon curd, and crystallized ginger that follow through in the taste. The balance is well nigh perfect, the zippy acidity playing counterpoint to the dense fruit in the mid-palate.

This is truly great California Chardonnay in a style that too few of us taste because too many California winegrowers are, well, "mostpeople." The price is downright cheap ($32) for the stunning quality. It's one of America's greatest Chardonnays, bar none. *(2006)*

Mayacamas Vineyards occupies a particular place in my mind, palate, and heart, as well as in multiple references in the body of my work. I make no apology. I admire unreservedly what Bob and Nonie Travers accomplished since they bought their high-elevation vineyard and winery in 1968. (Nonie Travers died in June 2007 after a long illness.) Bob Travers makes his wines without regard to the commercially driven fashions of the moment. He is a traditionalist in the best sense.

To this day, some critics either scorn or ignore his wines. They are, to put it bluntly, wrong. Many of Mayacamas's wines—most even—mature into something exceedingly fine. But that can take upward of a decade or more. In our judge-in-haste-and-dismiss-at-leisure world, Mayacamas's austere wines are insufficiently come-hither for immediate gratification. The most extreme example of this is reported in the following article, which ran in the New York Sun, *of Mayacamas's improbable release of its 1970 Zinfandel— thirty-six years after it was made.*

AGING WELL—AN UNUSUAL 1970 ZINFANDEL GOES ON SALE FOR THE FIRST TIME

ONE OF THE BIG DIFFERENCES between British wine writing and the American sort involves old wines. The Brits are famously fond of old wines. American wine writers, for their part, tend to avoid going on about old wines. Since wine appreciation is relatively new here, tales of venerable vintages leave an undemocratic, no-room-at-the-inn aftertaste of exclusion.

I have been reminded of this unspoken taboo in the past week or so, having drunk a disproportionate number of mature wines. Most of them, I might add, came from my own cellar—which is, in itself, its own unique pleasure.

These wines were not "old," mind you. Rather, they were "mature." The difference is all about transformation. Many wines can endure, but only truly fine wines transform, becoming something far more dimensional and resonant with age.

Some wines, such as French Chablis, transform to such a degree that you would never believe, *à la* the caterpillar and the butterfly, that two vintages of the same Chablis from the same producer and vineyard could be related, let alone identical in origin. Yet it is so.

The chance to drink mature wine is available to anyone possessed of three things: a cool space in which to store the wine properly, enough money to set aside without feeling too much of a pinch (a wine cellar is like a collection of uncashed paychecks), and sheer patience. This last element is often the most trying.

Mayacamas Vineyards "Napa Mountain" Zinfandel may be the rarest wine I have ever written about that you can still actually buy. The vintage date is not a typo: 1970 is indeed the vintage. Until this moment, it has never been for sale, and *New York Sun* readers are the first in the nation to know about it.

I have long been a fan of Mayacamas Vineyards, which is one of Napa Valley's oldest estates. High atop Mount Veeder, the original winery began in 1889, replete with an old stone structure still in use today. It went out of business and was revived in 1941 and then purchased in 1968 by its current owners, Bob and Nonie Travers.

Mr. Travers, who is also the hands-on winemaker, is a traditionalist in the finest sense. He makes wines for the ages. Mayacamas Chardonnay, for example, comes into its own only after ten years. And it can mature for far longer than that. (The 1976 Mayacamas Chardonnay is still a marvel of freshness and minerality.)

Anyway, I was visiting Mayacamas Vineyards recently and Mr. Travers casually said, "Here's something you might be interested in tasting." He likes to serve visiting wine writers so-called off-vintages, the better to demonstrate that what might be true for Napa Valley in general isn't necessarily so for Mayacamas Vineyards, two-thousand feet above the valley floor.

Out comes a bottle of 1970 Zinfandel with the antique designation "Napa Mountain," a term no longer in use. (Thirty-five years ago you could pretty much say what you liked on a California wine label.)

Now, Zinfandel is not known for transformation. It tends to be best while its intense fruit is still fresh and vibrant. A thirty-five-year-old Zinfandel that's really worth drinking is not merely improbable; it borders on the preposterous. Mr. Travers said nothing.

The wine was poured and the color was awfully fresh, a bright (if slightly cloudy) garnet with no signs of the orange or brown tints that signal aging. On color alone, you'd say, oh, ten years old.

But it was the scent and taste that astonished. This 1970 Zinfandel was plumped—that's the only word—with vibrant, surprisingly fresh-tasting fruits such as wild cherry, strawberry, and black cherry. What's more, it was laced with Zinfandel's signature spiciness, which is often the varietal feature that diminishes first as a Zinfandel ages.

The experience grew more profound as we finished the bottle. The depth and density of the wine increased upon prolonged exposure to air. (Old wines, like fading opera singers, often deliver an aria of fragrant, delicate scent and then suddenly collapse, exhausted of fruit.) Finally we reached the blackish sediment. It, too, was "sweet" and flavorful.

I demanded to know the story on this wine. Mr. Travers obliged with a satisfied smile. "This Zinfandel came entirely from a one-acre plot of one-hundred-year-old Zinfandel vines on the old Jerry Draper vineyard on Spring Mountain," he said.

"Those vines were huge monsters with massive trunks and tiny berries. I was only able to buy the grapes that one year, though. The vines were later ripped out.

"I made the wine here at Mayacamas. There wasn't much, a total of thirty-five cases. Our old stone cellar is very cold. And for whatever reason—winter cold, low pH—this wine just wouldn't go through malolactic fermentation. So the hard malic acid never transformed into softer lactic acid. As a result, the wine was hugely tart. It was never fined and only coarsely filtered. We put it in bottle and forgot all about it."

Only now, Mr. Travers said, has his 1970 Zinfandel become "drinkable." That is an understatement. It is superb red wine: smooth, intense, astonishingly fresh, and perhaps the most characterful Zinfandel I have ever tasted. "We're keeping some for ourselves," he said. "After all, we did wait thirty-five years to drink it."

Mayacamas Vineyards is now releasing this "lost" 1970 Zinfandel for the first time. Available only from the winery, the price is $100 a bottle, with a maximum sale of six bottles a person.

While $100 a bottle is hardly chump change, keep in mind that several California Zinfandels now routinely ask $40 to $75 a bottle for the latest vintage—without throwing in thirty-five years of aging in a cold stone cellar. This is a great wine that obviously won't come our way again. Get it while you can. *(2006)*

I regularly sent my New York Sun *columns to a small group of friends and acquaintances, including Tom Ferrell, who is a longtime Napa Valley winemaker. In the 1990s, Tom was tapped by the secretive Swiss billionaire Jacqui Safra to put together the remarkable Spring Mountain Vineyards estate. It was cobbled together from four vineyard properties including the old Jerry Draper estate founded in the 1940s. Eventually Tom and Jacqui Safra parted company, although Tom's wife, Valli, still works at Spring Mountain Vineyards.*

Upon seeing the preceding column, Tom wrote back, saying, "In 1991, when I was trying to interest Safra in the Draper Ranch, I actually talked Bob [Travers] into selling me a bottle of his 1970 Cabernet which was also 100 percent Draper. When we bought the Draper property in 1996, Safra had no interest in Zinfandel. In fact, he didn't even want me to make that vintage into wine.

"I pulled the fifty-year-old block in 1997 and replanted it to Cabernet per Jacqui's request. Then in 2000, he discovered Helen Turley and Zinfandel through some Los Angeles wine-snob friend. Matt, I swear I nearly burst a blood vessel when Jacqui announced to me he wanted me to plant him some Zinfandel on Draper. @#$%!"

A REVERED WINERY HAS LOST MORE THAN
ITS LUXURY WINE HOLDINGS

"SO WHAT DO YOU MAKE of the Mondavi mess?" a fellow journalist asked me.

The story, in case you missed it, is that the Robert Mondavi Corporation, which is publicly traded, announced on September 14 [2004] that it was selling off its luxury wine holdings: the namesake Robert Mondavi Winery in Oakville, Arrowood Winery in Sonoma County, and Byron Winery in Santa Barbara County. Also on the block are its 50 percent ownership of three joint ventures: Opus One in Napa Valley, a partnership with Château Mouton Rothschild; Tuscany's Ornellaia and Luce della Vite, a partnership with Marchesi de' Frescobaldi; and Chile's Seña, a partnership with Eduardo Chadwick.

Once stripped of this glossy veneer of brands and vineyards—which account for 14 percent of Mondavi's case sales and 23 percent of operating revenue in fiscal 2004—the new entity will focus, as the company puts it, on "lifestyle" wines.

Lifestyle refers to the sub-$15 a bottle brands such as Woodbridge, Robert Mondavi Private Selection, La Famiglia, Papio, Arianna, Kirralaa, Hangtime, and Oberon. This is the meat and potatoes of the business, accounting for 86 percent of case sales and 77 percent of revenue. Actions quickly followed words: in late September, Mondavi laid off 360 employees, all of them at the Robert Mondavi Winery in Napa Valley.

Why is Mondavi doing this? Here's the company line: "We believe that a lifestyle-focused company creates a new and unique business model with compelling future earnings growth, strong cash-flow generating capabilities, and relatively high financial returns, which provide an excellent profile for the investing public," said the company's president and CEO, Gregory M. Evans. "By contrast, because our luxury wine brands and assets are fundamentally agricultural in nature, with long-term investment horizons and lower financial returns over the next several years, they are better suited for a private entity that has different investment criteria."

Napa Valley, it's fair to say, is practically in mourning. Robert Mondavi, ninety-one, virtually invented fine California wine when he founded his namesake winery in 1966. He is the (gratefully) acknowledged messiah of the industry. Mr. Mondavi didn't merely sail his own boat; he raised the tide itself. He's given tens of millions of dollars to charitable causes, single-handedly created the Napa Valley Wine Auction event (itself a charity), and privately and discreetly offered money and assistance to numerous Napa Valley residents. Now you know why he's revered.

But when the company went public in 1993, making the family wealthy, the die was cast. Mr. Mondavi's two sons, Michael and Timothy, proved wanting as, respectively, CEO and winemaker, of the ever-larger operation. The family's squabbles have been widely reported, and the wines themselves have been assailed in *Wine Spectator* and Robert M. Parker's *Wine Advocate* as less than they should be. It's not been a pretty sight.

So what really happened? It's simple: the "suits" took over. "Suits" move boxes—wine-industry parlance for cases of wine. "Wine men," in comparison, make wine. They never lose sight of what really counts, which is quality. "Suits," of course, don't care. These managers now insist that the Mondavi empire, as currently constituted, can't effectively sell both up-market and commodity wines. This, in a word, is nonsense. After all, Beringer Blass, owned by Australia's Foster's Group, does just that. Beringer Blass makes some of Napa Valley's most acclaimed Cabernets, selling for upward of $100 a bottle, yet 40 percent of its total case sales is white Zinfandel, a low-priced commodity wine.

Ask anybody who knew Robert Mondavi in his prime. He was a wine man supreme. His sons aren't. And the people they hired (the Mondavis hold 85 percent of the voting shares) to run the ever-expanding company were strictly bottom-line men and women. Robert Mondavi, in comparison, was the sort who would do whatever it took to improve wine quality, even if it resulted in a short-term loss.

Mr. Mondavi himself conceded that the winery, under his sons' direction, had lost sight of its raison d'être. "We were interested in making money when I transferred the responsibility over to the next generation," he told Alan Goldfarb of Napa Valley's *St. Helena Star* newspaper in December 2002. "They were interested in making money and they forgot to promote Robert Mondavi Napa Valley wine. . . . We lost the image."

The suits now running the show (Michael Mondavi, sixty-one, first resigned as an officer and vice chairman, and on Monday, was booted off the board of directors altogether; Tim, fifty-two, remains as winemaker and vice chairman) find it much easier to juggle boxes than make compelling wine. In today's price-sensitive market, cheap wines sell easily.

But that won't last. It never does. Commodity wines are always, by definition, a race to the bottom. Someone, somewhere, has a cheaper wine yet. Ask any Chilean winemaker. Once a wine darling, Chile soon found itself superceded by better-marketed and equally cheap Australian wines. Now Australia's big brands are contending with a glut of excess production, with new, cheaper yet, Aussie labels emerging to take advantage of spot market deals.

What winegrowers at the high end don't want to tell you is that, actually, the best model for a big wine company is the fashion industry. Cathy Horyn, writing recently about the Calvin Klein fashion house in the *New York Times*, put her finger on it as well as any wine analyst: "If Calvin Klein is to avoid going the way of Perry Ellis—down market, in other words—it must keep its fashion culture."

Substitute the name Mondavi, and you've got it in a nutshell. They failed to retain their wine culture. The suits won. And the boxes are moving—for now. But ask any fashionista: Once your couture collection loses its luster, your money-in-the-bank inexpensive commodities no longer are. Who wants a perfume from a nobody? *(2004)*

The "Mondavi mess" concluded with the purchase of nearly everything Mondavian, lock, stock, and, especially, barrel, by the corporate wine behemoth Constellation Brands, Inc., for $1.03 billion in cash and $325 million in assumed debt in November 2004. Mondavi's sons, Michael and Tim, have both started small new wine companies, respectively, Folio Fine Wine Partners and Continuum.

❧

What Made Him Different

Robert Mondavi died at age ninety-four in May 2008. I wrote the following appreciation for Wine Spectator *shortly after his death.*

ALTHOUGH I WAS AFFORDED MANY opportunities over the past three decades to intersect with Robert Mondavi (at his winery, at his home, at public events, and crossing his path in Italy), I preferred to keep a certain personal distance. There is something about such Promethean personal capacity that can make you a little wary.

I've always been awed that Mondavi started his eponymous winery when he was fifty-three years old. Most people I know in their fifties are thinking of getting out, not diving in. And that's today, not back in 1966 when you didn't have people popping off about how sixty is the new fifty.

So what made Mondavi a man apart? He had the attributes common to all great successes: enormous drive, ambition, perseverance, creativity, and the benefit of good timing. Mondavi single-handedly made some of that good timing happen.

But he had something more. Robert Mondavi didn't just sail his boat; he raised the tide itself. He did this, I believe, not out of any grand strategy, but rather, because Mondavi always saw his success as inseparable from that of his friends, his family, his Napa Valley, his California, even his America.

In the years when he was running his winery, I never heard a vineyard owner complain about being badly treated by Bob Mondavi. When you think of the hundreds of contracts his ever-expanding empire issued, that tells you something right there.

Part of this had to do with something elemental: Robert Mondavi was a *wine* man. He was not a "suit." For all of his salesmanship, Mondavi navigated by the North Star of wine itself. He believed in fine wine like no one else I've ever met. Indeed, he practically *invented* fine wine, at least from a mass-market point of view.

You can make a pretty good case that the unraveling of his family business occurred when the "suits"—and their box-moving mentality—took over. They did so with Mondavi's active engagement, it should be noted. He later insisted that he had no choice, that his financial back was against the wall. I never believed that myself. Rather, it seemed that everyone involved thought they were being "Wall Street smart." The results speak for themselves.

Despite his bedrock conviction of the importance, even the transformative power, of fine wine, Mondavi was nevertheless reluctant to accept where his commitment to fine wine inexorably leads, namely, to a larger mentality of *terroir*.

"I have been in this business over fifty years," he said to me in a 1987 interview in *Wine Spectator*. "I have looked at each factor very carefully. *Terroir* has gone way beyond, in my opinion, what it should be. I think it's more PR than anything else."

This, in a word, was nonsense. He knew perfectly well that *terroir* exists and, furthermore, that he himself was in possession of one of Napa Valley's greatest examples, the To-Kalon Vineyard originally created by Hiram Crabb in 1866. Mondavi fought like a lion in the courts to get To-Kalon as part of his settlement when his family booted him from Charles Krug Winery.

To-Kalon was the source of the reliable goodness of his most pride-filled wine, his Reserve Cabernet. Yet, only with the release of his 1986 Fumé Blanc Reserve did To-Kalon appear on a label. Indeed, it was Mondavi's first vineyard-designated wine.

Why was Mondavi, a man almost preternaturally sensitive to the evolving American wine psyche, so dismissive of *terroir*? Because it was too confining and too passive for a man of Mondavi's let's-make-things-happen muscularity. *Terroirists* and their miniaturism struck him as Lilliputians. He would be nobody's Gulliver.

Of course, that interventionist muscularity created wonderful things, many of them charitable and community minded. "Why can't we have a charity auction like they have in Burgundy?" I can hear him saying in that curiously high, reedy voice of his. "We've got a hospital here, too, you know."

Robert Mondavi *believed* when no one else did. And his beliefs contained not a shred of irony, a whiff of cynicism, or even much guile, as best as I could tell.

He set about creating an American wine culture in that most American of ways, through inclusion, generosity, passionate perfectionism, and unembarrassed marketing. His charities and personal kindnesses (many of them very private and care filled) were expressions of his inclusionist conviction that his success should be yours, too.

What made him different was that, more than most of us, Robert Mondavi was fueled by a bottomless supply of that most American of beliefs: that the future was his friend. And so it was. *(2008)*

THIS LAND IS THEIR LAND

SANTA CRUZ MOUNTAINS, CALIFORNIA—ONE OF the differences between big California money and big East Coast money is that Californians seek agrarian bliss. They buy ranches and, especially, vineyard land. Of course, they've got their big house (or three), but the pull of place is strong in California. You've got to get rooted, literally.

That's certainly one of the impulses behind the newborn Rhys Vineyards in the Santa Cruz Mountains that arch above the Santa Clara Valley, aka Silicon Valley, south of San Francisco on what everyone calls the Peninsula.

Rhys Vineyards (pronounced "reece") is the passion and money pit of Kevin Harvey, a forty-something Silicon Valley software entrepreneur and now venture capitalist. "It all began as recently as six years ago," said Mr. Harvey, who admits that his pursuit of great Santa Cruz Mountains Chardonnay and Pinot Noir borders on obsession. "Once I start something, I guess I become totally enraptured," he said. "My wife likes wine, but she's, well, not quite so nuts," he laughed.

The California wine rapture is hardly a new phenomenon. It first began more than a century ago, when big San Francisco money showed off its wealth in the now-traditional California fashion: by buying vineyard land in Napa Valley and building show-off wineries in the 1880s such as Beringer and Inglenook, among many others.

Winegrowing in the Santa Cruz Mountains is equally venerable, although the scale was and is different. Then and now, these coastal mountains (the Pacific Ocean is always less than ten miles away as the seagull flies) are surprisingly rugged, wild, and remote. The difference between the valley floor, encrusted with sleek Silicon Valley campuses housing the likes of Intel, Hewlett-Packard, and Apple, and the untouched, above-it-all Santa Cruz Mountains is extreme to a degree best described as shocking.

As we drove along the breathtaking ridgeline road called Skyline Boulevard, upward of 1,500 feet above the valley floor, we saw unfenced, pristine open space as far as the eye could see. "It's all owned by the Peninsula Open Space Trust," Mr. Harvey explained. "They even have the right of eminent domain, although I don't think they've ever used it."

The Peninsula Open Space Trust, founded in 1977, owns 55,000 acres of land in San Mateo and Santa Clara counties, an area twelve times the size of Yosemite Valley. Given the extraordinary cost of housing in the Peninsula, the sight of so much untouched open land is almost surreal.

Rhys Vineyards plantings, however, are not only legal but also are even encouraged. As we visited Mr. Harvey's four vineyards—Family Farm Vineyard (6.2 acres at 400 feet elevation), Alpine Road Vineyard (13 acres at 1,200 to 1,500 feet elevation), Skyline Vineyard (3.5 acres at 2,300 feet elevation), and Horseshoe Ranch Vineyard (17.5 acres at 1,300 to 1,600 feet elevation)—I mentioned the protracted land-use battles now common in Napa and Sonoma counties, especially for hillside sites.

"I didn't have any problems at all," Mr. Harvey replied. "Everything sailed right through. It's all zoned agricultural, and since we did virtually no grading, we needed no additional permits."

Nevertheless, vineyards in the Santa Cruz Mountains are rare. It has long been one of the most profound locations anywhere in California, proved today by such stellar producers as Ridge Vineyards (whose Monte Bello Cabernet Sauvignon is routinely cited as one of California's greatest) and Mount Eden Vineyards (whose estate Chardonnay is many tasters' choice for California's single best Chardonnay).

Yet only the most impassioned venture in. According to the Viticulture Association of the Santa Cruz Mountains, little more than 1,100 acres of vines are planted in these hills. (Napa Valley has thirty times as much.) Most of the vineyards are tiny; only fourteen vineyards exceed twenty acres.

The reason is simple, if painful, economics. Not only is land expensive, but the deal-killer is low yields. No one in the Santa Cruz Mountains gets much more than 2 tons of grapes to the acre. Many get only half that. In comparison, a low yield in Napa Valley is 4 tons to the acre, with greedier growers getting more. In wine economics, yield is everything, as all your other costs (land, irrigation, sprays, labor) are largely fixed.

Mr. Harvey's passion, like so many others in this determinedly idiosyncratic zone, is Pinot Noir. "I dream about Pinot Noir," he said. And he tastes them constantly, comparing California Pinot Noirs in numerous, extensive tastings with red Burgundies, which are 100 percent Pinot Noir.

His vineyards are models of the most advanced vineyard thinking in California today. Mr. Harvey has planted nearly two dozen clones, or strains, of Pinot Noir in his four vineyards, many of which are very closely spaced, which means many more vines per acre than usual.

The vines are cultivated along biodynamic lines, a form of ultra-orthodox organic cultivation, although Mr. Harvey pointed out that he has not applied for biodynamic certification from Demeter, an organization created for that purpose.

Although creating great Pinot Noir is his goal, Mr. Harvey also planted Chardonnay and a small amount of Syrah. "Actually, I don't think we planted enough Chardonnay," he said. "People who have tasted our first Chardonnay have really loved it, and we probably should have more to offer."

He's right. Rhys Vineyards Chardonnay 2003 (never released commercially) is exceptional wine: dense, suffused with a minerality that a traditionalist would call Burgundian, and blessedly devoid of the excessive oakiness that mars several other Santa Cruz Mountains–grown Chardonnays. A not-yet-released 2004 bottling is equally rewarding.

Rhys Vineyards' first Pinot Noirs are still in the barrel. And a good portion of the vines are not yet even bearing. (It takes three years for a vine to first bear fruit.) The

Pinot Noirs tasted from the barrel, all from the 2004 vintage, are more than merely promising. They are characterful, with a resonant smack of the earth, and typical of other Santa Cruz Mountains Pinot Noirs in their sizable scale and likely longevity. (Wines from these mountains are among California's most age worthy.)

Other wines—Pinot Noir and Syrah—are offered from fruit purchased elsewhere and sold under the Alesia label. This practice is universal in the Santa Cruz Mountains as nobody can really make a living from vines offering such meager yields. So they buy fruit (or wine) from elsewhere.

The Alesia bottlings are very fine, especially the Syrahs, which are nothing less than extraordinary.

Rhys Vineyards is, obviously, still in its infancy. But it has the potential of becoming one of California's most compelling estates, given the location of its vineyards and the sure and rigorous palate of its owner. That's an unbeatable combination for wine greatness anywhere in the world. *(2006)*

A reader of the New York Sun *who lives in the Santa Cruz Mountains area corrected my misunderstanding of the public ownership of the vast open spaces above Silicon Valley. "Most of the open space around the Skyline Vineyard is owned and managed by the Midpeninsula Regional Open Space District, a public agency, not the Peninsula Open Space Trust, a private group," she wrote. "Other nearby open space is part of the Santa Clara County Parks system. The Midpeninsula Regional Open Space District, not the Peninsula Open Space Trust, does have the power of eminent domain and has used it on several occasions in the past."*

Since this was written, Rhys Vineyards has applied for certification as a biodynamically cultivated vineyard.

AN ISLAND OF VINES—A CALIFORNIA WINERY STANDS OUT IN A SEA OF McMANSIONS

SARATOGA, CALIFORNIA—ALTHOUGH the popular vision of California wine is dazzled by the starburst likes of Napa Valley, the fact is that California has hundreds of wineries that trade less on glitter and more on grit.

Usually these are small family wineries committed to a personal vision that pays little heed—and often receives the same in kind—to the handful of powerful critics whose high scores and worshipful words translate into big bucks. Of course, the small wineries would be pleased with such recognition. But to live and strive for it? Such is not their way.

A good example is Kathryn Kennedy Winery in Saratoga, close to the likes of Apple Computer and hundreds of other Silicon Valley moneymakers. Saratoga is an old town at the foot of the Santa Cruz Mountains in what Bay Area denizens call "the Peninsula," the tip of which is San Francisco. Until recently, it was largely devoted to agriculture, horse farms, and logging.

Saratoga does have a history of gentility. Fifty miles south of San Francisco, it was first a logging community. That gave way to agriculture (apricots, cherries, and French prunes). But its sunny hillsides proved ideal for wine grapes, and in 1890, the French winegrower Paul Masson made Saratoga the home of his eponymous winery.

Today, Paul Masson wouldn't recognize the place. The hillsides he treasured are now encrusted with steroidal suburban "McMansions" invariably described as Tuscan-style. (The locals in Tuscany would be agog—and aghast—at the comparison.)

Kathryn Kennedy Winery is a literal island of vines—just seven acres—in a sea of these houses. When you approach the entrance on Pierce Road (the original Paul Masson winery was on the same road a century ago), you discover a pocket of thirty-three-year-old Cabernet Sauvignon vines surrounded by manicured suburban lawns. Two small, ramshackle houses occupy the property. It is so odd, so disconcerting, that you expect Edward Scissorhands to come out to greet you.

Instead you get Marty Mathis, forty-eight, who makes the wine and tends the vines that Kathryn Kennedy, his mother, planted more than three decades ago. Mrs. Kennedy, seventy-nine, is now slow of step but quick of mind and always proudly stubborn. "We're not selling," she said firmly, with a smile.

She did, in fact, toy once with the idea of selling up and getting out, applying for and receiving a city permit to subdivide her property into one-acre housing sites, the minimum lot size in Saratoga. Each site would now sell for $1 million an acre. Two years ago, she intentionally allowed the permit to lapse. "My family can sell it when I'm gone," she said. One of Mrs. Kennedy's other sons is a real estate developer.

Mr. Mathis, for his part, is steeling himself for that day, which he knows will happen. "There are four of us and there's no way one of us could buy the others out in order to keep the vineyard," he explains.

In the meantime, Mr. Mathis tends the vines lovingly and creates one of California's most profound—and expensive—Cabernet Sauvignons. Designated the "Estate" bottling, it is dense, rich, structured wine notable for an entrancing amalgam of violets and iron, a combination this taster is hard-pressed to recall in any other Cabernet Sauvignon from anywhere. Typically, just seven hundred cases of wine emerge each year from those seven acres, thanks to yields of little more than 1¾ tons an acre (a low yield in Napa Valley is 4 tons an acre).

Mr. Mathis and I tasted fourteen vintages of Kathryn Kennedy "Estate" Cabernet Sauvignon and this iron-and-violets quality appeared more often than not. (Older vintages, from the early 1980s, showed more tobacco and cedar, partly from sheer age and partly from a less "clean" winemaking style; newer vintages, starting in the 1990s, are more berryish, with better flavor delineation.)

Three Estate Cabernets are currently available directly from the winery (www. kathrynkennedywinery.com): 2000, 2001, and 2002. The 2000 and 2002 vintages are $145, with the 2001 asking $160 a bottle.

Of the three, the 2000 was my favorite, with an intense scent of black cherries and dark chocolate and an enticing suppleness, with shy hints of the iron minerality and violets still to come. The 2001 is, thanks to the heat of the vintage, a bit over-ripe and alcoholic for my taste, but this lush style is now fashionable and sought after by some tasters, hence the higher price. The 2002 was back in form, in a lighter (relatively speaking) fashion, which itself may have seemed that way coming as it did after the ponderous 2001.

Mr. Mathis makes other wines as well. Look for the less expensive ($45) Small Lot Cabernet Sauvignon, which shows that Saratoga's viticultural heritage is not lost altogether. "It's called Small Lot because it comes from five or six tiny vineyards in the neighborhood," says Mr. Mathis, waving his arm to encompass the high-end housing sprawl on the hillsides around him.

"You see, because the minimum lot size is one acre, there's enough land after the house is built to put in a quarter-acre vineyard," he explains. "So the owners put them in, kind of like a front lawn. There are enough of them that you've got firms that work only on microvineyards, not only installing them, but also doing all the pruning, fertilizing, and picking.

"Ironically, I now have more Santa Cruz Mountain Cabernet available to me today than before all these houses were built," Mr. Mathis said with a laugh. "Who could have imagined that?" *(2006)*

Kathryn Kennedy died from cancer in August 2009. She remained steadfast in her refusal to sell her vineyard while never denying that eventually the vineyard would succumb to the irresistible economics. As of this writing, the estate vineyard remains, but probably not for long. However, Marty Mathis reports that the winery retains a sizable inventory of older wines, as well as extensive sources for purchased grapes from the Santa Cruz Mountains. So the Kathryn Kennedy Winery will continue, the fate of its original estate vineyard notwithstanding.

HANZELL VINEYARDS—DUE FOR A COMEBACK

"YOU WILL IN YOUR BUSINESS ultimately go out of business," declared the chief executive officer of American Express, Harvey Golub, in a recent profile in the *New York Times Magazine*. "You can do it yourself in organic ways by shaping your business with new products. Or somebody else will do it for you. It is only a matter of time."

But what is true for American Express may not, in fact, hold true for great vineyards. After all, such vineyards are deemed great by their very uniqueness. If someone could create—or rather, find—the likes of La Tâche or Montrachet, you know they would. The "business" of great vineyards is, more than anything else, simply to persevere.

But perseverance is no easy matter, especially these days. Even the greatest vineyards, with the longest and most distinguished histories, now require promotion, as well as careful winemaking management. Château Lafite Rothschild went through a slump in the 1970s, as did Château Ausone. In Burgundy, the fabled Domaine de la Romanée-Conti—repository of Burgundy's greatest vineyards—is currently being outshone by neighboring Domaine Leroy. Brunello di Montalcino's founding winery, Biondi Santi-Il Greppo, is now eclipsed by the upstart Case Basse estate.

In California, perhaps the most striking example is Hanzell Vineyards, high above the town of Sonoma. Something about Hanzell Vineyards calls to mind a once famously beautiful Hollywood star who, although remembered fondly, is no longer lusted after. Everybody shrugs. "You will in your business ultimately go out of business," they say. Younger, newer beauties come along.

We know how it happens: lack of marketing savvy, shifting tastes in wine styles, newer and flashier wineries slaking the need for razzmatazz. And, yes, sometimes less-than-ideal wines. But mostly it's the market need for novelty, never mind how shallow.

Yet no winery in California is more due for a comeback in public acclaim than Hanzell Vineyards. No winery in California has more perseveringly demonstrated the singularity of its vineyard site—especially for its landmark Chardonnay.

So why haven't we heard more about Hanzell? Partly it's the reasons cited previously. Partly it is the winery's fault. Virtually since the death of its founder, James D. Zellerbach, in 1963, Hanzell has lacked the driving force that only a dedicated owner can project. There have been two other owners, both of whom believed in Hanzell's significance, but neither of whom defined themselves by its accomplishments. Currently Hanzell is being held in trust for its twenty-year-old owner, Alexander de Brye, who inherited the winery as part of his mother's very substantial estate.

Nevertheless, Hanzell has persevered. What has sustained Hanzell is Zellerbach's legacy: a Burgundian conviction about the primacy of place. Where others merely employ Burgundian techniques, Hanzell *is* Burgundian.

Being Burgundian involves an acceptance—an embrace, even—of a constricted vocation. You do what your site allows you to do. Its limitations are yours. This submissiveness to site is not easily transferable to California's restless, investigatory spirit. Burgundians, after all, have known their particular winegrowing "truths" for centuries. This is unavailable in California, except in a very few locations. Hanzell's is one of them. Its original vineyard was planted in 1953. The same vines still are there.

That said, Hanzell had a few soul mates in its early years, such as the still-thriving Mayacamas Vineyards (founded 1948) and Stony Hill Vineyard (founded 1951), as well as more erratic aspirers to the fine-wine ambition such as the old Martin Ray Vineyard (now Mount Eden Vineyards) and Hallcrest Vineyards. But none of these wineries had such riches lavished upon them as were bestowed on Hanzell. None were furnished with a more transcendent, chaste ambition.

The source of this privilege came, as is traditional, from Hanzell's paternal creator, James D. Zellerbach, heir to one of the West's great timber fortunes.

But it was not just the Zellerbach money—critical as it was—that made Hanzell Vineyards unique. More important yet was Zellerbach's knowing ambition. After all, California had then—and has even more today—plenty of rich men and women who haven't a clue about taste, let alone an informed refinement. Hanzell was the first post-Prohibition California winery consecrated to refinement. It was born with the American equivalent of a patent of nobility.

Having lived in Europe in the 1940s—and later serving a stint as ambassador to Italy during the Eisenhower years—Zellerbach was exposed to fine wine. Much more important, he was sensible of its particular beauty. Considering that his was an era, and a social set, that prized Bourbon over Burgundy, this says something about Zellerbach.

It was Burgundy—that most seductive of all wines—that entranced him. Zellerbach returned to the United States determined to create Burgundian greatness in his native California. With that resolve, he purchased a two-hundred-acre property in 1948 just north of the town of Sonoma, in the hills above Sonoma Valley. There he installed fourteen acres of Chardonnay and Pinot Noir.

Although it seems painfully obvious today that if you want to create the equivalent of a great white Burgundy you need Chardonnay, keep in mind that few vineyards in California at that time were growing Chardonnay. It was so little grown as to be virtually unknown. Writing in 1941, Frank Schoonmaker and Tom Marvel in their landmark book, *American Wines*, observe: "There exist no accurate statistics concerning the present acreage in California of distinguished wine grapes. The following estimates are, in the authors' opinion, decidedly on the high side. . . ." By their estimate, California had no more than fifty to one hundred acres of Chardonnay, tops.

In the years—generations, really—that followed, Chardonnay progressed by arthritic half steps. Two decades after his first report, Schoonmaker noted in his *Encyclopedia of Wine* (1964) that, statewide, Chardonnay still occupied just six hundred acres. Today California is plumped with sixty-six-thousand acres.

HANZELL THEN

That Zellerbach's Burgundian zeal led to planting Chardonnay and Pinot Noir is predictable enough. But what he did inside his winery—a woodsy miniature loosely modeled on the château in Burgundy's Clos de Vougeot Vineyard—was unique. In one place, in one swoop, Zellerbach fathered the two features of California winemaking that continue to define it to this day: the use of temperature-controlled stainless steel fermenting tanks and small French oak barrels. It was as if a spacecraft had landed at Hanzell in 1957, leaving behind instructions for a better wine culture to come. Assuredly, both developments would have emerged anyway, but it was no coincidence that they happened first at Hanzell.

Hanzell's stainless steel tanks look like no others, as they were personally designed by Zellerbach in 1957. One dozen in all, at first glance they look like a single, unbroken bulwark. But, clambering up a ladder onto a catwalk, you peer down into them and discover a row of separate rectangular vats hollowed within the bulwark, each four feet long, three feet wide, and more than three feet deep, with sloping bases. The walls of each tank are empty jackets through which cool or warm water can circulate for temperature control. Each vat holds exactly one ton of grapes.

As for the French oak barrels, the story of Zellerbach's discovery of their qualities has become almost legend. Unlike the careful custom-crafting of his stainless steel tanks, the appearance of the small Burgundian oak barrels was less a matter of inspired planning than of simple traditionalism. Intending to create Burgundy-style wines, Zellerbach felt it self-evident to use Burgundian barrels. On a visit to Burgundy, he arranged with the local coopers, Sirugue, to ship their rustic, wood-hooped French oak barrels to Hanzell. The rest, as they say, is toast.

Although Zellerbach was the muse (and the money), the actual working of the winery was thanks to Hanzell's original winemaker, Brad Webb, who arrived in 1956. By then, the winery was designed and under construction, overseen directly by Zellerbach. It was Webb who worked with the then-unknown French oak barrels and who navigated day-to-day the winegrowing course laid out by Zellerbach. With Zellerbach's blessing, Webb created Hanzell's then-futuristic wine laboratory, replete with a gas chromatograph. At the time, the only other gas chromatographs devoted to wine research were found at the laboratories of University of California Davis and Gallo.

The fantasy came to an end upon Zellerbach's death at seventy-one in 1963. His wife, Hana, sold all of the wine that remained in bottle, as well as the two vintages still in barrel. (The few bottles of old Hanzell wines reposing today in the winery's library had to be bought back later.) The wines in barrel eventually reappeared under the Heitz label, one of which became legendary as Heitz Pinot Chardonnay 1962 Lot C-22. It sold for a then-boggling $9 a bottle, the same asking price at the time as 1962 Le Montrachet.

With the winery's contents emptied, no wine was made in the 1963 and 1964 vintages, the grapes having been sold to others. In 1965, Hana Zellerbach sold the estate—vineyards, winery, and family house—to Douglas and Mary Day. Whatever her feelings, they were resolute: She never returned to Hanzell, even though she only died last year, at age ninety-three.

The Day family owned Hanzell for ten years, selling it in 1975 to Barbara de Brye (pronounced duh-BREE), an Australian-born heiress who lived in London and had married Count Jacques de Brye, a Parisian banker. Subsequently divorced from the count, she later died unexpectedly in 1991. The sole heir to her considerable fortune is their son, Alexander, now twenty.

Hanzell today is overseen by three trustees administering Alexander de Brye's extensive inheritance. Even upon his mother's death, when he was only sixteen, Alexander insisted that Hanzell be retained. The trustees, although unimpressed with Hanzell's economic performance, have deferred to his wishes. Hanzell is, after all, only a small element of the de Brye fortune, which came from mining.

HANZELL NOW

Hanzell today is a perfumed whiff from California's past. Aesthetically, the buildings and grounds of Hanzell are the 1950s ideal—the epitome, really—of what was once called "gracious living." Today, the phrase seems mocking, but for postwar Americans pursuing the booming prosperity of the 1950s, "gracious living" was a motivating vision. This is not to say that Hanzell is showy, like Jordan. Or ostentatious, like Opus One. Instead, it is *Sunset* magazine genteel.

The winery seemingly floats above the town of Sonoma, which today is abuzz with traffic and tourists. Zellerbach surely would be shocked at Sonoma's transformation from a proverbially sleepy village to tourist mecca and bedroom community. But Hanzell remains literally above the fray.

To reach Hanzell, you turn off a frenetic urban arterial onto a narrow road that leads uphill, seemingly to nowhere. The elevation is deceiving, largely because of the numerous curves and the almost instantaneous serenity. Hanzell actually is only 750 feet in elevation, which is not that high compared to other nearby Mayacamas Mountain vineyards in Sonoma, such as Louis Martini's Monte Rosso vineyard (900 to 1,200 feet), Carmenet (1,000 to 1,750 feet), and Kistler Estate vineyard (1,800 feet).

What strikes the visitor, apart from the beautifully kept grounds and curving, private asphalt road, are the vines themselves. This is the founding vineyard: seven acres of Chardonnay and Pinot Noir which were first planted in 1952, only to be replanted a year later after a harsh winter eroded the soil. Another seven acres of vines were added in 1957. Set in gentle terraces, they are arranged in concentric, widening arcs that literally lap up against the winery.

That Hanzell pursues a Burgundian fidelity to place is further demonstrated by its allegiance to this founding vineyard. The child being the father of the man, Zellerbach's original fourteen acres are the progenitors of Hanzell's younger vines. As cuttings, all the vines are kin to the patriarchal vineyard.

The Day family planted three more acres of Chardonnay in 1972; Barbara de Brye added another ten acres of Chardonnay and Pinot Noir. This clonal continuity is admirable, even essential, as Hanzell's Chardonnay is a very low-yielding clone (2 tons to the acre), with tiny berries. Ditto for the Pinot Noir (1¾ tons to the acre).

This fidelity has proved a boon in yet another way: Hanzell is unconcerned about phylloxera. "Only 1 percent, about two hundred vines, of our vineyard is planted on A x R No. 1 rootstock," reports Bob Sessions, Hanzell's longtime manager and winemaker. The A x R No. 1 rootstock, on which roughly 80 percent of Napa's and Sonoma's sixty thousand acres of vines are rooted, is now susceptible to a new strain of the root louse phylloxera. "We never used that rootstock, except experimentally, because it was too vigorous. Virtually everything we have is grown on the same *rupestris* rootstock originally used when Zellerbach planted the original vines. And it resists phylloxera perfectly."

The primacy of the vineyard apart, to talk about Hanzell today is really to discuss the achievements and struggles of Bob Sessions. Arriving in 1973, he saw the sale of the winery from the Day family to Barbara de Brye, then witnessed yet another— more unsettling—transition, from her personal stewardship to the more cost-conscious oversight of the trustees of the de Brye estate.

During his twenty-two-year tenure, Sessions has watched Hanzell's production increase from eight hundred cases a year to three thousand. With that came a corresponding decline in exclusivity: Hanzell wine once was as unseen as a unicorn. Still, three thousand cases is not much wine. But the increase was not accompanied by much of a marketing push. Hanzell traded on its lustrous name and—in the case of the Chardonnay—its extraordinary quality.

Simply put, Hanzell creates one of California's greatest Chardonnays. Without question, it is demonstrably one of California's longest-lived white wines, transforming as it matures but aging only grudgingly. Wines from the 1970s are only now reaching maturity. Chardonnays older yet are far from fatigued. Few white Burgundies can claim as much.

But it is not just endurance or longevity that sets Hanzell Chardonnay apart. Rather, it is sheer goodness. When young, they are generous in their fruit flavors. With maturity, real distinction becomes apparent, with a whacking amount of mineral- ness underlying still-vibrant fruit. All of this is accomplished—as it always has been—with few of the winemaking flourishes considered so necessary by others.

Take, for example, the chorus testifying for barrel and malolactic fermentation. As the believers tell it, you just can't make a decent, let alone great, Chardonnay unless you adhere 100 percent to these practices. This will be news to Sessions, who barrel ferments only 10 percent of Hanzell's Chardonnay.

"Barrel fermentation can help obscure the fact that there isn't much going on elsewhere in the wine," he says. "I'm not opposed to barrel fermentation. Look, a lot of this has to do with the fruit you're using. For example, I was really impressed with the Au Bon Climat Chardonnay when I was down in Santa Barbara recently. And if I were using their fruit [from Santa Barbara's Santa Maria Valley] I probably would use more barrel fermentation. But I do think that the Hanzell fruit, wonderful as it is, would really get lost if it were 100 percent barrel fermented."

As for malolactic fermentation, Sessions takes a similarly judicious approach: 30 to 40 percent of the Chardonnay undergoes malolactic. "I'm not convinced that malolactic fermentation is the great answer that so many people think it is," he says. "I love the Chardonnays from Mayacamas Vineyards, where I worked for seven years before coming to Hanzell. I was the winemaker at Mayacamas for the 1965 through '71 vintages. Also, Brad Webb consulted there in 1965 and 1966. And Mayacamas doesn't use any malolactic fermentation at all in their Chardonnay."

Pinot Noir has, naturally, been more problematic. In fact, it's been downright aggravating, both to Sessions personally and to Hanzell's loyal following. According to some, the site simply is too warm for Pinot Noir greatness. Others point to how Sessions once handled the fruit, using techniques that extracted too much tannin.

Sessions is not one of your diseased-ego winemakers. While he will defend the goodness of his Chardonnay with the fervor of a grizzly protecting a cub, he is more openly self-doubting about the performance of his Pinot Noirs—especially those made before 1985. "Maybe the wines should have been a little more user- friendly," he says half-apologetically.

Having said that, he becomes a touch more defensive. "It may not be Burgundy—I *know* it isn't—but it's distinctive and it gratifies a good number of people. Our Pinot Noir is a damn good red wine experience. I draw a lot of strength from that."

Sessions is fighting ghosts. Hanzell's Pinot Noirs now are startlingly good. Starting with the 1985 vintage, and progressing noticeably with every vintage thereafter, Hanzell Pinot Noirs have transformed from pruney, Port-reminiscent "red wine experiences" to distinctive Pinot Noirs.

What changed was not the fruit, but Sessions's handling of it. The key point is Sessions's change of palate. He now seeks to extract Pinot Noir's ethereal berry flavors allied, as much as possible, to a delicacy previously absent in the old style. The old-style Hanzell Pinot Noirs always had a savor of site. But they lacked a taste transparency. An absence of delicacy—which is *not* the same as lightness—prevented this singular savor from showing through. No longer do the bitter, tannin-laden stems get tossed in as in the late 1970s. Instead, whole, unruptured clusters of grapes are used during fermentation.

All this has shown itself since the 1985 vintage. But the triumph—the finest Hanzell Pinot Noir this taster has experienced—is the newly released 1990 vintage (12 percent whole cluster). Here, finally, is what Hanzell's exceptional site and old, low-yielding vines can deliver: an intense *goût de terroir* wrapped up in a berryish, delicately delivered fruit. This Pinot Noir could not have come from just anywhere. And it is powerfully, unmistakably Pinot Noir in taste, character, and texture, in a husky fashion.

Where Sessions has had to concede defeat, unwillingly, has been with Hanzell's Cabernet Sauvignon. It was a new winemaking wrinkle for Hanzell, a twist added by Barbara de Brye, who loved Bordeaux wines. Five acres of Cabernet Sauvignon and its blending cohorts, Merlot and Cabernet Franc, were planted at her direction in 1976. The wines—the first vintage was 1981—failed to seduce the market. Just why is an intriguing question. One reason, I believe, is that they were *too* distinctive. There's something powerfully strong about the Hanzell site, which is apparent in the Chardonnay and Pinot Noir. And it comes through equally powerfully in the Cabernet. Still, even with only five acres and the formidable Hanzell name, an audience could not be captured.

After Barbara de Brye's death, according to Sessions, "The trustees gave me one year to do better in selling the wine. It wasn't selling through. I couldn't make it happen. So they decided in 1993 to graft over the Cabernet vines to Chardonnay and Pinot Noir. The last Cabernet vintage we made was 1992."

To Sessions, this decision, although done for good business reasons, is somehow wrong. It's the Burgundian in him. One must stay the course. "Grafting over is like channel surfing," he says disapprovingly. His only consolation, he admits, is that vines could be grafted back again. Perhaps a mature Hanzell Cabernet will one day sway the young Alexander de Brye. But for now, Hanzell has returned to its original, purely Burgundian, mission. *(1995)*

When this article first appeared in Wine Spectator *in 1995, Hanzell had yet to return to the spotlight. Since that time, however, it has returned not only to its full glory, but also to a revered status, which is its right. Bob Sessions retired as winemaker in 2002, but his legacy remains intact. Owner Alexander de Brye, now a grown man, is fully involved with Hanzell and dedicated to it. Cabernet Sauvignon has not been replanted.*

❦

THE END OF AN EMPIRE? CALIFORNIA PINOT NOIRS ARE CHIPPING AWAY AT BURGUNDY'S DOMINANCE

WHAT'S HAPPENING BEFORE OUR EYES today is something I never thought I'd see: Empires are falling. Everywhere, the old order is undergoing change on a scale, and with a speed, that no one could have predicted only a decade ago.

Let me first give you an anecdotal example. Lately, Pinot Noir has been much on my mind. It always is, but it's been more pressingly so than usual. As previously chronicled in this column, I was in New Zealand's Central Otago district—Pinot Noir country—as well as Australia's Mornington Peninsula and Tasmania (ditto). These visits included two Pinot Noir conferences as well as independently visiting producers. So I've been steeped like a tea bag in Pinot Noir.

Anyway, I returned home and found myself having lunch with a Burgundy shipper I've known for decades—a good, honest guy who's in the top echelon of Burgundy shippers. It was just the two of us, so the conversation was, as the State Department likes to say, frank and honest. I told him, hyperbolically, that Burgundy was dying. (Actually, what's happening is that the less prestigious subregions such as

Côte Chalonnaise and Mâconnais really are declining, with increasing bankruptcies. The heart of Burgundy, the famed Côte d'Or, is so far unaffected.)

As you might imagine, this took him aback. I said that although Burgundy was hardly going out of business, it will certainly steadily lose business, pointing out that California alone has the same Pinot Noir acreage (24,000 acres) as Burgundy, never mind Oregon, New Zealand, and Australia. I told him that I had recently recommended in this column a California Pinot Noir that—if I were tasting it blind—I would have sworn was a really good Bourgogne rouge. And it sells for $16.

My guest was (understandably) skeptical. The wine in question wasn't on the restaurant's list, so I excused myself, dashed across the street to a nearby wine shop, and snared a bottle of 2003 Saintsbury Garnet Pinot Noir. It was $15.99. I took the receipt for proof.

Like a cat proudly coming home with a captured mouse, I plopped the bottle in front of him. The sommelier hurried over with three glasses (one for him, too, after all), and we sampled the Saintsbury wine. The Burgundy shipper's eyes opened wide in honest amazement. "This is very good," he exclaimed. "This is very, very good," he repeated. "It absolutely smells and tastes like Pinot Noir. And the delicacy! I never suspected," he added, shaking his head.

Then I went in for the kill: Saintsbury makes 18,000 cases of this stuff. And that's just one winery in Carneros. There are plenty more grapes where those came from.

"How much would this be wholesale?" the Burgundy shipper asked the sommelier, who was swirling and tasting and loving every minute of it. "Oh, it would be $12 a bottle wholesale," he replied. "But with a volume discount, you could probably get it for as little as ten bucks."

I asked my friend if Burgundy could create a Bourgogne rouge as good as the 2003 Saintsbury Garnet and put it on the street for $10 wholesale. "There is no way," he conceded. "Absolutely no way."

I tell this story not to put Burgundy in a bad light, but rather to underscore the sweeping changes we're now seeing throughout the wine world. Burgundy producers will have to face the fact that, like it or not (and they won't), their Pinot Noir monopoly is finished. After one thousand years, the Burgundy empire is crumbling.

Burgundy's new reality is as clear as it is challenging: It should make half as much wine (by lowering its excessive yields) and sell it at twice the price. It should transform itself into what Burgundy alone can be, namely, an elite source of the world's greatest Pinot Noirs and Chardonnays. To be anything less—which is today's situation—is to continue to lose its centrality in the world's fine-wine culture, which is already happening.

Not long afterward, I was invited to a high-end California Pinot Noir tasting put on by a wine-enthralled Silicon Valley venture capitalist. (The West Coast rich are different from the East Coast rich—no fusty old Bordeaux for them.) He wanted to take a *tour d'horizon* of some of California's best Pinot Noirs and asked a few of us to come along for the ride. Thirty Pinot Noirs were rounded up, including such prestige brands as Marcassin, Rochioli, Calera, Williams Selyem, and Kistler, among others.

I thought of my Burgundy shipper friend as I tasted through the offerings. Were they as good as Burgundy's best? Not quite. But Satchel Paige's famous advice, "Don't look back. Something might be gaining on you," came quickly to mind. Some of these Burgundy-busters were coming on strong, especially if compared to the thinned-blood versions of Burgundy's more diluted *grands crus* made from vines with excessive yields.

What stood out? As a group—four wines were on offer—it was tough to deny the goodness of the Pinot Noirs from Rochioli Vineyard in Sonoma County's Russian River Valley. All four 2002 vineyard-designated Pinot Noirs were lovely renditions, with Rochioli's famed "West Block" bottling taking the prize for its berryish flavors, delicacy, and finesse. (And, yes, I could easily have confused it with a good Volnay.)

Equally satisfying, if different, was Rochioli's neighbor, Williams Selyem. Originally created by Burt Williams and Ed Selyem and sold in 1998 to John S. Dyson, a former New York City deputy mayor and owner of Millbrook Vineyards in the Hudson Valley, Williams Selyem put California Pinot Noir on the world map in the 1990s.

And how good are they today? I can answer that pretty definitively, thanks to spending a day recently with its winemaker Bob Cabral. This latest tasting of some of their 2002s was an added dollop. Williams Selyem is as good as it ever was, maybe even better thanks to a more extensive array of offerings.

The five 2002 Williams Selyem Pinots in the tasting lineup were all, at minimum, intriguing and, at maximum, flat-out beautiful. The stars were the 2002 Allen Vineyard from Russian River Valley, as well as the more easily obtainable 2002 "Sonoma Coast" bottling. If Williams Selyem has a flaw, it's that all of its wines are too strongly marked by oak, specifically the smoky bacon scent and taste of the heavy toast François Frères barrels the winery uses almost exclusively. It's become a bit of trademark for them, unfortunately.

The third standout—the best wine of the tasting for me—was the 2002 Flowers "Camp Meeting Ridge" Pinot Noir from the extreme western portion of the Sonoma coast. Barely two miles inland from the ocean, Flowers Vineyard and Winery has consistently issued *grand cru* level Pinot Noirs from its signature vineyard called Camp Meeting Ridge.

The 2002 Flowers "Camp Meeting Ridge" Pinot Noir may be their best yet, with its characteristic power and mineral notes allied to a greater degree of finesse and delicacy than in previous vintages. Experience reveals, by the way, that this wine rewards cellaring, which cannot always be said for some California Pinots.

Can you get these wines? Yes, with a bit of looking—and a fat wallet. All of the preceding wines sell for between $35 and $100 a bottle. The best chance of tasting them is at restaurants, especially the Williams Selyem and Rochioli wines. Both wineries have lengthy waiting lists for retail customers, but restaurants have dibs. One effective and convenient way of tracking down many wine rarities is the Web site www.wine-searcher.com.

Are these high-end California Pinot Noirs worth the money? As an education, absolutely. And as a profound Pinot Noir experience comparable to equally expensive red Burgundies, you ask? Here again, the answer is absolutely yes. Empires are falling. You can taste it. *(2005)*

THE MONEY BAMBOOZLE

IN WINE AS IN LOVE, money and attraction are widely considered directly related. ("It's as easy to love a rich man as a poor one.") That an expensive wine *must* be better is considered self-evident.

This explains much about a letter I received from Tom Linde of Seattle, Washington. "I'm all for the free-market system and I realize that if it sells, it was priced correctly for the market," says Linde. "My occasional purchases of premium wine at ridiculous prices makes me part of the problem. My only hope is that someone will still find it reasonable to produce a wine that will age well for 5+ years and not cost $100."

"Gotcha!" That's what more than a few California wine producers would surely say—if only to themselves—upon hearing Tom Linde's hope that just maybe, somehow somebody can make a good wine that could sell for less that $100 a bottle.

California wine producers are hugging themselves at their astounding good fortune. Despite the very real setbacks of phylloxera and the impending threat of Pierce's disease, they're raking it in like never before. Prices—and profits—have never been higher.

It's not just the Californians, although they're the masters at this game. An Oregon winegrower had the effrontery to write that "$50 a bottle is a bargain . . . $50 per bottle hardly covers expenses."

Tom, let me give it to you straight. The only reason for selling a wine for $100 a bottle—or $50 for that matter—is that you'll pay it. Production costs have nothing to do with such high retail prices.

You don't believe me? Well, maybe you'll believe David Coffaro, a vineyard owner and winemaker in Sonoma County's Dry Creek Valley. Coffaro makes terrific wines that easily will last "5+ years" and sells them for $20 a bottle or less. Why? Because he believes high prices are—and I quote—"ripping off the public."

David Coffaro is an affable guy. And he's not going broke, either. He just doesn't subscribe to the "shake 'em until their teeth fall out" school of wine marketing.

Coffaro has an entertaining Web site (www.coffaro.com), where he publishes a weekly diary. Enraged at one winery's assertion about why it had to charge so much, Coffaro sat down and ran the numbers. This is what he wrote on his Web site:

> One ton of grapes produces about 750 bottles. Or $75,000 gross at $100 a bottle. If you assume they are paying $10,000 a ton for their grapes (I am sure they are paying more like $3,000 to $4,000 a ton), that leaves $65,000.

> It costs them no more than $150 (20 cents a bottle) to bottle. If they are using 200 percent new French oak (I use 20 percent), that would amount to $4,000. They could be paying as much as 10 cents per label—another $75.

> Gee, let's see? I guess they could be paying as much as 12 cents for their capsules—$90. Gosh, they could be paying $2 for their glass (I pay 50 cents and the most expensive bottles are about $1.50)—$1,500 more.

If we total this up, it amounts to $15,815. That leaves them with $59,185. I am sure I forgot something. Maybe it takes many employees to handle this bottle? Maybe their distributor is making a bundle?

Let's be realistic. Their costs are probably well under $15 a bottle including replanting and all the other overblown expenses. If they sell all their wine through a distributor at $50 per bottle and none at retail, they are still making a profit of over $35 per bottle.

The point is obvious: Truly great wines don't have to cost anywhere near $100 a bottle. Want proof? Look at Mount Eden Vineyards "Estate" Chardonnay, which I consider California's single greatest Chardonnay. It comes from vines that give little more than one ton to the acre. Now *that's* expensive. The winery's retail price? $45.

Or there's Mayacamas Vineyards's extraordinary Chardonnay, also from one-ton-to-the-acre yields. Their 1997 vintage, perhaps their best in a decade, sells for just $32 at the winery. Or Joseph Phelps Vineyard's excellent 1997 Cabernet. The winery's retail price? $35.

The list of real-world prices from producers who haven't convinced themselves that "$50 a bottle is a bargain" is longer than you might think. But you can't be blamed for having an impression otherwise. The forces of bamboozle are out there, sure enough.

You don't have to spend $100 a bottle. And wineries don't *have* to charge it, either.
(2001)

CRYSTAL BALL

I t's the nature of pundits to make predictions. Not only are critics know-it-alls, but we collectively fancy ourselves as futurists, trend-spotters, and pulse-takers. I'm no exception. Over the years, I've generated my share of predictions and prophecies. Some of them turned out correct; others proved to be piffle.

PINOT GRIS: CALIFORNIA'S NEXT BIG WHITE

IT'S EARLY MORNING IN THE California wine country. You're staying in a little Victorian bed and breakfast. You step out onto the porch, a mug of coffee in hand, to savor the fresh, morning country air. Vines with gnarled trunks surround you, looking as fixed as if screwed into the soil. The scene feels timeless, serene, immutable.

Suddenly, this gossamer serenity is shredded by the scream of a chainsaw, which methodically reduces vine after vine to amputated stumps. Now you're *really* in California wine country: You are witnessing grafting-over. It is an everyday occurrence almost everywhere in California where they are not replanting altogether because of phylloxera.

Literally overnight, acres of unwanted varieties—Riesling, Gewurztraminer, Chenin Blanc—will change allegiance. Knowingly, you say, "Ah, more Cabernet or Chardonnay." But you'll be wrong—sometimes, anyway. It's going to be California's next "Big White"—Pinot Gris.

Pinot Gris? Who's ever heard of Pinot Gris? Granted, at the moment, very few. But it is destined for fame and (winegrower) fortune. Right now, there is no significant acreage of Pinot Gris in California. But that's meaningless: Grafting-over can create 1,000 acres in no time. And just one year later, the vines will bear almost a full crop.

But really, Pinot Gris as California's next Big White? That's a bit much. Yet a market test study has already been performed. And the results are convincing. It's all about dazzling profitability and marketability. Here's the scoop:

Pinot Gris is a white wine mutation of Pinot Noir. The name rhymes with "free," which it certainly isn't. But compared to Chardonnay, let alone Cabernet Sauvignon, it's virtually a free ride for the winemaker. Making Pinot Gris is about as straight-line as winemaking gets: You ferment the wine in stainless steel tanks, let it sit in those same tanks—or maybe a big oval cask—and then bottle the wine. Pinot Gris doesn't take to oak. There's no need to age it for two years like Cabernet. As early as six months after the harvest—one year, max—it's out the door to restaurants and wine shops.

The key, though, is this: Nearly everybody who likes Chardonnay also likes Pinot Gris. The average person who tastes Pinot Gris for the first time says, "Gee, this would go pretty well with chicken or pork or fish." That's part of the popular appeal of Pinot Gris: Instantly and intuitively you *know* it will go with whatever you're eating. Free at last!

What's more, it ages magnificently. If you ask an Alsatian winegrower to show you the oldest, still-drinkable bottle of wine in his cellar, he'll point to Pinot Gris. Unlike, say, Viognier, it has shelf life. Restaurants will be able to serve rewarding older bottles at premium prices.

But as all savvy marketers know, before you take the plunge, you've got to have a test market. There happens to be one: Oregon. It grows America's only significant supply of Pinot Gris. That's not much—530 acres, only half of which were bearing in 1993—but it's enough to currently crank out about fifty thousand extremely profitable cases. No Oregon wine sells more speedily—at a minimum price of $9.95 a bottle, no less. Remember, an early-release, no-oak white wine that blows out the door at ten bucks a bottle is more profitable than a $15 French-oaked Chardonnay.

So far, Oregon winegrowers have the market to themselves—until the California bear comes lumbering in. Keep in mind what Pinot Gris likes most: deep, rich soils, preferably volcanic or silty clay, and a warm, dry climate. Does this ring any geographic bells? California has dozens of such spots. Probably the Mayacamas Mountains in Napa and Sonoma are close to ideal. Then there's the vast Sierra

Foothills region. And Mendocino County. And who knows what the Salinas Valley in Monterey County or Santa Barbara's Santa Maria Valley can do?

Everything about Pinot Gris lines up: taste affability, European pedigree, a pronounceable French name (several trend-licking California producers are foolishly planning to use the Italian name, Pinot Grigio), a popular price point, and an already proven American test market.

You read it here first: California is about to see an outbreak of Pinot Greed. *(1994)*

A certain amount of, ahem, journalistic license was taken in calling Pinot Gris the next "Big White." On the one hand, I wasn't entirely wrong in my prediction. And, in fairness, I was way ahead of the curve when I wrote this. Pinot Gris now occupies more than 7,300 acres in California, which is hugely more than the few dozen acres that existed back in 1994. Oregon's acreage has also increased to more than 1,800 acres. But next "Big White"? Hardly, at least not when compared to California's 91,348 acres of Chardonnay in 2007.

One thing I did not predict: the preference for the Italian name Pinot Grigio over the French Pinot Gris. You can thank America's ongoing love of all things Italian, especially restaurants. This was captured in a 2002 New Yorker cartoon in which a man, looking at the wine list in a restaurant, says to his companion, "I want Chardonnay, but I like saying 'Pinot Grigio.'" I was wrong to call California winegrowers who preferred that name "foolish."

Syrah: The Next Really Big Red

THE MOST EXCITING WINE IN America today is Syrah. I'd love to say that it's Pinot Noir, but I cannot tell a lie. It's Syrah that's slated for stardom.

Big deal, you say. Syrah has *already* arrived. Sure, it's clearly moving up the charts. But I'm talking about something bigger than just the newest wine darling. I'm talking about—reverent voice here—Really Big.

The category of Really Big is a different order than just popular. Really Big is when golf courses and bed-and-breakfasts use the name. When it becomes a lipstick shade or a paint color. This is precisely what's going to happen to Syrah.

But in order for that to occur, you always find certain prerequisites:

Really Big Rule 1: I recently spoke with a California grower who was worried that there was too much Syrah in the ground. Actually, it's quite the opposite: There's not enough.

- For a wine to become Really Big, there has to be a lot of it. You think you're already hearing about Syrah? Think again. California has just 16,000 acres of Syrah planted; Washington has only 2,100 acres.

- That may sound like a lot, but compare it to such Really Bigs as Chardonnay (98,000 acres), Cabernet Sauvignon (76,000 acres), and Merlot (52,000 acres).

- What's more, it helps if there's plenty of the same wine from elsewhere in the world. It's all to Syrah's advantage that 40 percent of everything grown in Australia is Shiraz (63,000 acres). The Rhône Valley has at least 100,000 acres of Syrah, with Languedoc-Roussillon kicking in another 62,000 acres.

- Why is a vast supply so important? Because for a grape to become Really Big, it first has to be commodified. And that takes massive, even excess, supply. This, in turn, makes Rule 2 essential.

Really Big Rule 2: The grape variety has to have a "pinnacle wine." A "pinnacle wine" commands an outrageous price and achieves phenomenal fame and respect. It occupies an acknowledged peak of a pyramid, never mind how limited the actual supply.

- Cabernet Sauvignon has its Bordeaux first growths. Chardonnay has Montrachet (and other *grands crus*). Pinot Noir has Romanée-Conti (ditto). Merlot has Château Pétrus.

- "Pinnacle wines" serve two purposes. First, they set a price cascade, creating the classic sales pitch: "If

Château Lafite Rothschild gets $400, my wine is a steal at $100."

- Second, "pinnacle wines" validate quality. Recognized as unquestionably great, they confirm a grape's intrinsic quality. Without a "pinnacle wine" (or two or three) a grape that gets commodified becomes just that—a commodity confined to a price ghetto and an image from which it cannot escape. Think Chenin Blanc or, until very recently, Zinfandel.

Really Big Rule 3: The grape variety has to grow successfully in multiple climates and soils. And it has to deliver commercial yields, which means at least three tons an acre (or roughly forty hectoliters of wine per hectare, in European terms). Better yet, it should perform at even twice these yields and still retain discernible quality.

- Pinot Noir, for example, will be popular, but it will never be Really Big. Its yields are too low and it's too finicky about sites.

Really Big Rule 4: The wine has to be "obvious." This is a variation on H. L. Mencken's immortal observation about how "Nobody ever went broke underestimating the taste of the American public."

- Subtle wines don't sell—not in the Really Big leagues anyway. Most Cabernets, Chardonnays, and Merlots are pretty "obvious"—which is to say, accessible—wines, full of flavor, color, and fruitiness. Yet these same wines, no matter how basic, must still have cachet (see Really Big Rule 2).

Syrah has it all. The worldwide supply is generous and growing. It has its "pinnacle wines" in Côte-Rôtie, Hermitage, and Australian Shiraz such as Grange and Henschke Hill of Grace, with some California Syrah stars soon to shine.

Syrah grows wonderfully well in both cool climates (look for a blueberry scent) and warm (a whiff of leather) and in seemingly any soil. Its yields are legendarily large.

What's more, not even Syrah's most ardent defenders would suggest that it's subtle. Syrah is always, at minimum, a lush gush of fabulous fruit. You can't miss it.

And it won't, either. Syrah is the next Really Big Red. *(2003)*

Here I was doing all right. But then, what I was seeing with Syrah in 2003 wasn't anywhere near as far into the future as my prediction for Pinot Gris back in the mid-1990s. Syrah currently occupies 18,085 acres in California (in 2007), which is pretty respectable compared to its powerhouse red rival, Cabernet Sauvignon (74,643 acres in 2007).

What really matters in this prediction are the rules of "Really Big." These, I believe, are structural and will continue to hold true.

—⁓—

SO WHAT'S THE NEXT REALLY BIG WHITE?

RECENTLY, I WAS EXPLAINING TO a friend—who has only a casual interest in wine—my recent contention that Syrah will be the next Really Big Red. He listened politely and said, "Okay, fine. But what's the next Really Big White?"

For once in my life, I was momentarily stumped. I simply hadn't thought about the next Really Big White. After all, my criteria for Really Big status are

a) there's a lot of it grown, preferably worldwide;

b) it has to have what I call "pinnacle wines" which are bottlings that are universally recognized as profound and emotionally thrilling;

c) the grape variety must grow successfully in a variety of climates and soils; and

d) the wine has to be "obvious," which is to say that it's not overly subtle or inaccessible.

When you think about it, there simply aren't many plausible candidates for the next Really Big White.

Oh, there are plenty of swell whites yet to be fully celebrated. But none fulfill all of the criteria for Really Big status. Chenin Blanc? A wonderful white grape, but it falls short on most of the above. Sauvignon Blanc might be a contender, but it doesn't have "pinnacle wines," although it does perform well in many locales. Also, it doesn't transform with age the way other Really Bigs do.

Forget Gewürtzraminer, Muscat, and Viognier: they don't grow well in numerous climates and soils, to say nothing of lacking multiple pinnacle bottlings. Ditto for Marsanne, Roussanne, Trebbiano, Vermentino, Garganega, Grüner Veltliner, Pinot Gris, and just about any other white wine variety you'd care to name.

Only one wine fills the bill: Riesling.

But nobody *wants* Riesling, you say. Tut-tut. That's what they say now. But the business of Really Big is about two things: fashion and economics. Sure, right now Riesling is not ardently pursued. But it once was beloved by every strata of winedom, from experts to Sunday sippers. It's a matter of fashion—which is, by definition, changeable.

Don't forget economics. To be Really Big, a variety has to deliver high quality at generous yields. If Riesling has a problem it's that it's *overly* generous. Greedy growers in Alsace can easily crop seven tons an acre. And the Australians can (and do) deliver double-digit yields. Riesling puts out.

Of course, when everybody thinks of Riesling they think of Germany, which has more than fifty thousand acres of Riesling. No one disputes that it is the epicenter of great Riesling, with more "pinnacle wines" than any other nation.

But what's less often recognized is just how successful Riesling is elsewhere. Washington State has more Riesling planted than any other state (about 2,200 acres). Indeed, Chateau Ste. Michelle sells six-hundred-thousand cases of "Johannisberg Riesling" each year, making it the American market leader.

California, once a bastion for Riesling—twenty years ago they had more than 11,000 acres—still issues some mighty fine Rieslings. Trefethen Vineyards in Napa Valley and Navarro Vineyards in Mendocino County's Anderson Valley are two stalwarts that have actually planted *more* Riesling, as their wines are simply so good. Riesling is successful in numerous spots in California, such as Monterey and Santa Barbara counties, to name but two.

Then there's Australia. I don't know how many wine lovers associate Australia with Riesling, but once you taste some of the better bottlings from Clare Valley, north of Adelaide, you'll know that Australian Riesling is a world-beater. (And, to their everlasting credit, the Riesling producers of Clare Valley have collectively agreed to bottle their Rieslings using screw caps. Good on ya, mates!)

Of course, there's Austria, which makes famously good Riesling. (Interestingly, though, they grow more Grüner Veltliner than any other variety.)

Not least is France's Alsace region, which still creates the world's greatest dry Rieslings. Alsace remains the benchmark and rightly so. Once you've tasted a mature (ten to fifteen years old) Riesling from a producer such as Trimbach (to cite one of several dozen superb contenders), you know why Alsace is the motherhouse of dry Riesling.

Right now, *nobody* is betting on Riesling. If you say, "Hey, how about putting in some Riesling? It's gonna be the next Really Big White," you'll be classed as a *grand cru* loony.

Nevertheless, no other white grape fills the bill like Riesling. It's the only possible choice. *(2003)*

If there's much statistical proof about my prediction of Riesling as the next Really Big White, I haven't seen it. But them's my words and I'm sticking to 'em. Besides, Riesling is really wonderful and it ought to be the next Really Big White.

FIGHTING THE FUTURE

THE ISSUE KEEPS BUILDING. AND it surely won't go away—either its controversy or pressing reality. What am I talking about? Genetic modification.

If you're an American reader, chances are you'll roll your eyes and say, "Oh, lordy, not that again." If you're European, it's a good bet your blood pressure will rise and you'll say, "It's twenty-first-century evil and must be stopped." This, of course, is a broad brushstroke, but no less accurate for that.

Wine drinkers *really* don't want to hear about this. Why? Because we like our romantic reverie. (Me, too.) We love the age-old traditionalism of wine, its fingertip-touch across the ages, from Burgundy's Cistercian monks to Bordeaux's fairy tale châteaux to Napa Valley's fantasyland.

In the wine world, the most outspoken voices on the subject are Burgundians. In July 2000, a manifesto of sorts against genetically modified organisms (GMOs) was published, signed by twenty-four of Burgundy's most prestigious producers, including Aubert de Villaine of the Domaine de la Romanée-Conti and Pierre-Henry Gagey of Maison Louis Jadot, among other notables.

Their document notes, "No GMO vine or wine has as yet obtained marketing authorization in Europe." But studies are at a "very advanced stage, especially for genetically modified yeasts."

In the works, they say, are such genetic modifications as

- yeasts that secrete enzymes, antibacterial agents, varietal aromas, etc.

- rootstocks that are resistant to leaf roll.

- grape varieties that are resistant to oidium (powdery mildew), eutypiose, flavescence dorée (a yellowing viral disease), and phylloxera.

- grape varieties with low potassium absorption.

Gee, that sounds pretty good. A "cure" for phylloxera? It's a winegrower's dream.

Apparently not. The Burgundians are famously close to the land, what with so many owners of so many small plots. And they grow the world's most sensitive red wine grape, Pinot Noir.

But there's another, less conspicuous, feature to why Burgundians in particular are so concerned about "progress." Back in the 1970s and 1980s, they screwed up their vaunted vineyards pretty badly.

Burgundian growers were advised by academic researchers to replace their old vineyards, with their array of ancient Pinot Noir clones (or strains), with a handful of newly selected clones. It was a mistake. Yields were excessive and flavor shadings nonexistent.

They were advised to freely use newly developed antirot sprays to ward off rot at harvest time. After a few years' application, the easy-but-expensive sprays proved ineffective. And the vines were weakened, as well.

They were counseled to liberally use fertilizers, resulting in pumped-up vines and soil that was excessively rich in potassium. Intensive application of herbicides and fungicides created nearly sterile soil.

By the 1990s, Burgundy's best growers realized that it was madness. They were seduced by "progress."

Above all, they had an acute sense of moral lapse. Burgundy is an ancient and spiritually vital community. After all, Catholic monks and nuns created it. Modern-day Burgundians feel a strong tug from across the centuries. Lulled by assurances from scientists, as well as by the sheer ease of these wondrous new inventions, they had compromised their moral obligation as guardians of the world's most profound vineyards—and they knew it. So you can see why the French revolt started in Burgundy.

Their arguments struck home. In March 2001, a new organization emerged after winemakers elsewhere in France heard Burgundy's warning. After meeting in Burgundy, they created a new organization called Terre et Vin du Monde. It endorsed the plea for a ten-year moratorium and has asked winegrowers and wine drinkers everywhere to join their ranks.

Which leads to the question: Are they right? Should reasonable wine lovers everywhere rally—if only in spirit—to this cause?

I, for one, say yes. Genetic modification is surely the future—and not necessarily the scary "Franken-future" that some would have us believe. Still, Burgundy's recent experience with "progress" is a worthy cautionary tale. As the Burgundians who signed the original plea for a moratorium rather poignantly note:

> It is of the utmost importance that the future of our profession does not
> develop under the sole influence and interests of scientists, industrialists,
> and technocrats. The past has taught us a few lessons in this connection.

Fighting the future? Not necessarily. But is there any need to rush into it? *(2001)*

As is well known, the issue of genetically modified organisms (GMOs) has not gone away. However, it appears to be only simmering in recent years, especially in the wine world. Little has changed since this was written, which is not a bad thing. Time will allow proponents of GMOs to make their case, and for opponents to recognize and accept whatever turns out to be worthwhile and agitate against proposals that seem unnecessarily risky.

WINE HOKUM

I take the title "Wine Hokum" in homage to the late Frank Schoonmaker who, with co-author Tom Marvel, wrote a landmark book in 1941 called *American Wines*. The first chapter of that book was titled "Wine Hokum," which they defined as "all the things people can find out about wine without ever drinking."

"The victim of Hokum," diagnose Messrs. Schoonmaker and Marvel, "exhibits symptoms of nervousness in the presence of wine, followed by a mounting fever of pretense and snobbishness." The cure? "Where wine is abundantly enjoyed, Hokum withers and dies."

Like the deserving poor and the undeserving rich, wine hokum will always be with us, so much so that it's hard to know where to begin (or end) sticking in the pins—or even whether to bother. Still, there are times when a writer has to saddle up and joust.

WHY WINE ISN'T ART—AND WHY THAT MATTERS

RECENTLY I FOUND MYSELF IN one of those wine wrangles that, truth to tell, I usually try to avoid. (Check out any wine chat board on the Internet if you've got a taste for this sort of thing.)

The wrangle was with, natch, a winemaker at a social event. It involved the winemaker's assertion that, "Fine wine is art." I pointed out, as modestly as I could, that there's no denying that nature surely doesn't make wine on its own, let alone fine wine (vinegar is more like it). I then went on to say that fine wine is, at best, a high craft both in the vineyard and the cellar.

Probably, if I had stopped there, the discussion would have proved amicable. But I took the matter one step further. (You're shocked, I know.) I submitted that saying that winemaking, and therefore its result, is "art" was self-aggrandizing. You can imagine how that was received.

Now, I admit that the self-aggrandizing bit was a low blow. Still, it's true. If wine-makers can get you, me, and, especially, their employers to see them as artists, you know what'll happen: Their salaries will rise and producers, for their part, will start pricing wine as "art." And you know what *that* means.

So why isn't fine wine "art"? The answer is surprisingly simple. Art is creation; wine is amplification. The big difference between an artist and a winemaker is that an artist starts with a blank sheet while a winemaker works with the exact opposite. A grape arrives at the winery with all the parts included—a piñata stuffed with goodies just waiting to be cracked open.

Is there a craft to doing that? You bet there is. But where an artist conceives of something out of the proverbial thin air, no winemaker anywhere in the world can do any such thing.

For example, when my wine heroine Lalou Bize-Leroy bought the former Domaine Noëllat in Vosne-Romanée and transformed it into Domaine Leroy, she did not create her magnificent wines from scratch. It was all right there in the hallowed ground and old vines of her newly acquired pieces of Richebourg and Romanée-St. Vivant. She didn't create something from nothing. Quite the opposite.

Fine wine is not creation. It is refinement. If it were otherwise, then everybody would be "creating" Château Lafite Rothschild or La Tâche or any other wine masterpiece of singular, irreproducible expression and high price. Counterfeiting aside, I don't see anybody doing that, do you?

They don't because they can't. That's precisely why fine wine is not art. It comes from all the forces that create a particularity of site. Great winemakers—which is to say, expert practitioners of wine craft—tease what they can from the sites available to them by planting the right grapevines, growing them astutely, harvesting the fruit at an ideal moment (a problematic issue today given some winemakers' and critics' preferences for ever greater ripeness), and handling the fermented juice in the cellar with deft control.

This is no small charge, and I, for one, do not seek to diminish it in any way. But art? Not a chance. The poet E. E. Cummings put his finger on it better than anyone else: "A world of made is not a world of born." Wine is no more a blank canvas than the Grand Canyon.

Why does this distinction matter? Because abstract though it is, if winemakers and, yes, wine lovers see wine as "art," then the essential connection between what a grape expresses from its site and what we expect is severed. If a winemaker is an "artist," then he or she, by artistic right, can and should modify the result to suit a personal vision separate from a "mere" expression of place.

However, if the finest winemaking is seen as a high craft, rather than an "art," the expectation changes subtly yet substantively. Where art presumes a blank slate upon which a personal vision necessarily is writ large, the notion of craft is more deferential. Like great parenting, it's a guardianship of something already largely complete. The goal is refinement and amplification of what's inherent. Think of what happens when parents do otherwise.

So it is with wine. All sorts of technological deconstruction and reconstruction now occur in many wineries today, especially ones creating high-end—or at least high-priced—wines. They see themselves as artists and would like to convince you of same. If they can, well, you know how distorted the results can be—and who pays. *(2008)*

ALL IS NOT AS IT SEEMS IN *MONDOVINO*

A YEAR OR SO AGO, I was contacted by Jonathan Nossiter, the creator of the wine documentary *Mondovino*, which opens today in New York. He importuned me to appear in his forthcoming movie. I'd never heard of Mr. Nossiter and have never met him. But as he described his documentary, something didn't smell right. So I declined with thanks. Subsequently, he tried again to enlist me—to no effect.

I had the chance to finally see *Mondovino* at a private screening and found myself breathing a huge sigh of relief at having dodged a bullet. The documentary, so-called, turned out to be nothing of the sort. *Mondovino* is, instead, pure agitprop, a willfully deceitful piece of antiglobalist propaganda of the heavy-handed sort unseen since Greenpeace started filming the bludgeoning of baby seals.

Mr. Nossiter, forty-three, was previously a waiter and sommelier in New York and Paris, as well as the creator of other documentaries. He is the son of the late Bernard Nossiter, a foreign affairs reporter for the *New York Times*. Because of his father's peripatetic job, Mr. Nossiter is enviably multilingual, which talent is on display in *Mondovino* as he interviews subjects in French, Italian, Spanish, and English.

Mondovino purports to reveal the underbelly of soulless globalist wine forces such as the Robert Mondavi Winery, wine critic Robert Parker, and France's globe-trotting wine consultant Michel Rolland, whom the movie portrays as a villainous profiteer. In contrast, Mr. Nossiter parades a variety of French, South American, and Italian winegrowers who are meant to represent the threatened but oh-so-soulful "real people" of wine.

The problem is, these voices of humble wine humanity are often nothing of the sort—and Mr. Nossiter surely knows it. For example, the star of the show is Hubert de Montille, an entertaining, articulate, Burgundian winegrower who is, effectively, the voice of the romantic winegrower. An unknowing viewer—which means most viewers—would have no reason to believe that Mr. de Montille is anything other that the dirt-under-his-nails Burgundian vigneron displayed in the documentary. Yet he's far from that.

Mr. de Montille does indeed make wine in the village of Volnay. But he's no *paysan* as Mr. Nossiter would have you believe. Rather, Mr. de Montille has long been a prominent lawyer in Burgundy with a lucrative career in Dijon. He's no more a "man of the land" than George W. Bush is a cowboy. But nowhere in *Mondovino* are you told—or even given a hint—that Mr. de Montille is anything other than a genial old Burgundian codger wresting a precarious living from his handful of precious acres in Volnay and Pommard.

This duplicity flickers through *Mondovino* like a kind of cinematic Potemkin village. Little is as it seems. Producers in Bordeaux and Tuscany whom Mr. Nossiter dislikes are pointedly, and gratuitously, asked about collaboration with the Nazis or involvement with Mussolini—which subjects are apropos of nothing in the film. It's maliciously done to discomfort those being interviewed. The "good guys" are asked no such historical questions.

Much is done, subtly and unsubtly, to make the "bad guys"—the moneyed producers, consultants, various globalists—look grotesque. They are often shown in close-ups, the better to convey their purported grotesquerie. The camera work is literally jiggly. I'm told that Mr. Nossiter used a small camera placed on his hip, the better to make people less self-conscious. It also has the effect of making you feel like you're often peering up at the subjects being interviewed.

The good guys are always shown in their vineyards, while the bad guys are in offices or getting in or out of expensive cars. The implication is that the good guys are somehow peasants, which is laughable indeed in the case of Mr. de Montille, as well as another featured producer, Aimé Guibert of Mas de Daumas Gassac in the southern French town of Aniane.

Mr. Guibert spearheaded the opposition to Robert Mondavi establishing a vineyard and winery—and thus competition—in his village. Railing against big producers and wine consultants, Mr. Guibert is neither shown inside his own sizable winery (he has ninety-nine acres of vines), nor is any mention made of Mr. Guibert's own use of consultants when he established his winery.

And so it goes—excruciatingly slowly. *Mondovino* is a two-hours-plus exercise in malice aforethought. If that turns out to be your cup of overbrewed tea—to mix a metaphor—you'll be delighted to hear that Mr. Nossiter plans to release a ten-part DVD series to exploit the hundreds of hours of film never used for *Mondovino*. *(2005)*

BARBARIANS AT THE CORK

SPURRED BY THE POPULARITY OF inexpensive Australian and other New World wines, the drumbeat about making wine less snobbish and more accessible has grown louder in recent years.

Actually, there's *always* been such a movement. You can find books and articles dating back decades that decry the pretension of wine jabber. My favorite is a chapter in *American Wines*, a 1941 book by Frank Schoonmaker and Tom Marvel. It's titled "Wine Hokum."

So let's not imagine that today's trend toward making wine more consumer-friendly is anything new or original. But what *has* changed—and not for the better—is the attitude, a new kind of "off with their heads" arrogance.

Raising the revolutionary banner, today's proselytizers for the "people's wine" spend their time denigrating—indeed, seeking to destroy—the painstakingly constructed coral reef of wine appreciation created by wine lovers over decades, even centuries.

I'll give you an example. Here's Australian-now-living-in-England sommelier Matt Skinner (of chef Jamie Oliver's restaurant, Fifteen) in the British newspaper the *Observer*:

> "If you think of the wine industry as a pie, then the snobs are a tiny slice of it. But they're the slice that f***s it for everyone. Yeah, they've got a bit of a conspiracy to mystify it for everyone, to keep the younger generation out of the club. But fortunately, they're quite old now, so they're literally dying out."

> "But oh God," he continues, "I'd always rather serve a table of women than men. Men—your average Friday lunchtime table of w**kers—don't want to listen, they're competitive with me and they want to get one up on each other by pretending they know the most about wine when blatantly they don't . . . Tossers."

Here's a young sommelier, described as "twenty-something" by the *Observer*, who has decided that his male clients don't know anywhere near as much as he—"they're competitive with me"—and even worse, they're "tossers." (Off with their heads!)

Then along comes Richard Branson, the billionaire entrepreneur and owner of Virgin Atlantic Airways. He's decided to enter the wine business here in the United States. What's Branson's angle? He's offering a label called Virgin Vines along with the motto, "Unscrew it, let's do it." So far, so hip.

Then comes the skewer: "Wine, like life, is meant to be enjoyed," he says. "All the pomp and ceremony currently associated with wine just gets in the way of enjoying it."

How easy it is to pretend that in order to save the village you first have to destroy it. Everything that once existed about wine is worse than worthless: it must be eliminated in the name of wine democratization.

It's a conspiracy to mystify it for everyone, you see. And anybody who might believe, or even suggest, that there's merit to the old ways is a snob.

This is a new kind of wine barbarism. It's nihilistically premised on author Gore Vidal's immortal line, "It's not enough to succeed. Others must fail."

What was once an enduring wine beauty is now under siege. And what are these paragons of wine populism putting in its place? Nothing. Absolutely nothing.

It's so easy to decry wine pretension and pomposity. Yet the irony of this—the very vacuity of it—is that there's so little of that arrogance left today. The old tuxedo-clad wine waiter with the leather apron and the ridiculous silver tastevin hanging from his neck is not only a dog that won't hunt, it's a dog that's been dead for years.

Nonetheless, a denigration of thoughtful, carefully considered wine appreciation is growing. Those who take wine seriously, who care about fine wine served well and lovingly, are increasingly seen as the enemies of wine populism.

I wonder how much Branson would enjoy his wine if he went to a restaurant and the sommelier first did a little air guitar with his bottle and said, "OK, let's unscrew it. Let's do it!" I rather doubt that he'd clap his hands with delight.

Much of the beauty of wine today comes from the insight and care of those who preceded us. Not just in its service, but also in the creation of wines that are far more than mere brands with feel-good slogans.

Portraying these wine lovers as doddering fools who have prevented the world from enjoying wine is today's new *Clockwork Orange* wine hipness. *(2005)*

A GIANT SUCKING SOUND—AND THAT'S ALL

"IF I HAD TO LIVE my life over again," reflected Louis Pasteur, "I would try always to remember that admirable precept of Bossuet: 'The greatest disorder of the mind is to believe that things are so because we wish them to be so.'"

No doubt, neither Pasteur nor Bossuet was thinking of holiday shopping or pondering the purchase of wine tchotchkes. Yet Bossuet's maxim comes to mind every time I see a wine preservation gizmo called the Vacu-Vin. It is a little hand-pump device made in Holland that ostensibly creates a vacuum in a partially empty wine bottle. Merchants everywhere will tell you that it's a best seller.

The idea behind the Vacu-Vin—Pasteur's as it happens—is that degradation of wine cannot occur in an oxygen-free environment. There's only one problem: Vacu-Vin doesn't work. It never has. But that apparently hasn't stopped people from buying the gizmo, which has been on the market for years.

Its appeal is that it looks like it *should* work. You put the special flexible stopper where the cork used to sit. Then you place the gizmo on top of the stopper and pump up and down. It seems so gratifying. It makes so much sense. And the instructions even tell you that, "When resistance is felt on [the] upward stroke, your bottle is vacuum sealed."

Six years ago I was asked by the *Wall Street Journal* to evaluate the Vacu-Vin, the design of which remains unchanged. I agreed to do so, provided that I configure the evaluation, which involved five bottles of three different wines: a six-year-old Chambolle-Musigny, a two-year-old Oregon Pinot Noir, and a two-year-old California Chardonnay. Moreover, I insisted that the *Journal* engage someone to measure the vacuum created by the device, as I had my doubts as to its efficacy. They agreed.

The sensory part of the investigation took five days of preparation. Eight ounces (one-third of a bottle) were removed. The wines were then immediately "vacumated." On the day of the blind tasting, what was in front of me was a freshly opened control bottle of each wine; a second that had been "vacumated" for five days; a third simply recorked for five days; a fourth "vacumated" for three days; and a fifth "vacumated" for two days. All were stored upright at 65 degrees. Everything was witnessed by the *Journal* reporter.

The blind tasting confirmed my doubts. I am not one of winedom's better blind tasters. The young Chardonnays were difficult: I couldn't tell the samples apart with much discernment. But with the red Burgundy I was, as the *Journal* put it, "Right on the money for most of the samples." And for the Oregon Pinot Noir, I called every one correctly.

Sensorily, to me anyway, the Vacu-Vin was a shuck. You could track the deterioration in each sample. Indeed, just recorking the wine worked equally as well—or as badly. Even the *Journal*'s reporter could tell the difference. "One thing was perfectly clear, however, even to my untrained nose," she wrote. "The earlier 'vacumated' Burgundies smelled distinctly like pungent sherry—not a whiff similar to the fruity, delicately fresh control sample."

And what about the actual vacuum? The *Journal* asked Professor David Roe of the Portland State University chemistry department to test the gizmo. He put a little hole in a two-third's full wine bottle, inserted a short glass tube and a length of plastic tubing, and attached a vacuum gauge. Professor Roe ran the test several times. At best he achieved a vacuum of somewhat less than 70 percent.

Then, Professor Roe left the gauge attached to the bottle to see if the seal would hold the vacuum that was achieved. It didn't. In just ninety minutes, he reported, the vacuum pressure diminished by 15 percent.

I recently asked Professor Roe to repeat his test with a newly purchased Vacu-Vin. The results? "The pump is more efficient, but no more effective," he reports. "The vacuum is the same, around 70 to 75 percent. And the leak rate is the same: After two hours you lose 25 percent of the vacuum. Overnight—twelve hours—the vacuum is totally gone."

Bossuet was right: "The greatest disorder of the mind is to believe that things are so because we wish them to be so." *(1994)*

When the story first appeared in the Wall Street Journal, *neither I nor the* Journal *heard from the folks who make the Vacu-Vin, nor was any scientific evidence offered to refute the findings of Professor Roe. Six years later, after the preceding piece appeared in* Wine Spectator, *with updated findings that confirmed the original findings, there was again no evidence offered to refute the findings. This gizmo continues to sell well to this day. So much for the awful power of the press.*

NUTRITIONAL LIES

LIKE MANY WRITERS, I'VE HAD a book idea rattling in my brain that's never gone anywhere (and never will). I even have a title for it: *The Book of Truths.* In it there's a chapter about, ironically, what I call "nutritional lies."

Now, a nutritional lie is something that, once upon a time, all parents fed to their children. They probably still do, but I get the impression that today's kids are, in this context, a bit undernourished. A nutritional lie is something like the classic, "You can be anything you want to be if you try hard enough." Every adult knows this is a flagrant lie. But it's nutritional when fed to children.

All of this is a (long-winded) way of getting to the point of this column, namely, the nutritional lie about wine cellars. No "wine adult" wants to tell the truth about storing wines to those just starting out because it would hobble them. So we tell the second greatest nutritional wine lie: Any old place will do. (The greatest is: "If you like it, it's good.")

This past summer, during the heat, the *Wall Street Journal* ran a feature story that fed its readers the nutritional wine cellar lie as shamelessly as a parent wheedling a kid into bed. The headline alone told you about the whopper to come: "Do You Need A Wine Cellar?"

What was so interesting was how all the "wine adults" quoted dutifully told the same nutritional lie about storing wines. For example, wine adult Joshua Wesson, the 1984 winner of the Best French Wine Sommelier competition, assuredly knows the truth about wine storage. Yet he reassuringly says, "For 99 percent of the wine lovers of the world a closet is as good as a cellar."

Josh told the *Journal* that his own nine-case collection "is in boxes in the back of my closet, just to the left of my socks." The *Journal* lapped up that populist piffle like free beer at a labor rally.

Lest you think I'm singling out my old drinking buddy Josh, let me assure you that he was just doing his (adult) job. Who wants to tell the truth to would-be wine drinkers? Do *you* want to tell general-interest readers of a nationally distributed newspaper that their Chardonnays will die in the Kansas heat before this year's crop is hauled in? Of course not. Thank God (and Robert Mondavi) that they're willing to drink wine in Kansas. Let's not make matters more complicated.

This is the basis of the (highly nutritional) lies of Lettie Teague, wine editor of *Food & Wine* magazine and her husband, Alan Richman, food writer and movie star interviewer for *GQ* magazine. They, too, know better. (They're friends of mine, so I know.) Their twenty-case collection, "including a few 1982 Château Mouton Rothschilds," has been kept "baking and freezing in the hall of a New York apartment," among other venues.

The *Journal* approvingly notes that Lettie is "unrepentant." "The wine-cellar business," she says, "has gone too far. There has to be a happy medium between us [i.e., Real People] and people who are obsessed [i.e., anyone who doesn't bake and freeze 1982 Moutons]."

Nutritional liars tell themselves—and this was the gist of the *Journal* story, too—that almost no one actually keeps wine for long. That is a fact. Half of all the wine purchased is consumed within twenty-four hours, we're told by market surveys.

So why are Josh, Lettie, and Alan so willing to boldly lie where others have lied before? Because no one devoted to wine—such as they are—wants to tell those who aren't that they shouldn't lay in a few bottles unless they've got just the "right" space.

Not least, it's good, popular copy. The *Journal* wouldn't publish such nonsense if it was something important, like pork bellies. But, hey, it's only wine. And it's a Good Thing to demystify it and take it out of the hands of people who might "obsessively" put their $500 bottles of Mouton Rothschild into an elitist cool space.

Here's the nutritional *truth*: If you don't store your wines in a cool spot, say, 60 degrees or less, they're gonna fade. Then they're gonna die, like goldfish flopping on the floor. Just how long it takes will vary, but it's a sure thing. If anyone tells you differently, well, it's just a bedtime story to help you sleep. *(1998)*

Lettie Teague and Alan Richman have since divorced. (This column was not cited as contributory.) I have no idea who got the 1982 Mouton Rothschild in the settlement, but I do have a very good idea about what its condition was wherever it landed.

A GROWING MYSTERY

AS THE SMOKE CLEARS ON the twentieth century, it's safe to say that the century's most important wine event was estate-bottling. It was a revolution. Now it's so common as to seem uneventful. We *assume* a wine is estate-bottled if the label is strongly associated with a grower's name. Not so fast.

A funny thing happened on the way to the bank: many seemingly estate-bottled wines aren't. Oh, they have a "grower" name on them, which makes us innocently assume that they grew the grapes that made the wine.

We *know* that there's a vast difference between the grapes someone grows himself or herself and the stuff that gets bought. They told us so, remember? That's why savvy wine buyers everywhere are so avid for the best grower bottlings. It's a form of insurance.

Nowhere is this more true than in Burgundy. Yet an increasing number of seeming "grower bottlings" are anything but. Take the Burgundies of Domaine Jean-Marc Boillot. Not all of them are, in fact, "domaine." The estate stuff reads: *"Mis en bouteille par J. M. Boillot, propriétaire à Pommard."* However, the purchased wines read: *"Mis en bouteille par J. M. Boillot, Pommard, Côte d'Or."*

Got that? Otherwise, the labels look identical. Wow! You'd have to be one savvy insider to know which he grew and which he bought.

Ditto for the famous Etienne Sauzet, a domaine that now sells its own grapes to its own shipping company, thereby allowing them to buy grapes or wine and augment their production as they like. Which is the historically thrilling estate stuff? And which is the purchased goods? You can't tell from the label, as everything reads the same: *"Mis en bouteille par Etienne Sauzet."*

In these cases, and many others, they have the precious domaine *image*. The letter of the labeling law is "correct." But you can be damned sure that, like canny hostesses, no one is going out of their way to distinguish the home-baked goods from the store-bought.

It's no better on these shores. You see a California district appellation, say, Oakville or Dry Creek Valley. Not unreasonably, you figure that the wine in the bottle comes from the place named on the label. You figured wrong. The law says that only 85 percent of the wine has to come from that appellation.

It's a sweet deal. They get the luster of a named-district wine without all the wine actually having to come from it. How much difference can it make?

Imagine a Bordeaux-shaped bottle. Now imagine almost a half-cup of wine missing from it. The wine level would be what's called "low shoulder" in the auction trade. Now imagine how you'd feel if this high-priced "appellation" wine you just bought was topped up with bulk stuff from Fresno.

Ah, but what's a half-cup between friends? If you multiply four ounces by, say, 10,000 cases—why, it's the equivalent of 18,926 bottles of wine! At $50 a bottle . . . you figure it out.

How about the phrase "Produced and Bottled By"? This may be the most commonly used designation by many wineries—and not just big ones, either. It sounds straightforward, doesn't it? It isn't. You only have to make three-quarters of the wine to proudly and convincingly say you "produced and bottled" it. The rest could be a bulk purchase—and usually is.

Even more conniving is "Vinted and Bottled By." It means absolutely nothing. You can buy 100 percent of the finished wine in bulk, bottle it, and declare "Vinted and Bottled By" on your label.

Increasingly, producers seek to capitalize on their "grower image." The line between what we want (wines exclusively from grapes they grow) and what they want to sell us (the image, not the original substance that created it) is blurred.

The worst part is that the *real* growers, the ones who really do make 100 percent of their wines from grapes they grow, are hard-pressed to distinguish themselves.

If I were such a grower today, I'd trumpet that fact on a back label as loudly and clearly as I could. I'd say "100 percent of the wine in this bottle was grown by me, made by me, bottled by me, and comes 100 percent from the appellation designated." That's what the front labels are supposed to indicate clearly—but they don't. *(1999)*

Nothing has happened between then and now that would require me to change a single word of what I wrote a decade ago. By the way, 18,926 bottles at $50 a bottle works out to $946,300.

HOW DO THEY LIVE WITH THEMSELVES?

THE GUY WHO BROUGHT THE wine was generous indeed. But he got shafted, big-time. It wasn't by the restaurant, though. It was by the wines or, more specifically, the corks.

My host, who brought the wines, first pulls out a magnum of 1985 Dom Perignon rosé (cost: $500). As soon as the wine was poured I knew it wasn't right.

This presents an interesting social dilemma, by the way. What do you say (if anything) when someone else is serving you wine that you suspect—or worse, *know*—is corked? I waited to see if anyone, especially the host, made any comment. No one did.

Now, if it were a table where wine is no big deal, I wouldn't say anything. But this was a bunch of wine hounds. So I put my toe in the water. "I'm not that familiar with 1985 Dom Perignon rosé." (Which happens to be true.) "Is this what it should smell like?"

One of my tablemates gave a thin little smile and replied, "Well, actually it's not. I think the wine might be slightly corked." The stinky cat was out of the bag. Our host took another sniff, shrugged, and said, "You're right."

I felt sorry for the guy. Five hundred bucks down the drain. He'd had the wine for years, waiting to serve it for just such a special occasion. What are you going to do? Call Moët & Chandon and demand another magnum? I don't think so.

But wait, it gets better—or rather, worse. Our hapless host then pulls out a bottle of 1999 Richebourg, Domaine de la Romanée-Conti (cost: $700). The wine is served first to the host. He takes one sniff, grimaces, and tells the sommelier to take it away.

I reached for his glass to taste for myself. The wine was corked—not lightly, but badly and unmistakably. I wanted to weep, but the host was the model of a graceful loser at a high-stakes poker game. When I suggested that he return the wine, he explained that he had bought it in Europe. *Tant pis* (tough luck), as the French would say.

But where you buy your wine begs the question. A wine shouldn't come from a winery already tainted. Which brings us to an uncomfortable ethical issue: Is it morally acceptable to knowingly release defective products?

That's what we're talking about here: defective products. That's what corked wines are. And let's not kid ourselves. Every winery that uses corks knows full well that somewhere between 3 percent and 5 percent of everything they send out the door is defective. You can quibble about the percentage, but the fact remains that *nobody's* cork-sealed wines are guaranteed taint-free.

And I don't think that asserting, as I've heard countless times, "We do everything we can to get the finest corks" is any kind of self-absolution. Do you think that the Domaine de la Romanée-Conti stints on cork quality? Hardly.

If there was nothing wine producers could do about it—if cork closures were the only recourse—then you could honestly tell yourself that this is how the world is. But that's not the case here.

It's a smokescreen when producers hide behind traditionalism: "We don't know how well these synthetic corks or screw caps hold up over time."

Actually, with screw caps we do know that they hold up pretty well, although the oldest screw caps, dating to the early 1970s, had a less reliable lining of paper and cork than today's tin foil layer. The jury is still out with synthetics, but they're more than merely promising

The key point is that alternatives exist. And the jury is in on corks: they can—and do—ruin wines.

It's increasingly unacceptable that wine producers everywhere—and I include such properties as the Domaine de la Romanée-Conti, the Bordeaux first growths, and any other producer for whom traditionalism is part of their *pain et beurre*—don't give us a choice. They happily take our money up front on futures, so we're taking all the risk anyway.

If you knew that 3 percent to 5 percent of everything you sell is defective—when it doesn't have to be—could *you* look at yourself in the mirror and whistle a happy tune?

An increasing number of wine producers find that they can't. Take Dark Star Cellars in Paso Robles. Each of their synthetic corks reads: "No need to thank us for this synthetic cork . . . Last year our natural cork cost our customers $8,000 in purchasing wine that was 'corked.' This was acceptable to our supplier. It was unacceptable to us."

Wine producers of the world: How do you live with yourselves? *(2003)*

The debate and even rancor over cork-tainted wines has, if anything, increased. Synthetic corks have proved in laboratory tests to offer a less-than-effective seal after a year or two in the bottle. Screw caps, however, seem to be gaining in winemaker acceptance and consumer acceptance, although there's still resistance in both camps.

Worth noting is a report from my Wine Spectator *colleague James Laube who noted that in 2008, out of a pool of 4,295 California wines, most of which were new releases, they found 388 wines to be "corked." That's a "taint rate" of 9 percent, well above the 3 percent to 5 percent rate usually cited.*

Adding financial insult to the palate injury is the fact that the "taint rate" was 12.5 percent for wines priced at more than $200; 13.8 percent for wines priced between $100 to $200; and 10.8 percent for wines that cost between $50 to $99.

And what about the cheap wines? Of the 905 wines tasted that cost less than $20 a bottle, the rate was only 5.3 percent.

WINE AND WORDS

It seems impossible to drink wine silently. More than any other comestible, wine somehow demands a gush of words. You don't see anywhere near as much written about, say, beer or orange juice as you do about wine, never mind that both are consumed in vastly greater quantities than wine. Even food, no matter how great or refined, doesn't bear the brunt of words that wine does.

People can (and do) say what they like about the prevalence of scores in today's wine world. But words still rule. I know of no wine critic who is content with assigning a score and then shuffling away silently like a Trappist monk. Today's wine lovers are besotted with words, never more so than with the blossoming of personal wine blogs on the Web.

THE DEVIL'S WINE DICTIONARY

AMERICANS, IT OFTEN IS NOTED, are uncommonly serious folk. Some attribute this to our ceaseless quest for self-improvement. Maybe so. Still, we're not *that* unleavened. For example, there's the somewhat forgotten Ambrose Bierce, a deliciously witty (and sometimes bitter) humorist and journalist who had a large following at the turn of the nineteenth century.

One of Bierce's choicest efforts was *The Devil's Dictionary*, which first appeared in book form in 1906. It offered Bierce at his most trenchant. Try this, for example: "Dice, n. Small polka-dotted cubes of ivory, constructed like a lawyer to lie on any side, but commonly on the wrong one." And you thought lawyer jokes were new.

Bierce liked his wine, too. For example, there's this delicious entry: "Geese, n. The plural of Prohibitionist."

In the end (which in Bierce's case was mysterious, as he left for Mexico the day after Christmas in 1913 to travel with Pancho Villa's army and was never heard from again) he was devoted to "enlightened souls who prefer dry wines to sweet, sense to sentiment, wit to humor, and clean English to slang."

With Bierce in mind—and with no illusion of being a worthy competitor—I offer this variation of Bierce's diabolical theme, "The Devil's Wine Dictionary."

> **Connoisseur**—Someone who appreciates a wine paid for by someone else.
>
> **Wine Steward**—Someone who simply appreciates a wine being paid for.
>
> **Tastevin**—An unpronounceable piece of hardware that keeps wine stewards from being confused with busboys.
>
> **Wine Shipper**—A winemaker with no vineyards.
>
> **Master Blender**—A winemaker who lacks great grapes. Always applied to wine shippers who have just fed a wine writer a good lunch.
>
> **Wine Writer**—A sheep in wolf's clothing.
>
> **Wine Columnist**—A sheep in wolverine's clothing.
>
> **Scoring System**—A way of making your point without bothering to do so. (See also Hedonistic.)
>
> **Blind Tasting**—Method perfected during the Spanish Inquisition for getting experts to confess that they are not.
>
> **Wine Experts**—Those who have successfully avoided blind tastings.

Master of Wine—Name for version of British high school equivalency degree. In America, equal to Mr. Goodwrench diploma.

Master Sommelier—Someone who sells you wine at three times its cost and expects to be thanked for it.

Wine Auction—Free market device for distinguishing rich rubes from poor ones.

Wine Auctioneer—Wolf in wolf's clothing.

Wine Collector—Anyone with a wood crate of Bordeaux against which he or she can be photographed.

Serious Wine Collector— Anyone with a row of double-magnums against which he or she can be photographed.

Collectible—Anything that auctioneers can sell to anybody who decides he's a collector.

Champagne—Proprietary name for successful alchemy process in which carbon dioxide is added to otherwise undrinkable wine, turning it into gold.

New Oak—The wine equivalent of making hay whether the sun shines or not.

Chardonnay—A way of adding wine to new oak without anybody noticing.

AVA—Acronym for "Anybody's Variation Accepted." Mistakenly thought to also stand for American Viticultural Area.

Wine Futures—New wine in no bottles.

Pre-Arrival Offering—Technique by which the wine impotent seduce the wine lustful.

Low Yield—What my vineyard produces.

Excessive Yield—What their vineyard produces.

Consulting Enologist—Sleight-of-hand trick in which a winery owner's pocket is picked, with the pickpocket then taking credit for making the owner's fortune. Term first used by former bank examiner Willie Sutton, who said, "I rob wineries as a consulting enologist because that's where the money is."

Hedonistic—Wine tasting term applied to any wine that a taster likes but can't explain why. (See also Scoring System.) Always used in conjunction with "voluptuous," "creamy," and "skin contact." Known in academic circles as the Russ Meyer School of aesthetics, after the Hollywood filmmaker.

Goût de Terroir—French, for "corked."

Vino da Tavola—Italian, for "new oak." (See also Chardonnay.)

Unfiltered—American, for "The risk is all yours, bub."

Hospices de Beaune—Burgundian dialect phrase for "Gotcha!"

Terroir—French, for "birthright." Paternity is hard to prove, yet impossible to deny. Like good dancing, you know it when you see it. Often confused by Americans with new oak; by British with a free lunch.

Somewhereness—Wine tasting term applied to any wine that a taster likes but can't explain why. (See also Hedonistic.)

Meritage—Consumer protection label term. Signals a blended wine worth $10 trying to sucker a buyer into spending $20. *(1995)*

MAKE THAT A DOUBLE SUPER-TUSCAN

THE SINGLE MOST RECURRING WHINE in wine is, "We've got to make wine simpler for people." It's the perennial rallying cry for anti-elitist populists; for let's-make-a-buck bulk blenders; for corporate brand-name builders; for hand-wringing wine evangelists; and for everyone else who's paternalistically afraid that "ordinary folk" just won't be able to understand wine's finer points.

Well, I'm here to tell you that it's hokum. Why? Because those of us with any interest in wine, whether private or commercial, haven't a clue about making wine sufficiently simple. Really, we don't know nothing about "simple."

Typically, the wine world's notion of simplifying wine is much too complicated. What's more, it's wedded to niggling little laws such as appellation. Let me give you an example.

In America today there's only one Italian wine and food: Tuscan. Whatever the wine or the dish, it's Tuscan. For the average person—hell, for the average doctoral candidate—Italy is far too complicated to grasp. Geeks like me go on about Friuli or Umbria or beloved Piedmont. That's like wearing a "kick me" sign.

You want to know how real consumers see Italy? It's Tuscan. It's that simple. Look at the real estate pages for expensive new suburban homes. Everywhere, from Tuscaloosa to Tacoma, new suburban homes are described as "Tuscan," never mind that nothing built in Italy since the Etruscans resembles what's on offer.

People love Italian wine. In a pure marketing play, all Italian wines, regardless of grape variety or geography, would be Tuscan. All Italian wines would be either northern Tuscan, central Tuscan, southern Tuscan, or Super-Tuscan.

"It's a northern Tuscan wine from Piedmont." This, I swear, would sound right to the average American wine buyer—and I'll bet the average British, German, and Japanese consumer, too.

When the term *Super-Tuscan* first appeared, nobody here in the land of the Whopper thought twice about it. Hey, you've got Tuscan. So why not Super-Tuscan?

You think I'm joking, right? Well then, go figure this: Angelo Gaja, who makes northern Tuscan wine from Piedmont as well as central Tuscan wine from Tuscany, recently announced that with the 1996 vintage, his most expensive wines—his three single-vineyard Barbarescos and his two single-vineyard Barolos—would no longer display their appellation names.

That's right. The single-vineyard Barbarescos will no longer be *Barbaresco* and the Barolos will no longer be *Barolo*. So what will they be? Technically, they'll be labeled Langhe DOC Nebbiolo. Effectively, they'll really be Super-Tuscan wines from Piedmont.

And you know, it makes sense.

But there's more: It's not just labels. There's also the actual wine in the bottle. Way back in the 1970s, the Big Marketing Thought was varietal wine. It was honest (no more phony California "Chablis"). It carried a certain prestige. And, not least, varietally labeled wines commanded a higher price. "We're making the world simpler for wine," said everyone with great self-satisfaction.

Yes, it was simpler. But now we know that it wasn't simple enough. "What, they want Blue Nun again?" you ask. Not at all. Forget brand names. That's not how wines are divided in the public mind.

A stockbroker friend of mine said it best, "I like a stand-alone wine."

When I heard that, for a moment I thought I saw the rocket's red glare, the bombs bursting in air. By God, this was it! The real simplicity. Not the *faux* simplicity foisted by marketing departments everywhere. Never mind whether the wine is Chardonnay or Cabernet, Australian or Tuscan. It's *much* simpler than that. A wine is either a stand-alone or it's not.

What's a "stand-alone" wine? It's one that doesn't need food. If a wine only tastes good when served with food, then it's not a stand-alone. And my friend—and tens of millions like him—isn't interested.

Now we're talking simple: A world neatly divided between stand-alone wines and food-crutch wines. Since we know that the race goes to the swiftest, no prizes for guessing the winner. It really doesn't matter what's on the label, except the producer's name.

Before you declare this preposterous, please imagine overhearing the following at a party:

"It was great. It was a northern Super-Tuscan from Gaja that really stood alone. I mean, it was like, wow! I don't know what was in it, but we almost forgot to order dinner."

Admit it: That made sense, didn't it? *(2000)*

HELLO, YOU'RE ON THE AIR

Hi, welcome to *Don't Keep It Bottled Up!* where the wine elite meets to bleat. Hello, you're on the air.

Hi, this is Denise from Wooster, Ohio.

Welcome, Denise. What's on your mind?

Well, it's my husband. I don't know how to say this, because I've only just found out. I was going through his sock drawer. I wasn't prying, mind you, just checking to make sure that he didn't mix the black socks with the browns. He does that, you know. Anyway, I came across this magazine. And I don't know how to tell you this . . .

Just come right out and say it, Denise. You're among friends here.

Well, all right. Like I said, I saw this magazine and I just couldn't believe it! I guess I just have to say it: My husband is an oenophile. I mean, I'd heard about this sort of thing before, but I never believed.

So what's your problem, Denise?

What's my problem? Well, I'm not sure he's the man I married. I mean, it's one thing for him to bring home a bottle now and then. I could even look the other way when he brought a case into the house. But an oenophile! We have children. Is there anything I can do? I love my husband, but I'm not sure I can live with an oenophile. I mean, other men aren't like that, are they?

Denise, if this is any consolation, you should know that there are women oenophiles, too. Nobody knows the percentage of the population that become—or maybe always were—oenophiles, but it's larger than you might think. And you might be surprised. They lead happy, healthy lives. They raise good children. And they do add to the economy. I'm sure that if you give it some thought, you'll realize that now that you know he's an oenophile, you'll see that you're not losing a closet, you're gaining a wine cellar.

•

Hi, welcome to *Don't Keep It Bottled Up!* where the cork meets the dork. Hello, you're on the air.

Yeah, hello. This is Slade from Phoenix.

Thanks for calling, Slade. What's on your mind?

Not much. This is Phoenix. Heh, heh, heh. Just a little joke. Anyway, I was at a wine tasting here in Phoenix, and some guy said he didn't like Zinfandel.

So?

Well, isn't that un-American or something? I mean, I can understand not liking, say, white wines. Or French wines. But Zinfandel? Doesn't seem right to me. What do you think?

I'll tell you, Slade. Have you ever considered running for office? Of course it's un-American not to like Zinfandel! I myself have wondered about all those fuzzy Cabernet drinkers out there. Anyway, you're right, boy. This country was meant to be a nation of Zinfandel drinkers—even in places uninhabitable without air-conditioning.

•

Hello, welcome to *Don't Keep It Bottled Up!* where a magnum is more than a gun.

Hi, this is Suzy from Venice, California. I'm wondering how I could join one of those wine cults.

Wine cults? What sort of wine cults, Suzy?

Oh, I'm sure you know about them. A friend of mine, he's this movie producer, see, and he and his friends are in something they call the Lalou Cult. They are, like, really weird, but they dress well. So I was wondering if, you know, I could write away some-where to join?

Suzy, I'll tell you straight. You sound like a nice person. You don't want to get involved with the Lalou Cult. It's really expensive and, frankly, their Hostess Twinkies aren't fully stuffed, if you know what I mean.

But I'm so sorry, we're out of time. Tune in next week, when our special guest will be Michael Broadbent discussing his latest tasting of nineteenth century Beaujolais Nouveau. In the meantime, remember, if you keep it bottled up—well, you won't have any friends. *(1998)*

THE FEAR OF AUSTERE

MY EARS PERKED UP WHEN I heard it. "This wine is austere," said the taster. "And that's not a good word in my book." The other tasters nodded in agreement. Keep in mind that the knock against "austere" wasn't that it's uncommercial—which is doubtless true—but that austerity in wine is undesirable, even a flaw.

This was offered during a blind tasting in Napa Valley of a couple dozen high-end Napa Cabernets, along with a few star-studded red Bordeaux. This wasn't some suburban wine-and-cheese nosh. The group was, to a man and woman, knowledgeable and accomplished. They were pros, literally.

This is why I was so surprised—flabbergasted, really—when the descriptor "austere" was knocked out of contention like a croquet ball in a high-speed game. So apparently self-evident was it, it incited no discussion.

Is this, I wondered, why so many Napa Valley Cabernets taste the way they do: ripe (or overripe), luscious (or voluptuous, even *zaftig*), and devoid of any edge? When did austere become pejorative? And why?

My guess is that austere went out of fashion—and became a negative tasting term—sometime in the 1990s. That's when Napa Cabernets (and the winery owners, for that matter) got a lot richer.

As to why, I'll bet your guess is similar to mine: The world loves "ripe" rather than "restrained," "lush" rather than "detailed," and "accessible" rather than "ageworthy." This is not confined to Napa Valley Cabernets, to be sure. Longtime Bordeaux lovers have noted the change in red Bordeaux, from relatively low alcohol wines to lush, ripe wines without any "edge."

Now this may seem to be much ado about words. Yet wine and words have never been more entangled than they are today. Never have so many individual wines been lavished (or subjected) to so many words. Today we're more besotted by words than, ironically, by wine. Ask any retailer selling futures.

But why should austere be pejorative? And what does it tell us about ourselves as tasters if we find ourselves agreeing that a wine judged austere is, by definition, lesser?

When I heard this, I thought of what Nelson Riddle, the great arranger who helped create Frank Sinatra's finest recordings, said about Sinatra's singing. "I didn't care for his original voice," said Riddle, referring to Sinatra's early years as a singer in the 1940s. "I thought it was far too syrupy. I prefer to hear the rather angular person come through in his voice."

It's no different with wine. We're not finding the "angular" in today's wines—at least not as often as we once did. And when we do, it's often marked down, disregarded, or dismissed as—you guessed it—austere.

We now have winemakers and wine tasters who will say flat out that you can't create a good Cabernet Sauvignon at less than 14 percent alcohol. Anything less and the grapes, they submit, simply aren't ripe enough. Of course, if that is the minimum level of acceptable ripeness, it takes no imagination to see how desirable it would be to ratchet up the ripeness (and the resulting alcohol) yet more. This is precisely what's happened in the past decade or more.

This is why, by the way, we're not seeing the likes of such once-revered (and rightly so) wines as the Inglenook Cask Selection Cabernets from the 1950s and 1960s. They probably never nudged much past 13 percent alcohol, if that.

Do such wines exist today? They do, but they're increasingly rare and not always celebrated or held up as exemplars. And it's not confined to Cabernet Sauvignon, either. The red Burgundies of Domaine Henri Gouges in Nuits-St.-Georges are nothing if not austere. The Zinfandels of Saucelito Canyon Vineyard in San Luis Obispo share a similar restraint. Chardonnays from Mayacamas Vineyards and Stony Hill Vineyard are bracingly austere, as are many Chablis and the white Burgundies of Domaine Matrot, among others.

The list of true-to-their-austere-school Cabernets embraces the likes of various wines from Napa's Howell Mountain, Spring Mountain, and Diamond Mountain districts; the best reds from Renaissance Vineyard in the wild reaches of North Yuba County; an assortment of offerings from the Santa Cruz Mountains (Kathryn Kennedy, Mount Eden, Ridge); and Cabs from such places as Australia's Coonawarra zone.

If we can eat our words, we can drink them, too. A large glass of austere might be just right for what ails some wines today. *(2008)*

DO TASTE BUDS MAKE THE WINE CRITIC?

CRITICS HAVE ALWAYS VIED WITH one another, typically seeking to increase their own authority and influence at the expense (and disparagement) of the competition.

What's happened recently, however, is an almost desperate attempt by some of today's wine tasting potentates to bolster their credibility by suggesting a physical superiority, like 1950s Hollywood starlets insisting that their acting ability was inseparable from their mammary endowment. In wine's case, it's papillary.

This was brought home recently upon reading that Jancis Robinson, a well-regarded British wine taster, announced that she had her tongue tested and that, lo! she is a "supertaster." More about that in a moment.

Wine critics have lately come up against new competition. Previously, it was a matter of who got published. Today, A. J. Liebling's famous dictum that "Freedom of the press is guaranteed only to those who own one," generates a new kind of freedom: the ability to run for wine office without the nomination of an established publishing party.

The line between amateurs and professionals in wine tasting is increasingly erased with today's every-man-a-king proliferation of wine blogs (a number of which are proffered by queenly women, it should be noted).

Consequently, professionals' desire of being seen as superior in literal matters of taste has become more pressing.

Keep in mind that wine criticism, more than other forms, relies almost entirely on perceived—and largely unprovable—credibility. What credentials exist are either highly technical, such as winemaking degrees from schools like Cornell or the University of California at Davis, or patently self-promoting, such as the transparently trumped-up Master of Wine designation. (The name alone is a giveaway to its priestly pretensions.)

The result of this arms race is that critics make ever-grander, even scientifically tested, claims to authentic credibility.

Linda Bartoshuk, a professor of otolaryngology and psychology at Yale University, published research in the 1990s about what she calls "supertasters." They are people with a higher density of taste buds. Professor Bartoshuk's research shows that among American Caucasians about 35 percent of women are supertasters and about 15 percent of men are supertasters.

The test that Ms. Robinson recently took is straightforward: Blue food coloring is swabbed on part of the tongue. The fungiform papillae do not absorb the food coloring and thus appear as pink dots on a blue field. Within a small defined area, the pink dots are counted. Supertasters have at least twice as many taste buds as others.

This sounds good, doesn't it? Being a supertaster would seem an incontestable boon, like an acrobat being double-jointed. Not so fast. The problem with having a lot of taste buds is that taste sensations are intensified to the point of pain.

Supertasters, Professor Bartoshuk reports, typically dislike spicy foods, which irritate, as do fatty foods, which literally weigh upon the touch sensors in the fungiform papillae. (Supertasters also have more sensitive touch receptors in their tongues.)

Doesn't sound so inviting now, does it? Indeed, being a so-called supertaster is as much a prescription for painful sensitivity as it is an asset. A supertaster has to work around his or her genetic inheritance as much as with it.

However, saying you're a supertaster sure does sound good. It suggests a physiological gift, which is about as plausible as a film critic asserting superiority because of unusual light sensitivity. But in today's wine-writing free-for-all, any edge in credibility is considered a well-placed elbow in the ribs of the competition.

Indeed, no sooner did a member of the chat board sponsored by über-taster Robert M. Parker Jr. report Ms. Robinson's self-discovery as a supertaster than Mr. Parker quickly allied himself among the physiological elect, asserting that "I don't care for even mildly spicy or seasoned food." (Previously, Mr. Parker had ascribed his tasting acuity in part to having unusually deep crevices in his tongue.)

What we really need is less Yale and more Saul Steinberg. More specifically, we need Mr. Steinberg's famous 1976 *New Yorker* cover depicting the parochial world map of a New Yorker reconfigured to reflect various tasters' tongues.

Mr. Parker, for example, would have broad swath for Bordeaux receptivity on his tongue, as he is a famously good taster of red Bordeaux. Ms. Robinson, for her part, would vie similarly, although the lingual zone for California would likely be quite small.

And what of my own tongue, you ask? It would likely shift with the seasons, showing a rosé zone blossoming like a summer algal bloom, only to contract in winter and be replaced by a vast swath for Italian reds.

Actually, such maps exist. Every writer draws one for his or her readers. It's called judgment, which is always on display. Suggesting a linkage of taste buds to wine judgment is like confusing eyesight with insight. Otherwise, Ted Williams—with his legendary 20-10 vision—would be renowned today as an art critic. *(2006)*

I did make an error in the preceding article which I regret. Jancis Robinson did not have her taste buds counted but rather, was administered what's called a "PROP test" (6-n-propylthiouracil, which is a prescription thyroid medication) where a piece of paper is soaked in the compound to see if a taster can detect it. Those who do are identified as supertasters or the term Jancis Robinson prefers, "hypertasters."

Although Jancis was (understandably) dismayed by this column—and expressed it to me privately by e-mail—the fact remains that it was she who reported her own hyper-tasting facility. Had the test shown her to be an underachieving "hypo-taster," I rather doubt that we would have heard about it.

THE NO-WINE MAGAZINE

IN MY "MISCELLANEOUS" FILE—BY FAR the most bulging in my cabinet—I have a check stub. Now, I'm not a check-stub-saving sort. I cash my checks, spend the dough, and move on, looking for my next financial killing. Stubs are literally worthless. I toss 'em.

But I have kept one stub. It comes from *The New Yorker* magazine and reads "Kill Fee—$15,000." It's not every day that a wine writer (or any other sort, for that matter) sees a check for fifteen grand, let alone as a fee for the acceptance of a story that the publication has no intention of using. It was for a profile of Italian winegrower Angelo Gaja commissioned by then-editor Robert Gottlieb and discarded by succeeding editor Tina Brown along, I'm told, with a lot of other pieces commissioned by Mr. Gottlieb. If it had run, it would have been the first substantial wine writing in *The New Yorker* for many years.

I thought of this check stub when I picked up the September 5 *New Yorker*, called "The Food Issue." I groaned inwardly because I knew what was coming—or rather, not coming. Once again there would be nothing about wine in the magazine. This from a publication that, more than any other, sees itself as an arbiter of sophistication.

Actually, there was something about wine: There were three wine advertisements. The back cover is a full-page ad for Turning Leaf (owned by Gallo). Château Ste.

Michelle Winery (owned by U.S. Tobacco Co.) took another full-page ad. There was also a small, three-inch long ad from Bonny Doon Vineyard, which is owned by one of America's more bizarre marketing geniuses, Randall Grahm.

A winemaker with a doctorate in philosophy, Mr. Grahm comes up with goofy labels like Le Cigare Volante, a Rhône-style red wine whose label celebrates an ordinance passed in the 1950s in Châteauneuf-du-Pape which forbids landing rights for flying saucers (which the French call flying cigars).

However oddball he may seem, Mr. Grahm knows how to sell. Bonny Doon's yearly production makes his winery the twenty-eighth largest in the country according to *Wine Business Monthly*, with an estimated yearly production of 365,000 cases. It's bigger than, say, the well-known sparkling wine producer Domaine Chandon.

Anyway, that was the full extent of the wine presence in *The New Yorker*'s latest annual food issue. This is nothing new. There's almost never any mention of wine in *The New Yorker*. And when it occurs, it's almost always sneering.

You don't believe me? Try this from one of *The New Yorker*'s undoubtedly best writers, Adam Gopnik, in last year's annual food issue musing at length about wine writing: "Remarkably, nowhere in wine writing . . . would a Martian learn that the first reason people drink wine is to get drunk. . . . Wine is what gives us a reason to let alcohol make us happy without one. Without wine lore and wine tasting and wine talk and wine labels and, yes, wine writing and rating—the whole elaborate idea of wine—we would still get drunk, but we would be merely drunk."

How's that for a sophisticated analysis of wine appreciation? We drink wine to get drunk. We choose wine, rather than the much more economical and fast-acting booze, out of sheer pretension. A similar depth of art appreciation would have us viewing paintings as nothing more than a way to look at naked women.

What is it about wine and *The New Yorker*? Two years before Mr. Gopnik's assertion came Calvin Trillin's gleeful (and, of course, always witty) examination of the not-quite-fact that some wine drinkers cannot distinguish a red wine from a white when they can't see the color of the wine.

This is not really true, which Mr. Trillin eventually concedes only in the final paragraph of the piece. "I concluded that experienced wine drinkers can tell red from white by taste about 70 percent of the time, as long as the test is being administered by someone who isn't interested in trying to fool them."

These two articles, both denigrating, constitute pretty much everything *The New Yorker* has published on wine in recent years, never mind that the latest food issue is an ongoing enterprise of several years standing. Wine is worse than esoteric or even unimportant. Wine and its culture smack of fraudulence. (Mr. Gopnik again: "The end of wine writing is to turn drinking into a metaphor for judging. Since we know that this is false, we feel the falsity, and the pathos of the falsity.")

I mention all this because it's not insignificant that a magazine such as *The New Yorker* steadfastly refuses to address the cultural significance of wine in American life. Worse, it indulges in a double whammy, reverse flippancy that scoffs at wine as having any substance at all.

I was reminded of historian Richard Hofstadter's succinct definition of the key word in the title of his landmark book, *Anti-Intellectualism in American Life* (1963): "The common strain that binds together the attitudes and ideas which I call anti-intellectual is a resentment and suspicion of the life of the mind and of those who are considered to represent it; and a disposition constantly to minimize the value of that life."

Wine is more than a fancy way of getting drunk. There is, in fact, a "wine mind." It's been present for centuries, first in Europe and now in America. And there is, even more so, a "wine life," a culture and a form of civilization that has recently put down its deepest-ever roots in modern American life.

The evidence is all around us. Wine has become normal in American life. That alone is a far-reaching change. Its economics are considerable, worth $33 billion a year in California alone in wages, revenues, and economic activity. Every state in the nation now boasts wineries. Its issues reach the U.S. Supreme Court, such as the recent matter of interstate wine shipping.

Wine is increasingly intrinsic, and informing, to American culture. Yet *The New Yorker* continues to believe otherwise, engaging in an odd defiance—either through a willful silence or an occasional fling of the mud of disdain—of one of the more significant transformations of modern America.

It's too bad for us writers (I enjoyed spending that fifteen grand), but it's really a loss for readers everywhere including, yes, *The New Yorker* itself. *(2005)*

The profile of Angelo Gaja mentioned in this column appears starting on page 264.

The Decline of the Heroic Palate

SHOULD YOU EVER FEEL OVERWHELMED by wine, take heart: The professionals in the field apparently feel the same way. Years ago, such über-tasters as Robert M. Parker Jr. of the *Wine Advocate* and Stephen Tanzer of the *International Wine Cellar* were one-man bands. They trumpeted Bordeaux, banged the drum for Burgundy, and strummed about Spain, often all in the same issue of their personal newsletters.

But lately it's clearly become too much. The one-man-band wine newsletter is today almost a thing of the past. Recently, Mr. Parker replaced his one full-time tasting comrade (who covered Burgundy and anything else that Mr. Parker chose to personally forego) with no fewer than three new full-time employees, one of whom is devoted exclusively to Italian wines.

Mr. Tanzer, for his part, previously employed part-time tasting help. These free-lance palates offered tasting notes from locales such as Australia and Hungary. But until last year, Mr. Tanzer never had a full-time palate partner to help ease the load. Now he does.

What this tells us is that a certain fatigue likely has set in. After all, Messrs. Parker and Tanzer have been in the tasting-note trenches for decades; both are in their mid- to late-fifties. More than this, though, they are overwhelmed by wine itself. The world is issuing more must-be-tasted fine wine than even these stalwarts can take on.

We've reached the end of the Age of the Heroic Taster. It began in earnest in 1972 with the wine newsletter of San Francisco–based Robert Finigan (who eventually fell by the journalistic wayside) and expanded most significantly a few years later with the still-vibrant efforts of Messrs. Parker and Tanzer. It was a kind of Faustian era, in which tasters exchanged seemingly all their waking hours to taste all wines worth a sip and a score.

Their newsletters were all about the primacy of the "hero palate." Now, however, they are of necessity ceding or at least sharing the field with others, with the implication that their employees are reliable extensions of themselves. (Mr. Tanzer, introducing his full-time tasting employee, Josh Raynolds, wrote, "Josh's scores for wines he has tasted blind with me have been within a point or two of mine upwards of 90 percent of the time.")

These newsletters are changing not just because of the sheer grind of one person tasting thousands of wine a year for nearly three decades, but also from the new realities of Web-based wine writers.

Messrs. Parker and Tanzer still are tethered to print, although both offer their readers Internet options. But others, such as Allen Meadows of Burghound.com and Jancis Robinson of JancisRobinson.com, float expansively, and far less expensively, in cyberspace.

Mr. Meadows, for example, specializes in Burgundy, offering far more extensive coverage and tasting notes than any competing print-based newsletter could afford to deliver. He now dominates the subject, with thousands of subscribers worldwide paying $125 for four exclusively Web-based issues a year.

Mr. Meadows represents today's new heroic taster in the classic all-knowing and all-tasting mode but only in a narrowly defined field where it's feasible for one person to seal the Faustian deal and financially plausible for him to do so thanks to the near-absence of production costs. Print newsletters such as those of Messrs. Parker and Tanzer (neither of which carries advertising) are dinosaurs, eventually to be made extinct by Web-based vehicles.

When that happens, we will see yet more changes. New Web newsletters like Burghound.com will emerge for categories such as Bordeaux or Italian wines, which enjoy a sizable worldwide audience of enthusiasts. And what about the all-wines-all-the-time approach? With three full-time tasters, Mr. Parker's *Wine Advocate* is edging ever closer to a magazine model, never mind the absence of advertising or graphics.

In a Web-based world, these employees can be milked for ever-larger numbers of tasting notes and in-depth reportage, which can be conveyed on the Web far better and more comprehensively than in prohibitively expensive paper-based print.

Ironically, such a twenty-first-century newsletter then finds itself cheek by Internet jowl with conventional magazines such as *Wine Spectator* (where I have a column, it should be noted) or *Food & Wine*. Both have increasingly potent Web presences; both accept advertising. Not least, these and other deep-pocket publications can ramp up with ever more content if need be.

"On the Internet, nobody knows you're a dog," said the now-famous 1993 *New Yorker* cartoon by Peter Steiner. The question soon will be: if you're not a heroic taster but instead more a drum major in a parade of palates, will anyone know you're a newsletter? *(2006)*

In October 2009, Stephen Tanzer of the International Wine Cellar *announced that his newsletter would become an exclusively Web-based publication with no print version.*

❦

THE PERILS OF PANELS

THE LATEST TREND IN NEWSPAPER wine journalism—the *New York Sun* happily excepted—is the tasting panel, wine writing's version of a group grope. You will find tasting panels on the *New York Times*, the *Chicago Tribune*, and the *San Francisco Chronicle*, to name but three prominent newspapers that have succumbed to the safety of a tasting herd.

Put simply, wine tasting panels are useless. They're about as instructive and usable as asking directions from five people at the same time.

On the *Chicago Tribune*, for example, their tasting panel recently surveyed thirteen different bottlings of Viognier, an aromatic white grape originally from France's Rhône Valley and now popular among Rhônistas in California.

Now, thirteen wines in a blind tasting is hardly a daunting number. With twenty, thirty, or forty wines, you'll inevitably get some "judgment drift." But a mere baker's dozen of wines allows focus—or so you'd think.

Yet tasting panels, like too many cooks, structurally sully the soup. What are you, the reader, supposed to do with advice such as "Flinty, dusty taste," said one taster; "A wee bit sharp," said another; but a third panelist gave the wine a perfect 10, praising its elegant balance?

Or this: "One panelist gave this Aussie wine a perfect 10, calling it 'lovely, elegant, balanced, nuanced' with a 'great tingly mouth feel.' Another praised the 'stunning' tropical fruit aroma and dry styling. Those less enchanted complained of a slightly bitter finish and 'new eraser' smell." Now that's useful: Either it's a perfect wine or it smells like a new eraser, a descriptor not commonly raised in worshipful wine praise.

You can peruse the tasting reports from any newspaper wine panel you'd care to inspect. The message comes back loud and muddy: There's no "I can use this" kind of consensus. And when it does emerge, I'm here to testify—having partici- pated in panel tastings in wine judgings and the like—that the middle-of-the-road, least "offensive" wine wins. Wines have significant variation in quality and style; in panels, the really characterful version comes off as idiosyncratic rather than benchmark.

No one is served by this journalistic nambypambyism. So why are newspapers doing it? A. J. Liebling, the great *New Yorker* writer and press critic, put his finger on it best. Newspapers "know and revere their awful power," he said. "Like a prizefighter in a bar full of nonprizefighters, they are loath to loose it." The current trend toward newspaper wine-tasting panels is based on such self-awe. To invest this "awful power" in the palate of one man or woman, well, an editor just couldn't sleep at night.

Insecurity is the driving force. It's a rare editor who actually knows about wine and thus feels capable of judging the house critic. Everyone's an expert on food, music, and art and consequently restaurants, performances, or exhibitions are never subjected to group judgment. Only wine requires a "let a thousand palates spit" tasting-panel populism.

Not to be ignored is the class element. Wine still seems hoity-toity. And there's a whiff of sin about it, too—something faintly corrupting. This grates on the sensibili- ties of many newspaper editors. They want to take it down a peg. What better way to do this than subject it to the vox populi of a panel tasting, where Joe and Jane Everyman can take a righteous swing at it? They wouldn't dare do this with, say, art or music, both of which are institutionalized and powerful. But wine is fair game, like dunking the banker's kid at a neighborhood carnival.

The result, of course, is a kind of "median mediocrity" of taste. But there's safety in (wine taster) numbers. Editors are off the hook and readers, well, they're more baffled by wine than ever. How can a wine be "lovely, elegant, balanced, nuanced" and have a "new eraser" smell? Beats me. *(2004)*

GETTING "RICH"

THERE'S A TRIBE THAT LIVES deep in the Amazon jungle called the Pirahã that has excited intense interest among linguists. The Pirahã language, you see, does not define numbers above two, as far as researchers can tell. They've only got words for *one* and *two*. After that is *many*.

A series of tests with members of the Pirahã tribe by Peter Gordon, a Columbia University psychology professor, offers the strongest evidence yet for what's called linguistic determinism. Put in plain English, it's the notion that language shapes thought.

Professor Gordon's research offers real-world evidence that lacking words for certain concepts can effectively prevent the understanding of those concepts. (Think it can't happen here? Try "*terroir*.")

I thought about the Pirahã tribe, of all things, when drinking a 1985 Bonnezeaux from Château des Fesles in the Loire Valley. What's the connection? The word *rich*. Or rather, the critical absence of that concept.

Instead we use the word *sweet*. We say *dessert wine*, banishing it to the end of a meal, like keeping the family loony in the attic. The Aussies say *stickies*, which is about as inviting as finding gum on the bottom of your shoe.

Like the Pirahã, we don't have a commonly understood concept for what might be called the rich-wine experience. Consequently, *à la* the Pirahã, these wines don't really exist for us. They've become wine ghosts, sensed but not participatory.

How did this happen? What occurred in our wine comprehension that the very vocabulary of rich wines—which reflects an active existence in our lives—has eluded us?

The French, for example, developed an extensive vocabulary for the rich-wine experience, employing such poetry as *moelleux*, which translates into English as "soft," "mellow," "tender," or "moist." (Think of a muffin with a soft center, and you've got it.) There's also *liquoreux*, which is best translated as "luscious."

The Germans, for their part, express their understanding of rich wines not, as is commonly thought, as gradations of sweetness but, rather, in naturalistic reflections of the grapes at the moment of harvest: *spätlese* means "late harvest"; *auslese*, "selected harvest"; *beerenauslese*, "selected harvest of berries"; and so on.

Although increasingly more selective (and later), harvesting does result in sweeter wines; the German vocabulary reflects a greater understanding that these wines acquire not merely more sugar, but a greater richness and dimensionality of flavor. This is why it's not a contradiction—to the Germans anyway—to offer a wine labeled *spätlese trocken* (dry) or *auslese trocken*.

So what happened to our understanding of rich wines today? The answer is not just the usual one that's trotted out, that these wines are no longer fashionable, that we now prefer dry wines. This is true, but it explains little.

Instead, the answer lies elsewhere, in something more fundamental than mere fashion. The answer is that today we drink nearly all wines when they are very young. Nowhere has drinking wines so young been more inimical to understanding—to connoisseurship, if you will—than with rich wines.

When tasted young, nearly all rich wines—whether Sauternes, Tokaji, Chaume (the new name for the former Côteaux du Layon), Quarts de Chaume, Bonnezeaux, Vouvray moelleux, various German and Austrian Rieslings, Australian Muscats, and Italian Picolit, among others—taste more of sweetness than of anything else. They give only a hint, if that, of the massive depths of flavor and dimensionality that lies beneath.

This is why that 1985 Bonnezeaux that I was drinking was such a world-rocker of a wine. We had it with some guests as a kind of treat after a hike of several hours high in California's Sierra Nevada. It came from my cellar, where I have been nurturing a good number of rich Loire wines, especially Bonnezeaux and Quarts de Chaume.

That 1985 Bonnezeaux was, in fact, barely sweet at all. Instead it was as layered and dimensional as the greatest white Burgundy, although it tasted completely different, of course. You had an almost electric minerality allied to hints of honey. Your palate was constantly refreshed. It was a rich wine, not at all a sweet one.

Lately, we've all seen an ever-larger contingent of gotta-have-it wine buyers chasing after the same few wines. None of those wines, except for the trophy of Château d'Yquem, is rich. Yet today's rich wines are, in fact, some of the world's finest. We have become (most of us, anyway) a Pirahã tribe of collectors who can't see greatness—for want of a word that opens a world. *(2008)*

THERE'S A PLACE FOR US—
SOMEWHERENESS

No single word has transformed American wine—and American wine drinkers—as much as the French term *terroir*. In trying to render this supremely ambiguous notion into something comprehendible in English, I coined the word "somewhereness." Much more important is that the concept itself is now fundamental.

The idea of *terroir* permeates my writing. No more important concept in wine exists. It is impossible to create—which is to say, discover—truly fine wine without accepting the primacy of the idea of *terroir*. I have written at length about it, most notably in the essay "The Notion of *Terroir*," as well as in numerous columns.

THE NOTION OF *TERROIR*

Always the beautiful answer who asks a more beautiful question
—E. E. Cummings, *New Poems*

THE "MORE BEAUTIFUL QUESTION" OF WINE is *terroir*. To the English speaker, *terroir* is an alien word, difficult to pronounce ("tair-wahr"). More frustrating yet, it is a foreign idea. The usual capsule definition is site or vineyard plot. Closer to its truth, it holds—like William Blake's grain of sand that contains a universe—an evolution of thought about wine and the

Earth. One cannot make sense of Burgundy without investigating the notion of *terroir*.

Although derived from soil or land (terre), *terroir* is not just an investigation of soil and subsoil. It is everything that contributes to the distinction of a vineyard plot. As such, it also embraces "microclimate": precipitation, air and water drainage, elevation, sunlight, and temperature.

But *terroir* holds yet another dimension: It sanctions what cannot be measured, yet still located and savored. *Terroir* prospects for differences. In this, it is at odds with science, which demands proof by replication rather than in a shining uniqueness.

Understanding *terroir* requires a recalibration of the modern mind. The original impulse has long since disappeared, buried by commerce and the scorn of science. It calls for a susceptibility to the natural world to a degree almost unfathomable today, as the French historian Marc Bloch evokes in his landmark work, *Feudal Society*:

> The men of the two feudal ages were close to nature—much closer than we
> are; and nature as they knew it was much less tamed and softened than as we
> see it today. . . . People continued to pick wild fruit and to gather honey as in
> the first ages of mankind. In the construction of implements and tools, wood
> played a predominant part. The nights, owing to wretched lighting, were
> darker; the cold, even in the living quarters of the castles, was more intense.
> In short, behind all social life there was a background of the primitive, of
> submission to uncontrollable forces, of unrelieved physical contrasts.

This world extended beyond the feudal ages, as rural life in Europe changed little for centuries afterward. Only the barest vestiges remain today, with the raw, preternatural sensitivity wiped clean. The viticultural needlepoint of the Côte d'Or, its thousands of named vineyards, is as much a relic of a bygone civilization as Stonehenge. We can decipher why and how they did it, but the impulse, the fervor, is beyond us now.

The glory of Burgundy is its exquisite delineation of sites, its preoccupation with *terroir*: What does this site have to say? Is it different from its neighbor? It is the source of Burgundian greatness, the informing ingredient. This is easily demonstrated. You need only imagine an ancient Burgundy planted to Pinot Noir and Chardonnay for the glory of producing—to use the modern jargon—a varietal wine. The thought is depressing, an anemic vision of wine hardly capable of inspiring the devotion of generations of wine lovers, let alone the discovery of such natural wonders as Montrachet or La Tâche. *Terroir* is as much a part of Burgundy wines as Pinot Noir or Chardonnay; the grape is as much vehicle as voice.

The mentality of *terroir* is not uniquely Burgundian, although it reaches its fullest expression there. It more rightly could be considered distinctively French, although not exclusively so. Other countries, notably Germany and Italy, can point to similar insights. But France, more than any other, viewed its landscape from the perspective of *terroir*. It charted its vineyard distinctions—often called *cru* or growth—with calligraphic care. Indeed, calligraphy and *cru* are sympathetic, both the result of emotional, yet disciplined, attentions to detail. Both flourished under monastic tutelage.

Italy, for all of its ancient winegrowing tradition, never developed a mentality of *terroir* to the same or even similar extent as France. It lacked, ironically, the monastic underpinning of the Benedictine and Cistercian orders, which were represented to a far greater degree in France and Germany. An ecclesiastical map of western Europe during the Middle Ages (*Historical Atlas* by William R. Shepherd) shows hundreds of major monasteries in France and Germany, nearly all of them Benedictine or Cistercian. In comparison, Italy had less than a dozen.

The phrase "mentality of *terroir*" is pertinent. The articulation of the Burgundian landscape increased steadily long after the decline of the feudal ages. Ever-finer distinctions of site mounted along the Côte d'Or through to the Revolution of 1789, when the Church lands were confiscated and publicly auctioned. The monks and nuns, whose wines and vineyards remained the standard for nearly a millennium, never wavered in their devotion to *terroir*. If only by sheer longevity, their vision of the land became everyone else's. Wherever the Church shaped the viticultural landscape, *terroir* was the means by which that world was understood.

But in France there exists, to this day, a devotion to *terroir* that is not explained solely by this legacy of the Church. Instead, it is fueled by two forces in French life: a longstanding delight in differences and an acceptance of ambiguity.

The greatness of French wines in general—and Burgundy in particular—can be traced to the fact that the French do not ask of one site that it replicate the qualities of another site. They prize distinction. This leads not to discord—as it might in a country gripped by a marketing mentality—but consonance with what the French call *la France profonde*, elemental France.

This is the glory of France. It is not that France is the only spot on the planet with remarkable soils or that its climate is superior to all others for winegrowing. It is a matter of the values that are applied to the land. In this, *terroir* and its discoveries remind one of Chinese acupuncture. Centuries ago, Chinese practitioners chose to view the body from a perspective utterly different than that of the dissective, anatomical approach of Western medicine. Because of this different perspective, they discovered something about the body that Western practitioners, to this day, are unable to independently see for themselves: what the Chinese call "channels" and "collaterals," or more recently, "meridians." The terminology is unimportant. What is important is that these "meridians" cannot be found by dissection. Yet they exist; acupuncture works. Its effects, if not its causes, are demonstrable.

In the same way, seeking to divine the greatness of Burgundy only by dissecting its intricacies of climate, grape, soil, and winemaking is no more enlightening than learning how to knit by unraveling a sweater. Those who believe that great wines are made, rather than found, will deliver such wines only by the flimsiest chance, much in the same way that an alchemist, after exacting effort, produces gold simply by virtue of having worked with gold-bearing material all along.

Today, a surprising number of winegrowers and wine drinkers—at least in the United States—flatly deny the existence of *terroir*, like weekend sailors who reject as preposterous that Polynesians could have crossed the Pacific navigating only by sun, stars, wind, smell, and taste. *Terroir* is held to be so much bunk, little more than viticultural voodoo.

The inadmissibility of *terroir* to the high court of reason is due to ambiguity. *Terroir* can be presented, but it cannot be proven—except by the senses. Like Polynesian seafaring, it is too subjective to be reproducible and therefore credible. Yet any reasonably experienced wine drinker knows upon tasting a mature Corton-Charlemagne or Chablis "Valdese" or Volnay "Caillerets," that something is present that cannot be accounted for by winemaking technique. Infused in the wine is a *gout de terroir*, a taste of the soil. It cannot be traced to the grape, if only because other wines made the same way from the same grape lack this certain something. If only by process of elimination the source must be ascribed to *terroir*. But to acknowledge this requires a belief that the ambiguous—the unprovable and immeasurable—can be real. Doubters are blocked by their own credulity in science and its confining definition of reality.

The supreme concern of Burgundy is—or should be—making *terroir* manifest. In outline, this is easily accomplished: small-berried clones; low yields; selective sorting of the grapes; and trickiest of all, fermenting and cellaring the wine in such a way as to allow the *terroir* to come through with no distracting stylistic flourishes. This is where *terroir* comes smack up against ego, the modern demand for self-expression at any cost. Too often, it has come at the expense of *terroir*.

It is easier to see the old Burgundian enemies of greed and inept winemaking. The problem of greed, expressed in overcropped grapevines resulting in thin, diluted wines, has been chronic in Burgundy, as are complaints about it. It is no less so today, but the resolution is easily at hand: lower the yields.

But the matter of ego and *terroir* is new and peculiar to our time. It stems from two sources: the technology of modern winemaking and the psychology of its use. Technical control in winemaking is recent, dating only to the late 1960s. Never before had winemakers been able to control wine to such an extent as is available today. Through the use of temperature-controlled stainless steel tanks, computer-controlled wine presses, heat exchangers, inert gases, centrifuges, all manner of filters, oak barrels from woods of different forests, and so forth, the modern winemaker can insert himself between the *terroir* and its wine to a degree never before achieved.

The psychology of its use is the more important feature. Self-expression is now considered the inalienable right of our time. It, thus, is no surprise that the desire for self-expression should make itself felt in winemaking. That winemakers have always sought to express themselves in their wines is indisputable. The difference is that today technology actually allows them to do so, to an extent unimagined by their grandparents.

Submerged in this is a force that, however abstract, has changed much of twentieth-century thinking: the transition from the literal to the subjective in how we perceive what is "real." Until recently, whatever was considered "real" was expressed in straightforward mechanical or linear linkages, such as a groove in a phonograph record or a lifelike painting of a vase of flowers. Accuracy was defined by exacting, literal representation.

But we have come to believe that the subjective can be more "real" than the representational. One of the earliest, and most famous, examples of this was Expressionism in art. Where prior to the advent of Expressionism in the early twentieth century, the depiction of reality on a canvas was achieved through the creation of the most lifelike forms, Expressionists said otherwise. They maintained that the reality of a vase of flowers could be better expressed by breaking down its form and color into more symbolic representations of its reality, rather than by straightforward depiction.

How this relates to wine is found in the issue of *terroir* versus ego. The Burgundian world that discovered *terroir* centuries ago drew no distinction between what they discovered and called Chambertin and the idea of a representation of Chambertin. Previously, there were only two parties involved: Chambertin itself and its self-effacing discoverer, the winegrower. In this deferential view of the natural world, Chambertin was Chambertin if for no other reason than it consistently did not taste like its neighbor Latricières. One is beefier and more resonantly flavorful (Chambertin) while the other offers a similar savor, but somehow always is lacier in texture and less full-blown. It was a reality no more subject to doubt than was a nightingale's song from the screech of an owl. They knew what they tasted, just as they knew what they heard. These were natural forces, no more subject to alteration or challenge than a river.

All of which brings us back to Burgundian winemaking. In an age where the subjective has been accepted as being more "real" than the representational, the idea of an immutable *terroir* becomes troublesome. It complicates ego-driven individualism, the need to express a personal vision. In an era of relativism and right of self-expression, Chambertin as *terroir* has given way to Chambertin as emblem. The notion of *terroir* as an absolute is rejected. All Chambertins therefore are equally legitimate. We have come to accept that a grower's Chambertin is really only his or her idea of Chambertin. The vineyard name on the label is merely as a general indication of intent.

How, then, does one know what is the true voice of the land? How does one know when the winemaker has interposed himself or herself between the *terroir* and the final wine? Discovering the authentic voice of a particular *terroir* requires study. The only way is to assemble multiple examples of a wine from a particular plot and taste them side by side. Ideally they should all be from the same vintage. This eliminates at least one distracting variable.

In seeking to establish the voice of a *terroir*, one has to concentrate—at least for the moment—not on determining which wines are best, but in finding the thread of distinction that runs through them. It could be a matter of structure: delicate or muscular, consistently lean or generous in fruit. It could be a distinctive *gout de terroir*, something minerally or stony; chalky or earthy. Almost always, it will be hard to determine at first, because the range of styles within the wines will be distracting. And if the choices available are mostly second-rate, where the *terroir* is lost through overcropped vines or heavy-handed winemaking, the exercise will be frustrating and without reward. *Terroir* usually is discovered only after repeated attempts over a number of vintages. This is why such insight is largely the province only of Burgundians and a few obsessed outsiders.

Nevertheless, hearing the voice of the land is sweet and you will not easily forget it. Sometimes it only becomes apparent by contrast. You taste a number of Meursault "Perrières," for example, and in the good ones you find a pronounced minerali-ness coupled with an invigorating, strong fruitiness. You don't realize how stony or fruity, how forceful, until you compare Perrières with, say, Charmes, which is contiguous. Then the distinction of Perrières clicks into place in your mind. It's never so exact or pronounced that you will spot it unerringly in a blind tasting of various Meursault *premiers crus*. That's not the point. The point is that there is no doubt that Perrières exists, that it is an entity unto itself, distinct from any other plot.

Such investigation—which is more rewarding than it might sound—has a built-in protocol. When faced with a lineup of wines, the immediate impact is of stylistic dif-ferences, a clamor of producer's voices. Once screened out, the lesser versions—the ones that clearly lack concentration and definition of flavor—are easily eliminated. Some are so insipid as to make them fraudulent in everything but the legal niceties. Then you are left with the wines that have something to say. At this moment, you confront the issue of ego.

The ideal is to amplify *terroir* without distorting it. *Terroir* should be transmitted as free as possible of extraneous elements of style or taste. Ideally, one should not be able to find the hand of the winemaker. That said, it must be acknowledged that some signature always can be detected, although it can be very faint indeed when you reach the level of Robert Chevillon in Nuits-Saint-Georges; Bernard Serveau in Morey-Saint-Denis; or the Marquis d'Angerville and Gerard Potel, both in Volnay, to name a few. The self-effacement of these producers in their wines is very nearly Zen-like: their "signature" is an absence of signature.

Such paragons aside, the presence of a signature is not intrinsically bad, as long as it is not too expensively at the cost of *terroir*. A good example of this is the winemaking of the Domaine de la Romanée-Conti. The red wines of this fabled property—Echézeaux, Grands-Échézeaux, Romanée-Saint-Vivant, Richebourg,

La Tâche, and Romanée-Conti—all share a stylistic signature that becomes immediately apparent when the wines are compared with other bottlings from the same
vineyards. (Only two of the properties are exclusively owned or *monopoles*, La Tâche
and Romanée-Conti.) All of the wines display a distinctive silkiness, almost an unc-
tuosity, as well as a pronounced oakiness.

Nevertheless, the wines of the Domaine de la Romanée-Conti do overcome this
stylistic signature to display a full measure of their particular *terroirs*. This is confirmed when tasting other good examples of Richebourg or Grands-Échézeaux or
the other properties. The reason is that the yields are admirably low; the clonal selection is astute; the harvesting punctilious in discarding rotted or unhealthy grapes;
and the winemaking—stylistic signature aside—devoted to expressing the different
terroirs to the fullest degree. The wines could be improved if the signature were
less pronounced, in the same way that a beautiful dress could be improved if the
designer's initials were eliminated.

This matter of signature only becomes apparent when tasting multiple examples
of the same *terroir*. Although the ideal is what stereo buffs call a "straight wire,"
where the signal goes through the amplifier without any coloration, this simply is
impossible given the intervention of both grape and grower. In this, winemaking in
Burgundy really is translation. The poet W. S. Merwin maps out the challenge:

> The quality that is conveyed to represent the original is bound to differ with
> different translators, which is both a hazard and an opportunity. In the ideal
> sense in which one wants only the original, one wants the translator not to
> exist at all. In the practical sense in which the demand takes into account
> the nature of translation, the gifts—such as they are—of the translator are
> inescapably important.*

A good example of this would be the various Meursaults of the Domaine de
Comtes Lafon and those of Jean-Francois Coche-Dury. Stylistically, the Lafon wines
are more voluptuous, more apparently oaky when young, but impeccable in their
definition and separation of flavors. There is no mistaking one *terroir* with another
when tasting their wines. The same may be said of Coche-Dury, except that his style
is more austere and somehow leaner, with distinctions of *terroir* that are almost painfully precise. The depth and concentration are the equal of Lafon, yet the delivery is

---

* *Selected Translations 1968–1978* (Atheneum, 1979)

slightly different. In both cases, the distinctions of site are preserved at all costs. Both accomplish what W. S. Merwin intends when translating someone else's poetry: "I have not set out to make translations that distorted the meaning of the originals on pretext of some other overriding originality."

Awareness of the existence of signature in a Burgundy is critical, if only because it is easy to be seduced by style at the expense of *terroir*. A surprising number of Burgundies, especially the white Burgundies, do just that. Character in a white wine is much more hard-won than in a red, if only because white wine grapes usually have less intrinsic flavor than red wine grapes. This is very much the case with Chardonnay compared to Pinot Noir.

Moreover, much of the flavor in a wine is extracted from the skins during fermentation. Where many red wines, and certainly Pinot Noir, are made with extended skin contact, most white wines see little or no skin contact. This is true for Chardonnay as it is produced in Burgundy, although there are exceptions. At most, a white Burgundy will see no more than twenty-four hours of its Chardonnay juice fermenting or simply macerating in contact with its skins; most Pinot Noirs are given anywhere from seven days to three weeks on the skins.

Because of this, the temptation is strong for the winemaker to infuse flavor into white wines by means of various winemaking techniques in lieu of winning it in the vineyard. The most common of these is the use of brand new oak barrels, which provide an immediately recognizable scent of vanilla and toastiness. Another approach is to leave the young but fully fermented wine on its lees or sediment while aging in the barrel and stir up this sediment from time to time. Here the winemaker is seeking to capitalize on the subtle flavorings of autolyzing or decomposing yeasts. Sometimes, though, the result is a wine with off flavors from microbial deterioration.

Too often, signature substitutes for insufficient depth. It is easier, and more ego-gratifying, to fiddle with new oak barrels and winemaking techniques than to toil in the vineyard nursing old vines and pruning severely in order to keep yields low. Character in a white Burgundy, even in the most vocal of sites, does not come automatically. One need only taste an overcropped Montrachet—it is too common—to realize how fragile is the voice of the land when transmitted by Chardonnay. As a grape, it is surprisingly neutral in flavor, which makes it an ideal vehicle for *terroir*—or for signature.

Character in a red Burgundy is just as hard-won as in a white, but its absence is not as immediately recognizable because of the greater intrinsic flavor of Pinot Noir.

That said, it should be pointed out that flavor is not character, any more than a cough drop compares with a real wild cherry.

Where Chardonnay is manipulated to provide an illusion of depth and flavor, the pursuit with Pinot Noir is to make it more immediately accessible and easy down the gullet. An increasing number of red Burgundies now are seductively drinkable virtually upon release only two years after the vintage. Such wines can be misleading. Rather than improving with age, their bright, flashy fruitiness soon fades, like an enthusiasm that cools. The wine drinker is left stranded, stood up by a wine that offered cosmetics rather than character.

All of which underscores why *terroir* is the "more beautiful question" of wine. When the object is to reveal, amplify, and transmit *terroir* with clarity and resonance, there is no more "beautiful answer" than Burgundy. When it is ignored, wine may as well be grown hydroponically, rooted not in an unfathomable Earth that offers flashes of insight we call Richebourg or Corton, but in a manipulated medium of water and nutrients with no more meaning than an intravenous hook-up. Happily, the more beautiful question is being asked with renewed urgency by both growers and drinkers. A new care is being exercised. After all, without *terroir*— why Burgundy?

From Making Sense of Burgundy *(1990).*

<hr>

TERROIR MATTERS

WHEN I WAS A CHILD, fairy tales often struck me as vaguely deceptive. Take, for example, the saga of Sleeping Beauty. Who got the credit? The Prince, of course, for giving Sleeping Beauty the smooch that brought her back to life.

I think of Sleeping Beauty whenever the subject of *terroir* crops up. For reasons that continue to surprise me, a vocal contingent—call it the Prince Faction— insists that it's the Prince who did all the work. Without him, the whole Sleeping Beauty thing was a snore.

This, in a nutshell, is the anti-*terroirists'* position. It's the Prince who counts, the fellow with the magic touch who prunes the vines just so, puts the wine in the right barrels, and eventually presents to the world a Beauty.

All right, fine, give credit where credit is due: The Prince did wake the Beauty. But remember, Sleeping Beauty was already there.

This is why *terroir* matters. Because you can do all the grape growing and wine-making smoochery you like, but the Beauty has got to be there all along.

Want proof? Look at Chardonnay. Everywhere in the world, winegrowers have gone to elaborate lengths to be Burgundian. They use Chardonnay clones painstakingly plucked from Burgundy's most prized plantings. They use the same barrels as the Burgundy producers they so admire, toasted on the inside just so. They slavishly emulate the same winemaking techniques, such as stirring the lees. In short, they follow the Prince everywhere, taking copious notes on his osculatory technique.

Now, think about all the Chardonnays you've had from California, Australia, South Africa, Chile, Oregon, Washington, and Italy. How many of them were Sleeping Beauties, real stunners that drew us peasants from our huts to cheer madly for the gorgeous, golden-tressed beauty? Damned few. The vast majority of the world's Chardonnays are dull.

Of course, you know the reason why. The Prince Faction has folks believing in the wrong thing. Instead of seeking sites where Chardonnay can shine, their belief in the power of technique led them to plant Chardonnay in sites where, because of excessive warmth or unpromising soils, its beauty will never awake.

Actually, the Prince was lucky, because no one ever said, "Do it again, somewhere else." If they had, he would have been revealed as a fraud. It was Sleeping Beauty who had the magic in her. Anyone with a princely pedigree could have woken her.

Terroir is all about the second kiss. And the third. And the fourth. You and I and generations yet to come will awaken every time to the beauty of, say, Ridge's Monte Bello vineyard or Meursault Perrières, never mind who's making the wine (assuming a minimum degree of competence).

Which brings us to an unspoken element in today's aggravated *terroir* debate: Why is *terroir* so threatening to the faction that insists it isn't so?

I know of no *terroir* believer who doubts or dismisses the importance of the essential smooch, if you will. We know that clones matter, that pruning matters, that the thoughtful considerations of winemaking matter.

Yet the anti-*terroirists* are often far less accommodating. They rail against *terroir* with Jacobin-like zeal. They dismiss the virtues of the senses as unreliable.

The received wisdom of generations of "discoverers" of Wehlener Sonnenuhr Riesling or Volnay Clos des Ducs is dismissed as unreliable because you or I can't spot the same wine twice in a blind tasting. (All that really proves, by the way, is the fallibility—and often a mere lack of training—of an individual taster.)

Terroir is actually wine's version of a so-called prediction market, where groups of people opine on something, the results coalescing into a remarkably accurate consensus.

According to Michael Maboussin, a Wall Street strategist and an adjunct professor at Columbia University Business School, prediction markets are uncannily accurate. "All of us walk around with a little information and a substantial error term," he recently told the *New York Times*. "And when we aggregate our results, the errors tend to cancel each other out and what is distilled is pure information."

Think of *terroir* as pure wine information, distilled over generations of tasters—most of whom, individually, probably got it wrong in a blind tasting. But collectively, over generations, we nail it every time. And that's no fairy tale. *(2006)*

How the Land Became the Brand

ONE OF MY FAVORITE READS—IN addition to the letters page of the *Wine Spectator*—is the weekly British magazine, *The Economist*. I thought about that estimable publication when I read a letter to the *Wine Spectator* from Tom Wark, of Tiburon, California.

Tom takes me to task because my "obsession with *terroir* borders on the dictatorial." He believes—if I understand him rightly—that growing only certain grapes in spots where they have a vocation is unnecessarily limiting.

I have no objection to this accusation. To columnists of all stripes, being dictatorial is *grand cru* mother's milk. And he has a point—if dictatorial wine writers had such legislating powers. But we don't.

Which brings me to the heart of the matter: Why are California's vineyard areas subdividing into legally delimited districts? I can say straight off that it has nothing whatever to do with dreamy, impassioned wine columnists mooning about somewhereness. Instead, the answer is found in *The Economist* magazine.

The Economist doesn't ordinarily write about wine. In fact, it didn't even mention wine in a recent cover story about the business of brands, "Don't Get Left on the Shelf." But it nevertheless explained the inevitability of appellations in California as lucidly as any analysis I've read.

It all comes down to brands versus commodities. "If you are in the business of making something that has become indistinguishable from its rivals," instructs *The Economist*, "it has in effect turned into a commodity and will, therefore, sell chiefly on price. A few years ago, this happened to personal computers and so enabled cheap clone makers to knock famous names such as IBM off their pedestals. Makers of consumer goods, especially of food and drinks, now live in daily terror of the same thing happening to them."

In fact, just such a terror is sweeping California's wine producers. Everybody is making Cabernet Sauvignon and Chardonnay. These two names—never mind the vines—have been cloned to meaninglessness. Even entry-level wine buyers know they want Chardonnay and Cabernet.

Once, a varietal name signaled a premium wine. That's long gone. Witness the booming success of so-called "fighting varietals"—popularly priced wines that sport varietal names, none more prominently than Chardonnay and Cabernet. The consequences are clear. "If there is little or no difference in the perceived qualities of a range of products," observes *The Economist*, "the rational buyer will go for the cheapest."

This is why California is subdividing into appellations. It's the consequence of commoditization. The two grapes that the market demands—and nearly every winery survives on—have long since ceased to be differentiated in the public mind. Cabernet and Chardonnay have become commodities, like pork bellies.

Price alone won't serve to distinguish, as it once did. Winemaking won't do the trick, either. After all, *everybody* is using French oak barrels, malolactic fermentation, and lees contact. And relying on the fame of your winemaker is all washed up: Winemakers move around so much that they obviously are interchangeable.

Yet *The Economist* says brands will survive. "The point of brands is, and always has been, to provide information." Once, that information was of the most conventional, minimal sort: a family name like Martini, Mondavi, or Heitz. Later, varietal grape names served to inform. The two combined still can be a potent combination, but only for a fortunate few. Family names are tattooed to tanker loads of varietal wines.

So what's left? Only one thing: appellation. The French learned centuries ago that there's no other way to advertise your wine's distinction from your neighbor's except by pointing to where the grapes are grown.

Nowhere is this more economically pressing today than in California. If everybody is growing the same two grape varieties and fashioning them pretty much the same way, appellation is the only meaningful brand information left.

Once a grape variety becomes a commodity—it's now starting with Pinot Noir—the land becomes the brand. A pedigree of place emerges. For example, a ton of Cabernet with papers confirming a Howell Mountain or Mount Veeder pedigree gets about 30 percent more than a mutt with a "Napa Valley" lineage.

The inevitability of appellation is a matter of economic fact—not a wine writer's fancy. *(1994)*

It's nice to know that, sometimes, you can sway your audience. In 2005, in his wine blog called "Fermentation," Mr. Wark admitted to a change of perspective. "Many years ago I fired off a letter to the editor of the Wine Spectator. *The letter was aimed at* Spectator *columnist Matt Kramer. It was a not so subtle attack on what I recall was his contention that one day, when California vintners got it right, only one or two varietals would be planted in the States' appellations . . . I called Mr. Kramer a 'Terroirista.'*

"Since then I've become a bit more sophisticated in my thinking on terroir, *in large part, ironically, due to reading Matt Kramer's fantastic* Making Sense *series of books as well as following his writing in the* Wine Spectator.*"*

━●～

THE REAL SCOOP ON DIRT

RECENTLY, THE WORLD WAS ELECTRIFIED to hear about how—just maybe, mind you—there once was life on Mars. As you doubtless recall, some fossilized microbes were reported found inside a meteorite from Mars, a galactic version of finding a note inside a bottle washed up on the beach.

Call me unimaginative, but the whole event failed to move me. Not for the first time, I felt out of step with the fabled Zeitgeist. But I brightened considerably upon reading Edward O. Wilson's latest work, *In Search of Nature*. A Harvard professor, Wilson is renowned as the leading proponent of biodiversity and single-handedly created a new discipline called sociobiology.

"More organization and complexity exist in a handful of soil than on the surfaces of all the other planets combined," declares Wilson.

Boy, was I glad he said that. Because here-and-now dirt moves me much more than Martian meteorites. Not least, it also spotlights one of the most important, if subtle, trends in fine wine today: a growing awareness about dirt. The complexity of it. The life diversity within it. And, somehow, wine's ability to reflect the living world of dirt.

This last point is key. What sets wine apart from, say, orange juice, is its transparency to place. Much attention has rightly been paid to such site-specific features as temperature, air and water drainage, mineral constituents, soil structure, and so forth. But until recently, little has been said about dirt itself.

In a word, it's alive. Or should be. The famous soils scientist Hans Jenny of University of California Berkeley once estimated that if you tot up all the microbial, invertebrate, and vertebrate life underground, one acre contains the biomass equivalent of ten draft horses.

The problem is that in the last few decades a lot of dirt is literally dying in intensively cultivated spots such as vineyards. Some people believe that, over time, our best wines will suffer from this.

Perhaps because their soils have been cultivated for so long, European winegrowers are at the forefront of addressing this problem of the leaching of life itself from the soil. But why are they concerned only now? After all, the great vineyards of France and Italy have been around for centuries.

The answer is that never before have traditional vineyard areas been so cultivated to a single crop. Never before were they so monocultural. The unbroken carpet of vines of the Côte d'Or, the Médoc, Barolo, and Barbaresco didn't exist until the 1960s. Before then, it was more a checkerboard of pasture and vineyard.

Plenty of people still are up and about in Burgundy, Bordeaux, and Piedmont who can tell you about when fields were left fallow for years, with oxen and horses grazing on them, their manure used for fertilizer.

André Gagey, the former director of Louis Jadot, recalls it well. "There's no question that the fertilization is completely different now than it was when I started in 1947," he says. "Back then we used manure, a lot of manure. Natural fertilizer. Now, we don't use any manure, or very seldom anyway. As a result, the composition of the soil has certainly changed a lot."

What's happening in today's most intensively cultivated vineyards is a disturbingly rapid process of soil life exhaustion. That it happens so quickly makes it an important matter even for intensively cultivated New World districts such as Napa Valley.

The leading researcher is the aptly named Claude Bourguignon, who is an agronomist working in a laboratory in southern Burgundy. His most famous quote—cited in Anthony Hanson's second edition of *Burgundy*, which has a superb discussion of Bourguignon's investigations—is his declaration: "Many of the Côte d'Or's vineyards are more devoid of microbial life than the Sahara Desert."

This has alarmed a squadron of France's best winegrowers. Bourguignon has consulted to Burgundy's "great *L*'s": Leroy, Lafon, Lafarge, and Leflaive, as well as to Château Latour, Coulée de Serrant, and others. They are making mighty efforts to recall their soils to life.

Can you taste the difference in their wines? Hard to say. It's too early to tell. But these producers, among many others, can at least prove that their soils now are more alive, more vital. That alone makes their efforts worthwhile.

William Blake's famous line about "seeing a world in a grain of sand" is almost right. Really, it's a grain of dirt. *(1996)*

SHERRY BABY

READERS PLAGUED WITH RETENTIVE MEMORIES will recall one of my resolutions for 1999: "Visit Spain's Jerez district. (I'm embarrassed to say that I've never been there.)"

A man of my columnist word, I acted. Now, I have to tell you that I did not go to the Sherry district—centered around the city of Jerez in southern Spain—with much knowledge in my head or lust on my palate. Sherry is like the Oldsmobile: It's your father's drink. Actually, it's your *grandfather's* drink. So who knows? Maybe it's due for a comeback.

I've had my share of sherries—the light, delicate finos; nutty amontillados; dark, sweet olorosos—but I can't say I was transported. Truth to tell, I'm still not. Sherry is strange stuff. But it *is* intriguing, I'll give you that.

I discovered a kind of *Alice In Wonderland*, topsy-turviness to the whole affair. Take, for example, the fino-type sherry called Manzanilla. Now, of all the sherries, this is the one I like best. Fino sherries, by definition, are those protected from oxidation by a thick, white layer of floating yeasts called *flor*, or "flower." It's *flor* that makes fino. Without it, the wine would become oxidized and fated as something darker and nuttier, called amontillado.

Then there's a fino called Manzanilla, which is a delimited district near the sea around the lovely, deliciously seedy town of Sanlúcar de Barremeda. So, Burgundy boy that I am, I figured that the lovely, delicate tang of Manzanilla sherry has to do with the vineyards. *Terroir*, remember?

Not a chance. All these years I've been trying to decipher the received message of the land, teasing out the source of a wine's fundamental distinction, and then I get to Jerez. The following is verbatim, I swear to you:

ME: This fino called Puerto Fino is coarser and heavier than the Manzanilla, which is wonderfully delicate, finer, and lighter.

SHERRY PRODUCER: That's right.

ME: I assume that's because of the grapes grown in the Manzanilla district?

SHERRY PRODUCER: I'm sorry, I'm not quite following you.

ME: Well, I mean, you agree there's a definite difference between the Puerto Fino wine and the Manzanilla—which is consistent. So I assume it has to do with where the grapes are grown. Isn't that right?

SHERRY PRODUCER: Oh, no. The grapes could come from almost anywhere in the whole area. It has to do with where the *barrels* are located.

ME: What?

SHERRY PRODUCER: Oh, sure. If the barrels are in Sanlúcar, where it's cooler and more humid, you'd get a Manzanilla. That's because the *flor* layer doesn't thin out in the summer. But if the barrels are here in Jerez, where it's farther inland and consequently warmer and less humid, then you'd get a Puerto Fino.

ME: From the same grapes?

SHERRY PRODUCER: Exactly.

I was so boggled by this that on my next stop, in Sanlúcar as it happens, I repeated this conversation to another sherry producer. He looked at me a bit mystified and said, "Well, of course."

What a fool I've been. All these years I've been traipsing through vineyards, practically licking the dirt, and now it turns out that, really, it's where the *barrels* are stored that matters.

This, folks, is a whole new concept. Never mind about delimiting a district by vineyard location. What a silly idea. *Terroir* is where you put the barrels. This is genius.

But why limit it to barrels? Bulk winemaker Fred Franzia says it's the bottling line. He's planning an 18-million-case bottling plant in Napa Valley, near the airport. (This, all the insiders know, was choice bottling-line *terroir*.) His wines will say "Cellared and Bottled in Napa, California." How's *that* for *terroir*?

But why stop there? Why not winery consultants? Consultant *terroir*. What a concept. After all, every winemaking consultant I've ever met is quick as a dragster off the line to claim—or at least charge for—a wine's greatness. (Actually, "consultant *terroir*" is already operational in Tuscany.)

I'm glad I went to Jerez. Those sherry producers have been around. They obviously knew what I had yet to learn: *Terroir* is what you say it is. *(1999)*

Fred Franzia did build an 18-million-case bottling plant in the city of Napa. And although in 2004 he was forbidden by the California State Supreme Court from continuing to sell not-grown-in-Napa-Valley wines with brand names such as Napa Ridge, Napa Creek Winery, and Rutherford Vintners, nothing in the law prevents him from labeling his wines as "Cellared and Bottled in Napa, California."

～～

CLUELESS IN CARNEROS

FOR A WHILE, IT LOOKED like fine wine in Napa and Sonoma was growing up. Over the past few years, the Valley boys and girls had slowly dropped their University of California Davis techno-jargon and replaced it with what seemed to be, well, adult wine talk.

For the first time ever, there is widespread discussion about nuance, such as choosing various rootstocks for different soils in the same vineyard. You hear less of the old, "We're gonna bring in a D-9 Cat and rework the site." Or, my favorite: "A vineyard is just a factory. We can modify it just as we want with fertilizer, drip irrigation, and canopy training." I always asked for a free gimme cap when I heard that.

Lulled into thinking that winegrowing in Napa and Sonoma had irrevocably changed its old University of California Davis science-leads-the-way chest puffing, I was astounded by a newly released twenty-page tract titled "Towards Defining *Terroir* with the Carneros American Viticultural Area" by McCloskey Arrhenius and Co., a consulting and research firm in Sonoma, California.

Paid for by the Carneros Quality Alliance, an organization of Carneros district growers and wineries, the study was initiated to *prove* that Carneros exists. I imagine the Carneros growers wondering, existentially, "Is there really such a place as Carneros? And how will we know unless we can trot out scientific proof to that effect?" Apparently, the Carneros Quality Alliance doesn't really believe what it finds in its own wine glasses (never mind whose glasses).

In the bad old European days of *terroir*—from the folks who brought you such wonders as all of the great wines of Burgundy, Champagne, Mosel-Saar-Ruwer, and the Loire Valley—you looked for it in the glass. Wine was a proof complete in itself, vetted over generations.

Now, you'd think that the Carneros crowd would be feeling pretty good about themselves. After all, anybody can now pick up a glass of Carneros Pinot Noir or Chardonnay and establish for himself or herself in just a few sips that, "Yes Virginia (or New York), there really is a Carneros."

Despite this, McCloskey Arrhenius and Co. was hired, like tech-talking gumshoes, to track down Carneros. Here's what they wrote in the abstract: "The goal of this extensive study was to investigate regional *typicité* (*terroir*) of premium ($12 to $25 a bottle retail) Chardonnay wines using only industry quality experts (e.g., winemakers) as judges. The hypothesis was that if regional *typicité* is linked to grape-based aroma attributes, then this may be used to define California *terroir* and to support the creation of appellations."

Allow me to put this in English: We want to prove that Chardonnays from different areas taste different. And if they do, then we can make a case for all the appellations that have already been created anyway, such as Carneros.

Here's the best part: "*Terroir* may be the theory needed by California producers to guide researchers and technologists. Although it was not based upon scientific principles, producers need an equivalent concept to establish appellations." An equivalent? After all that Burgundy, Champagne, the Loire, Mosel-Saar-Ruwer, the Rheingau, and the Rheinpfalz have told us about *terroir*, California needs an *equivalent*?

The authors oblige. "We propose the following definition," they write (in boldface, no less). "The 'modern *terroir*' is the unique ecotypic expression of region grapes which causes differences in the secondary chemical flavorants detected in defect-free bottled wines."

Blown away, aren't you? This is an equivalent that surely will inspire generations of future California winegrowers to—in Robert Louis Stevenson's words—"grope about for their Clos Vougeot and Lafite." What blunderers those old monks must have been not to see that "*Terroir* may be studied within the context of ecotypic expression to create a scientific view based on both chemical and sensory assessments."

As if this isn't enlightenment enough, the authors make an even bolder claim to furthering the frontiers of wine knowledge. "The modern *terroir*," they announce, "is an ecological theory we are advancing which allows us to expect regional variations in wines based upon regional physical environmental differences." In other words, you can expect wines to taste different when they are grown in different places.

And with this powerful new paradigm in hand, what did their industry quality experts discover? "Regional *typicité* was most easily detected in high quality wines and the industry panel did not detect regional *typicité* in low quality wines." You heard it here first. *(1996)*

THE FIGHT FOR THE SOUL OF WINE

WHETHER WE HUMANS HAVE A soul I'll leave to theologians, but I have no doubt about wine: it has a soul. I'm not talking about the everyday stuff, which, admittedly, is pretty soulless.

Fine wine, the sort that gets us dreaming, surely has a soul. Its source is clear: It's the voice of the earth. Call it *terroir* if you like. This natural expression of site is what makes wines so rewarding over so many generations.

But what happens when winemaking technique so distorts a wine that it literally could not possibly come from nature? We're now seeing such wines.

Take, for example, reverse osmosis. This is the wine version of a complete transfusion via an ultrafine filtration. Reverse osmosis is increasingly used in California, Bordeaux, and Australia.

What's reverse osmosis like? This is a description from Vinovation, Inc., a major supplier of reverse osmosis equipment to California wineries:

> A common experience when you begin your first reverse osmosis application is that it may be disconcerting that the filtrate is obviously stripped of vinous character. It takes time to realize that unlike all other filtrations, *the product is not the filtrate; it is the retentate!* [emphasis theirs] The filtrate "has the appearance of water."

In other words, the technique is to deconstruct wine and then reconstruct it, eliminating water, alcohol, or volatile acidity.

Now, guess who's using these gizmos? Californians and Australians certainly, but the real fanciers are the Bordelais. It's estimated that Bordeaux has at least sixty reverse osmosis machines in use. What's more, it's not necessarily Bordeaux's wine cooperatives using reverse osmosis. Rather, it's the expensive classified growths, because they can afford the devices.

The Bordelais are not eager for you to know this. Neither are the Californians or the Aussies. That alone tells you something.

California producers, for their part, are using reverse osmosis to allow them to harvest ultraripe grapes. If made naturally, the resulting alcohol from such overripe grapes would be excessive. No worries. Just run it through reverse osmosis and take out however much alcohol you want. Voilà! A creation previously unseen in nature.

It's tempting to shrug and say, "Well, it's just another tool in the winemaker's toolbox." Maybe so. But what are the tools being used to build? The issue is no longer whether technology can change wine. The issue is, are the wines we're tasting "real"?

The effect of reverse osmosis is not unlike plastic surgery. It's one thing to have a little nip or tuck to restore you to your original beauty. But it's quite another to become Michael Jackson, reconfigured out of all recognition from the original.

The importance of the natural cannot be overstated. Think of the effect in, say, bodybuilding. It's widely acknowledged that many bodybuilders use steroids to acquire mass. What chance does the natural bodybuilder have in competition? None. The aesthetic is changed—and not for the better.

We can see the same effect in sports. When Mark McGwire revealed his use of a performance-enhancing drug, it somehow gave fans pause about his record-breaking achievement of hitting seventy home runs. Was it truly human? Was it natural?

A similar specter haunts the Tour de France. Even when the bicycle race is won by someone who steadfastly denies using performance-enhancing drugs and has always tested clean (Lance Armstrong), he's on the defensive. Cynical suspicion unfairly taints his achievement.

Now, think of the disadvantage faced by natural winemakers. Either their wines seem puny (the bodybuilder syndrome) or, if they achieve heroic concentration through superlow yields, their wines are suspect (the Lance Armstrong syndrome).

Wine's most profound appeal is its thrill of the wild. It's that Michelangelesque fingertip touch between nature and us. If wines lose this birthright expressiveness of place, then they've lost their soul. We, in turn, can quickly forget what the real thing is supposed to taste like.

Want proof? Recall (if you can) the taste of real cream compared with today's ubiquitous ultrapasteurized versions. Or real tomatoes. Or real corn compared with the genetically fixed "supersweet" varieties.

We're at a crossroads. The fight for the soul of wine has begun. *(2001)*

THE WINE BEHIND THE MACHINES

IN HIS TOUGH-GUY FASHION, RAYMOND CHANDLER—or his alter ego, private detective Philip Marlowe—would have made a terrific wine critic, especially these days. Today's calculated wine commercialism employs practices designed to make wines seem better than they really are.

For example, in California it's now common practice to allow grapes to become overripe, the better to create outsize flavors and soft tannins. A traditional wine made from such sugar-rich grapes would be very high in alcohol. California winemakers turn to a high-tech device called a spinning cone to lower the alcohol level. You can "dial it in," they say.

In Europe, especially in Bordeaux, winemakers create a kind of false concentration by removing water from the unfermented juice using yet another high-tech gizmo called a vacuum concentrator. A godsend in a wet vintage—when grapes get bloated from harvest rains or when a mistake is made in picking times—it's also mighty handy if you over-crop your vines and then reduce the dilution later. It's estimated that Bordeaux alone has some two thousand vacuum concentrators, including many at the most famous châteaux.

Also, wineries in California, Europe, and Australia frequently use a technique called reverse osmosis, which is an ultra-fine filtration that literally deconstructs wine at the molecular level and then reconstructs it. You can remove alcohol or water molecules as you like.

Are these high-tech tools intrinsically bad? Not at all. They have their place as recourses of last resort, something you employ in a wet vintage.

However, these deconstructionist gizmos are increasingly used as part of many wineries' annual protocol, never mind the need or the vintage. Too often, the resulting wines are like a Miss America smile—glossy and insincere.

Raymond Chandler put it best: "From 30 feet away she looked like a lot of class. From 10 feet away she looked like something made up to be seen from 30 feet away." *(2008)*

An Open Letter to Natural Winegrowers

DEAR NATURAL WINEGROWERS,

I call you "natural winegrowers" for lack of a better phrase. Who are you? You are winemakers for whom wine is not merely an end product (indeed, it's not a "product" at all), but a fulfillment of what you created and nurtured in your vineyard.

But it's not just growing grapes. Rather, it's a whole attitude about why you've consecrated your lives to wine. You don't need to be told about *terroir*. You're living it. Maybe your wines have it (and maybe they don't), but it's not for lack of trying.

I've met you in Walla Walla, Washington, patches of Australia, and in Napa Valley, too. At the risk of seeming gloomy, I've got to tell you this: You're in trouble.

I'm sure it doesn't feel like that right now. The last decade has been good for winegrowers. So what's the problem? It's this: The meaning is being sapped from your wines. You're not making a case for your way of wine.

I'll give you an example. Recently, I was walking in the vineyard with a California winegrower. I commented on the absence of drip irrigation in his vineyard. "All our wines are dry-farmed," he said proudly. "Of course, that really lowers the yields, but I'm convinced that dry-farming, if you can do it, really makes a difference. It's all muscle in the glass. No flab."

When I asked if he told his customers this, he shrugged and said, "Nah, I've never bothered. It's just what I do, that's all."

Such modesty is a lovely thing. (I'll have to try it sometime.) But it's wrong. Not only is he doing himself a disservice, he's allowing his competitors an advantage they haven't paid for the way he has. He's not setting himself apart from them in a very legitimate, meaningful way.

Then there's winemaking. I've written before about the radical interventionism in today's most expensive wines, such as vacuum concentrators, which can make wines seem more concentrated by removing excess water.

Reverse osmosis and spinning cones, for their part, allow winemakers to remove alcohol from wines created from intentionally overripe grapes, the better to make massive wines without the excessive alcohol that would normally accompany over-ripe grapes.

You might think that it's all a matter of winery size. But it's not. For example, I recently spent most of a day visiting Gallo of Sonoma's winery, which is tucked away in tiny Dry Creek Valley. I'm a big admirer of Gallo of Sonoma, especially their single-vineyard bottlings. As you might imagine, it's not a small winery.

Anyway, I decided to broach the topic of vacuum concentrators, reverse osmosis machines, and spinning cones. Frankly, I figured they'd dance around it or refer me to someone higher up.

"We don't use any of these things," unhesitatingly replied winemaker Eric Cinnamon. He seemed genuinely surprised at my question. "I guess you could say that our winemaking is really traditional. I've never heard anybody here even consider using any of those things."

How ironic, I thought. Here's Gallo of Sonoma which, I imagine, most folks would figure as a likely user of just these sorts of devices. In comparison, a majority of Bordeaux's classified growths—which cultivate an aura of traditionalism—now own (and presumably use) vacuum concentrators or reverse osmosis machines to concentrate their wines.

Technologists talk *terroir* but they don't necessarily practice it. Rather, their intent is to design wines to their own specifications.

Think of the difference between growers of heirloom tomatoes and growers of those "improved" tomato varieties created by nurseries and universities serving the industry. Who do you think has it easier? And who gives us the better tomato?

What do I want you to do as a natural winemaker? I want you to declare yourselves. I'd like to see something like this on your back labels:

> This wine was made from grapes we grow that were made into wine with as little intervention as possible. Think of it as high-fidelity wine. Here's what we do, etc.

If you don't make your case, my cherished natural winegrowers, then your efforts will continue to be diminished by those who want your image, but who are not willing to pay your price. *(2002)*

Gallo of Sonoma has since changed its name to Gallo Family Vineyards.

ANGELO GAJA—NOT QUITE THERE AT *THE NEW YORKER*

In 1991, I wrote a proposal letter directly to Robert Gottlieb, then the editor of *The New Yorker*. I didn't know him, and he certainly didn't know anything about me. Yet just a few days later, the phone rang and a warm voice at the other end said, "Hi, this is Bob Gottlieb."

Even though *The New Yorker* had not published anything about wine for years, even decades—and despite the fact that Gottlieb himself had no personal interest in wine—he liked the idea and commissioned the profile.

Then, like something out of *Mission: Impossible*, he said, "you will never hear from me again. Of course, if you should need to speak to me, feel free to call. But we won't be calling you. There is no deadline. Whenever you have finished the profile, that's when it's due. The fee will be $15,000 with a 100 percent kill fee. Your expenses will be reimbursed as you incur them. Simply send us the bill, and we'll send you a check."

I submitted the profile about a year later from Piedmont, where I had moved to research my cookbook on the region's cuisine. By then, Gottlieb had been replaced by Tina Brown, who reportedly wanted no part of anything to do with wine. I received a check for $15,000 with a stub declaring "kill fee." The piece was mine to do with as I pleased.

Of course, there wasn't any other market for such an extended profile, as *The New Yorker* magazine, then and now, is unique. I have, over the years, cannibalized one or another part of the profile for use in essays, columns, and other books. So if something sounds familiar to you, that's why.

It hardly needs to be said that, since this profile was first written in 1992, much has happened to wine in general and to Angelo Gaja in particular. Nevertheless, Gaja's saga is still one of the most extraordinary. (Only those of Baron Philipe de Rothschild and Robert Mondavi rival it.)

Most importantly, what follows captures the flavor of how radical and recent is Italy's rise to wine fame. Back when I wrote this, if I had predicted to Piedmontese producers that their Barolos and Barbarescos would one day command the same prices as *grand cru* Burgundies, they would have been incredulous.

I have made no changes to what I originally submitted to *The New Yorker*. I have added an appendix that briefly updates Gaja's trajectory since this was originally written, as well as refreshing some factual information.

THE EASTER SUNDAY MORNING THAT Angelo Gaja and I set off for a walk—more like a wind sprint, given Gaja's usual mode of overdrive—was a rare day. We were on Gaja's native ground: the Langhe hills of the Piedmont region of northwest Italy. Too often the Langhe is shrouded in winter fogs or veiled in spring and fall rains. This leaves the occasional visitor with a nagging sense of Brigadoon, that somehow you have witnessed something not merely foreign, but transitory and secretive. Even after living in the Langhe for a year, I still feel this way.

Yet that Easter Sunday, the Langhe was radiantly, innocently, on display. You could see the full breadth of its plunging, freestanding hills that, at such moments, make it look like a vast, repeating terrestrial bosom. In the distance lay the Alps, toothachingly white with unmelted winter snow.

Part of this sense of Brigadoon—that mythical place which can be seen by outsiders only once a century—is due to language. A visitor to Italy comes equipped with, or at least braced for, the sound of Italian. Yet in Langhe, especially in its rural reaches, the sound is disturbingly foreign. Even the untutored ear can hear that, whatever is being spoken, it certainly isn't mellifluous Italian, with its springboard vowels that send each word hurtling toward the next, only to be briefly caught and immediately forwarded, like a package in a post office manned by jugglers.

Instead, what one hears is Piedmontese, which is one of Italy's many dialects. A dialect usually implies a subsidiary language, a variation on an acknowledged mother tongue. In the Langhe, Piedmontese is the preferred language and Italian not only is subsidiary, but barely even maternal. Italian is only modestly related to Piedmontese, which shares more in sound and individual word with such antique tongues as Provençal and Languedoc.

At first, the dialect sounds almost Germanic, so abrupt and guttural is it. Far from the springy quality of Italian, with its penchant for words ending in a vowel, Piedmontese tends to finish in consonants, giving the language a cropped, heel-digging, reluctant sound. Upon closer listening, you pick up something undeniably Italian. *Va bene?*—how's it going?—emerges in Piedmontese as *va bin.* Or, *va ben.* Every town in Piedmont has its own pronunciations and, frequently, wholly localized vocabularies that are foreign even to other speakers of Piedmontese. Still, the Italian connection is gratifyingly clear.

But then you hear a relatively simple sentence such as, "There is a lot of snow today." In Italian it is simply: *Oggi c'é molta neve.* But in Piedmontese, you lose all linguistic bearings: "*A-j' moto-ben ed fiòca ancheuj.*" The vowels are elongated, yet the words typically are expelled forcefully, even explosively. The effect is like harbor seals barking in French.

No matter how unusual it sounds to outsiders' ears, including those of other Italians, the dialect is to the Piedmontese their most natural, expedient expression. This particular Easter Sunday, when the narrow roads that thread through the Langhe's complicated hills were clotted with groups of families and friends slowly making their way to church, it was Piedmontese that filled the air. Italian may as well have been Tahitian.

To reach the trailhead of our walk, we left Gaja's hometown of Barbaresco (population, six hundred and fifty) in his massive, dark blue Seven Series BMW. It filled the road. Big European luxury cars are sizable even in America's generous landscape. In a place as confined as rural Piedmont, on roads custom-fitted for a plump goat, a car such as Gaja's seems like an aircraft carrier. Usually, Gaja, fifty-three, drives it like a kid on a Vespa with an overfull bladder, weaving through traffic and rocketing along momentarily empty roads. And although the car is fitted with an automatic transmission, Gaja fiddles with it like a manual, constantly jiggering the shift lever through first, second, and third gears.

On Easter Sunday, though, his driving was more restrained. The weather was soothing. Also, the fact that it was Easter Sunday, even though a day of apparently no personal significance to Gaja, surely had a psychic effect. Easter permeates Italy like Thanksgiving does in America. (His wife, Lucia, was attending church with Gaja's elderly parents in San Remo, a two-hours' drive from Barbaresco over the mountains to the Mediterranean, where his parents spend part of the winter.) For once, the BMW's transmission was allowed to proceed in its orderly Teutonic fashion without Gaja's anarchic interference.

The greatest impediment to speed, or even efficiency, was the clumps of church-going locals. It wasn't just their presence on the road. (Even Italian schoolchildren know that pedestrians have no rights worth mentioning.) What really slowed our progress was Gaja's obligation to acknowledge his neighbors. Time and again, the electrically controlled windows of the car whirred down to allow Gaja to converse in Piedmontese with well-wishers along what was, effectively, Barbaresco's Easter parade.

The locals seemed pleased—and a little surprised—with their opportunity to chat with Gaja (whose name rhymes with "hiya"). For his part, Gaja exuded a convincing and sincere warmth and animation. Clearly, he was himself pleased with the contact, and also, one suspected, his ability to remove himself with a flick of the electric window button.

After our halting procession out of Barbaresco, the car picked up speed, and we careened through the hills in search of the trailhead. Gaja was as relaxed as I've ever seen him, although a witness to the walk would hardly have described it as a leisurely stroll. Still, for him, it served.

We talked, as we always have, about wine and business. The conversations can often start on a matter seemingly unrelated to wine. But in the end, all roads to Gaja are puddled with wine. Wine and Italy. Italian wine and Americans. Wine and the British.

"England, for example, is a very difficult market, a shit market," he offers. I was delighted to hear this, not so much for the sentiment—which, for Italian wines, is largely accurate—but for its uncharacteristic acerbity. Usually Gaja is a paragon of tact, even though his rat-a-tat speaking style makes everything he says sound insistent and dramatic. He is almost never bloodyminded, as the British themselves would put it. And when he is, he is even less likely to reveal it.

"It's always been difficult," he continues. "When I first started going to England in the early 1970s, this strong category, these connoisseurs, these Masters of Wine, they approached the Barbaresco, always sniffing, saying 'salami skin' or 'chicken skin boiled in water with cabbage' or 'animal smells.'

"It was really a surprise, because we were offering what we considered our best wines. And they were going 'Ptui! Ptui! Ptui!'" Gaja mimes an elaborate spitting motion to further convey the point. "My dear, they were not appreciating at all," he adds dryly. Gaja rolls his *r*, so that the phrase "My dear" comes out sounding something like "My dearrr." Oddly, he says this only in English, never in Italian.

"So I believed that two attitudes were possible. To say, 'These people don't understand anything.' To be a little bit offended. Or, trying to taste again, to reconsider our wine, trying to see it from their perspective. To try to become more of a critic of the wine.

"When I repeated the same tasting in Belgium—they have a little bit of a complex about not being French—they were even worse than the English. For them, the wines were always too tannic, too aggressive, too, too, too bad. Coming back home, I was a little bit frustrated. It's not easy for me to be frustrated. But I was. When I returned, I was saying, 'Look, the wine is so, so, and so. We will have to change. We will have to think. We will have to do things differently.' But it was difficult. You know that a lot of people were not endeared by this."

While he was talking, I recalled a weekend five months previous, when Gaja invited me to join him when he hosted the British wine auctioneer and standard-bearer of London's clubby wine trade, Michael Broadbent. It was Broadbent, along with others, who helped found the Master of Wine Institute, which creates these same self-styled Masters of Wine who so coolly appraised Gaja's (then different) wines in the early 1970s.

With a full head of silver hair combed straight back, longishly curling at the nape of his neck, Broadbent looks like the American and Italian image (or caricature) of a certain sort of elegant yet physically awkward Englishman. He stands uncomfortably stiff, with his knees locked inward and a pleasant, unintentionally smirking smile pasted on his face. He also has a soothing, comforting voice. The accent, as one might expect, is plummy but not overripe.

Broadbent's professional specialty is auctioning old and rare wines, especially Bordeaux and Port, for Christie's auction house. He is, by his own admission, an assiduous, obsessive notetaker about every wine he drinks, no matter how social the occasion. Some of these scribblings have been assembled in two massive books of published tasting notes, which have been well received. In both books, Piedmont wines barely figure. They are not much in demand at the Christie's "Fine and Rare" wine auctions over which Broadbent presides. An American magazine, *Wine Spectator* once headlined him as "The World's Most Experienced Wine Taster."

During the first night's dinner, I asked Broadbent when he was last in Piedmont, which is universally recognized as Italy's finest wine region. He wasn't quite sure, he had to admit, but he did recall driving through once about twenty or twenty-five years ago. In comparison, Broadbent has been a regular, and frequent, visitor to California's Napa Valley, where he has presided over various auctions.

Clearly, getting Broadbent to the Langhe—an area that, in his line of work, is nothing less than a backwater—was something of a triumph for Gaja, who single-handedly enticed Broadbent and his wife, Daphne, to be his guests for a weekend. Ever diplomatic, Gaja made sure to include local wine organizations in the Broadbent visit, but it was openly and unmistakably Gaja's show.

For somebody such as Gaja, who makes what are deemed "collector's wines," a person in Broadbent's position can be invaluable. At the most rarefied levels of wine, to ascend to regular auction status both confirms and reinforces your position as a blue chip. No Italian wine has ever insinuated itself into that winner's circle. Gaja's wines, and their world reputation, are still too new to be auctionable, but the time is fast arriving and the Broadbent weekend was an essential, even critical piece of road paving.

Often, when Gaja takes out visiting wine writers for lunch or dinner, he chooses not to serve his own wines, preferring instead to expose his guests to other wines of the area. It is partly a function of his genuine pride about the Langhe and partly a savvy insight into the mentalities of the American, Swiss, and German writers who are the most frequent foreign visitors. Usually finding such lunches and dinners to be hard-sell extensions of the preceding winery visit, they are relieved, and gratified, to see a winemaker serving someone else's wines. Gaja comes off as a magisterial practitioner of noblesse oblige.

The first Broadbent dinner, however, was strictly a Gaja affair. Partly, this was because Gaja had already arranged the next day for a monumental tasting of other producers' wines, with the winemakers in attendance, as well as local political dignitaries. It was, by the way, an unprecedented wine fest, with some fifty producers and three times as many wines put forth for, really, just one person. All the rest of us were merely along for the ride, like small sucker fish that attach themselves to a big shark in hopes of snagging a few scraps.

Virtually every winemaker who was anybody in the Langhe was present, serving their most stupendous wines. They all knew, of course, who had gotten Broadbent there, although Gaja tactfully left Broadbent's side, letting him engage the producers on his own. You had to feel sorry for Broadbent, who surely knew that the whole thing was exclusively for his benefit and, therefore, not only had to be gracious to every producer (which came naturally and easily to him) but also had to taste everyone's wines (which is brutal).

That first night's dinner, therefore, had only Gaja's wines. As might be expected, Broadbent was tasting carefully and thoroughly, taking notes with seemingly every sip. Everyone else at the table—Broadbent's wife, Daphne; the Austrian glassmaker Georg Riedel and his wife, Evi; American writer Edward Steinberg, who lives in Rome and is writing a book about Gaja's wines; and Gaja's wife, Lucia—engaged in discreet, bilingual chitchat.

At the midpoint of the dinner, just after the best Gaja wine of the evening was served—one of his "collector" Barbarescos from a single vineyard that never produces more than one thousand cases—Broadbent tasted the wine and then looked up, hoping to catch someone's eye around the circular table. He caught mine. "This is terribly interesting wine, don't you think?" Clearly it was a rhetorical question. He continued, "It really reminds me of nothing so much as Château Mouton Rothschild. Wouldn't you agree?"

Château Mouton Rothschild is a Bordeaux icon, a first growth that regularly sells for $75 to $100 a bottle for the latest vintage. It is made almost exclusively from the Cabernet Sauvignon grape variety. Old vintages command phenomenal prices. Broadbent, naturally, is intimately familiar with them all.

It was a flattering comparison, just the sort that Gaja could not help but enjoy. The only problem was that The World's Most Experienced Taster apparently didn't have much experience tasting wines made from the Nebbiolo grape variety, which is the sole grape of Barbaresco. To conclude, however complimentarily, that a Barbaresco resembles a Bordeaux is like a man admiring a woman's fashions only when they resemble his own tailoring. A certain understanding is missing, a recognition of another legitimacy, with its own needs and expressions.

In fairness, Broadbent was set up. His response was precisely what Gaja set out to achieve after he returned from that deflating foray into Great Britain and Belgium twenty years earlier. For Gaja had learned that if his wine was ever going to be acknowledged, let alone endorsed, by the thousands of Broadbents whose understanding of great red wine has been shaped on the template of red Bordeaux and red Burgundy, then his Barbaresco wine would have to speak to them in the same stylistic vocabulary.

When I asked Gaja about this later on, he protested that it was not so. "No, I don't believe that it was the impact of England," he says. "Frankly, I was not really offended. I have always maintained a respect for these people. They have another taste. Another parameter. You know, I can't easily eat in the French way. But there are forty-five million French who like to eat butter and so on. I can't! I recently went with my family to Paris. We went to various two-star restaurants and so on. We didn't eat lunch, only dinner. And even then we didn't choose a full menu. How can you stay at a table with two young daughters, eating six or seven dishes? So we chose only two dishes. But after some time eating this food, I was stopped. I couldn't do it." Gaja accompanies this declaration with a birdlike fly-away motion with his hands, along with a tweeting whistle sound, laughing at his own audio-visual antics.

"What can I say? That French *grande cuisine* is boring? That it's no good? This would be stupid. It's a question of parameters, of education, don't you believe?" Here his voice rises as the passion grows. He is too refined a fellow to pound the table, but you sense that if he were less disciplined, the table might have something to fear. "I have the habit of drinking Barbaresco. I drank Nebbiolo from the beginning, when I was very young. I like this aggressivity in the wine.

"So I was not particularly offended," he insists. "When I listen to people I try not to consider the bad things they say. I try instead to understand what is good from what they say. In England, you have people who have discovered many wines in the world, such as Champagne. I have a respect for the people there. Unfortunately, we have two different life interpretations."

That said, Gaja's actions speak louder—or at least more convincingly—than his words. His action, on the broadest scale, was to sandpaper this "aggressivity" in Nebbiolo that he professes to like into something so smooth, so polished, so admirably elegant that it could be presented at court. (Which is precisely where both Bordeaux and Burgundy first gained their reputations centuries ago.) And indeed, today there still is a court of sorts, with courtiers (or kings) such as Broadbent sitting in instant, often harsh judgment on any country bumpkin wines that have the temerity to try to pass themselves off as something aristocratic. To succeed, they must have the fine-wine versions of patents of nobility, the wine equivalents of certain standards of dress, bearing, speech, and accent.

The French are no less demanding. In fact, it is their wine politesse that remains the standard for all aspirers to greatness. And its requirements are clearly stated. This was fully in evidence when Michel Bettane came to the Langhe for his first visit. At forty years old, Bettane is France's most formidable wine critic. A former professor of the classics, Bettane writes lengthy, learned, detailed, and controversial—the French, who enjoy argument for its own sake, as do the Italians, prefer to say "provocative"— articles for *Revue du Vin de France*, which is France's leading wine journal.

Bettane was herded into the Langhe with a group of other Frenchmen by an ambitious Italian wine exporter who wanted to create a market for Piedmontese wines in Paris, an admirable exercise with about as much chance of success as selling boxing reform to a bunch of fight promoters. After all, they put the fix in for themselves long ago, so why change?

After the group departed, Bettane remained behind, and we traveled together around the Langhe, tasting wines and comparing notes. Although no French chauvinist, Bettane—like everyone else—tastes wines within a certain cultural framework. As a Frenchman deeply immersed in aesthetic matters (he once seriously examined pursuing a career as a pianist), Bettane's considerations about wine quality derive from explicit criteria. He believes, with justification, that although these criteria may have been articulated first, and probably best, in France, they are universal. For example, he insists, "A wine cannot be great unless it is *harmonieux*." This view is endorsed by every stripe of French aesthete. Harmony is not an end, but rather, simply a beginning. A wine—or a dress, or a plate of food—must first be presentable, and graceful. Only then can it even begin to be considered as something fine.

Underlying this principle of harmoniousness is that nothing can be out of whack. A wine, for example, cannot have too much mouth-rasping tannin. Or too much or too little acidity. Yet other elements come into play, such as the quality and intensity of the fruit flavors. As in a chess game where no move is, or should be, evaluated merely on its own, various elements in a wine can only be judged in relation to their overall, interactive effect—which must be harmonious. For Bettane, tasting Barolo and Barbaresco was disturbing. Frequently he found them intriguing, even endearing. But too often, they were not *harmonieux*. They lacked aesthetic traction.

Partly the difficulty lies in Nebbiolo itself. For centuries it has been the pride of the Langhe. It is a beast of a grape, highly acidic and ferociously tannic. Its flavors, though, are original and somehow magical. Classically described as having intermingled tastes of tar and roses, only in the Langhe, specifically in its Barolo and Barbaresco districts, is Nebbiolo fully resonant. The Langhe is to Nebbiolo what Burgundy's famed Côte d'Or is to Pinot Noir.

The locals long ago learned to live with the beast, even to love its beastly qualities. They tried to tame it, sometimes harshly so. "I remember when my father, and other winemakers of his generation, used to put their Barolos on the roof to soften them up," recalls Aldo Conterno, who at sixty-two is one of the Langhe's most deft, and modern, winemakers. (Bettane considered his Barolos to be *harmonieux* when he tasted them.)

"In the old days the Barolos were so tannic, because of how they were fermented," explains Conterno. "They used to leave the juice and then the brand-new wine in the vat with the tannin-rich grape skins for two months or more. Today, the whole maceration process rarely goes for much more than thirty days. After the wines were drawn off from the skins, the Barolo would remain in casks for five, six, seven years, sometimes even more. And then it would be transferred from the cask into glass demijohns. Even then, the wine could still be pretty tannic. So sometimes, to soften it up, they would put the demijohns outside, on the roof, for the summer and part of the winter. Of course it was oxidized all to hell by then, but anyway, they liked that taste."

Gaja recalls—and recoils from—the same memories. "When I first had an impact on the way we made wine, this was in the early 1970s, some longtime customers were beginning to realize that the wine was changing, compared to the wines of the 1950s," he recounts. "At that time, there were maybe only ten winegrowing families offering wines to customers, including the big merchants. So the change was imposed on them. They had to accept it.

"The change we imposed was a wine that was darker in color than in the past. This was because we started to reduce the wood aging in casks. Starting in 1970, we realized that the longer the wine aged in cask, the more the coloring material would become orange. But the taste of my father's customers was in the direction of this kind of oxidation. I remember some older customers coming here. And my father would open old bottles. They were enthusiastic, exclaiming, 'This is like Marsala! It's fantastic.'"

Gaja still can't get the taste of the memory out of his mind. Or forget the indignity of an aesthetic that valued Barbaresco or Barolo looking like Sicily's famous amber-hued sweet wine. "My God, Marsala!" he groans, his lips contorting into a pained grimace like a cheese fancier who had bit into a morsel with mold. "I remember this happening many times. I decided that if they wanted Marsala, then they could go to Sicily."

It must be said that, although now long gone in Italy, a taste for old, oxidized, exhausted wine still can be found in unexpected quarters. I thought of Gaja when I picked up the December 1992 issue of *Decanter* magazine, the house organ of Britain's wine establishment. The editors had asked various wine luminaries to recount their six best wines of the year. No less a figure than Hugh Johnson, the world's best-known wine writer and a superb stylist, lauded as one of his six best wines a forty-year-old French Champagne, Pol Roger 1952. "The last taste was almost like iced coffee," he enthused.

The problem Gaja had with his father's old customers—who were even then willing to pay a premium price for Gaja wines—was not just a matter of taste. It was the more intractable problem of tradition itself, nowhere more tenacious than in Italy's many mountainous, tucked-away wine districts. The Langhe is one of these. But as the recognized repository of Italy's greatest red wine, Barolo, it had self-consciously become a fortress, its ramparts bricked with tradition and mortared with pride.

This, despite the fact that the audience for Barolo was both local and dwindling, extending not much farther than to Turin and Milan, which is like shipping New Jersey's famous tomatoes no farther than to Philadelphia and Providence. Some of the larger commercial shippers did get their wines to the United States and Argentina (the destinations of choice for many Italian immigrants, especially Piedmontese, over the last century). But the prestige failed to translate.

Barbaresco—now famous thanks to Gaja—was utterly unknown. In fact, Barbaresco didn't even exist as a wine until 1894, when a liberal-minded local aristocrat, Domizio Cavazza, formed a growers' cooperative. Previously, all the Nebbiolo grown in the Barbaresco area was sold as Barolo. Barbaresco is an arriviste compared to Barolo, and a conspicuously successful one at that. Inevitably, claims of Barbaresco having a more prestigious, and ancient, heritage are now submitted with assiduity, reminding one of Giuseppe di Lampedusa's immortal line in *The Leopard* when the Prince, of impossibly ancient lineage, remarks about a newly rich and eager arrival to the upper classes, "His family, I am told, is an old one or soon will be."

Gaja's family itself is far from being a Barbaresco purebred. The name is thought to be of Spanish origin, the family having arrived in Piedmont sometime between 1820 and 1830. Gaja is not absolutely sure, because the family records were destroyed when the church in nearby Vezza d'Alba, where the Gajas first arrived, was bombed during World War II. The Gaja wine business began in 1859. The maternal side of his family is not at all local. His grandmother, Clotilde Rey, had French parents and, although born on the Italian side of the border near France, was effectively French in language, culture, and habits. His mother, Giannina, came from Biella, a town in the northern reaches of Piedmont which saw Italy's first Industrial Revolution with Biella's still-vibrant textile industry.

Gaja's father, Giovanni, is, however, a Langarolo. Even so, his own occupation—and the source of considerable income—came not from wine but from his profession as a *geometra*, a sort of combination land surveyor and real estate agent. Angelo did not grow up in the tiny village of Barbaresco, but rather in the nearby, much larger town of Alba, which is the commercial hub of the Langhe.

It was in Alba that Giovanni Gaja practiced his profession as a *geometra*, and, during Alba's industrializing boom years of the fifties, both made and lost a considerable sum investing in real estate. As a *geometra*, Giovanni Gaja was in a good position to know about potential vineyard acquisitions. And although never a winemaker, he knew choice vineyard land when he saw it. In fact, the three named vineyards that are today Angelo Gaja's most sought after wines were acquired by his father in the early- and mid-sixties.

Although Alba still is a provincial town by anyone's standards (population, thirty thousand people), it today boasts substantial wealth, thanks to its three post-war industrial giants: the food processing firm of Ferrero (which makes Nutella, a chocolate-flavored hazelnut butter, among other items); Miroligio (a clothing and textile empire); and the delightfully named Mondo Rubber (which is self-explanatory). All three are homegrown and headquartered in Alba.

The Gaja family also was headquartered in Alba. It was instead Angelo's great-uncle and great-aunt who lived in Barbaresco, in a row of rooms that have since been converted into offices for the business. Only several years after they died did Giovanni Gaja move to Barbaresco. Still, the locals must have felt some affinity for, and identification with, the Gaja family because they elected Giovanni Gaja their mayor in 1958, despite the fact that he remained living in Alba until 1963 when he finally moved to Barbaresco. He held the post of mayor for twenty-four years, relinquishing it in 1982. Today, he is eighty-five years old and strikingly handsome.

Barbaresco is only six-and-one-half miles from Alba, but it is reachable only after traversing a steeply inclined, twisting road. It takes just eleven minutes to make the run, if you drive like an Italian, but this is a modern twist. Barbaresco remained effectively cut off, a remove demonstrated by the fact that its town residents did not have water piped into their homes until 1964.

By the time his father moved to Barbaresco, Angelo had already graduated from Alba's winemaking school, the Instituto Technico Agrario ed Enologico. Unlike the American system, where students interested in learning how to make wine pursue such studies only at the college level, the Italian system has students enrolled in a six-year program that combines conventional high school academic studies with specialized subjects, such as enology or wine science. Graduates usually are twenty years old upon completion, as was Gaja.

Unusually, Gaja subsequently pursued a degree in economics from the University of Turin, which degree he acquired only in 1970. Working at the family winery, he did not take any courses at all for several years. Gaja readily admits to having always been an indifferent student. He was, however, an Eagle Scout, a boyhood pursuit that he almost never mentions. When I once teased him about it—the go-it-alone Gaja being the unlikeliest of Boy Scouts—he looked a little embarrassed, then recovered quickly. "But I never wore all my merit badges! Not many people knew I was an Eagle Scout."

When Angelo landed in Barbaresco to work in the winery in 1961—he moved there with his parents in 1963—he was twenty-one years old. And he surely was restless. The thought of what he must have been like at that age is disconcerting. For Gaja today, at fifty-three, quivers with barely contained energy, like a springer spaniel about to be taken for a walk.

Everyone's first impression is of something electric, even crackling. His speech amplifies this sense of an intensive charge, his tip-of-the-tongue *r*'s spraying forth, giving the impression of ammunition being prodigiously expended from an automatic weapon. This is accompanied by exaggerated, yet balletic, body motions.

When Gaja strides from his offices into the courtyard of the winery to greet a guest, he has the politician's capacity of laser-beam directness. "My dearrr, it is good to see you!" he purrs. "Everything okay? Very good," he says hurriedly, satisfied that the world still is spinning on its proper axis for his guests. (Gaja does not enjoy hearing about difficulties, which he takes personally and immediately sets about trying to correct.) "All rrright, 'nduma!" he exclaims in Piedmontese, adding in Italian, "andiamo, we go." This is punctuated, Victor Borge style, with forefinger extended and his arm jerking a full circle and simultaneously corkscrewing forward, as if forcefully hand-cranking an antique car.

His walk is brisk, verging on a trot. Although neither especially tall nor big, he has a disproportionately large trunk which leaves you with an impression of size. He carries his shoulders almost unnaturally squared, so much so that he appears to be leaning backward. Gaja once had back problems requiring surgery and this may account for the posture. His chest consequently juts forth, giving him a strut when he walks. If he had any pomposity at all—which, thankfully, is absent—the effect would be like that of a tinhorn dictator striding about in riding boots. Instead, his relentless enthusiasm washes away any such thoughts. The squared, leaning-back shoulders and resulting cock-o'-the-walk swaying strut calls to mind Bob Hope swiveling about onstage.

But the most attention-getting physical feature—apart from the inhuman energy—is Gaja's head. It is oversize, and unusually square, and bobbles slightly on his neck, like those spring-loaded doll's heads that used to adorn the rear windows of cars. His black hair is increasingly flecked with steel gray, but is mostly intact. It is combed straight back, almost short enough to be a brush cut, which further accentuates the squareness. A widow's peak effect, created by a receding hairline at each temple, points to an expansive, expressive forehead, which billboards Gaja's every emotion: furrowing, wrinkling, arching, seemingly even darkening, as his moods and thoughts take him.

As is so often the case, the eyes have it. They are deep-set, pleasantly blue, although not magnetically so, and lodged under the formidable brow of his forehead. Nothing about their color or size sets them apart. Rather, it is their roving intensity. They are Holy Roller eyes, the sort that can look out over a sea of sweating, expectant revivalists and transfix them by sheer conviction and fervor, as well as seduce them with playfulness. When combined with Gaja's almost wolfish grin and his ever-present charge of crackling energy, the effect is like nothing so much as a happy demonic possession.

"After I arrived at the winery, I was becoming nervous, impatient," he recalls. "I was not happy with the idea that I had to do exactly what my great-grandfather did. At the time, producers here were very proud to say—although it really couldn't be true—'I am making the wine exactly as my grandfather.' But in fact, the times were different. And surely they were not exactly doing the same. Hah! Because the great-grandfather didn't even have any water, probably. It was difficult to wash anything. Anyway, the idea that in my life I would have to do the same as my grandfather, that my destiny was already sliced like a salami, this I didn't like.

"The first big change started in 1961, when I entered the cellar. It was a decision of mine, made with my father's consent, of course, to reduce the crop by 50 percent, by pruning the vines more severely in order to have more concentrated grapes. With more concentrated grapes there is more concentration to the wine. Then it is possible to have lower acidity in the grapes. This was a step in trying to smile at the English!" he points out, recalling our earlier conversation.

"At the time, my father was the mayor of Barbaresco. Because of that, he always had local grape growers close around him. When they looked at this severe pruning, they told him, 'You're losing all the crop.' As you might imagine, he was disturbed to hear this.

"As bad luck would have it, in 1961 it rained through June, and then also in the first half of July. Incredible! This disturbed the flowering of the grapes. So we lost a part of the flowers in that time, and consequently, we didn't have many grapes. As you know, one flower means one grape. Few flowers, few grapes. And remember, the pruning occurs before the flowering, in the late winter.

"As a result of having pruned so severely, our crop was 30 percent or 35 percent less than others people's crops. And everybody already had small crops to begin with because of the bad flowering. Oh my God!" cries Gaja, pantomiming the sort of exaggerated anguish seen on World War I memorial sculptures of stricken mothers grieving for their dead. "My father was not happy at all. Anyway, that next year, 1962, the vintage was large. An excellent vintage. We had a reasonable-size crop. My father was more relaxed."

Equally as radical was his insistence, again with his father's assent, to no longer purchase grapes from other growers. Until Angelo's arrival in 1961, the Gaja winery was not making wines exclusively from its own grapes. Like nearly all of the other (relatively few) profitable wineries in the Langhe, roughly half of the winery's production was from purchased grapes.

This was the norm everywhere in the Langhe. Until the late 1970s or even into the early 1980s, it was a buyer's market. The prices paid for grapes were derisory. Other successful Langhe wineries never bothered to own even a sliver of vineyard land. For example, not until 1989 did Prunotto, a first-rate producer founded in 1924, buy its first piece of vineyard. With grapes selling so cheaply from so many sources, there was no need.

"Easily 90 percent to 95 percent of all Langhe wines came from *négociants*," Gaja points out, using the French term for "wine shippers." But the Gaja winery was different, thanks in large part to Giovanni Gaja's love of land and his insider's acumen as a *geometra*. "My father was always looking to enlarge our vineyard ownership," he adds. "Making wine exclusively from your own grapes was very unusual at the time. I don't think that any winery before 1961 was exclusively estate-bottling. In fact, there were very, very few wineries even making wines from their own grapes and selling any of them under their own label.

"The tradition was that the vineyards were in the hands of rich people: nobles, bourgeoisie, the upper-middle class. They never made wine. They always sold the grapes to *négociants*. Before World War II, when they owned everything, this was even more extreme: It was absolute! The phenomenon of grape growers becoming wine producers—which is common today—was unknown. Yet it took us a long time to get to this: Estate-bottling was largely unknown in the Langhe all through the 1960s and even into part of the 1970s."

Ironically, Angelo Gaja's ambition exactly paralleled those of the late Baron Philippe de Rothschild. When the twenty-four-year-old Philippe de Rothschild was given stewardship of his father's Château Mouton Rothschild in 1926, the wines of even the most famous estates, such as Châteaux Lafite Rothschild, Margaux, and d'Yquem, were not cellared and bottled on the estates. Neither was that of Château Mouton Rothschild.

Instead, the young wines were sent in barrels to the powerful *négociants* in the city of Bordeaux. It was they who "raised" the wines and slapped a label on the bottle. In the case of the great estates, the label did proclaim Château Mouton Rothschild or Château d'Yquem, but the owners of these same properties had virtually nothing to do with the wines that bore their names. Too often, even these wines were not pure expressions of the properties, as the shippers happily modified the taste of the wine by blending to suit the demands of the buyer.

This accommodation to individual markets was a longstanding practice. In the nineteenth century, a wine as fine as Château Lafite Rothschild was augmented with a dose of Hermitage, a strong red wine from the Rhône Valley. For this the client paid extra and the wine was referred to as being Hermitage. Cyrus Redding, in *Every Man His Own Butler* (1852), felt free to reveal: "The Bordeaux wines sent to England are not pure growths, but mixed with second-class Hermitage, and sometimes Benicarló, adding a little spirit of wine [brandy]." Benicarló is a Spanish village on the Mediterranean once noted for its deeply colored, heavy red wines which, as Redding pointed out, were popular for blending with lighter-hued Bordeaux.

Such practices did not sit well with the young baron-to-be. So with the sort of crust for which the Rothschilds were famed throughout Europe, the twenty-four-year-old Philippe de Rothschild convened a gathering of the owners of Châteaux Lafite Rothschild, Haut-Brion, Margaux, Latour, and Yquem.

He implored them to no longer send their unfinished wine to the *négociants*, but instead bottle it themselves. He succeeded. Most of the rest of Bordeaux's many hundreds of estates did not follow suit for another forty years or more. They couldn't afford to, as they lacked both the capital to cellar their own wines for two, three, or four years, as well as access to the foreign markets—or even just to Paris—that have always been important to the sales of Bordeaux wines.

When, in 1961, twenty-one-year-old Angelo Gaja urged his father to make wine only from vineyards they owned, and then prune those vineyards so severely as to reduce their annual yields by 50 percent, his challenge was not so much convincing his father. Like Philippe de Rothschild, he had the parental approval, as well as some reservoir of financial strength, although hardly like that of the Rothschilds. Still, he enjoyed far more resources than most in his neighborhood. Despite Gaja's talk of "the rich people," the fact is that his father could afford to be indulgent. The winery was already in its third generation when Angelo arrived with his ideas. And it had established itself among its local audience as a producer apart, charging prices well in excess of most of its competition. "My father was selling his wine for a very expensive price in Lombardy and Liguria," Gaja points out with pride. "He was selling his wine in demijohns, and his price was three times that of the others. And people were willing to pay."

But unlike Philippe de Rothschild who was, after all, an aristocrat in that most aristocratic of vineyard districts, Gaja had to contend with social and cultural forces in a stubbornly rural corner of Italy. And where Rothschild secured the prestigious support of the acknowledged greatest properties of Bordeaux, Angelo Gaja was going it alone.

"I insisted that we continue keeping our crop reduced by pruning. But the problem was to convince the vineyard manager to continue. This was not easy," says Gaja. "And in the winery, it was not easy either! I will remember always how difficult it was to change anything in the cellar. You see, the master of cellar was very well considered by my father. And, okay, probably my knowledge of cellar work was limited, as I had not worked in any other wine cellars. I had spent some time in France, in Montpellier, but just a one-week stage. It was not practical work in the cellar, only theory. As far as the master of cellar was concerned, I knew nothing.

"I'll always remember when I proudly suggested to him that we introduce a big thermometer in the cap of grape skins that float at the top of the fermenting tank. This way, you could know the temperature of the wine, which is critical. It gives you more control, more opportunity to prevent bad things happening." By modern winemaking standards, this suggestion is as sweetly reasonable as feeling a child's forehead for fever.

"The master of the cellar thought otherwise. He suggested that I put this thermometer to another use! But this is normal," he adds charitably, laughing at the old cellar master's pungency. "After all, doing things his way, he was able to sell Gaja wines at the most expensive prices compared to many other producers in the area. So why should he have changed? And he never did. He stayed very strongly in his ideas. It was only much later, in 1970, that we started to take the temperature of the fermenting wine."

Neither in the winery nor in the vineyard nor among other winemakers did Gaja find consent to any ideas not previously consecrated by tradition. His father's concurrence, it turned out, was only a permission to enter the battle, rather than a victory in itself.

The battle was against a force that, in the end, only death (or at least retirement) could vanquish. I, myself, see this force, in fact, weekly. It can be found every Friday at the farmer's market near where I live, which is forty-five minutes from Barbaresco. Standing next to sometimes embarrassingly small quantities of vegetables and fruits is the tradition itself, in human form.

This tradition doesn't look formidable, although you can see its stubbornness easily enough. Mostly, they are old peasant farmers, *contadini*, with outsize knobby hands, and weathered, sun-beaten skin. Invariably, they have not shaved for several days. Their tough, grizzled, old men's beards make their faces look like worn, furrowed lava fields through which a crop of tiny cactuses are pushing up. They speak Piedmontese insistently. A handful still do not know Italian, which now is unusual in the Piedmont, but fifty years ago was common.

Not knowing or speaking Italian still afflicts the poorer, typically southern, regions of Italy. According to Tullio De Mauro, an Italian language scholar, 13 percent of the population in the southern Italian regions of Calabria and Basilicata still cannot speak or understand Italian and rely exclusively on dialect.

These men, their wives, and even some of their older children once were *mezzadri,* or sharecroppers. They were not, however, migrants. Rather, they had long lived in the Langhe, many of them able to trace their families back far further than Gaja can. But they were excluded from owning land by the feudal system of *mezzadria.* The word *mezza,* meaning "half," reveals clearly enough how the system worked. In exchange for their labor, they got half of the crop. They were allowed to live on, and off of, the land they tended. Sometimes a house, really a hut, was included. Sometimes they had to build one for themselves. The landowner provided seed and sprays and little else. The Langhe was like a hive abuzz with *mezzadri.* It was no different in many other parts of rural Italy.

While we were walking along the trail on that sunny Easter Sunday afternoon, a day so bright that one could imagine only success, I brought up the darker matter of *mezzadria*. "It was different in the Langhe compared to, say, Tuscany," Gaja points out. "There, the concept was different, at least for the large properties. The landowner normally had a *fattore*, a factor or overseer. Here in the Langhe sometimes there was somebody we called, in dialect, a *fator*. But in Tuscany the *fattore* was totally independent. He would decide himself what to do, what to plant and when to plant. He would establish new contracts with new *mezzadri*. He would give to the proprietor an accounting of what was happening, financial accounts and so on, at the end of the year. That was if the proprietor even wanted to know.

"Here in the Langhe the proprietor was probably a bit more involved. And in any case, in this area there were no properties as large as in Tuscany. I remember reading that, before the war, the property of the Barone Ricasoli in Tuscany was more than twenty-five thousand hectares (61,775 acres). This did not exist here. The landholdings were already divided, although nowhere near as much as they are today." The landholdings in the Langhe are almost unworkably fragmented; the average vineyard holding is just 3.7 acres. In the best vineyards, parcels are even more fractionalized.

"You have to remember," continues Gaja, "that in those days the Langhe looked completely different than it does today. Today it's all grapevines everywhere you look. A monoculture. But back then, when I was a boy and even a young man, it was a polyculture. Normally, the *mezzadro* liked to have stalls, where he could keep cows and oxen. Cows meant milk and meat. For example, our Sorì San Lorenzo vineyard used to be planted one-fourth to grass for grazing. But the yield even for grass was poor. You could cut the grass no more than three times a year." Today, the eight-acre Sorì San Lorenzo vineyard is the source of one of Gaja's "collector" Barbarescos. It sells for as much as, or more than, a first growth Bordeaux, or about $125 a bottle.

For most *mezzadri*, though, theirs was a world with little possibility of ownership of any really decent land and, of course, no incentive toward energy or ambition, as there was no reward for such exercise. "Normally, a farm was split into grain, corn, grassland, and a little bit of vineyard," points out Gaja. "In the 1800s and the early part of the 1900s, the principal owners were noble people such as the Marchesi di Grésy and various counts. For example, I don't believe that the Marchesi di Grésy had a larger property than he does today—maybe a little bit. Regardless, *mezzadria* was the way agriculture was conducted. Because the noble people were not interested in investing. Some families did have a chance to buy small pieces of land. But even so, they were not cultivating it intensively. Mostly, it was just subsistence farming."

The Marchesi Cisa Asinari di Grésy are an old aristocratic family that now lives in Milan. Unlike most of the other aristocratic families in the Langhe, which either died out or sold out, the di Grésys kept both their ancestral vineyard in Barbaresco, called La Martinenga, as well as their turn-of-the-century house crowning the top of a nearby hill, from which you can see not only the family vineyard, but very nearly all of the Langhe itself. Both the vineyard and house are two of the choicest properties in the area.

The estate, the proper name of which is Tenute Cisa Asinari dei Marchesi di Grésy, is administered by Alberto di Grésy who has infused into it an ambition that, by his own admission, previously was absent. Slender, in his mid-forties, with a full head of gray hair, and scrupulously elegant in the tweedy, beautifully tailored country clothes that the Italians call *moda inglese* and is nothing of the sort, di Grésy is open about his family's fortunes. "My father died when I was only six years old," he explains. "La Martinenga Vineyard, which has been in the family for generations, was always farmed by *mezzadri*. In fact, that changed only in 1980, when we left the Produttori del Barbaresco."

The Produttori del Barbaresco is a revival of the town's original cooperative, founded in 1894, which had winked out of existence by 1930. Where the original cooperative was started by a liberal-minded aristocrat, the new impetus came in 1958 from a liberal-minded priest who was determined not to see his flock remain perpetually impoverished by the low grape prices paid by the area's wine shippers. The only way for them to make money, as in so many other forms of agriculture, was to be their own processor—in this case, to make and sell their own wine. Today, with a growing market for fine wine, it is a matter of hanging out a shingle. Back in 1958, it was a matter of helping create a market altogether.

From the start, the Produttori limited itself exclusively to Nebbiolo, which gave the cooperative rigor and direction—just what other winegrowers' cooperatives always lack. This prevented it from pursuing the easier, and more lucrative, markets for the early maturing Dolcetto and Barbera wines. But the initial rigor has paid off: Its members now make far more money from Nebbiolo than they ever would have from Dolcetto and Barbera, to say nothing of greater public esteem. Not least, the worth of their Barbaresco vineyards has increased dramatically, if for no other reason than being able to take advantage of the public relations groundwork achieved by Gaja. (The Produttori, like all winegrowers' cooperatives, is institutionally incapable of public relations flair.) Today, the Produttori's sixty-six members—originally there were nineteen—collectively own about one-quarter of all the Nebbiolo vineyards in the Barbaresco zone. And if you look at the best vineyards in that zone, the Produttori's members probably own about half of all the really good sites.

The commitment to Nebbiolo and to the Barbaresco zone is the more evident upon discovering that the cooperative began issuing single-vineyard or *cru* bottlings, starting in 1967. Although a tentative practice at first, it nevertheless put them in the unlikely position of being in the vanguard with no less an avant-guardist than Gaja himself, whose own first single-vineyard bottling also appeared in 1967. (You can walk from the Gaja winery to that of the Produttori in one minute and fifteen seconds.)

Today, these top-of-the-line single-vineyard bottlings account for 40 percent of the Produttori's production, at least in good vintages. They also command the highest prices, from which all of the members benefit equally. In lesser years, the wines from these vineyards are blended with those from lesser sites, the better to create only one (good) wine labeled simply as Barbaresco.

La Martinenga Vineyard, which today is fifty-four acres, is reckoned by Barbaresco locals to be the single best site in the zone. But like virtually every other wine in the Langhe, its wine never was issued under its own name. For generations, the estate was worked by *mezzadri*. And in recent years, the family sold its share of the grapes to Barbaresco's winegrowers' cooperative, the Produttori del Barbaresco.

"We were sorry to lose the di Grésy grapes from La Martinenga," admits Aldo Vacca, the thirty-year-old director of the Produttori who, in fact, previously worked for Gaja for five years. Aldo Vacca assumed the position from his father, Celestino, a founding member in 1958 and the Produttori's longtime director. "I remember that they did everything they could to entice di Grésy to remain, even offering to pay them more money for their grapes than they did other members. This was very unusual and not really how we work here. But it's a great vineyard and everybody knew it, so there was a willingness to bend the rules." No doubt, also, the growers liked having aristocracy among their ranks.

But di Grésy's problem was finding people to work his vineyard economically. While virtually all of the other members of the Produttori work their own land, di Grésy was in no position—in every sense—to do so. Vineyard workers are expensive and increasingly scarce. "Frankly, we wanted to continue using *mezzadri*," admits di Grésy. "Because it was easier for us. But in the end it became too expensive. It used to be that they got 50 percent of the harvest. And then the contracts began to change: they got 60 percent. And then it went to 70 percent. Finally, to keep them, we would have had to give them 90 percent of the crop, which was ridiculous." For di Grésy, the only way to afford workers, as well as improvements, was to set out on his own, creating his own wine that he hoped would command a premium, which it now does. Di Grésy freely admits that Gaja was his model and inspiration.

When Angelo Gaja was born in 1940, it was to an agrarian culture in stasis: Nothing changed because there was no motivation for it to do so. Before the war, the owners didn't want it to change; the *mezzadri* were helpless. "I remember when my father changed from the *mezzadria* in the early 1950s," recalls Gaja. "At that time, *mezzadria* still was very strong. The system was only just starting to change. Lawyers, notaries, professional class people were still leaving their property to be worked by a *mezzadro*. My father wasn't the only one to want to change. But unlike other property owners, he wanted to have greater control over his own land.

"Because my father was thinking about buying more vineyard in the early 1950s, he realized that the only way to manage the vineyards effectively was to pay salaries. Because with a *mezzadro* you could have conflicts. A *mezzadro* always wants higher yields, for obvious reasons. Secondly, it was difficult to convince the *mezzadro* to do anything different than he did before in managing the vineyard. He had no reason to change. Even after we switched to paying salaries, this problem of getting them to change their ways continued. Why? Because many of the people we gave salaries to previously were *mezzadri*, that's why."

It is also why, in the end, Giovanni Gaja was unwilling to disagree with his old winemaker, despite his son's mounting frustration. He was unwilling to upset the equilibrium of Barbaresco's social microculture. Being mayor of Barbaresco meant, even into the late 1960s, being an arbitrator among disputes and difficulties formed and nurtured by the limitations of the old *mezzadri* culture and the security of its old, established forms.

Nevertheless, the system did change, although, as it turned out, the demise of *mezzadria* was slow and lingering. To this day, many of its survivors—and even their children—think, and above all, act, as if its still-warm corpse is in the same room with them. The beginning of the end can be traced to World War II, which brought with it a glimmering of awareness that things could be different. "If the *mezzadri* and the poor of the village didn't go about the world themselves, the world had come, in the war years, to awaken them," commented Cesare Pavese in his 1950 novel about the Langhe countryside, *The Moon and the Bonfire.*

After that, two forces aligned to firmly usher its exit. The first was Italy's post-war industrialization. After Italy picked itself up from the devastations of the war, the cities and mid-sized towns everywhere north of Rome began to industrialize. Nowhere was this activity—which by the 1960s created Italy's first economic boom and by the eighties made its economy reportedly the fifth largest in the world—more intense than in Piedmont. Turin is Piedmont's largest city and is home to Fiat, which has long been Italy's largest privately owned company.

Decades, if not centuries, of agricultural lassitude had, by the war's end, made Italy's farms literally and figuratively untenable. For example, writing in 1901, Bolton King in his book *Italy Today* compared the wheat yields of various European countries. Even though a higher proportion of Italy's farmland was devoted to producing wheat than in any other European nation, its average yield was just 11½ bushels per acre. France, in comparison, produced almost one-third more at 16½ bushels per acre. Great Britain reported 30 bushels per acre, or more than 2½ times that of Italy. Only Russia, itself struggling with its own agrarian feudalism, reported lower wheat yields than Italy.

With urban industrialization offering an alternative, to say nothing of a siren call, the glacial *mezzadria* system began to dissolve. The lawyers, doctors, and other upper-middle-class professionals, who owned two, three, or four farms, as well as the landed aristocracy, soon found themselves saddled with properties that, because they were so badly managed, could not support workers earning a decent wage. Certainly they could not compete with factory wages. Only the cheap labor of *mezzadria* kept these farms economically plausible for their owners. Even the farms owned by the peasants, which were equally badly run, if not worse, also could not compete with the new factory wages. Everywhere in Italy the countryside began to be drained of its workers, all of whom fled to the cities in search of a living or at least a future.

The government was rightly alarmed at this prospect of deserted farms. So, in the 1950s, it offered Italian farmers a deal that they hoped they would not refuse: If the farmers stayed on the land and made money only from crops on land they owned or leased, they would be excused from paying any business income tax. Effectively, they paid no income tax at all, since most farmers had no other sources of income. This law proved enticing. And in the beginning it probably didn't cost the Italian government very much simply because the farms generated so little income anyway.

But when the Italian economy improved, these once negligible incomes became increasingly more substantial. In the case of winegrowers, as long as they made wine only from grapes they grew on land they owned or leased—buying not a single grape or a drop of juice or wine from anyone else—their income was gravy. And in the 1970s and early 1980s, that gravy was lip-smacking.

I recall being baffled in the early 1980s when I would visit tiny Italian wineries whose owners would proudly show me their gleaming new stainless steel fermenting tanks and their $100,000 German-made sterile bottling line. All to produce, say, five thousand cases of wine that sold locally for maybe five bucks a bottle. It didn't pencil out. Only later did I learn about the tax exemption law.

Given the notorious inefficiencies of Italian government, to say nothing of its endemic corruption, allowing farmers to legally keep their money was probably the best use of that money that Italy could ever have hoped to achieve. Italians, despite their preposterous image as endlessly lunching layabouts, actually are insistently industrious. It was trickle-up economics at its best. They took their money and reinvested it. They bought more land, better machinery, and sent their sons—and sometimes even their daughters—to agricultural schools. In the case of wine, the result was better-quality wines, an awareness of marketing and, eventually, a higher return. Only in 1987 was the law rescinded.

For their part, the previously landless *mezzadri* benefited from yet another critical piece of 1950s legislation: a low-interest loan program for *mezzadri*, as well as an option to buy the land they worked if the owner put it up for sale.

Without the cheap labor of the *mezzadri*, the professional and aristocratic landowners found their farms an insupportable burden. They had no choice but to sell, which they did in droves. The government, for its part, recognized that what the *mezzadri* lacked was not a willingness to work the land, but access to capital with which to buy it. If a landowner put up for sale a property worked by a *mezzadro*—which he was not, in any case, compelled to do—the *mezzadro* had first rights of refusal to buy the property. The government made available low-interest loans to the *mezzadro*, with the stipulation that he work this land himself for a certain number of years. It was a clever idea, serving the interests of both the landowners—they had a ready buyer already on the property—as well as the *mezzadro*, whose labor could make the land economically viable.

When I mentioned this legislation, admiringly, to Aldo Conterno, he grunted and said, "Let me show you something." Frankly, I didn't know what Aldo thought of the program. Professionally adventurous but politically conservative, Aldo is forever complaining about the government. "Nobody wants to work anymore," he says with mantra-like repetition. In English, this sounds vaguely like it's coming from someone from Brooklyn. This is because, in December 1954, his father sent him to California to help some uncles start a winery. The uncles had money and some influence and arranged for Aldo to get a permanent visa, which was then tantamount to citizenship.

At the time, a military draft was still in effect. Aldo was in California six months when he was drafted. "I called my father and said 'Pop, what should I do?' My father said, 'Go in the army. That way you'll learn English.'" When I asked him if, in fact, he really didn't know any English at the time, he declared, "I thought I knew English. But I didn't know anything." So he learned English, as well as spent time in Korea as part of the occupation forces. The experience was profoundly influential. Inducted into the U.S. Army in July 1955, he spent twenty-one months in the service.

After his discharge from the army in April 1957, Aldo went back to his uncles in California, only to discover that one of them had become seriously ill. The winery plans were shelved. He hung around California, soaking up the swaggering confidence of a 1950s America that exuded ambition. It made an everlasting impression. Aldo retains an abiding, passionate love of America and Americans, so much so that he will not countenance even the mildest whiff of criticality from me about American government or culture. "I still have my discharge papers," he once growled, with mock ferocity. "You want to see them?" (He was honorably discharged as a Specialist Three.)

Eventually, his father instructed him to return home. A farmer at heart, Aldo never returned to the States after he left in January 1959. For that matter, he has since rarely ever left the Langhe.

When Aldo was forty years old, he established his own winery in the Barolo zone in 1971, calling it Poderi Aldo Conterno. He broke away because of disagreements with his older brother, Giovanni. Although the separation was amicable, it was Giovanni who was allowed to keep the father's well-known label called Giacomo

Conterno. "I thought back in 1971 that just being a Conterno was enough to sell the wine. Well, I was wrong. My brother had a big advantage in having our father's label," Aldo says unequivocally. Although his brother's wine remains one of Barolo's best, the Aldo Conterno label today has equal luster.

So when I brought up the loan program for *mezzadri* to Aldo, I didn't know what to expect. Certainly, it wasn't a tour of the vineyard, which by now I've seen at least a dozen times. But I dutifully trotted along. "Look at that," barked Aldo. I looked across the valley to another Barolo vineyard. "You see that?" He likes to make sure that listeners, especially suspected liberals, are not about to miss a profound conservative truth. "That vineyard over there was worked by a *mezzadro* and his family since the 1950s. Then it went up for sale. And he was able to buy it by getting one of those loans you were talking about. You know how much he paid for it?" he demanded. I hadn't the faintest idea, especially considering how cheap vineyard land in Barolo was in the 1950s. "I'll tell you how much: eight hundred thousand lire. For something like twenty acres."

Frankly it sounded pretty cheap to me. When I said as much, Aldo looked at me with the same despairing forbearance for the perennially weak-minded that Jeeves had for Bertie Wooster. "Of course it was cheap," replied Aldo with asperity. Having got that clear, he continued, "You know Prunotto, of course?" I did, quite well in fact. Prunotto is one of Piedmont's best wine shippers and was recently purchased by one of the most successful and aristocratic wine merchants in Tuscany, Marchesi L. e P. Antinori. "You know their Barolo, the one they label Bussia Vineyard?" I knew that, too. I've sluiced down quite a lot of it over the years.

"Prunotto always bought the grapes for it from that guy down there," instructed Aldo, pointing to the nonexistent guy. "Well, anyway, in 1989 Prunotto bought the vineyard from him. And you know how much they paid?" his voice reaching a Pavarotti-like pitch of incredulity. "How much?" I asked, as meekly as possible. "Eight hundred and twenty million lire," replied Aldo, pronouncing each word slowly, with awe, satisfaction, and amazement. "Without that program, that *mezzadro* could never have bought that vineyard. He worked like a dog."

As soon as I heard this last remark, I knew how Aldo felt. He's all for hard work. By then, I was all for lunch, so we went up the hill to Monforte d'Alba, to Aldo's favorite restaurant, Il Giardino da Felicìn, which is good enough to get one star in the Italian Guide Michelin. Aldo could care less about what Michelin thinks, having enjoyed the food at Felicìn for decades. He goes to see his friend Giorgio Rocca, who is the chef and owner. Rocca also works like a dog, getting up at five in the morning every day to hand-roll the dough for his delicate *tajarin*, which is the Piedmontese word for tagliatelle pasta. Giorgio pulled up a chair, and he and Aldo bantered in dialect. I ate the magnificent food and pretended to follow the conversation, which fooled nobody.

It was at Felicìn that Gaja reminisced about one of the turning points in his struggle to free himself from the sticky grip of the Langhe's insularity. Being at the restaurant reminded him of the event. "I was very lucky," he began. "I had many sleepers." At first, I thought I had misunderstood. Sleepers?

"Yes, sleepers," he replied. "In 1973, Robert Mondavi came here to visit the winery." Mondavi, who started his own winery in Napa Valley in 1966, when he was fifty-three years old, was singularly instrumental in launching California wine to new levels of prestige, price, and accomplishment. He is a hero to Gaja, who is a full generation younger than the eighty-year-old Mondavi.

"It was the first time I met him. He spent the day. He asked me to accompany him to look at the other vineyards of the area. The day was very nice. We went and had lunch at Ristorante Belvedere in La Morra, which as you know has a good view of the Langhe. We spoke at the table about wine and so on. He offered a lot of compliments. I was so proud of the area. When we walked back to the car, he stopped me and said, 'Don't you hear a noise in the air?' I tried to listen. I didn't hear any noise. I said, 'No, I don't hear any noise.' So he said, 'Okay, probably I am wrong.'

"Then we went to Felicìn to say hello to Giorgio. And we went out on the balcony of the restaurant to look at the view. And again he mentioned the noise. And again I said, 'I can't hear any noise.' After that, we went to look at more vineyards. And again, he mentioned the noise. 'What noise?'

"Finally, we returned to Barbaresco and on the way back I said, 'Now look, what is this joke about the noise?' And he told me, 'Don't you hear it? The people in the Langhe are snoring. Not just at night, but during the day.'

"This was a very important lesson. So I told this story to some of my colleagues. They were not happy at all. In fact, they were offended. This surprised me. Only Aldo Conterno was capable of understanding. It was such a good lesson. Can you imagine what a man like Mondavi could be capable of doing in an area like the Langhe?"

As it happens, Gaja could. Moreover, he took his cues from California. Mondavi's achievement in California was convincing skeptical, if not outright contemptuous,

Americans that a California wine could be as good as the great French wines. Not least, he had to convince them to pay a comparable price. To do this involved both winemaking technique and not a little marketing psychology.

Gaja, for his part, faced comparable—although not identical—challenges. Unlike Americans, Italians were already convinced of the goodness of their own wines. But they were unwilling to pay anything more than a pittance. Wine in Italy has long been regarded as a cheap staple like bread or salt. Until the 1970s, the ceiling price for Barolo was just one thousand lire, which even then was a nominal sum. Barbera, in comparison, never topped a few hundred lire.

"The first step in increasing our prices was with the 1971 vintage," recalls Gaja. "We had sold the 1970 Barbaresco for one thousand six hundred lire a bottle. The 1971, we increased to three thousand five hundred lire. It was considered at the time to be an incredible price. You have to remember that the 1958 vintage, a very great year for Barbaresco, sold for one thousand lire. But the 1959 dropped back to the more usual seven hundred fifty lire. Only in the late 1960s did we get as high as one thousand six hundred lire. We doubled the price of the 1971, only because the crop was 40 percent less than normal."

In both California and Italy, if improvements were going to be made, somebody would have to have both ambition to burn and capital to risk. The goal, ultimately, had to be a place at the fine-wine pinnacle, which meant France.

The fine-wine-ambitious Californians discovered that the great Bordeaux and Burgundies that they and the rest of the world so admired, and would pay premium prices for, all were aged in small oak barrels called barriques. Each holds two hundred twenty-five liters, or fifty-five gallons. A big cask, in comparison, can hold thousands of gallons. Fashioned in France by coopers using oak from various French forests with names such as Limousin, Alliers, Nevers, and Tronçais, these barrels, especially when brand new, gave both red and white wines a distinctive flavor and a certain suppleness. Wines that spent time in them—anywhere from three months to two years—tasted better, finer, more complicated, in short, more like expensive French wines.

California producers were so fervent about barriques that they single-handedly revived the French cooperage industry, which until the 1970s had been languishing because Bordeaux châteaux and Burgundy winegrowers bought new barrels only reluctantly. Californians wanted new barrels because they needed them, their many new wineries having none to begin with. More important yet, the new barrels had the flavors they were looking for. Once a barrel has been used for three or four vintages, the oak flavor is largely exhausted. It becomes a useful, if neutral, container.

In Italy, barriques were unknown. Although barrels of all sizes could be found in every corner of the country, the idea of using oak to flavor a wine—and have that flavor be considered a good thing—was absent. An older Piedmontese winegrower once told me about how he had to sell a Barolo he'd made for half the regular price because he had stored it in a brand-new barrel and it had an oaky taste. "I should have asked for twice the price!" he laughed.

Gaja made no such mistake. As the first Italian wine producer to use French oak barriques, he knew exactly what he was doing. Or rather, what he intended to do. As it turned out, you can't just put Nebbiolo wine into the barrel and stand back.

"The idea of using barriques, frankly, was born from visiting California. Not from France," admits Gaja. "When I went to France in 1968, I saw that they were using barriques. They were using barriques because it was their tradition. It was part of their traditional ways of making Pinot Noir and Chardonnay in Burgundy and Cabernet Sauvignon in Bordeaux and so on. We had a different wine. And I was proud enough of my wines, in the style of my father. So why change the wines?

"It was only after I visited California that I began to think differently. The California producers would travel, to go outside of their world, to take the best of France, principally. They didn't have an interest in making more Lambrusco," he adds, referring to one of Italy's cheapest, most abundant red wines. "They were investing a lot of money, spending a lot of capital. So their interest was in making wines that were capable of giving them a return on their investment. This meant trying to equal the most expensive wines."

It was about at this same time that the normally buoyant Gaja had returned home, frustrated from his unsuccessful forays into England and Belgium. And it was the same time when he finally vanquished his father's winemaker, who was soon to leave the winery as much from declining health as from Gaja's dissatisfaction. Seizing the opportunity, Gaja had installed his own man, Guido Rivella. In him, Gaja had found someone both receptive to his plans for change and capable of transforming Gaja's ambitions into wine cellar realities.

"After I returned, I turned to Guido and said that we will have to do things in a different way. So we started to think about barriques. The idea was not so much to give the Barbaresco wine an oak taste, but to take the benefit from the great amount of oxygenation that the small barrels allow. They have a greater ratio of wine surface to barrel surface than in a big cask. So you can get more oxygen to the wine in a very slow, effective way. The idea was to smooth the wine."

Just how alien barriques were in Piedmont is revealed by how Gaja was suckered by a French barrel broker from Bordeaux in his first purchase. Because he was thinking only in terms of their ability to expose the wine to oxygen, rather than pursuing the oak taste as winemakers were doing in California, Gaja purchased used barriques. "They assured us that the barriques were three or four years old. That the barrels were young, young, young. When we saw these barriques for the first time, we didn't have any idea that the barrels we saw were twenty years old. So we accepted them. We were very happy to have these barriques," he says without a trace of rancor.

"But they were not three or four years old," he adds with a frown, his voice lowering like a doctor telling a family member that the patient will not pull through. "Also, unfortunately, the barriques were shipped, with wine inside, during the summer. So there was a lot of evaporation. And the bung became dried. The wine inside took on some acetic acidity. Vinegar! We were not able to remove the acetic acidity that seeped into the staves."

Gaja likes telling this story of his naiveté, French duplicity, and the sheer challenge of attempting something utterly new in the Langhe. "Later, Monsieur André Noblet of the Domaine de la Romanée-Conti came here and looked at the old barrels." The late André Noblet was an earthy, jovial giant of a man whose favorite sport was copping a quick feel from awed female visitors in the dark cellar of Burgundy's greatest wine estate. Recalling his comments, Gaja laughs. "He looked at my barriques and said, 'These are older than my grandmother! This is stupid. Don't do this. You have to come back and buy brand-new barriques.' 'But they will be too oaky,' I replied. 'No,' he said, 'too oaky is not a problem. You will see.'"

Noblet was right. After all, the Burgundians had centuries of experience with barriques. Gaja had none. But no one, anywhere, had any experience with aging tannic Nebbiolo wine in barriques. Because a new barrel imparts its own oak tannins to a wine, putting already-tannic Nebbiolo into one is like adding a new tea bag to an already brewed cup.

On the other hand, oak tannins have the desirable ability of bonding molecularly with the color pigments of the wine, thereby preventing them from oxidizing. The wine emerges both darker and brighter—which was just what Gaja wanted, among other things. "The color of the wine surely has changed in the last fifteen years. This is due partly to the reduction of the yields. But it is also due to the use of barriques. Because barriques add a little part of wood tannins. And these wood tannins help the polymerization by making bigger molecules. And these bigger molecules reflect a deeper color. I prefer this deep color. Most consumers prefer a deeper color. We did experiments for seven or eight years with barriques," reports Gaja. "Hah! We had problems with volatile acidity, a smell like airplane glue. Sometimes the oak taste was too strong. And we didn't know the best time to blend the wines from barrels. It took time. We started with thirty-six barriques, experimentally, in 1969. Then it went up to sixty barrels in 1973. It was only later, closer to 1978, that we started to introduce a larger volume of barrels."

What Gaja and his winemaker, Guido Rivella, finally discovered was that new barrels were indeed best—they, too, liked the taste—but the oak tannins had to be reduced. Soaking the barrels with wine or salt water—two common techniques— were insufficiently extractive. Steaming proved effective, but ordinary steamers lacked punch. Convinced that steaming was the answer, Gaja purchased a huge industrial steamer and with this new capability was able to subject the new oak barrels to relentless, pressurized steam continuously for one hour. It did the trick. Barbaresco aged in these barrels emerged as supple and faintly sweet-smelling as a baby from a happy bath.

"The 1978 vintage was the first Barbaresco that I can say was truly mine, an expression of Gaja. First, I had to lower the yields, to get more concentration. Then Guido Rivella arrived in the cellar in 1970. And the old master of cellar finally left. Then it took seven or eight years to figure out how to use barriques. It all came together, finally, in the 1978, or maybe the 1979, vintage.

"So, when I tell people that my first wine was 1968—the first one that I had an effect on after coming into the winery in 1961—that's not totally right. That wine was 40, 50, 60 percent Angelo Gaja and the other part was of the master of cellar. And later, slowly, with Guido, it surely became more his project, as I spent more time outside pursuing foreign markets.

"Guido was the right man. It was impossible to do this with the old master of cellar. With Guido I had an excellent partner. Immediately I found a good feeling with Guido Rivella. He's not a man who speaks on the outside. He's not a man who goes to conferences. He's proud of his job. He has a little bit of vanity, like everybody, but he has kept very quiet. For example, I never would have accepted a winemaker who consulted to outside clients. Guido never asked me to do something like that. And I never would have accepted it if he had."

Gaja knew that by putting Barbaresco in barriques, he was cocking a snoot at virtually everyone in the Langhe. During the 1970s, the Langhe still adhered to tradition with unquestioning fervor. The few exceptions, such as Aldo Conterno, at least paid lip service to the old ways. Gaja was having none of it. He had set his sights on the outside world, in the process beginning a pattern of isolation that has since become almost hermetic. This is why, during our slow processional drive through the Easter Sunday throng of Barbaresco, so many locals were pleased to have a chance to chat with him.

Virtually none of them has seen the winery. Indeed, almost no fellow winegrowers from the Langhe has laid eyes on it. Situated near the center of the town, the only access is a fifteen-foot-high green metal folding door fitted under a massive wood-beamed overhang. It is the only opening in a street-long barricade of newly painted but otherwise anonymous contiguous buildings, some of which are Gaja's offices. To enter, you must present yourself in front of a television security camera, press the admittance button, and state your business. There used to be a plastic lettered sign explaining, in Italian, French, German, and English, that although visitors were welcome, the winery could not receive anybody without a prior appointment. Now, there's no sign at all. It was removed when the great metal folding door was repainted from red to green. Gaja's architect wanted to replace it with something cast in bronze. It still hasn't appeared. Gaja doesn't seem to feel its absence keenly, either.

The winery itself plunges five floors down the slope of the hill on which the town of Barbaresco is perched. Gaja is constantly expanding it, making more room for the almost annual stream of expensive, high-technology equipment that he pursues avidly, as well as more barriques. At last count, the Gaja wine cellar held one thousand one hundred barriques of varying age. Each barrique costs between $400 and $500. The oak flavor, for which they are prized, is exhausted after a few years. Stripped of their precious flavor, they become, like little Cinderellas, workaday barrels like any others.

In addition to the barrels in the cellar are yet nine hundred more future barriques lying in crisscross ricks outside the back of the winery. Not yet assembled, they look like neatly stacked elephant bones, gray-white from years of exposure to the elements. These one-inch thick, rough oak staves are brought directly to the winery from France, so that they can dry in the open air for several years before Gaja turns them over to a local cooper to fashion into barriques. "The best barrels come from air-dried, seasoned wood. You can dry the wood in kilns, which is quicker, but the result is not as good," says Gaja. "Since air-drying is so expensive because it's so slow, the barrel makers can't afford it for very long. So we do it ourselves. We have to do it if we want absolutely the best barrels.

"Some of my success occurred when American wine writers, particularly, started visiting the winery. Having a strong link with technology, with the French barriques and so on, they saw what I had here, and seeing this, they were happy. Because in their eyes this was similar to California. And so they wrote articles. But for a long time, nobody was allowed even to take photographs of the barrels. So my colleagues here in Langhe had an idea about the barrels, but I never pushed it.

"I was not open like the California producers, who exchange experiences in the cellar. And open their cellars to their colleagues. Here, the door was totally closed. It was not easy for them to enter and see what I was doing. It was easier for me to speak with other people outside the Langhe.

"My colleagues were not exactly jealous. But not giving them the opportunity to enter the winery and visit easily was a way of not giving them ammunition. I had some enemies. In our field, professional jealousy is a grass that grows up quickly. This takes place everywhere, not only among winemakers. Sometimes I heard voices about my friends not being happy about what I was doing. But at the end, they were not aggressive about it. And they are still not. I have always tried to keep a low profile. You can't push up the flag."

When Gaja said this, I had to laugh. A master of creating publicity for himself and getting it, Gaja can hardly be described as shy. When I remonstrated that not only does he push up the flag, but does the bugling, too, he happily conceded the point, which was undeniable anyway.

"Okay. Good. Fine. This is true. You are right. But you must remember that it was not *here*. They didn't know *here*. I can assure you. I never tried to achieve popularity here. I have friends here, some writers, etc. But I always asked them not to write about Gaja in the local press, unlike my colleagues, who want to be spoken about locally.

"The reason was not to impose my success on them. Success is not something that makes your colleagues happy. More in Italy than any other country, you can't impose your success upon your colleagues. We say, '*Farsi perdonare il successo*'—to have your success forgiven. If you want to live peacefully among your neighbors, it becomes important to obtain this forgiveness. And it gets you more respect.

"I was a little bit isolated, yes. I created it more by not giving my colleagues any opportunity. For example, many of my colleagues were talking often about the price for the new vintage. I never entered into these discussions. First, because it was difficult for me to tell them my selling price. Second, it was difficult to have a good suggestion from them. My idea in setting the price was first the connection with the demand, of course. In setting the price, it was important to look at the Bordeaux prices and the evolution of Burgundy prices. I looked more to France than to my colleagues here in Italy."

Gaja's prices, as much as his winemaking, have always been the sticking point. They offend people. They are, and continue to be, a provocation like no other. For so long, Italian wines were synonymous with cheapness, in much the same way that in the 1950s and 1960s, "Made in Japan" evoked an image of flimsy, cheap goods. And in Italy itself, no self-respecting Italian could imagine paying anything like a respectful price for a bottle of wine. For that matter, most Italians didn't even buy wine in bottles. Instead, they purchased wine in bulk, carrying it away in demijohns and bottling it themselves, if that. This practice still is common, if not quite so universal. Language, as always, reveals much: cheap in Italian is *buon prezzo*—a good price.

Not only was a low price reflective of Italy's longstanding poverty, and the ubiquity of wine, but it also was reflective of a cultural imperative about being modest. As Gaja noted, in Italy you have to have your success forgiven. This is especially forceful in the countryside. When asked how they make their wines, winemakers of an older generation still protest strenuously that "I do like my father."

This is precisely what occurred when, years ago, I visited one the Langhe's finest traditional winemakers, Elvio Cogno. His wines came from a section of the Barolo zone called La Morra. After averring that I considered his Barolos the finest that I knew from La Morra, Cogno accepted this praise without demurring, as the Italians themselves are used to laying it on with a trowel. That I was sincere was, effectively, irrelevent.

I asked him what he did that made his wine so superior. I already knew the answer. It's the same everywhere in the world of fine wine: very low yields, old vines, careful winemaking. But I wanted to hear it from Cogno himself. "I do like my father did," he replied. With a sinking feeling, I said, "All right. How did your father do it?" As expected, Cogno replied, "He did like his father." After two hours, I finally broke the man and got the answers: low yields, old vines, careful winemaking. Not least, this same modesty extended to pricing, resulting in derisory prices even for wines as fine as Cogno's Barolos.

Gaja isn't having any of this forelock tugging. "Here there is a fantastic heritage," he proclaims. "But you have to believe. Not to believe is to be a loser. I'm not sure that I have a superiority complex. But I haven't an inferiority complex, either, I assure you. I have a lot of respect for some of my colleagues. But some of them say about my prices, 'It's not right. It's crazy. It's stupid.' Their wines are good. I respect them. Okay, fine. But I am sure that I can sell my wines. That I can find customers for my wines! And I have! That's all," he adds petulantly, his chin jutting out.

Gaja is very nearly beside himself with richly savored righteousness about his pricing. "It's easy to say that the price of my single-vineyard Barbarescos are near the price of first growth Bordeaux," he declares. "But the first growth Bordeaux châteaux each sell twenty thousand cases. And Gaja sells just one thousand cases of each of the three single-vineyard wines. These wines are never in a duty-free shop. Maybe these wines actually create problems. I have no more Sorì Tildin, Sorì San Lorenzo, or Costa Russi, the three single-vineyard Barbarescos. There is no more availability. What can I do? It's not easy. You'd be surprised. To sell a thousand cases of each of these for a company that has at least ten thousand customers in the world?

"But when you go up in price, they become severe. So, you have to feel the responsibility. But this is not only for Gaja. This is also true for Château Petrus, for the Domaine de la Romanée-Conti. It's true for everybody, my dearrr. Because prices everywhere are going up. Perhaps one grows stronger, but at the same time, you will also get more beat up."

More galling, though, is the censure for his presumptuousness. Occasionally this is openly voiced; more often it is whispered maliciously. Either way, it always gets back to Gaja. His fellow Italian winegrowers, nowhere more so than in the Langhe itself, suggest that Gaja's high prices are somehow traitorous. Traditionalists elsewhere harrumph about the audacity of an Italian wine presuming to position itself alongside the great Bordeaux and Burgundies. Oddly, even some Italian Americans seem to think that flying so high is somehow un-Italian in its immodesty.

All of these murmurings of disapproval are constantly present, never quite drowned out by the vocal praise that also has been heaped on Gaja and his wines. It is a kind of inversion layer, where the cold air of disapproval lies just below the warm layer of praise.

Gaja is confident enough to know that inversions blow off. "I have always been aware that to push up the price is not easy. You have to have a high demand. Higher than your supply. But at the same time you have to remember that going up, up, up, and up, there is a responsibility that you have about the worth of the wine. I don't know if the wine has to absolutely reflect the land. But the wine has to be capable to have a message in a blind tasting. Look, there are people in such blind tastings who are *maltesta*, whose minds are set against the high prices. Or, some others, who just don't like Nebbiolo. They have a message in the mouth only for Bordeaux wines."

Gaja's problem is that there aren't any museums of fine wine. At first glance, a museum of fine wine seems absurd. But museums play a sanctioning role in contemporary society. They are essential in the selling of aesthetics, nowhere more so than in setting prices.

Witness the pricing of modern art. By now, it is freely admitted that no one knows anymore—as people once presumed to—what is art and what is not. We look to museums to give us a clue. Museum curators assume the priestly role, sanctifying what to most people looks like a huddle of rocks arranged in a circle or a splattering of paint, into Art.

More to the point, without this curatorial version of turning what might otherwise be considered tap water into Holy Water, those in the business of selling the goods cannot dare ask the high prices that only art can command. This is why we see timepieces trademarked as The Museum Watch and glass objects trademarked as Museum Crystal. Or endless other items positioned as "museum quality," or, more boldly yet, simply declared as art and priced accordingly.

Wine has none of this. Yet it has its hierarchies. The French government, in the 1930s, assumed a kind of curatorial role when it established its system of *appellation contrôlée*, which legally delimited both district and individual vineyard boundaries all over France. The key stroke, though, was that it established official quality rankings among these newly delimited vineyards. In Burgundy, for example, the best vineyards are designated as *grand cru*, or great growth. Below that comes *premier cru* or first growth. The pyramid broadens significantly below these two elevated levels.

Bordeaux has a different quality ranking, also sanctified by the government. This was a classification of the best châteaux in Bordeaux in 1855 performed by a group of Bordeaux wine merchants at the request of Napoleon III for the Exposition Universelle in Paris that year. Somehow it stuck. With *appellation contrôlée*, the French government formally confirmed these 1855 rankings of first, second, third, fourth, and fifth growths. The rank, by the way, attaches not to the vineyard site as it does in Burgundy, but to the château brand name itself. This is why virtually all of these *crus classés*, or classed growths, have significantly expanded their vineyards in the past two decades, the better to take advantage of their privileged rank.

The only curatorial change the French government has ever made in its codification of the antiquated 1855 classification was upgrading Château Mouton Rothschild from its original second growth standing to first growth status. This was performed in 1973, and was the result of a fifty-year-long crusade on the part of the late Baron Philippe de Rothschild. After that, the doors slammed shut.

The government's curatorial function in both confirming and designating quality differences among French wines has had a calculable effect in setting prices. Pricing for Bordeaux wines are set by the opening prices asked by the first growths. Everyone else follows in lockstep, each at prices corresponding to their rank. In Burgundy, a vineyard designated *grand cru* always fetches a much higher price for its wine than a *premier cru*, regardless of their qualities. In both cases, aspiring but unknowing drinkers take understandable reassurance in the fact that what they just paid (dearly) for is, after all, a first growth or a *grand cru*. "It's in a museum," they might say to themselves or their guests, much in the same way that they might justify a high-priced piece of otherwise incomprehensible art on their wall.

Wine, of course, shouldn't be incomprehensible. But as in artworks, some media are more difficult than others. Gaja's experiences in England and Belgium, and elsewhere, quickly taught him that, in Nebbiolo, he was working with perhaps the most difficult wine medium of all. "When I was offering Barbaresco, the foreign customers didn't know it at all. Comparing it with my Barbera, they were largely preferring Barbera to Barbaresco. My God! First, because they didn't know. And then when they tasted the Barbaresco with food it was different. And finally, they realized. Many times they were ignorant, in the kindest sense: They just didn't know. It was difficult."

Making matters more difficult yet was the fact that Italy had no version of *appellation contrôlée* until 1963 when, modeled openly on the French system, it created various *denominazione di origine controllata*, or DOCs. This was known as the Law 930. But unlike France, the Law 930 establishing DOCs did not install either quality rankings or even attempt to define vineyard boundaries. It did, however, create an authority that set broad district boundaries and officially confirmed various local winegrowing traditions.

Italian wine producers, characteristically, chafed under the DOC regulations. The system has long since been outmoded. In fact, the old Law 930 has recently been overhauled and will be replaced with another version of the DOC system. Although the new system calls for delimiting single vineyard boundaries for the first time, no provision whatever is made for establishing quality rankings.

Gaja, more than some other Italian producers, has praise for the original DOC system, despite the fact that he himself chafed under its restrictions, more vocally so than most. Still, he retains an awareness that some sort of system, however flawed, was necessary to impose order on Italy's wine anarchy.

"The old 930 law, which will cease to exist in February 1995, was criticized because, in the minds of Italians, all of the wines were effectively of the same level," notes Gaja. "There was no pyramid. In Italy, it is very difficult to make a pyramid! But despite all the defects of the old 930 law, it made places for everybody. It created the possibilities for grape growers to become wine producers. Because it at least formalized and legalized what was Barolo and what was Barbaresco, and many other wines. At least you could say that your wine was a DOC wine, which was some distinction, anyway.

"In the past, Barolo and Barbaresco were made by *négociants* such as Prunotto, Pio Cesare, Borgogno, and so on. Their object was to select different wines from different villages and blend them, to create a single standard wine labeled Barolo, or sometimes Barbaresco.

"It was only in the beginning of the 1980s that, in reality, single vineyards began to be named on labels. Only then did the big *négociants* finally realize that it was important to create a pyramid. Not just of quality, but of price. Making only one Barolo, and producing eight hundred thousand bottles, you are obliged to follow the market, staying in line in matters of price. But if you produce single vineyards, then you can sell at other, higher prices—according to quality, of course. And you still can continue to have a basic Barolo."

However sympathetic Gaja may sound about the old system, the fact is that he is Italy's most prominent flouter of some of its more restrictive provisions. Gaja was having none of the old deference to tradition required of dutiful Italian sons of the land. Once again, his independence further isolated him, as well as further upsetting envious onlookers.

This time it was his insistence on planting unauthorized grape varieties, specifically Chardonnay and Cabernet Sauvignon. The DOC regulations for the Barbaresco zone, where his vineyards are located, authorized only certain traditional grape varieties, such as Nebbiolo, Barbera, and Dolcetto. In this, the DOC regulations are of a piece with other European wine regulations, which also restrict vineyard plantings to certain grape varieties. Nevertheless, all over Italy, producers were secretly and not-so-secretly challenging what they saw as a fossilizing of Italian wines, with inflexible regulations embedding outdated traditions.

Starting in 1979, Gaja secretly planted Chardonnay. Technically, he could plant whatever he wanted—if he was given prior approval, which was problematic, at best. But even with that, the authorization probably would be only for vineyard experimentation purposes: An unauthorized grape variety would not be allowed to be sold as anything other than anonymous bulk wine. Gaja had no intention of growing Chardonnay only to sell it for bulk. He was going to make a Gaja Chardonnay, aged in barriques just like white Burgundies. Only when he was ready to bottle his first vintage, the 1983, did he turn to the authorities and ask for authorization. This he did one year before he was ready to release it.

Tactician that he is, he had calculated, correctly, that his action was fait accompli. By then he was already prominent and an idol to the new generation of young university-trained winegrowers. Not least, he had already garnered huge publicity, so the spotlight was on full glare. His Chardonnay was by then not so secret. Gaja figured that the authorities would bumble and grumble, but in the end do nothing. Which is precisely what happened. Later, like politicians caught short on a popular issue, they subsequently declared that they, too, were in favor of authorizing all "reasonable" experimentation. Gaja, ever sensitive, humbly agreed that he, too, was in favor of such experimentation being "reasonable." Obeisances made, he then went ahead and planted no fewer than two dozen other grape varieties.

When he unveiled his 1983 Chardonnay, the first such bottling ever seen in living memory in the Langhe, the reaction was tumultuous. After the business of barriques, Gaja was a known firebrand. But his success was undeniable and for his part, Gaja was endlessly diplomatic. As might be expected, others have followed Gaja's lead. The Langhe has always been a red wine area. It never had any white wines of note. And white wines are commercially attractive. Like using barriques, which can now be seen in hundreds of Italian wineries, making Chardonnay became a signal to onlookers that a producer is modern and forward-thinking. So now even the Langhe abounds in small quantities of Chardonnay from various producers. Gaja was the first producer in Italy to use barriques and then became the first to make a Chardonnay using them.

No sooner had the Chardonnay ruckus died down than Gaja revived controversy by issuing a Cabernet Sauvignon, a red wine grape as alien to the Langhe as a skyscraper. Actually, he had secretly planted Cabernet vines in 1978, a year earlier than he had the Chardonnay. But Cabernet vines take longer to give good quality fruit. Also, Cabernet needs more time in the barrel to mature properly. So it had to be released later than the Chardonnay.

By then, everything Gaja did was closely watched by his colleagues and the press, as well as the wine bureaucrats. This high profile, coupled with a restlessness among many of his colleagues, made everything he did tantamount to legal, never mind the regulations. The Cabernet Sauvignon plantings were again authorized shortly before Gaja was ready to release his first 1982 vintage, in 1985.

But more than the Chardonnay—which after all is white and, therefore, doesn't really count as a real wine in the minds of the Langaroli—Cabernet Sauvignon is red. Local disapproval was vocal and instantaneous. Why should someone bother with Cabernet Sauvignon in an area long since recognized to be supreme on the planet for Nebbiolo? This was not experimentalism. This was a slap in the face.

Even his father, always publicly supportive, openly confessed his disapproval. Gaja was unperturbed, even amused. The Cabernet vineyard literally surrounds his house, which itself is on the most prominent hill just outside the town of Barbaresco. Like many Italians, Gaja's parents live in the same house with their son. So his father, then still mayor of Barbaresco, had no choice but to view the Cabernet vines every day upon leaving the house and returning to it. The site, an unusually good one, previously was planted to Nebbiolo. According to Gaja, every day as he walked through the vines to town hall, his father invariably would mutter, in dialect, "*darmagi*"—what a pity. So that was what Gaja named his Cabernet: Darmagi.

He enjoyed the witticism, the more so for its being in dialect. Nearly all of Gaja's wines sport dialect names, which is a point of pride with him. Two of his named-vineyard Barbarescos employ the dialect term *sorì*, which refers to a site's favorable exposure to the sun. In Barbaresco the word, despite its spelling, is pronounced su-REE. But in neighboring Barolo, *sorì* becomes *sirì*. And outside of the Langhe, in the Asti area, little more than twenty miles north of Barbaresco, it becomes *solì*. In this version one can see the etymology: *sole*, Italian for "sun." Gaja was the first to use the old dialect word on a label. Other wines display more Piedmontese, such as Vignabajla (a vineyard once owned by a nanny or *bajla*) and Vignaveja (the old vineyard).

For Gaja, planting Cabernet Sauvignon and Chardonnay is a matter of marketing. For others, including foreigners, it is a shameless, even whorish, pursuit of public relations glory at the sacrifice of a great local distinction. Gaja has heard it many times. "The real goal in planting Cabernet Sauvignon and Chardonnay was to show what the land was capable of. To put a spotlight on the Langhe. This was the principal object," he insists. "The idea of Cabernet Sauvignon opening new doors has been, in effect, a less important reason. The principal reason was to help people focus more on the Langhe area. This has happened, absolutely. I believe that planting the French varieties has been a perfect market strategy. And in keeping it in small quantities. Because my goal is Barbaresco.

"In some tastings, particularly in Europe, tasting the Cabernet Sauvignon or Chardonnay, they were surprised about the quality coming from the Langhe. And I was thinking in my heart, 'You should not be surprised, my dears. This is a fantastic land.'

"In Piedmont there are one hundred sixty thousand acres of vines planted. Chardonnay occupies three hundred seventy acres. Less than one-quarter of one percent! Cabernet Sauvignon is one hundred eleven acres. That's less than, what?" Gaja rummages for a pocket calculator, punching furiously at the buttons. "It's point zero seven. What is that? Less than one tenth of a percent. My God, it's nothing! It's a strategy, a marketing strategy.

"Cabernet and Chardonnay have offered me many opportunities to enter into blind wine tastings in Europe that I couldn't enter with the Nebbiolo grape. Because, for example, when Georg Riedel had a tasting with his wine glasses in London, it was with Cabernet Sauvignons and Chardonnays from around the world. How could I enter with Nebbiolo? When you are speaking about a competition of Nebbiolo, what are you speaking about? Piedmont. But with

Cabernet or Chardonnay, it's all over the world. So you can enter there. You have the right to open the door.

"If you are good, people will then say, 'What is this? Italian? Piedmont?' All right, maybe they will continue drinking only Burgundy and Bordeaux. But something stays in their minds. Probably some of them don't know about Nebbiolo. Or they have a bad idea about Nebbiolo. But the collective image of the Langhe goes up a little bit. Thanks maybe to Gaja or to other people. I believe that we will have to play this way. The problem is to be capable to manage it in the right way. Not to lose your mind, planting Chardonnay and Cabernet everywhere. This would be a mistake. You have to be capable of playing your cards—if you have some."

One of the cards Gaja plays with consummate skill is packaging. But perhaps it is better described as framing. Here again, the late Baron Philippe de Rothschild led the way when, starting in 1945, he began adorning Château Mouton Rothschild's labels with different artworks every vintage, making the labels themselves collectible. In fact, some of Mouton Rothschild's worst vintages, such as 1956, are among its most expensive and sought after wines. Unlike great vintages, a wine such as 1956 was such a poor year that nobody had any intention of keeping it. The empty bottles—this was before everything became a "collectible"—were discarded. Today, people seeking a complete set of Château Mouton Rothschild wines since 1945 will pay a fortune for a bottle of the 1956 just for the label.

Gaja, for his part, had yet a different card to play. By the time he had arrived on the world's fine-wine scene, Mouton's art-on-the-label ploy was already being knocked off. Besides, Gaja is no knock-off artist. He recognized, rightly, that many, if not most, buyers of fine wines have little or no understanding of what makes such wines so good. After all, wine is a language unto itself. People willing and able to pay a premium for wine usually are fluent in other languages, most particularly the languages of money and rankings. They instantly comprehend Bordeaux's first growth through fifth growth classification. And they easily swot up the few necessary French words to grasp Burgundy's *grand cru* and *premier cru* categories.

Gaja knew that how he packaged his wine—how he framed what he, at least, considered his art—was critical. He had to signal to these same buyers of Bordeaux and Burgundy that his wine was somehow "important." After all, even the most implausible painting, if framed artfully, inspires a second glance, whether or not it's hanging in a museum. "I want people to know that they are drinking Gaja," he once said to me.

His label is as calculated as an optician's eye chart. The design is austerely modern, three-quarters of it white, with a one-inch-wide black band at the top. The white part has several eye-straining lines of information swimming about: two squeezed lines at the base and three squeezed lines near the top. Otherwise, the space is blank. The eye instinctively looks for something more visually congenial. Gaja provides. With relief your eyes rest upon fat, white letters luminous against the black band: *GAJA*. Experiment discovers that, in daylight, you can read the name at a distance of thirty-two feet. The name "Barbaresco," however, can be made out only at eight feet. And the type telling us that the wine is classed by the Italian government as a *denominazione di origine controllata e garantita*, Italy's highest wine distinction, is discernible at two feet.

The effect is dramatic and intriguing. The spelling alone piques interest: What is a "Gaja"? How is it pronounced? The design is bold, so forthrightly black and white that the last place one thinks of is Italy, which still is burdened with an outdated image of straw-wrapped wine bottles holding candles dripping red wax. But ignorance is no obstacle to effect: Whomever or whatever this Gaja is, must be important. The name was even more outsized in the 1970s, when the *GAJA* on the label was half again as large as it is today. Of this downsizing, Gaja grins, "Well, when you get a little more famous, you have to be a little more modest."

Gaja's awareness of the importance of packaging in sending a message of quality dovetailed neatly with his own love of obsessive perfection. Witness the great cork pursuit, which will probably be the basis of a Freudian doctoral thesis with a title such as "Eros and Oenology: A Study of the Crypto-Phallicism of Men and Wine."

Corks can sometimes impart bad flavors to wines. Just why is the subject of intense discussion among winegrowers everywhere in the world. Cork producers, mostly Portuguese, are defensive, but now reluctantly acknowledge that a problem exists. Depending upon whom you talk to, the percentage of so-called "corky" wines is between 2 percent and 10 percent of a producer's production. No single solution presents itself, in part because the exact cause of everything loosely (and often inaccurately) categorized as "corky" in a wine has yet to be determined. In the meantime, wine producers agonize over the problem.

Gaja, however, decided to act, sooner than most. He began in the mid-seventies, a full decade before the great majority of wine producers in France and California decided to even think about the matter. Seeking a resolution, he went to Sardinia, which has ancient cork oaks, the stripped and processed bark of which create corks for wine bottles.

"The cork companies in the 1970s in Sardinia were tiny and badly organized," he recalls. "I had the impression that, although they were doing their best for Gaja, they lacked ambition and drive. I knew that I had to get them to give me better quality corks. But I had to figure out a way to get them to do it, as they had no drive of their own. I had to find some argument, some way of getting them to pay more attention.

"I realized that, by asking for a longer cork, it would impose upon them a rigor and severity, a selectivity, that they didn't have. So I went to my most important supplier and asked him to produce a cork for me of sixty-three millimeters or almost two-and-one-half-inches long. The longest cork then made was fifty millimeters or fifty-five millimeters or two-inches long. They were a little bit astonished to be asked this, because it would require them to be more selective than they ever had been.

"Also, you cannot get corks like that from only one producer. You must use five or six. They have to sort from a very large amount of raw material. No one producer has enough. So we had to find small artisans who would be curious enough, willing enough to do this. Of course, price could not be an issue. But even with price not being a problem, it was difficult."

Nevertheless, after numerous trips to Sardinia, Gaja lined up his suppliers. His corks, of necessity, were coming from the oldest trees, with the thickest bark. And the quality was unsurpassed. "I don't want to say that the only way to have a good cork is to have a sixty-three millimeter cork. This is stupid. I'm not saying that our corks never have problems. Everybody gets bad corks. But I believe that we have reduced in a large way the risk of bad taste." He had solved, as best as possible, the real problem of imperfect corks. But he also had something instantly recognizable, something dramatic and different: the world's longest corks. Gaja was happy.

The first vintage to sport the new two-and-one-half-inch long cork was the 1979 Barbaresco. But Gaja soon discovered that the new cork created a new problem: the cork machine couldn't handle it. The standard corking machine, including Gaja's, could hold corks no longer than fifty-five millimeters. Gaja had no choice. He had to have these corks. So he went to the corking machine manufacturer and arranged for a first-of-its-kind prototype corking machine capable of holding his one-of-a-kind cork. "It was expensive, but worth it," says Gaja with undisguised satisfaction. Gaja was now very happy.

But no sooner was the cork capable of being driven into the bottle than Gaja discovered that the neck of his existing bottle simply wasn't long enough to accommodate the full length of his sixty-three millimeter cork. "So we had to change the neck of the bottle," he says. "This is not easy. You have to get the glassmaker to create a special mold, which was very expensive. We still have a little bit of a problem with the bottle. We need one centimeter more in the neck. That's why, now, the cork we buy is sixty millimeters long or two-and-one-third inches." With his one-of-a-kind corks, one-of-a-kind corking machine, and custom-made long-necked bottles, Gaja was happier than ever before. He rested, content with his good works.

But this was not to last. "I remember when, in the autumn of 1982, I introduced the Barbaresco 1979, which was the first wine with the new long corks. I was very proud. I went to a customer in Milan who was then selling between sixty and one hundred cases of Barbaresco a year. A very important customer. I told him, 'Look, the Barbaresco has a special long cork. Be careful.' He said, 'No problem, no problem.' A week later, he called me and said 'This is a disaster.' 'What's happened?' I said. He told me, 'The waiters don't like opening the bottle.'

"The problem was that the corkscrews used by the waiters in Italy, given to them as gifts by big wine companies, were too short. It was impossible, or nearly so, for them to pull out the cork. Customers get a little bit nervous, watching a waiter struggling with a wine bottle, you know," adds Gaja with a laugh.

Gaja now had a new problem: He had introduced a cork so long that no one, with a conventional corkscrew, could easily extract it. Now, everyone who wanted to drink Gaja wine had to have a special corkscrew. Fortunately, such a corkscrew already had been invented, by a Texan who was marketing them under the brand name Screwpull.

"As it happens, I was just back from the States. And when I was in New York, I had bought about one hundred Screwpulls. So I gave thirty or forty to that restaurant. I gave the rest to my agents with instructions to show them around. I had no choice, my dear. I had to import Screwpulls to Italy!" says Gaja, radiantly happy.

A close friend of Gaja's, the late Giacomo Bologna, was a roly-poly Piedmontese winegrower who was a great favorite among his colleagues for his generosity and wit. He delighted in Gaja's new long corks and immediately used them to tweak the already tetchy jealousies of Gaja's fascinated competitors. Once, at the Vinitaly trade show in Verona where every Italian winegrower can be found, Bologna was telling an enthralled audience of fellow producers about Gaja's new long, longer, longest corks. Like a talented older boy telling scary stories around a campfire to impressionable younger boys, Bologna described how impressive it was to see these Gaja bottles opened.

"You know this Gaja is smart," he proclaimed, like a carny barker setting up the rubes to be fleeced. "You know how much that cork costs? One thousand lire!" The audience shook its collective heads in amazement. Gaja was *matto, pazzo,* crazy. At that time, a cork cost two hundred lire, tops.

"Sure, Gaja is crazy," confirmed Bologna. "But Gaja is not crazy. He spends one thousand lire for a cork, yes. But he saves one centiliter of Sorì Tildin with the longer cork. And you already know how much he gets for that wine. This is not so dumb. He always has money in his pocket!"

In the penny-counting mentality of this rapt audience of Italian winegrowers, many of whom were one generation away, if that, from being *contadini* or peasant farmers, they could see that, in so expensive a wine, all those one centiliters (one-third ounce) could add up. In fact, Gaja's wines, like everyone else's, contain the legally required seventy-five centiliters, or 25.3 ounces. But Italians, especially Italian farmers, are sure that the smart ones, the rich sorts, such as Gaja, are forever *furbo*—foxy, admirably crafty.

But Bologna was not finished with them. "And there's another reason," he exclaimed. "You know why else?" All the men said no, they couldn't think of another reason why someone would spend five times more on a cork than he had to. "Maybe *bella figura*," offered one, referring to the Italian love of beautiful style. Many otherwise unjustifiable expenses in Italian life are done in the name of *bella figura*.

Everyone agreed that this must be the other reason. "No!" cried Bologna. "The other reason is that with these corks, he obliges all the restaurants in Italy to use the Screwpull. Which he imports and sells to them!" It was so obvious, so deliciously *furbo*, they wondered how they could have missed it. *Gaja is smart*, they said in awe and envy.

That envy was not entirely benign, which resulted in a turning point in Gaja's ever-more-strained relations with his fellow Langaroli. His determination to play upon a larger stage—and never mind what others say—was already resolute. But it was further stiffened by what could only have been a betrayal. In 1981, shortly before Gaja intended to roll out his tradition-shattering Chardonnay, it appeared that he was untouchable.

Someone made a telephone call to the local wine authorities, suggesting that they have a look around Gaja's winery. Italian wine regulations allow the authorities to enter a winery at any time, to inspect that wines are being properly labeled, that hygiene is maintained, and so forth. Usually the visits, if they are made at all, are perfunctory.

But this suggestion had to have come from someone on the inside. Because what the authorities discovered when they visited the Gaja winery was a half-ton of sugar. To Italian wine insiders, familiar with the arcana of Italian wine law, this is a disastrous piece of news. It is one of those ominous facts, the sort said in deadpan tones by *Dragnet*'s Sergeant Joe Friday. The long arm of the law was about to come snaking around, like a boa constrictor with a grudge.

To understand why having a half-ton of sugar lying around a winery could be considered so heinous—in certain circles, anyway—it helps to know that grape juice is transformed into wine by yeasts consuming the natural sugar of the grapes. The amount of alcohol in the eventual wine is directly determined by the amount of sugar in the juice. But if a harvest is poor, meaning that the grapes are less than fully ripe, the resulting wine might be too low in alcohol, with only, say, 10 percent alcohol rather than a much more desirable 13 percent. When a wine has too low a level of alcohol, especially if it is meant to spend years in a barrel before being bottled, it rarely keeps well. It is vulnerable to microbiological disturbances that a higher level of alcohol would ward off.

Centuries ago, winegrowers discovered that yeasts are not particular about the sugar they consume. Grape sugar, beet sugar, cane sugar, fructose from honey, they can handle it all. And they will create alcohol equally well as a byproduct from any of these. So, centuries ago, during bad harvests, winegrowers would add some form of sugar to a vat, to raise the alcohol level of the wine to something a little safer. You need ten pounds of sugar for every sixty gallons of wine—one barrique's worth—to raise the alcohol one degree.

Originally, they used honey, as sugar was far too rare and expensive. But by the late 1700s, the importation of sugar from sugar cane growing in the West Indies and Brazil made sugar much more widespread. The only problem was that the British controlled the trade and, because all of it was seaborne, they could effectively block its arrival on the European continent if they wished. Which they did during the Napoleonic Wars.

However, half a century earlier, in 1747, a Prussian chemist discovered sugar in beet juice; by 1793, a Frenchman living in Berlin perfected a process to extract this sugar on a commercial scale. Napoleon consequently saw beet sugar as his salvation and ordered vast tracts of land in northern France to be planted to the beet.

For winegrowers, the availability of cheap sugar was a godsend. It allowed them to salvage otherwise hopeless harvests. Granted, unripe grapes never offer the same flavor qualities as ripe grapes, but sometimes the line between something undrinkable and something pretty decent could be a matter of only one or two degrees alcohol, especially in matters of a wine's "balance."

When Napoleon Bonaparte pursued his plans for widescale production of sugar beets, and their subsequent transformation into sugar (there is no difference, by the way, either chemically or in taste, between sugar from beets and sugar from cane), he turned to his minister of agriculture, Comte Jean-Antoine Chaptal de Chanteloup.

A chemist himself, as well as president of the French Academy of Science, Chaptal saw immediately the benefits to wine that cheap sugar afforded. And he gave his endorsement to the practice, which became known—as it still is today—as chaptalization. It is simply the addition of a measured amount of sugar to a fermenting vat of grape juice. Chaptal did not, however, invent the technique. The French chemist Maquer investigated and described the process as early as 1776, twenty-five years before Chaptal's endorsement.

When properly done, to no more than one degree to two degrees alcohol, chaptalization is a sound idea, as well as virtually undetectable to the palate. In France it is legal and is now performed virtually every year in Burgundy and Bordeaux, seemingly no matter how fine the vintage. It must be done with official permission, but that always is forthcoming.

The French wine critic Michel Bettane calls chaptalization "socialism in the vineyard." He says, "It's the civilization. France is a helped society. Every French person is helped by Social Security. Chaptalization is a type of help. It's a mentality. When you buy prescription drugs in France, you are reimbursed for part of the cost by the Social Security. The other part you have to pay yourself. So you have a second insurance policy, a private one, to pay for this part. This, we call the *ticket moderateur*. Chaptalization is the *ticket moderateur* of the grape. You pay people to produce grapes ripe enough for eleven degrees alcohol. Then you have insurance to produce thirteen degrees."

In Italy, chaptalization is illegal. Everywhere. The government knows that in northern Italian winegrowing regions, such as Piedmont, Alto Adige, Friuli, and Valle d'Aosta, among others, poor harvests happen, abounding in less than perfectly ripened grapes. But instead of allowing growers the option, as in France, of using sugar, they instead insist that growers firm up their wines only with grape concentrate. In other words, they want northern Italian producers to blend concentrated wine from the south into their more delicate northern wines. Not surprisingly, many northern Italian wine producers recoil at the idea. Where chaptalization is neutral, grape concentrate brings with it muddying flavors.

The authorities are unbending. It is a political issue with them, a means of justifying the huge, uneconomic investments that the government has made in supporting vast wine cooperatives in the south. Chaptalization is the sacred cow of Italian wine law.

The northern Italian producers insist that they never chaptalize. But privately, if you know them well enough and they've had a few bottles of wine down their gullets, they will confess to having discreetly dabbled in the practice.

With a half-ton of sugar sitting in his winery, nobody was about to believe that Gaja was putting up preserves. ("For coffee, my dear, coffee," laughs Gaja.) His defense was that he had been given permission to experiment with making sparkling wines, for which you need sugar to create a second fermentation to get bubbles into a wine already fermented once to complete, sugarfree dryness. Gaja insisted that the sugar was legal. But his evidence was vague.

The whole thing was splashed across the pages of the local newspaper, *Gazetta d'Alba*. Everyone knew. Gaja kept his head low. A few friends, such as Aldo Conterno, publicly supported him, but the majority of his colleagues kept mum. The most public supporter was, of all people, the late Renato Ratti, who at the time was president of the Barolo and Barbaresco growers consortium and an influential wine politico. Ratti was somebody in an official position. To Gaja's dismay—he wanted the thing to die down as quickly as possible—Ratti declared that Gaja had done nothing wrong. That plenty of other growers in the Langhe chaptalized their wines. That the whole thing was a ploy to embarrass Piedmont's most prominent winegrower.

Privately, Gaja was despairing. "I could not believe that this was happening," he confided during our Easter Sunday walk. It was a depressing subject for such a sparkling day. Clearly, it still was painful. When I suggested that it had to have been an inside job, Gaja refused to confirm it. "Maybe, maybe," was all he muttered. That said, he added, "I was very depressed, really. This is rare for me, I assure you. But after this, I really closed the doors tight. It became just me and Lucia and Guido Rivella. We became our own world."

The case dragged on for four years. Finally, in 1985, it was thrown out of court along with thousands of other minor court actions. The Italian judiciary is so over-worked that the only way for it to eliminate its backlog is simply to abandon all but the most significant cases. This occurs every few years. The Gaja chaptalization matter ceased to exist and appears to have long since faded from people's minds. At least it never gets mentioned, in part because it was so obviously picayune to begin with.

By the time of the chaptalization scandal, Gaja had been married for six years, to his former secretary, Lucia Giordano, whom he married in 1976. A small, dark-haired, pert-looking woman with luminous brown eyes, she is thirteen years younger than Gaja.

"I married late, no question. Lucia was working here. I began to look at her with different eyes. I had the goal to marry Lucia. Yet, at the same time, I was a little bit hesitant. There were differences—in terms of culture, habits, ways of life. Differences that were important. After all, I was thirty-six, and she was twenty-three."

Not least was the fact that Lucia was a local girl, born and raised in Barbaresco. Her Piedmontese probably is better than Angelo's. And, according to her, he has an Alba accent in his dialect while hers is "pure."

Their marriage took nearly everyone by surprise, partly because Gaja was not expected to marry anyone local. He was known to have had a relationship with someone in far-off Milan. Partly it was because of Gaja's strong urge toward isolating himself from local scrutiny. "Here in Barbaresco, there was a terrible amount of gossip when we announced our marriage. My parents, they didn't know. I had told my friends. But I only told my parents fifteen days before the wedding. They were happy anyway, because they knew her.

"At the time, I was still living at home with my parents. Here in Italy, your mother believes that only when you are married are you *systemato*, or settled. So my family was always pushing. Many times when I was here in Barbaresco I chose to eat outside the house. This caused a little bit of conflict with my father.

"When I started remodeling the house, every day my parents starting asking me if I was getting married. They knew about my relationship in Milan. And I told them that if we didn't make more room in the house, that I would move to another flat altogether. 'But why?' they asked. Because I would like to have more independence! My God, I am thirty-six years old!"

When I observed that it is no small trick keeping an impending marriage secret in a village as small as Barbaresco, Gaja smiled slyly and said, "Yes, probably. But if I don't want people to know, I am pretty capable of keeping things quiet." What was left unsaid was that Lucia, too, was capable of keeping things quiet as well. This must have pleased Gaja inordinately. He had chosen well—better, he admits, than he knew at the time. "Frankly—because she is not here I can say this—Lucia was a very good choice. I don't know when exactly, but my sense of her grew up. She is an important help. I was very lucky."

Lucia, for her part, surely grew up as well. In marrying Gaja, she had vaulted into another sphere of economics, culture, and exposure to the outside world. She runs the day to day administration of Gaja's ever-expanding business. And she accepts—although not always without complaint—her husband's relentless business ambition.

Gaja is frequently on the road. On some occasions, he is gone for as long as a month. Rarely a week goes by when he has not traveled at least overnight to some European city. In the early 1980s, he could be found in the United States for as much as two or three months a year. Lucia held the fort in Barbaresco, running the business and raising their two daughters, Gaia, thirteen, and Rosanna, eleven. This February, Lucia, now forty years old, gave birth to their third child, Giovanni. It was an unexpected, although welcomed, pregnancy. Noting Gaja's frequent absences for business travel, one local wag called it another Gaja "first"—conception by fax.

What Lucia handles these days—apart from a new baby, which lies and cries in a specially created nursery next to her office, attended by a full-time nanny—is not just Gaja's own wine business. He also imports other producers' wines into Italy.

"It began in 1977," he recounts. "They were bad times for expensive French wines. The former Italian importer of the Burgundy wines of the Domaine de la Romanée-Conti decided to stop bringing them in. But he agreed to help find a new importer. He called me to ask if I knew of anyone who might do it. Two months later, after asking around quite a lot, I called him to say that I couldn't find anyone to help him.

"And then I thought, 'Why not me?' So I arranged to do so. Actually, it was a very good thing for Gaja. Because when I first started to sell my wines in the United States, where nobody had heard of Gaja, every writer would say that Gaja distributed the expensive wines of the Domaine de la Romanée-Conti in Italy. It was a big help."

This was the beginning of Gaja Distribuzione. At the time, no one else had chanced on the idea that a successful winery could as easily sell other, noncompeting, wines as well as one's own. For Gaja, it was business at its best. It offers unlimited expansion. And he seized on it ravenously, signing on all the first growth Bordeaux, a clutch of major Sauternes producers, a prominent French Champagne house, and assorted other French wines, as well as some Austrian bottlings. Not least, in 1987 he also commenced importing several dozen of California's best bottlings, including the wines of Robert Mondavi, as well as an Oregon wine. "We bring in about three containers a year of California wine. This is about three thousand cases. It can be good business at the price levels I have."

Because Gaja Distribuzione also sells Gaja's own wines, he is his own distributor throughout Italy, thereby pocketing yet another slice of the wine business profits that usually goes to someone else.

Recognizing that his agents can sell many items on the same sales call, Gaja secured the rights to sell Riedel glassware in Italy. Riedel is an Austrian company that produces what are acknowledged to be the most intelligently designed wine glasses. Italian restaurateurs are wild about them. They now are obligatory in seemingly every restaurant in Italy with any pretension to quality, despite their expense. Every major wine producer uses them to present his wines to visitors. Gaja Distribuzione is responsible for every glass, as well as Riedel's many other items such as decanters, plates, pitchers, and the like. To complete the tabletop picture, Gaja also brings in a line of fine German porcelain. The second floor of Gaja's offices in Barbaresco resembles a wholesaler's showroom, which is, in fact, what it is. All of the items for sale, including the wines, are on display.

Gaja remains voracious. "I am thinking of something in the future for Gaja Distribuzione where we can sell directly to private customers. A mail-order catalog to sell all of the wines of Gaja Distribuzione as well as everything else in Gaja Distribuzione.

"In Italy, nobody has yet had any success in the mail-order business because the mails don't work. But now a lot of private mail services are starting up. Now, it's only the large cities, but eventually they will expand. Lucia is asking me if I am becoming crazy," he adds with evident satisfaction.

"When customers arrive here, Lucia welcomes them. And many times she handles the agents. Increasingly, most of my time now is spent doing public relations, because I speak English and French. And, in the public mind, Gaja is, well, me. Lucia is spending more and more time dealing with customers than in even running the office. She controls in large part the purchasing of bottles, corks, cases, and so on. We need more people in Gaja Distribuzione.

"You know in France the Moueix family [owners of numerous Bordeaux châteaux, including Château Pétrus] have become a large power. They sell by catalog. They are very strong. And they sell Château Pétrus, too, by catalog, as well as many other wines. The commercial aspect is becoming a very, very important element in fine wines.

"Today Gaja Distribuzione has fifty-eight to sixty agents here in Italy. Maybe in the future, this will increase to eighty or ninety agents. They sell also Gaja wines. This is a fantastic synergy. Maybe it will be possible in the future to sell Gaja wines directly to private customers—at a high price. My competitors have not yet realized the right connections. I have no desire to give them any lessons. It's very good that they stay asleep!"

Yet one market, perhaps the most obvious market, is something that Gaja will enter only in September 1993: selling a Gaja-made Barolo. While Gaja single-handedly made Barbaresco a force among Langhe wines, the unpicked plum hanging on the tree all along was the Langhe's already acknowledged great wine, Barolo.

Even the most cursory, dismissive discussions of Italian wines never fail to mention Barolo. Like Barbaresco, it is a geographic zone of the Langhe hills. Its wine, too, must be 100 percent Nebbiolo. Barolo is a larger area than Barbaresco, with many more microclimates. Above all, it has cachet, which even Gaja does not deny.

"I don't know why I didn't sell Barolo. But in any case, I stayed with Barbaresco exclusively. It was more difficult. This was a big stress. It would have been much easier to sell Barolo than to sell Barbaresco," he confesses. "Thirty years ago my colleagues saw being a leader in Barbaresco like being a leader in Grignolino," he adds with the barest tinge of bitterness. Grignolino is a grape that creates an inconsequential pale red wine that once was popular among the local farmers.

"I had many opportunities to buy land in Barolo over the years," he continues. "Not doing so was a bad decision. It would have been possible to have a second line of Gaja wine, exactly like the first line of Barbaresco. It would have helped much more the diffusion of Gaja wines in foreign markets. I would do it differently today if I had the chance to do everything over again."

This belief is underscored by the name Gaja gave to his new sixty-nine-acre vineyard in Barolo, which he purchased in 1988 for one billion, two hundred seventy thousand lire or about $900,000 dollars. At thirteen thousand dollars an acre, part of it already planted, it was a steal. Vineyard land in Napa Valley sells for at least $40,000 dollars an acre, and often much more. That he could walk off with one sizable vineyard parcel, in a site already known to be superb, in an area as famous as Barolo, confirms the truth of what Robert Mondavi revealed to Gaja twenty years ago: They are still snoring in Barolo.

Gaja, as always, is wide awake. The new name he has given to his Barolo vineyard, in full-throttle Piedmontese, is sure to have wine fanciers scratching their heads in a half-dozen countries around the world: *Sperss Ed Bareu*, which means "Nostalgia for Barolo."

There is an air of triumph in Gaja's "return" to Barolo. The vineyard he purchased once supplied the grapes that his father used to make a Barolo under the Gaja name. But after 1961, when Angelo convinced his father to make wines only from vineyards they owned, they left off making Barolo and turned exclusively to their own Barbaresco vineyards.

But the real triumph, the unspoken one, is that Gaja's Barolo will be sold for less than he asks for his three single-vineyard Barbaresco wines, or about $100 a bottle. Curiosity alone will drive the sales, at least at first. Confident as always, Gaja plans an unusual marketing twist: Releasing two vintages of his brand-new Barolo simultaneously, the better to drive home the point of the wine's quality.

"When I said that I wanted people to know that they were tasting Gaja, I was always aware that the image of Barbaresco was low. Many *négociants* were selling both Barbaresco and Barolo. But the more important wine had to be the Barolo. And that the Barbaresco had to be a little bit inferior in both price and perceived quality.

"I don't want to say that they were looking to do this, but probably it was in their subconscious minds. Even growers who owned vineyards in both Barolo and Barbaresco always sold their Barbaresco at a lower price than their Barolo. But starting from about 1975, and continuing today, they began selling their Barbaresco at a higher price than their Barolos. This had never happened before. Maybe this was thanks to Gaja," he adds with exaggerated choir-boy innocence.

With the new Barolo vineyard purchase, Gaja has become either the second- or third-largest owner of Langhe vineyards (depending upon who is counting), with two hundred and seven acres of vines. He also controls an additional fifteen vineyard acres through leases. For the Langhe, this is a stupendously big ownership. Characteristically, it has been effected quietly. When I casually asked several Langhe winegrowers how much vineyard they thought their famous neighbor owned, they put forth guesses that represented only a fraction of Gaja's holdings. I mentioned this to Gaja, who smiled and said, "They don't think about it, my dear. And I would like to keep it that way."

Despite this sizable holding, Gaja issues only a fraction of wine that the other two top vineyard owners do, one of which is good for two hundred thousand cases and the other for four hundred thousand cases.

In comparison, Gaja made just twenty-two thousand cases of wine before the Barolo vineyard purchase. The new vineyard acquisition won't drive this figure up dramatically, what with only fourteen hundred cases each of the 1988 and 1989 vintages of Barolo being released. Half of the new Barolo vineyard will be given over to new plantings of Chardonnay, Barbera, and other grape varieties. Gaja's eventual total production might reach thirty thousand cases.

However much his vineyard purchases might have escaped his colleagues' calculations, Gaja's latest venture is sure to wake them up: He has bought the biggest private building in Barbaresco and plans to turn it into a hotel. Or a reception center. Or a fancy winery facility. Or all of these. Gaja is not sure. "This is something that I have always dreamed of," he says. "And the opportunity to buy this building, well, this is fantastic!"

Its irresistibility is understandable, as the old brick building, locally known simply as Il Castello, happens to be directly across the street from Gaja's winery. "Who could resist buying it?" he asks joyfully. When it is pointed out to him, by his wife, Lucia, among a few other insiders, that Il Castello is in woeful repair and that Gaja has already remodeled, expanded, and then remodeled the expansion of his existing winery at obviously impressive cost, Gaja is unfazed. "It is once in a lifetime!" he exclaims.

Like many successful men entering their fifties, the spirit of Gaja's ambition is as willing as ever, but the flesh probably is hinting that it may not always be able to keep up. In the last three years, Gaja's hair has grayed noticeably. And he has put on a little weight, although he still cuts a reasonably trim figure. The new baby, however rejuvenating, surely gives him pause as well. After all, when the child turns eighteen, Gaja will be seventy-one years old. And Lucia will only be fifty-eight, just five years older than Gaja is now.

So the opportunities for the kind of full-speed-ahead achievement that Gaja has always pursued are narrowing. A new building project is just the ticket. Besides, it is time to make a public statement, as Gaja reluctantly concedes. Old habits of secretiveness die hard.

"Frankly, I am never content. I don't know why. This is a big stress. I have a lot of admiration for people who are entrepreneurs and at the same time are capable of a way of life that does not disturb others. If you have money, you have to be capable of spending the money without disturbing other people.

"*La borghesia*, the bourgeoisie, have a responsibility—I'm not saying to give a good example—but to live in a way that is not provocative to others. I like very much this restraint. But at the same time, I also like very much people who are capable of appreciating a quality of life. Life is also the table, the restaurants, and so on. I know many people who go to important restaurants only when someone else, or the business, is paying."

Gaja had been hinting at some kind of big new project for months. But he refused to say what was in the wind for fear, he later told me, of the negotiations falling through. In fact, the old Castello did slip through his fingers once, only to be bought by owners who subsequently decided that they really didn't know what they would do with their new acquisition. The second time, Gaja was resolute.

Frankly, I was pretty sure that whatever the new project was, it would be something concrete, some sort of capstone to his accomplishments. I saw it in his eyes when I was with him in Napa Valley while he was taking around a group of Gaja Distribuzione agents for their first-ever visit to America.

Gaja himself is an old Napa Valley hand. The group was also to attend the gala opening—for its foreign customers—of the brand-new winery of Opus One, which is a joint wine venture of Robert Mondavi and the late Baron Philippe de Rothschild. Making just one wine, a Bordeaux-type Cabernet Sauvignon blend that sells for about $50 a bottle, Opus One has been in production for a decade. But the joint venture only recently constructed its own winery facility, the wine previously having been made at the Mondavi winery just down the road.

Finally, in 1992, the lavish, Mayan-temple-like winery was completed. Even Napa Valley, which is inured to expensive temples to winemaking, was impressed by the lavishness of the project. The winery alone is reliably rumored to have cost its joint proprietors between $23 million and $27 million, which would easily make it the world's most expensive winemaking facility devoted to making about eighteen thousand cases of just one wine.

Like the Bordeaux châteaux it was intended to replicate—psychologically, anyway—the semicircular winery is designed to impress. To enter it, you must walk up a long series of steps to reach a half-enclosed courtyard that is embraced by opposing columnar arcs reminiscent of the Palais de Chaillot in Paris. You feel like a human sacrifice.

The reception for foreign clients was part of a three-day extravaganza, which occupied the time of Robert Mondavi, his two sons, Tim and Michael, and co-owner Baroness Philippine de Rothschild, the daughter of the late Baron. Descending into the underground cellars—which had to be air-conditioned at enormous expense after it was belatedly discovered that the winery is sited on a geothermal hot spot—the guests were soothed by a chamber music group.

Dinner was served at tables artfully maneuvered among the glistening stainless steel tanks. Gaja, too, has the very latest in temperature-controlled stainless steel fermenting tanks. But these were something else again, raised on stiletto-heel supports which give them a teetering elegance usually absent from conventional squat-on-the-floor tanks such as Gaja's.

But the best touch, real *bella figura*, was the engraving of the Opus One insignia on the door of each tank. It is not merely a designer touch. It is a territorial declaration, a squirt of ego on every fermenting tank like a dog making the rounds of the neighborhood hydrants.

This insignia is the centerpiece of the Opus One label, which is one of California's cleverest. Opus One, which is a blend of as many as a dozen different vineyards, is consecrated to the power of personality rather than site. Where nearly all of the world's best wines are expressions of place, rather than personality, Opus One is a brand, rather than an expression of land, a wine built, rather than found.

Naturally, the Opus One label celebrates its builders. But the equal time provision never was more demanding than this, given that it is the creation of two of winedom's most ego-swollen personalities. In a stroke of Solomonic insight, the designer cleverly conceived of a double profile of the two founders, the backs of their heads joined, with their distinguishable profiles looking out in opposite directions, like a double-headed eagle.

As Gaja looked around the winery, which he had seen before, he nodded approvingly. He had become an equal of these two formidable figures. His wine sold for more than Mondavi's and for as much as that of Château Mouton Rothschild. He was nearly as famous as they, from a place far less heralded, let alone visited.

But they had erected something that he, at fifty-three, had yet to do. Granted, in Barbaresco he was never going to create something as flagrant, even outlandish, as the Opus One winery. Gaja believes too strongly that the *borghesia* have a responsibility not to be too provocative to others. Still, these days you cannot shy from at least a bit of self-celebration, can you? Look where it got Mondavi and Rothschild.

But in Barbaresco, Gaja had only the big, closed green door. He had reached that time in life when a man has to put up at least a modest monument to his achievements. On the way back from our walk that sunny Easter Sunday, I asked Gaja about this, in an indirect way. He was steering the big BMW, energetically piloting around the curves of the Langhe. But he was relaxed. The walk, the sunshine, and the sense of control that comes from driving, made him more expansive than usual. He talked of himself in the third person, as he often does, downshifting from time to time into the first person. Lucia hovered as an unseen, but strongly felt, presence.

"We built this myth of Gaja, the man. What is becoming difficult, particularly for Gaja, is that there are people who want to meet me, to speak with me. The problem now is I need people who can assume more responsibility. The most important work in the next ten years is to grow men capable of working in the right manner, capable of taking more responsibility. And for Angelo Gaja, if it's possible, to stay more back. If not, I will go crazy!

"Ten years ago it was impossible even to think to close the winery on Saturday and Sunday. But today, we have arrived. We don't permit people to enter and to come like they once did. Still, we continue to work on Saturday morning.

"In the past we had a lot of people—excellent people, very nice people—wanting to come to have a private contact and so on. An important step will be to refuse to continue to go in this direction. It will be important in the future, especially in the project of selling by mail, to sell the picture of Gaja!"

"Like the pope," I suggest helpfully. Italian houses abound with pictures of the pope, their owners not for a minute thinking that they might ever meet the real man. Gaja laughs at the agreeable notion that a picture of him, allied to a vast mail-order marketing scheme, could provide a satisfying substitute for the real Gaja. "This is a little bit of a dream," he says wistfully.

"You know, maybe today it's just Italy, but why not later to commercialize mail order in other countries? You know there still are large areas where Gaja wines are—I'm not saying they are not existing—but surely they are not well known. I've never had a complex of jumping off the table in France or England. Or in Belgium. But you know, it has to arrive. Why not? It's another part of the market."

I add that, yes, this may be. But that it will take Gaja himself to do it, rather than just pictures of the pope. Momentarily he is deflated. "Yes, probably, you are right," he says ruefully. But the idea of new whirls to conquer invigorates him. "You are right!" he chortles, his right forefinger corkscrewing into the air. "They need me. Not just pictures of the pope!" The car rocketed forward, as if jerked by an unseen string.

Angelo Gaja is today in his seventies; he was born in 1940. Both of his parents lived to their nineties and are now deceased.

The prices of Bordeaux first growths such as Château Mouton Rothschild now command $500 to $700 a bottle upon release, depending on the quality of the vintage.

In comparison, Gaja's single-vineyard wines from the Barbaresco zone—Sorì San Lorenzo, Sorì Tildin, and Costa Russi—currently sell for $350 to $400 a bottle.

The Gaja winery today has a sign in several languages informing visitors that an appointment is necessary. Gaja no longer ages his own wood for his barrels. He now buys the quality of barrels he seeks directly from France.

Gaja's business ventures have expanded dramatically since the mid-1990s. His purchase of the Castello across the street from his winery and offices in Barbaresco proved to be an expensive misadventure. After remodeling the ancient structure with the idea of turning it into a small, ultra-luxury hotel—itself a tortuous affair requiring hard-won permissions from the local authorities for the historic structure—Gaja never did open it as a hotel as the idea was uneconomic. It's now used to receive visitors—but no one is invited to stay in one of its thirteen rooms.

Much more profitably, Gaja reached beyond Piedmont to create two wine estates in Tuscany. One is a small vineyard and winery acquired in 1994 in the prestigious appellation of Brunello di Montalcino called Pieve di Santa Restituta.

Much more ambitious and costly is Gaja's two-hundred-acre estate in the Bolgheri district of coastal Tuscany called Ca' Marcanda. Created from raw land starting in 1996, the new vineyard is planted primarily to Cabernet Sauvignon and Merlot, as well as Cabernet Franc and Syrah.

In Piedmont, Gaja now owns about two-hundred-fifty acres of vines in Barbaresco and Barolo. Although Gaja Distribuzione continues to sell Riedel glassware and other tabletop items throughout Italy, Gaja never did pursue selling his wines by mail order.

Although Gaja continues to be fully absorbed by his business—receiving visitors and journalists daily—his oldest daughter, Gaia (born 1979), has taken over a good portion of the worldwide traveling required to market Gaja wines.

Among those mentioned in the profile, the French wine writer Michel Bettane is still France's leading wine writer, although he is no longer associated with Revue du Vin de France.

Winegrower Aldo Conterno has turned over his winery to his three sons, although he remains singularly influential both with his family and in the Langhe wine community. Aldo Vacca continues as the director of the Produttori del Barbaresco winegrowers' cooperative.

ONE LAST WORD

A common, if unseen, thread runs through all the words on wine in this book: It's really all about time. Everything about wine, especially fine wine, involves time. Unlike slugging back a beer or a shot of whiskey, our appreciation of wine requires a longer, savoring moment. In an age in which seemingly everything is compressed and accelerated, wine takes time—which we willingly give it.

It's no different, by the way, at the production end. The richest winegrower in the world cannot make his or her vines grow any faster than the poorest peasant. A vine will grow at its own pace and pays no attention to our needs or desires. If you want a mature vine, you'll just have to wait the thirty, forty, or fifty years required, never mind your ambitions or bank account.

Similarly, although all sorts of winemaking techniques have been developed to make young wines drinkable sooner, none allows a young wine to have the nuance or character of a fully mature wine. Only time can do that. A wine can be made to taste softer and thus more accessible by eliminating harsh tannins. Or it can be made to seem more mature by cellaring it at a warmer temperature. This creates the wine version of wrinkles: it looks old, but is devoid of the character that only age can instill.

Time also affects words about wine. There simply is no substitute for decades of time spent tasting wines, following them from inception in barrel all the way through to authentic maturity. And there's no substitute for the accumulation of knowledge that comes from decades of talking with grape growers, wine makers, and fellow wine lovers. No immersion course, no matter how intensive, can allow you to both collect this knowledge and, more importantly, sift through it for nuggets of enduring insight.

Although we bring it into this world, once wine arrives, its pace is set by a measure not our own. Wine is time physically slowed. It makes us relax, in every sense. And that, in the end, is what we really savor. It's why we write and read and talk about wine, the better to continue to savor its captured moment.

SOURCE CREDITS

The sources for the columns and essays are in order of their appearance in the book, as follows:

The Tyranny of Being Well Brought-Up, *Wine Spectator*, April 15, 1995

Does America Need Masters of Wine?, *Wine Spectator*, April 30, 1994

Music to No One's Ears, *Wine Spectator*, December 31, 1995

More American than Ever, *Wine Spectator*, February 14, 2002

Rock, Paper, Scissors—Style Clobbers Character, *Wine Spectator*, September 15, 1997

Wine in the American Mainstream, *Wine Spectator*, March 31, 1994

Slipperiness at the Smithsonian, *Wine Spectator*, April 31, 1996

Gen X Nixes Wine? Aw, Quit Worrying, *Wine Spectator*, February 28, 1997

An Open Letter to Wining (and Whining) Gen Xers, *Wine Spectator*, November 15, 1997

Some Truths of Our Time, *Wine Spectator*, November 15, 2008

Fear vs. Conviction, *Wine Spectator*, January 31–February 28, 2005

Caught in a Blind, *Wine Spectator*, December 15, 1996

Yet Another Grand Tasting, *The New York Sun*, May 10, 2006

The Genius of Great Wine, *The New York Sun*, November 3, 2004

How to Be a Wine Guy, *The New York Sun*, October 5, 2005

The 25-Watt Wine, *Wine Spectator*, July 31, 2006

Tasting and Talking, *The New York Sun*, February 9, 2005

Buddy, Can You Spare a Paradigm?, *Wine Spectator*, May 31, 2008

Stop Me before I Judge Again, *Wine Spectator*, August 31, 1995

Judgment Day, *Wine Spectator*, October 31, 2005

Tree Hugging, *Wine Spectator*, June 15, 2002

Right Down the Middle, *Wine Spectator*, May 15, 1996

Wine Viagra, *Wine Spectator*, October 31, 2004

The Critical Half-Inch, *Wine Spectator*, June 30, 2008

What Makes a Wine a Landmark, *Wine Spectator*, September 15, 1996

Schlepping Old Wine Baggage, *Wine Spectator*, October 31, 2002

The Low-Cut Dress Syndrome, From *Making Sense of Wine* (Running Press, 2003)

All Noir, All the Time, *Wine Spectator*, February 28, 2000

The Myth of the All-Purpose Palate, *Wine Spectator*, August 31, 2003

The Rule of Good Bones, *Wine Spectator*, November 15, 1999

Fit for a Prince, *The New York Sun*, August 23, 2006

Beyond "I Like It" and "I Don't", *The New York Sun*, May 2, 2007

Telling the Difference, *Wine Spectator*, November 15, 2007

10,000 Hours, *Wine Spectator*, September 30, 2007

Voting (Wine) Conservative, *Wine Spectator*, October 31, 2008

My Wine, My Self, *Wine Spectator*, June 15, 2009

The Mentalist of the Menu, *The New York Sun*, September 13, 2006

An Open Letter to America's Restaurateurs, *Wine Spectator*, July 31, 1994

Was My Last Open Letter too Subtle?, *Wine Spectator*, November 15, 1995

Here's the Wine List, Heh, Heh, Heh, *Wine Spectator*, November 15, 1994

"Accommodate Them," He Said., *Wine Spectator*, November 15, 1996

Is It Real? Or Is It Pretentious?, *Wine Spectator*, May 15, 2001

You Have the Right To . . . , *Wine Spectator*, September 30, 2000

Why Today's Wine Lists Fail, *Wine Spectator*, June 30, 2002

OK, So It Was the Vintage of the Century, *Wine Spectator*, December 31, 2005

Finally, the Truth about Old Wines, *Wine Spectator*, October 31, 1997

When Good Wines Say Good-Bye, *Wine Spectator*, September 15, 1999

Counterfeit Confidential, *The New York Sun*, April 4, 2007

Real Collecting vs. Phony Collecting, *Wine Spectator*, January 31, 1998

This Bud's for Them: Women Are Better Tasters, *Wine Spectator*, May 15, 1995

The Heady Mix of Men and Wine, *Wine Spectator*, June 30, 1995

Your Cheatin' Wine Locker, *Wine Spectator*, October 31, 1998

This Just In! Women Collect Wine, *Wine Spectator*, September 30, 1995

Excerpt on *Bella Figura*, From *Matt Kramer's Making Sense of Italian Wine* (Running Press, 2006)

In Defense of France, *Wine Spectator*, August 31, 2002

Burgundy and Its Enemies, *Wine Spectator*, September 30, 2002

My Dearest France . . . , *Wine Spectator*, September 15, 2004

Forever Francoholic, *Wine Spectator*, December 15, 2006

The Folly That Is France, *The New York Sun*, January 23, 2008

Bordeaux Mega-Dough, *Wine Spectator*, September 15, 2001

To Splurge or Not to Splurge, *The New York Sun*, July 5, 2006

An Open Letter to Bordeaux Lovers, *Wine Spectator*, May 31, 1998

What It Means to Be Bullish on Bordeaux, *The New York Sun*, November 9, 2005

What It Really Costs, *The New York Sun*, April 5, 2006

Being An *"Esperto"*, *A Passion for Piedmont: Italy's Most Glorious Regional Table* (William Morrow, 1997)

Aged in an Attic, Enjoyed at the Table, *The New York Sun*, September 27, 2006

A Fortuitous Mistake, *The New York Sun*, November 29, 2006

A Tuscan Vineyard Keeps It Deceptively Simple, *The New York Sun*, November 15, 2006

The World's Best Lagrein. Now, What Exactly Is Lagrein?, *The New York Sun*, November 8, 2006

On the Waterfront, Fresh Fish and Great Wine, *The New York Sun*, November 1, 2006

Rare Treat, *The New York Sun*, August 3, 2005

Engagement with the Future, From *Matt Kramer's New California Wine* (Running Press, 2004)

Bottled Poetry, *The New York Sun*, October 4, 2006

Aging Well—An Unusual 1970 Zinfandel Goes on Sale for the First Time, *The New York Sun*, March 15, 2006

A Revered Winery Has Lost More Than Its Luxury Wine Holdings, *The New York Sun*, October 6, 2004

What Made Him Different, *Wine Spectator*, July 31, 2008

This Land Is Their Land, *The New York Sun*, February 15, 2006

An Island of Vines—A California Winery Stands Out in a Sea of McMansions, *The New York Sun*, May 31, 2006

Hanzell Vineyards—Due for a Comeback, *Wine Spectator*, December 15, 1995

The End of an Empire? California Pinot Noirs Are Chipping Away at Burgundy's Dominance, *The New York Sun*, April 6, 2005

The Money Bamboozle, *Wine Spectator*, April 30, 2001

Pinot Gris: California's Next Big White, *Wine Spectator*, September 30, 1994

Syrah: The Next Really Big Red, *Wine Spectator*, September 30, 2003

So What's the Next Really Big White?, *Wine Spectator*, October 31, 2003

Fighting the Future, *Wine Spectator*, October 15, 2001

Why Wine Isn't Art, And Why That Matters, *Wine Spectator*, October 15, 2008

All Is Not as It Seems in *Mondovino*, *The New York Sun*, March 25, 2005

Barbarians at the Cork, *Wine Spectator*, November 15, 2005

A Giant Sucking Sound—And That's All, *Wine Spectator*, December 15, 1994

Nutritional Lies, *Wine Spectator*, October 15, 1998

A Growing Mystery, *Wine Spectator*, June 15, 1999

How Do They Live with Themselves?, *Wine Spectator*, October 15, 2003

The Devil's Wine Dictionary, *Wine Spectator*, November 30, 1995

Make That a Double Super-Tuscan, *Wine Spectator*, September 15, 2000

Hello, You're on the Air, *Wine Spectator*, July 31, 1998

The Fear of Austere, *Wine Spectator*, March 31, 2008

Do Taste Buds Make the Wine Critic?, *The New York Sun*, July 19, 2006

The No-Wine Magazine, *The New York Sun*, September 7, 2005

The Decline of the Heroic Palate, *The New York Sun*, September 20, 2006

The Perils of Panels, *The New York Sun*, October 20, 2004

Getting "Rich", *Wine Spectator*, November 30, 2008

The Notion of *Terroir*, *Making Sense Of Burgundy* (William Morrow, 1990)

Terroir Matters, *Wine Spectator*, June 15, 2006

How the Land Became the Brand, *Wine Spectator*, September 15, 1994

The Real Scoop on Dirt, *Wine Spectator*, October 31, 1996

Sherry Baby, *Wine Spectator*, July 31, 1999

Clueless in Carneros, *Wine Spectator*, April 30, 1996

The Fight for the Soul of Wine, *Wine Spectator*, December 15, 2001

The Wine Behind the Machines, *The New York Sun*, May 30, 2007

An Open Letter to Natural Winegrowers, *Wine Spectator*, November 30, 2002